SINGING
JAZZ

SINGING
JAZZ

THE SINGERS AND
THEIR STYLES

Bruce Crowther + Mike Pinfold

BLANDFORD

A Blandford Book

First published in the UK 1997 by Blandford
A Cassell Imprint
CASSELL PLC
Wellington House, 125 Strand, London WC2R 0BB

British Library Cataloguing-in-Publication Data:
a catalogue record for this book is available from the British Library

ISBN 0-7137-2649-0

Designed and edited by DAG Publications Ltd.
Designed by David Gibbons. Edited and indexed by John Gilbert.
Printed and bound in Great Britain by Creative Print and Design
Wales, Ebbw Vale.

Front cover: Sue Storey of Focus on Jazz.
Back cover (top left clockwise): Concord Records,
Sue Storey, Kitty Margolis, Lee Richardson.

CONTENTS

ACKNOWLEDGEMENTS

We are very grateful for help we have received in preparing this book and we take this opportunity to express our sincere thanks to everyone who has assisted us. In particular, we are especially indebted to those singers who gave generously of their time in answering questions and sharing with us their views on the subject of singing in jazz. Inevitably, much that was said to us did not survive into the final draft but this was always by reason of space, not a reflection upon merit or value. In some instances we have also had to edit remarks, hopefully without adversely affecting the speaker's intentions. Any errors of fact that might occur are our responsibility alone.

Eddie Anderson, Mary Andrews, Audiophile Records, Betty Berry, Bill Berry, Terry Blaine, Lillian Boutté, Mike Campbell, Concord Records, Eddie Cook, Richard Cook, Laila Dalseth, Greg Dark, Dominique Eade, Dave Frishberg, Dardanelle Hadley, Joya Jensen, Marguerite Juenemann, Stacey Kent, Sue Kibbey, Barbara Lashley, Ron P. Lawlor, Nicki Leighton-Thomas, Tom Lellis, Mike Lovell, Mundell Lowe, Susannah McCorkle, La Velle McKinnie, Chris McNulty, Gill Manly, Kitty Margolis, Claire Martin, Susan May, Tina May, Helen Merrill, Mark Murphy, Nanette Natal, Jan Ponsford, Mark Porter, Keith Prior, Lucy Reed, Jean-Michel Reisser, Spike Robinson, Ellen Rucker, Michael Shera, Carol Sloane, Sue Storey, Brian Turnock, Christine Tyrrell, Marlene VerPlanck, William J. 'Billy' VerPlanck, Bert Warner, the late Don Waterhouse, Magni Wentzel, Weslia Whitfield, Jennifer Whittington, Marge Windus, Axel Zwingenberger and our agent, Carolyn Whitaker, and our commissioning editor, Stuart Booth.

PICTURE CREDITS

Marge Windus Archive: Louis Armstrong & Billie Holiday, Mildred Bailey, Betty Bennett, Sarah Vaughan.

Courtesy of the Artist: Terry Blaine, Mike Campbell, Laila Dalseth, Dardanelle, Dave Frishberg, Marguerite Juenemann, Sue Kibbey, Barbara Lashley, Nickie Leighton-Thomas, Tom Lellis, Chris McNulty, Kitty Margolis, Nanette Natal, Mark Porter, Lucy Reed, Ellyn Rucker, Marlene VerPlanck, Magni Wentzel.

Sue Storey of Focus on Jazz: Dee Dee Bridgewater, Betty Carter, Elaine Delmar, Slim Gaillard, Shirley Horn, Stacey Kent, Carol Kidd, Abbey Lincoln, Bobby McFerrin, Claire Martin, Tina May, Marion Montgomery, Dianne Reeves, Annie Ross, Cassandra Wilson, Norma Winstone.

House of Jazz Photo Archive: Cab Calloway, Ella Fitzgerald, Helen Humes, Julia Lee, Carmen McRae, Helen Merrill, Anita O'Day, Sister Rosetta Tharpe, Dinah Washington, Fats Waller, Ethel Waters.

William Rivelli: Dominique Eade.

Concord Records: Susannah McCorkle, Carol Sloane, Mel Tormé.

Bert Warner: Mark Murphy.

Jamoula McKean: Jan Ponsford.

Lee Richardson: Jimmy Witherspoon.

PREFACE

'After me there are no more jazz singers.' In 1986, when we wrote the concluding passages of our book, *The Jazz Singers: from Ragtime to the New Wave*, we found ourselves in general agreement with that sentiment, expressed by jazz diva Betty Carter some fifteen years earlier.

Happily, we now concede that in terms of both quantity and quality the intervening years have revealed a wealth of singing talent of every kind, pigeon-hole them as you will; modern, traditional, experimental, jazz fringe, jazz influenced, etc. The voices of Billie, Sassy, Dinah, Carmen and Ella may now be stilled, but throughout the world there are many wonderful jazz voices demanding to be heard. There are now literally thousands of young women and men willing to listen and learn and above all eager to sing – to sing jazz. Not pop or rock, where money is more easily made, but jazz, where, regardless of talent, ability, or determination, the chance of stardom is slim and financial security is virtually non-existent. The new singers are from many backgrounds and almost without exception they came up in ways that were different from those of their predecessors. They had to, because most of the old routes for jazz singers of earlier generations were gone and almost all those few routes that remained had undergone drastic change.

SINGING
JAZZ

ONE
I HEAR MUSIC

A jazz singer is a singer who sings jazz. — Mark Murphy

For many years singers whose careers had developed during the swing era had warned that the decline of the big bands had resulted also in what was essentially the demise of the best training ground for would-be vocalists. When popular singing star Peggy Lee spoke of both the benefits and the pitfalls of learning her craft during that era, she was speaking for a whole generation of talented artists: 'Band singing taught us the importance of interplay with musicians. We had to work close to the arrangement. Even if the interpretation wasn't exactly what we wanted. We had to make the best of it. I learned to do the best with what they gave me.' She went on to explain how she had learned more about music from the musicians in the bands than from anywhere else: 'They taught me discipline and the value of rehearsing and how to train.'

With on-the-road schooling virtually at an end by the 1950s, the lack of any other training arena in the 1960s and 1970s affected jazz singing and all but the most tenacious fell by the wayside, hence Betty Carter's comments. What has now filled that vacuum, in many ways distinctly for the better – in others perhaps for the worse, is Jazz in Education. Between the end of the academy of hard knocks and the flowering of orthodox academic training was a hiatus of almost an entire generation. Many singers who came along in this interim were thus obliged to create their own training ground. Some of them, such as Mark Murphy, continue to perform but also now take the time to pass on their expertise and experience to new crops of talent in the classroom.

That word – talent – is the right one to use because the new singers have it in abundance. Yet the very fact of their ability allied to their overwhelming numbers has thrown a harshly revealing light upon the acute and ever-present problems of the jazz singer, now, then and probably forever: Lack of opportunities, too few gigs, too little cash. Singer and teacher Mike Campbell highlights the problem he encounters at every new student intake: 'In five years' time, 95 per cent of them will be out of the business.' He explains that it has 'nothing to do with artistic ability. The business just beats you up.' Nevertheless, reality does not seem to deter would-be jazz singers – they just keep on coming. In terms of style and performance, however different they might be, all the newcomers are enthusiastic. Many are exciting new talents who somehow manage to create their own freshness of approach and readily demonstrate their individuality.

This overcrowded generation of new singers, this new era of jazz and jazz-orientated singing, although worldwide, is a largely underground phenomenon. From New York to Naples, London to Los Angeles, in Paris, Sydney, Tokyo, Oslo, Berlin, jazz singers abound but they sing to small

11

specialized audiences. In the past some jazz artists were able to reach out to the general audience. It was never easy and since rock became the dominant force in popular music it has appeared to be impossible without compromise. Perhaps a few of the newcomers have the potential to project jazz once again onto the world stage. If that should happen, then a possible side effect might be the creation of a new era of jazz associated popular singing when the music of a new generation of melodic composers and lyricists will be performed. Certainly such a thing happened in mid-century when the popularity of swinging jazz sparked one of several revolutions in popular music.

The golden age of popular singing is generally considered to be those years between the American Federation of Musicians' strike of the early 1940s and the rock 'n' roll invasion of the late 1950s and early 1960s. It was an era when good singers were valued, well represented and promoted accordingly; Frank Sinatra had Capitol Records, Ella Fitzgerald had Norman Granz. Popular singing, much of it jazz-influenced, was at its zenith.

Today, most young singers working in jazz have no one to champion their cause – no recording contract, no agent, no manager. The creed is: you fight your own corner, finance your own records, book your own gig – like it or not, your art is very much your own business. Most of today's jazz singers acknowledge that they will remain anonymous, known only to a limited, and often parochial, hardcore audience. This is not negative thinking, merely realistic. The singers know that jazz remains a neglected art. In Britain and America, those who control official arts funding look the other way at the mention of jazz. Meanwhile the music industry has inculcated millions worldwide with a taste for manufactured rather than creative popular music and has left itself, and in consequence large sections of the general public, indifferent to jazz and suspicious of anything that purports to be an art of improvisation. Improvisation, which lies at the core of the jazz singer's art, does not in any way equate with the preconceptions of an industry and an audience geared to accept a Star with Product in the charts.

This book, then, is not about man-made Stars or music that is Product (and profit) led. *Singing Jazz* is about a very special kind of singer, men and women, mostly women, who in the past changed perceptions not only of popular singing but also of popular music in general and today continue in that same innovatory vein. Popular music? Yes, because since its birth, jazz has been inextricably entwined with popular music. Jazz has influenced, affected and changed popular music; and, to be sure, popular music has had its effect upon jazz.

Knowledge that stardom is improbable will not deter the jazz singer; for while some might yearn for stardom, with all its glitzy trappings, this is not what drives them. The hard work, application and dedication displayed by all the singers appearing in these pages is prompted not by a desire for glittering success but by a need to express themselves in a manner and style that is inherent in their nature. They love and delight in the act of singing, but it is a form of self expression which they all take very seriously. Singing jazz is not something that artists do casually. The on-stage confidence and spontaneous creativity they display is not the effortless act it appears to be; it has been worked at long and hard and is the result, in most cases, of vocation. As singer Tina May says, 'You don't choose to be a jazz singer, it chooses you.'

In part, *Singing Jazz* is the story of a kind of singing that has been a feature of jazz throughout the years of the twentieth century. Sometimes it is integral with jazz, at other times it follows a parallel course. Also, it is the story of some of its practitioners both in the past and today. Wherever possible, the world of the singer will be seen through his or her own eyes. This way, all can experience the hard endeavour, suffer the rejection and despair, share the enthusiasm and momentary joy which justifies, for them, the hard knocks and tough times to which they willingly expose themselves.

First, however, a question needs to be asked: what is a jazz singer?

To the world in general, the sound of Ella Fitzgerald, swinging, scatting, improvising around a melody line, epitomises jazz singing. This surely is what jazz singing is all about. But what of her Songbook series recorded by Norman Granz? On her own admission, she changed her style to accommodate the Great American Song Book material which she sang, melody virtually intact, often with orchestral accompaniment that was tasteful but bland and plainly unjazzy. Critics of the time, concerned with the lack of improvisation but unable to fault the quality of her vocalizing, almost to a man damned her with faint praise. Many were the po-faced critiques admitting that her performance was superb but that 'of course she is not a jazz singer'. These earnest reviewers ignored her achievements of the previous twenty years, dismissing a career in jazz on the basis of half a dozen albums of popular songs sung in a manner intended to be faithful to the composers' aims. Even as critics condemned her, somewhere in the world she was delighting audiences with often wildly exciting and frenzied vocal performances, leaving little doubt of her authority as a jazz improviser.

Conversely, while critics agonized over Fitzgerald's perceived imperfections as a jazz singer, few of them troubled themselves or their readers with analyses of the style of Jimmy Rushing. A blues shouter, Rushing's place in jazz history is taken for granted yet he sang his songs unembellished, in a direct manner without recourse to scat or improvisation.

Regardless of opinion, if Ella Fitzgerald and Jimmy Rushing both have a place in jazz, what of a popular singer such as Rosemary Clooney? Widely acclaimed for her artistry outside the jazz idiom, in recent years Clooney has increasingly appeared in jazz settings and has been labelled accordingly. This prompted an impassioned response from Carmen McRae to the question, asked in a *down beat* interview, 'What is a jazz singer?' 'You know they call Rosemary Clooney a jazz singer,' she stated rather aggrievedly. 'This woman never improvised in her life. She sings a song exactly the way it's written.'

13

Do we accept McRae's point and discount Clooney for what she does not do, or do we attune our ears to what she does do and refer to singers of the past such as Mildred Bailey, Lee Wiley and Maxine Sullivan? Hardly improvisers in the accepted sense; but they are rarely omitted from discussion of jazz singers by virtue of their tonal quality, vocal timbre, phrasing, use of time and indefinable jazz feel.

Perhaps we can define a jazz singer as someone who uses his or her instrument in a disciplined and intelligent manner to sing songs in a jazz setting and who, during performance, will communicate not only a commitment to and love for the music to the audience, but will also, at times, improvise within the framework of the music to create a performance that demonstrates a kind of premeditated spontaneity. Terry Blaine says, 'You take a tradition and try to create your own unique style to it. Hopefully you evolve into something new, something different that is your own.' Mike Campbell is brief: 'Phrasing, individual concept, time, feel', is his definition; but Marguerite Juenemann takes a little longer to examine the inherent difficulties of reaching a satisfactory answer: 'What is jazz has come to include so much these days, I think its own label is somewhat vague. A traditional mainstream jazz singer will include improvisation in executing a tune, be it scat or lyrics. That kind of singer may also approach the same tune differently from one performance of it to another. Most traditional mainstream jazz singers will expand a tune as much as their understanding will tastefully allow, and will constantly challenge their musicality with what they choose for repertoire.'

Stacey Kent finds a neat turn of phrase to sum up herself which also effectively provides a definition: 'I am a singer. I sing jazz. I am a jazz singer.' Carol Sloane unequivocally states that, 'A jazz singer is one who takes risks. The improvisational element is what separates us from straight popular commercial singers.' Sue Kibbey pursues the importance of improvisation: 'A jazz singer takes a song and improvises over it, sings with a certain swing. It's about syncopation, timing, swing, improvising around a tune.' Kitty Margolis defines the necessary requirements for singing jazz: 'Improvisational skill, rhythmic complexity, sophisticated lyric interpretation, "soulfulness".'

For Magni Wentzel, a jazz singer 'has the ability to swing, the ability to phrase spontaneously, the ability to change the rhythmic patterns of a song and improvise and change a song and not be disrupted by the musicians behind doing something unexpected'. Jan Ponsford's view holds that, 'A jazz singer is a singer who has an extraordinary musicality, who doesn't just sing notes that are written in the song or lyrics that are written; who is skilled in interpretation, inflection, and sound placing. One who knows that the voice is an instrument and uses the voice as the instrument it is, who explores while they are singing, who explores the use of their instrument while singing. One who is fearless in their interpretation of a song.'

Implicit in all these definitions, of course, is the presence of an uneasily defined term which can unseat even the most positive response and which Laila Dalseth underlines: 'A jazz singer sings jazz. (What's jazz?)'

Does this bring us any closer to a definition of a jazz singer? No, it does not. If anything, it clouds the issue. Enquiring of singers does not necessarily lead to enlightenment. When that doyen of modern singing, Mark Murphy, was asked, 'What is a jazz singer?' he blithely replied, 'A jazz singer is a singer who sings jazz.' To clarify any confusion felt by those uninitiated into jazzspeak he added, 'Well, *we* know who we are.' But where does that leave the rest of us? Consider those singers who, like Murphy, wholeheartedly immerse themselves in improvisation, modal concept, chord changes and trading fours with the guys in the band; there is no confusion as to what *they* do. But what about singers who do not so readily delve into the realms of improvisation, preferring to concentrate more on tone, nuance, inflection and subtle interpretation? Are they to be excluded? Are we unconvinced that what they do should be designated jazz singing? There is, after all, a school of thought that would describe jazz as being as much to do with jazz feel as it is with improvisation.

Then there are those who might be called jazz singers by others but who categorically deny it. Marlene VerPlanck, a singer admired by jazz musicians and fellow artists alike, when asked the same question, commented forcefully, 'I have heard many singers that term themselves as jazz singers but who never "turn a phrase"... they never take a chorus! I never claim to be a jazz singer. I sing American popular song with jazz players around me with kind of a jazzy influence, but I think that the term is really reserved for a few very special people.' A singer who might qualify to be placed among those very special people is Helen Merrill who defined jazz singing thus: 'It's instinct, spontaneity, understanding of chord changes and being able to converse with your fellow musicians.'

So how can anyone define an area of song so diverse that it can include an untrained, corrugated voice like that of New Orleans barrelhouse singer-pianist Billie Pierce, and the superb vocal instrument that was Sarah Vaughan's? Or contrast the brash, unsubtle, shout of Ruth Brown with the fragile, bell-like tone of Teddi King? A category designed to fit Pierce would clearly exclude Vaughan; and how could a category designed for Vaughan sensibly include Pierce or Brown or King?

Customarily, the criteria by which singers are judged in the jazz world often are either harshly restrictive or absurdly indiscriminating. Taken to extremes, the former makes it almost impossible for anyone other than Billie Holiday and a handful of lesser mortals to qualify. The latter allows just about anyone who ever approximated 'Basin St Blues' in a Karaoke bar to wear the label. Of course, reality lies somewhere in between these extremes. Exactly where the boundary falls is profoundly subjective and if we lean in this book towards one extreme it will be to the broader view. This is not because we choose to be non-judgmental but because the art of singing jazz constantly weaves in and out of other forms and styles of singing, creating in its wake new and exciting concepts which, of necessity, demand singers with widely differing styles and qualities. And inevitably, given decades of interplay with other forms, many qualities of jazz singing are found in some non-jazz artists.

Noticeably, and instructively, jazz singers are much less restricted by the boundaries of appreciation which confine many fans, and often express admiration for singers outside the jazz idiom. For example, many admire the rhythmic qualities of Fred Astaire's singing and the interpretative skills of Mabel Mercer. Specifically, Connee Boswell learned much from operatic tenor Enrico Caruso's superb breath control, while Mark Murphy thinks soprano Maria Callas was a genius: 'She still raises hairs on your arms.' Kitty Margolis enjoys listening to rock singer Annie Lennox. Perhaps even more surprisingly, Anita O'Day, Jon Hendricks, Rosemary Clooney and Sarah Vaughan all expressed admiration for the singing of movie actress Martha Raye. Examples such as these are merely the tip of a deep and wide-ranging sense of unity between popular music forms and practitioners.

This drawing together of jazz and non-jazz forms has been a significant factor in the development of popular music, particularly since Louis Armstrong liberated both jazz and popular singing back in the 1920s. By recording Tin Pan Alley tunes he ably demonstrated that the origin of material makes little difference to jazz performance. It is in the performance itself that jazz is created. Armstrong enriched all areas of American popular music as he illustrated how to personalize written material. His influence, and the further success of other singing stars who followed, is responsible in part for any vagueness in definition. So many singers, in and out of jazz, adopted and adapted Armstrong's concepts that, directly and indirectly through the following decades, he touched almost every singer of popular music and his influence, recognized or not, lives on.

*   *   *

While the term jazz singer has probably been used to describe a certain kind of vocalist as long as the word jazz has been in use, it is only within the second half of the twentieth century that the term has taken on special significance and that singers have consciously described what they do as jazz singing.

During the first decade of the twentieth century the popularity of the minstrel show diminished. White performers who aimed with greater integrity to assimilate something of the rhythmic quality of black artists were identified as singers of ragtime or, more vulgarly, as 'coon shouters'. The earliest of these singers simply adopted black material. Canadian-born May Irwin, a star of farce-comedy, was the first to popularize the 'coon-song' on Broadway when she interpolated 'The Bully Song', actually written by a white man, in the première of *The Widow Jones* in 1895. In 1902, black composers Bob Cole and James Rosamond Johnson offered their songs to white

Broadway stars, including Marie Cahill who performed and popularized 'Under the Bamboo Tree' in the show *Sally in Our Alley*. The vaudevillian Emma Carus, described as a 'female baritone', first introduced Irving Berlin's ersatz ragtime novelty 'Alexander's Ragtime Band' in 1911, thus helping to create a worldwide misunderstanding about what ragtime music really was. Even Berlin himself was perplexed: 'You know, I never did find out what ragtime was.' It was a curious anomaly. Interest in black music was fired by a white singer performing a song in simple march time composed by a white man. Perhaps the most famous of all these early female singers was Sophie Tucker, the 'Last of the Red Hot Mommas'. In later years both Ethel Waters and Alberta Hunter confirmed that Tucker offered them payment to privately perform songs to help her absorb their style and delivery.

The 1920s, popularly known as the Jazz Age, was an era when popular singers increasingly adopted a veneer of jazz. Singers like Blossom Seeley, Lee Morse and Margaret Young continued the Red Hot Momma-strain of vaudeville hokum while other more stylish performers, like the splendid cabaret singer Marion Harris, Broadway artist Zelma O'Neill, recording and radio stars Annette Hanshaw and Ruth Etting, had a more modern appeal. In performance they might have been described in such endearing period terms as 'peppy' or 'hot', their delivery as 'sweet and lowdown'. Equally they may have been called jazz singers. Once the blues craze took momentum, around 1921, most black artists typecast themselves as blues singers; an alternative description often used by record companies being 'comedienne'. Sophisticated and dignified black singers such as Waters and Hunter were often described thus. Later in the decade, a sad-eyed white singer, Helen Morgan, along with other sweet young things on Broadway such as Libby Holman and Lillian Roth, helped popularize the term 'torch singer'. This term usually described female singers who sang yearningly and sensuously of lost, lacking or unrequited love.

In 1927, through the new and exciting medium of the Talkies, Al Jolson told the world about *The Jazz Singer*, but failed dismally to demonstrate what one was. Crooners forsook the megaphone for the new-fangled microphone and Bing Crosby proved that crooning was something to be taken seriously. Whereas a decade or so earlier white singers had tried to emulate black performers by mimicry, gradually a few began to absorb some of the true rhythmic qualities of the new music and learned how to express elements of their own personality in the new idiom. Through this personalization, they created in their wake their own lines of influence. An important singer of this period, Connee Boswell, later described how she and her sisters, Martha and Helvetia, had played an influential role. 'We revolutionized not only the style of singing, the beat, the placing of voices, the way-out harmony, but also the musical world in general.'

In the 1930s more rhythmically sophisticated singing became evident. Vocalists such as Boswell and Mildred Bailey, both of whom had begun to record in the late 1920s, showed how they were assimilating some of the musical innovations of Armstrong and Waters and the microphone technique of Crosby. As the decade wore on, singers were being described as able to swing. Crosby, Boswell and Bailey could swing; but Ella Fitzgerald and Maxine Sullivan excelled at it. And no one made better use of Armstrong's influence than Billie Holiday. She best demonstrated what jazz singing was all about, although it is unlikely that during those years she consciously considered herself anything other than a singer of popular material. In many ways Holiday illustrates why jazz singing is so difficult to define. It is rare to hear her sing a blues and she never used scat, a form of expression forever associated with her great influence, Louis Armstrong. What she did do, time after time on record, was to spontaneously compose music, subtly or even dramatically restructuring melodies in a manner that was as equally imaginative as the very greatest instrumental improvisers. Miraculously, at the same time she managed with artless simplicity to convey to her listeners a sense of uncontrived vulnerability that could be quite devastating to the emotions.

In the 1940s and in the wake of Holiday, some singers began to see that what they did was different from what was being done by the more popular singers. Swingers like Anita O'Day, beboppers such as Dave Lambert and Babs Gonzales, west coast coolsters like June Christy, were of a generation that sensed it operated in a different 'time' zone. The term 'jazz singer' took on a more positive role, became an identifiable pigeon-hole – you either were or you weren't. By the 1950s it had become a hip status symbol, something more than just showbiz hype. It was in the late 1950s, too, that a further long-standing influence was clearly identified; that of the church – the soul of black music – exemplified in the work of Ray Charles, Della Reese, Dakota Staton and later extended fully by soul singers such as Aretha Franklin.

Argument and debate also developed: how, for example, could Sarah Vaughan be a jazz singer when it was evident that her recordings at this time were clearly aimed at the Hit Parade? It went unacknowledged that some singers easily step in and out of the jazz arena at will without demeaning their status as jazz artists. It was always thus; take for example the veteran Adelaide Hall. Her 1920s recordings with Duke Ellington are treasured gems of jazz history, but her seventy-year-long career was successfully spent almost entirely outside jazz.

Choice of material is another source of confusion. 'On Green Dolphin Street' was written by Bronislau Kaper and Ned Washington and originally performed orchestrally for a film but is now almost solely associated with jazz performances. Alternatively, the tune 'Misty', written as a jazz vehicle by pianist Erroll Garner, is often performed by artists of very different persuasion. Meanwhile there are many stylish singers of popular song standards, like Marlene VerPlanck, who use jazz accompaniment and utilize jazz phrasing and nuance and who are perfectly acceptable to jazz audiences. Conversely, many of today's jazz singers are increasingly writing their own songs or writing lyrics to well-known jazz compositions and relying less on popular material, thus reversing the trend started by Armstrong and Waters in the late 1920s.

When considering jazz singing styles there are yet more anomalies. Scat, the impromptu use of rhythmic vocalized syllables, and vocalese, in which pre-determined lyrics are fitted to the transcribed notes of an existing instrumental solo, are ostensibly similar in sound, yet these two styles are essentially governed by opposing criteria.

A holier-than-thou attitude does still exist among some of today's jazz *cognoscenti*. To them an artist, once acknowledged, must never change; a point that rankles with some of the more progressive singers. As one particularly frustrated singer commented: 'These jazz purists drive you up the wall. They put us into a box and we can come out when they want us to. I have a problem with that, as a singer who sings jazz.' Fortunately, this narrowness of vision and unwillingness to accept change among some members of audiences seems to be on the wane.

Importantly, however, the debate continues, not only between jazz enthusiasts and critics but also among jazz singers themselves. It is healthy debate, demonstrating lively interest in an absorbing topic, although it is doubtful if the question, 'What is a jazz singer?', will ever be answered to everyone's absolute satisfaction. Indeed, we might ask why it is necessary even to ask and answer that particular question? Singer-teacher Dominique Eade responds to the question by suggesting that the qualities that make a jazz singer are 'probably a combination of interaction and success at realizing that intention. I answer that cryptically because, in general, I find there is too much emphasis on trying to define jazz singers with some foolproof, narrow definition that ends up tripping on its own rules. Is jazz saxophone Gene Ammons or Anthony Braxton? If every article about jazz saxophone began with that question, it would be pretty boring. The industry tries to pass off some obviously (to a jazz listener) non-jazz singers as jazz singers, but just as jazz listeners know the difference between Kenny G. and Wayne Shorter, so I think they are equally discriminating with jazz singers.'

But one thing is certain: in context or out, jazz continues to illuminate every form of music it touches and none more so than American popular song. And the illuminators include those women and men of many nationalities who elected to devote their lives to singing jazz throughout the twentieth century. The new singers are their heirs and successors and the women and men who will take jazz singing beyond the millennium.

*   *   *

Although the upsurge in jazz singing in the 1990s seemed to come from nowhere, like all revolutions it had been fermenting for some time. As is so often the case, the most visible revolutionaries were young people seeking means of expression different from those with which they were surrounded. During the previous decade the pop music scene had become increasingly synthetic and was thus unattractive to singers fired with any measure of creative impulse.

The sudden intensity of interest in jazz singing cast light not only upon singers with new careers but also on others whose careers had begun in earlier decades, in some cases as far back as the 1940s.

Among the latter is Sheila Jordan, whose inventive improvising and subtlety of phrasing and note displacement always show respect for a song's lyrics; Rosemary Squires, still an extremely versatile and respected popular singer, with a highly individual rhythmic feel for jazz; and Etta Jones, whose clear identifiable and distinct delivery retains vitality. Mel Tormé's precocious start did have its problems. In those years he sang mostly in head tones, creating a highly distinctive sound but at the same time placing limitations in the minds of his audience: 'I spent most of the 1950s getting over the Velvet Fog image.' More than forty years later he enjoys continued appreciation of his work: 'I'm grateful for the enthusiastic and warm responses of the audiences and the younger fans who are discovering me... I'm thrilled to be a part of this musical revolution.'

Starting out in the 1950s, sophisticated stylists Barbara Jay and Maxine Daniels remain delightfully melodic, straight ahead singers; Marion Montgomery is a talented and intimate performer whose long career continues unabated; Annie Ross also sings on and still strikes a responsive chord with her slightly acerbic delivery. Abbey Lincoln is another unpretentious and honest artist whose career illustrates many of the problems of the jazz singer. She had to wait until she was in her sixties before gaining a contract with a major label: 'I'm suddenly visible to people who never heard of me ... because of Polygram ... marketing my work.' Singer-pianist Shirley Horn, considered by many, including her peers, to be one of the finest jazz performers singing today, also displays great instrumental finesse; Betty Carter, still creative in a bebop style, is a brilliant if idiosyncratic scat singer and continues to delight festival audiences; Cleo Laine is a wide-ranging performer whose profile in the 1990s remains as high as ever it was in the past. Blues-balladeer Joe Williams had his first major hit back in 1954 but has lost little of his richness of voice and none of his enthusiasm. He told Brian Priestley, 'I'm still listening to things – Robert Cray kills me and Koko Taylor, she makes my body laugh... Dianne Reeves really, she frees the spirit.' And Mark Murphy, who continues to be a great influence on many of today's singers, is as hip today as he was in the 1950s. Importantly, he is also alert to developments. Speaking in 1996 of his new compact disc, he believes it to be 'more accessible than any I've done – ever. I mixed up the rhythms. I used some Latino rhythms, slightly younger hip-hop beats. I like them. If I don't like them I don't use them, if I like them I use them. If they swing for me, they swing. What the hell's the matter with that?' Jon Hendricks, a great exponent of vocalese and scat, is another extremely influential singer who still has amazing ideas. Some of the older singers have returned after a period in semi- or even full retirement. Chris Connor, to some extent overshadowed by June Christy in the 1950s, proved when she reappeared on the scene that she still had magic. Dutch singer Rita Reys came back after some inactivity to appear at front-rank jazz festivals. Carol Sloane, only sporadically active through the 1960s, 1970s and early 1980s, burst back to stake a convincing claim as one of the best singers of her generation.

Among the singers whose careers began in the 1960s are Carol Kidd and Elaine Delmar. Kidd, an artistic and witty singer with remarkable vocal clarity, returned to fulltime singing in the 1980s after a period in retirement. Delmar had bided her time, continuing to sing throughout the intervening years with considerable success and was as professional as ever.

Some of the singers in jazz whose reputations spread in the 1990s were new only to the genre, having gained singing experience in other fields. Terry Blaine and Helen Shapiro first sang pop music; Dominique Eade and Marguerite Juenemann spent time singing folk music before entering jazz in the 1980s, developing as singers and teachers during the following decade; Weslia Whitfield and Magni Wentzel trained as classical singers before deciding in the 1980s that it had to be jazz.

*   *   *

Just as their age range is wide, so too is there great stylistic diversity among singers active in the 1990s. There are innovative singers who include vocal gymnast Urszula Dudziak, uncompromising Jeanne Lee, and abstractionist and experimenter Jay Clayton, all of whom sing with great sensitivity. There is also the humour which emanates from free vocal spirits such as Lauren Newton and Norma Winstone, the latter a skilled exponent of wordless improvising who is an equally gifted interpreter of lyrics. Then there are Nanette Natal, Tom Lellis and Kurt Elling, the last influenced by Mark Murphy and Jon Hendricks. Both Elling and Lellis write lyrics to well-known jazz instrumentals. Sometimes working in a vocalese format, they also sing standards with lyrics relatively intact. Natal, who entered jazz from commercial music in 1980, ranges from standards through jazz originals and, like many of the new breed, also teaches her craft to still younger singers. Crossing over between jazz and classical music is the extraordinary Bobby McFerrin, a hugely entertaining and humorous improviser who makes unusual use of sound. There are also those who concentrate almost exclusively on modern scat. Carla White, famous or infamous in the 1980s as the Queen of the Two-hour Scat Set; Madeline Eastman, a virtuoso scat singer admired by her contemporaries; and Meredith Monk, a classically trained scat singer.

Lorraine Craig, Lianne Carroll and Ian Shaw are young improvisers who use a diversity of material from classic songbooks to originals. Along with Carol Grimes and Maggie Nicols, they ably utilize an amalgam of standards, scat, vocalese and original material. Jacqui Dankworth is another

21

young singer who favours original material and, like so many of her contemporaries, seeks to nudge the boundaries of jazz.

Bringing new depths and contemporary meaning to lyrical interpretation are a host of talented singers: Judy Niemack, a swinging, sometimes scatting, hard-bop singer on the scene since the late 1970s; Gill Manly, an uninhibited and imaginative improviser; Tina May, who handles intricate lyrics with an agile and expressive voice, fine dynamics and exquisite control; and Claire Martin, who employs her attractive voice with great fluency and command and has a fine sense of pitch. Chris McNulty is a subtle and sensitive interpreter of lyrics who swings; Nnenna Freelon favours original material, much of it in vocalese fashion; Jan Ponsford concentrates on use of voice as a musical instrument and draws from many musical and cultural roots. Kitty Margolis is a gifted singer with great flair and ingenuity; Mike Campbell is a teacher and consummate professional with a relaxed and intimate style. Dee Dee Bridgewater sings with respect for the song even when departing from the melody for some wild scat chorus and she has the ability to swing easily with attention to the tradition of past masters. Helen Merrill's cool delivery emphasizes considerable depths of emotion. Dianne Reeves uses a diverse range of material and is a mature and sincerely confident singer without affectation. Another fine interpreter of lyrics is Carmen Lundy whose good timing and clear diction illuminates her material, much of which is original. Kevin Mahogany sings ballads and blues with understanding, often extending into scat and vocalese. There is also Roseanna Vitro, a lively and vibrant singer from Texas; Vanessa Rubin, a swinging musical singer with great flair; Rebecca Parris, whose repertoire in the 1990s has moved from conventional to original and is delivered in an attractive manner in keeping with latter-day perceptions of the new jazz-fringe audience. Barbara Paris is content to work out of the mainstream in Colorado; Holly Cole and Ranee Lee, both with considerable talent, are Canada-based; and Karin Krog, mature now but a gifted stylist, is still prepared to be as adventurous in the 1990s as she was thirty years ago.

There are also the interpreters of classic jazz material of the 1920s and 1930s. Barbara Lashley's album *Sweet and Lowdown* was by far the best of its kind to be produced in the 1980s, and Terry Blaine's *Whose Honey Are You?* was the best-produced album of classic-style vocal jazz in the early 1990s. Blaine's conception of jazz singing is clear: 'A lot of young people are drawn to jazz because it allows you a lot of freedom and self-expression.' Also following the traditional repertoire are Carol Leigh, Sue Kibbey, Christine Tyrrell, George Melly and Marty Grosz, all of whom incorporate popular songbook material and blues in broad repertoires, while Gail Wynters takes a backward glance at the hip interpretations of the 1940s.

Among blues and gospel singers performing in the 1990s are Marilyn Middleton Pollock, a confident exponent of hot jazz and classic blues singing, and Lillian Boutté, whose straight ahead approach has essential qualities emanating from a background in gospel music. Ernie Andrews and Jimmy Witherspoon are still shouting the blues with enthusiasm and Jeannie Cheatham is an amiable and gifted performer who retains all the qualities of the great blues singer-pianists of the past. There are also r&b cross-over artists such as Ruth Brown and Etta James, who have the declamatory delivery of rock 'n' rollers, and raw-voiced Koko Taylor who is steeped in the ethos of the blues.

The area loosely termed 'jazz-soul' covers a wide stylistic range. Among singers with close links to jazz are Nancy Wilson, who gained a large international following for her popular repertoire while straining her jazz connections; Ernestine Anderson, a dynamic blues-tinged singer with enormous presence and authority; Mary Stallings, in the 1990s winning belated plaudits and recognition for her work; and Barbara Morrison, a lively singer with great panache.

Singers choosing to operate in the jazz fusion idiom include Gil Scott-Heron, a mannered jazz fusion rapper, and Al Jarreau, whose appeal to fusionists of the 1980s built a substantial following which he still retains.

Among a vast number of artists of all ages who show great enthusiasm for classic songbook material are Stacey Kent, a swinging singer with masterly interpretative skills; Nicki Leighton-Thomas, a rising young singer with a mature approach to her work; Lucy Reed, based in Chicago for many years, whose vocal skills are undimmed; Ruth Price, one of the overlooked singers of the 1950s, who has sung on in relative obscurity; and Laila Dalseth, whose sojourn in her native Norway kept her from centre-stage. Susannah McCorkle is an excellent interpreter of lyrics with a particular interest in Brazilian rhythms; Diana Krall is a young Canadian singer-pianist who sings with a maturity which belies her youth; and Sidsel Endresen is a cool Scandanavian stylist on the borders of jazz. Lena Ericsson, a well-controlled singer, makes good use of dynamics; Denise Jannah is a confident young performer from Surinam with great potential; Karrin Allyson is a convincing stylist, as is Eden Atwood, a pleasantly versatile singer, particularly able on up-tempo songs; while Oleta Adams shares her time between Top-40 work and jazz. Attracting considerable attention, publicity and plaudits are Cassandra Wilson and Rachelle Ferrell; sometimes over-dramatic but always listenable, Wilson is a credible nominee for tomorrow's title of World Jazz Queen, as is Ferrell, whose extraordinary voice can soar dramatically over many octaves with great accuracy and ease.

Jazz-informed popular singers who continued into the 1990s include veterans Frank Sinatra, Peggy Lee, Rosemary Clooney, Tony Bennett, Margaret Whiting, Barbara Lea and Buddy Greco; and much younger singers Harry Connick Jnr, Mark Porter, Joe Francis, Laura Fygi, Andy Prior and Gary Williams. These last six have helped re-popularize many songs from the American songbooks by bringing them to the attention of a new young

audience. Sue Raney and Salena Jones are consummate artists, fine interpreters of ballads and adept professionals with jazz associations, as are
Cheryl Bentyne and Janis Siegel, while Ricky Lee Jones, Basia, and Maria
Muldaur are jazz-aware pop singers who can deliver unusual and idiosyncratic material with considerable skill and conviction.

All of these singers have reasons for choosing their style of singing
and their material. A few have the ability to move between styles and material easily and convincingly without condescension. For example, Norma
Winstone may switch from songbook material to avant-garde innovations;
Lillian Boutté, between blues and gospel; Ian Shaw turns from songbook to
scat; while Jon Hendricks is at ease in both vocalese and scat. Singers such
as Dianne Reeves, Claire Martin and Tina May search for their material in
many music forms, creating repertoires which at times might include jazz
standards, originals, ethnic material and rock.

Performers in jazz-cabaret, still a viable form in the 1990s, usually
go without widespread acclaim either by the general public or jazz audiences. However, their craftsmanship and subtlety are often greatly admired
by other singers and musicians. They include Blossom Dearie, a small-
voiced and intimately hip singer who is extremely engaging in performance;
Dave Frishberg, distinguished by his witty lyric writing and exceptional jazz
piano playing; mellow-voiced Bob Dorough, and Nina Simone, whose often
burning intensity can sometimes tip over into despair. Ellyn Rucker is
another outstanding jazz pianist with a flair for singing; Meredith D'Ambrosio, a favourite singer of John Coltrane, sings in an intimate low-voiced
style, painting impressionistic variations on standards; and Dardanelle is
yet another fine instrumentalist for whom singing is a second but true love.

*   *   *

Quite clearly, the singers of the 1990s are a richly varied group. Divide
them by age or style, repertoire or musicianship, traditionalism or originality, there remain certain interconnecting threads that bind them
together. All of these artists – be they stylists, swingers, jazz-orientated
popular singers, jazz-aware pop singers, singers with 'jazz feel', vocalese
and scat singers, or jazz-soul singers – do what they do because it comes
from within and they do it with integrity. Those who found they had a lull
in their careers preferred to stop singing rather than change to a style for
which they felt neither emotional nor artistic affinity. No jazz singer sings
in a style or styles in which they do not believe simply to make money.
There is no such incentive in jazz. As critic Barry Ulanov observed: 'Getting
into jazz singing professionally is chiefly a matter of developing a stoical
disregard for decent food, decent lodgings and a decent income.'

As to what it is about jazz that generates this fierce loyalty – the
answers are almost as many as there are singers. High on most artists' lists
of motives might well be the opportunity for overlaying the material with
the singer's own concepts, the possibilities for endless stylistic variations,

the chance to make personal statements on established songs, or to introduce new and exciting songs and ideas. And to be able to do it all not merely during a long career but even in the space of a single album or on one night on the bandstand.

The variations and the opportunities, the ability to delight and surprise, are clearly enormously appealing to creative people. The singer can make her contribution unmistakably her own, however conventional the backing might be. Some may need to use scat, others can sing a lyric without changing one word. As already noted, some jazz singers have superb vocal equipment, others succeed despite barely having a voice at all but compensate through a certain dramatic power or through an ability to connect emotionally with song and listener. A constant source of fulfilment and rejuvenation comes from an ability to displace phrases and to use inflection to an extent that the song not only comes alive but also becomes essentially their own. Equally invigorating are the conflicting demands of interpretation and improvisation which can be met in many ways; melodic decoration is the most common, yet simplification of the melodic line can act just as well. Key to it all is improvisation, which can reshape material into a personal statement and turn the ordinary into art. It is not only the material that is reshaped, the singer too can be subject to the magical metamorphosis. As Mark Murphy says: 'You improvise yourself into being.'

Also adding to the excitement is the potential for either inspired interplay or breakdown in communication between singer and accompanying musicians. Jan Ponsford describes the uncertainties inherent in working in an improvisatory situation: 'If an arrangement changes on the stage, as it often does, that's fine by me. What tends to happen is that the people who can't go with the flow, who lack creative spontaneity, are the ones who panic when creativity happens. They'll stick to the original arrangement regardless of what everybody else is doing!' Such emotive situations inevitably colour performances and heighten interactive tensions with the audience. The altered harmonies of jazz singing can be as shocking to the non-jazz audience as they are a delight to the jazz fan. Some singers distort and fragment a melody to the outrage of the lover of conventional songbook material, perhaps reshaping and rearranging lyrics in a way that appears to mock the original lyricist's meaning. Others not only bring out that meaning totally, but through the use of delayed phrasing and a subtle use of inflection emphasize the original intention in a manner unimaginable to an orthodox singer.

In performance, the art of jazz singing is an incredibly exciting experience for singer and audience. Every night the singer is new, the audience is new. Young or old, inexperienced or mature, the singer is continuing a long tradition. Young or old, unaware or knowledgeable, the audience is also a part of the world of jazz singing. Yet for all its immediacy, the exciting jazz singing scene of the 1990s, shared by audiences and singers alike, came into existence almost a century ago.

TWO
THAT RHYTHM MAN

Music's my language... — *Louis Armstrong*

Viewed from the end of the twentieth century, the outstanding characteristic of American popular music is that it is so unmistakably American. A
hundred years ago, there was little that was exclusively American about
popular music in America. Authentic black music was only just beginning
to make an impression, and those areas of entertainment that carried
elements of Americana – minstrelsy, for example – by then had been largely
relegated to performances in second-rate provincial theatres. Big city
dwellers wanted sophistication and to them that meant European music.
Broadway echoed to songs from England, France and Austria by the likes of
Gilbert and Sullivan, Offenbach and the Strauss family. Audiences were
dazzled by the zest and gaiety of this music and the production values of
the shows in which it was performed. In the 1910s and 1920s American and
American-based foreign-born composers responded to these stimuli in a
variety of ways; some chose to found their work upon the European
example while others were convinced that the way ahead was to match
musical values, but to incorporate qualities that reflected America. The
former category included Sigmund Romberg, a transplanted Hungarian
whose operettas owed their shape, structure and sound to those of Vienna;
and among composers whose early work encompassed both imported and
indigenous forms were Jerome Kern, born in America, and Victor Herbert,
born in Ireland and educated in Germany. Representative of the new breed
of composer who sought to develop a uniquely American form of popular
song, and who became some of the founding fathers of Tin Pan Alley, were
Harry Von Tilzer, born in America of German stock, Irving Berlin, born in
Russia, emigrated to America at the age of four, and George Gershwin, born
in America.

Uniquely American the new songs most definitely were, but they
continued certain important characteristics of European music – romance
and delightful melodies. As composer and arranger Billy VerPlanck
observes: 'The American Popular Song is the last gasp of melody, the last
gasp of romanticism that came out of the last century. Of course Bach
wrote little gems of things, and Mozart, but the romantic era started in the
last part of the nineteenth century and the really great melodist was Rach-
maninov. There's no question that Puccini wrote marvellous things but if
you think about the absolute melodic content of the classic composers very
few had the melodic gift of, say, Cole Porter, Jerome Kern, certainly George
Gershwin.'

In the first decade of the twentieth century, American vaudeville
theatres echoed to sentimental ballads and comic ditties similar to those of
British music hall. Americanization of popular song came mainly through

the music and lyrics written for Broadway shows in the 1920s and especially in the 1930s by Berlin, Gershwin, Kern, Porter and their peers and
successors who include Richard Rodgers, Lorenz Hart, Harold Arlen, Jimmy
McHugh, Dorothy Fields, Harry Warren, Johnny Mercer, Buddy DeSylva, Lew
Brown, Ray Henderson and a host of others. New songs also developed
along Tin Pan Alley among the many geniuses and hacks who proliferated
there, labouring to fill the public's insatiable demand for new songs. The
term 'Tin Pan Alley' was probably derived from the constant racket of
pianos being rattled by a multitude of song pluggers churning out the latest
titles, and both Von Tilzer and Monroe H. Rosenfeld laid claim to coining
the expression.

A significant effect of the flood of vernacular love songs pouring out
of Tin Pan Alley was the death of ragtime and the syncopated music of
'coon-songs' – music which had itself previously hastened the demise of
sentimental drawing-room ballads. The songs that poured out were
frequently little more than workaday artefacts of popular culture, written
in the full and certain knowledge that they were ephemeral. Here today,
overwhelmed tomorrow by the next jingle on the conveyor belt. Inevitably
much was dross but here and there were musical gems which have endured.
That these songs live on in the way that they do is only partly attributable
to their composers. Neither is credit necessarily due to the original
performers in shows or on record. While some of these singers may have
been responsible for the initial success of many a tune, rarely did they
retain public affection beyond a generation: certainly not long enough to
claim that they alone have been the reason for a song's lasting popularity.
Credit for this is due to singers over the years, often jazz singers, who have
continued to sing, in contemporary vein, quality numbers rescued from the
past, breathing new life into half-forgotten but lyrically intriguing, melodic
songs. The Great American Song Book has been built from good songs,
consolidated by good singers, and has thus retained its popularity well past
the expected life span.

The majority of these songs are of 32-bar construction, standardized
into four sections each of eight measures, often with the third section,
known as the 'bridge', rhythmically and melodically different from the
others. This formula is designated AABA. With an introductory verse,
usually 16 bars, a standard song pattern was created. Intended or not, stan-
dardization served a useful purpose in allowing singers to approach new
material with a sense of its structure, regardless of whether or not they
could read music. The 32-bar song remained the dominant form of popular
music until the ascendancy of rock.

Songwriters Arthur Schwartz and Alec Wilder came independently to
the conclusion that Jerome Kern's composition 'They Didn't Believe Me',
written in 1914, was pivotal in the evolution of modern popular music.
Wilder explained, '... its melodic line is as natural as walking. It pointed in
a new direction and over the next few years Tin Pan Alley tunes increasingly

included a more substantial form of songwriting.' Kern, whose contribution to American popular song is all the more impressive when it is considered that in his formative years there was no music quite like the songs he would later write, had clear ideas about jazz and how his songs should be performed. He not only thought that jazz debased music but also argued that 'no author would permit pirated editions of his work in which his phraseology and punctuation were changed thereby giving to his work a meaning entirely different from what was intended'. Although the argument might initially appear reasonable, its total denial to the singer of any licence for interpretation is clearly restrictive. The interpretation of any written work, say a poem by Emily Dickinson or a play by William Shakespeare, can be word perfect and yet sound and feel completely different from another word-perfect version. The manner in which the words are spoken by reader or actor, how the work is presented to an audience by the director, must refashion the material. The importance of the role of the performer in readings, plays, films and music cannot be denied, and whereas Kern might be entitled to feel protective towards his creations, his condemnation of jazz is hard to sustain in the light of what really happens in jazz. What the jazz soloist, singer or arranger does is turn a standard popular song into a vitally creative interpretation, albeit one that is no longer totally owned by the composer. In so doing, using the composer's polished artefact as their own raw material, they have helped create something which is similarly original and just as characteristically American.

During the early years of the twentieth century, a steady acculturation of black musical forms was also taking place, gradually weaving them into the fabric of American popular music. Among the early black composers and performers who created a niche for black musical theatre on the predominantly white Broadway stage were Bob Cole and his partner John Rosamond Johnson, James Weldon Johnson, Ernest Hogan, Will Marion Cook, George Walker and Bert Williams.

After a hiatus, they were followed in 1921 by Eubie Blake and Noble Sissle whose energetic and tuneful score for *Shuffle Along* caused a furore on Broadway. Other black composers and lyricists of popular music of the period included Chris Smith, Perry Bradford, Sheldon Brooks, Spencer Williams, Clarence Williams, James P. Johnson, Andy Razaf and Fats Waller.

*　　*　　*

Just as music written in America before the advent of the new breed of composer was rooted deeply in the ways of the previous century, so too were performing artists mired in an ageing heritage.

Popular singers of the early twentieth century included Al Jolson and Billy Murray. Jolson, who was born in Russia and emigrated to America in 1893, became in time the best known and most popular all-round entertainer America (and probably the world) has ever known. Both in his choice of material and in his singing style, Jolson crossed and recrossed boundaries between operetta and minstrelsy, ballads and ragtime. He could be mawkishly sentimental and energetically rhythmic, he captivated audiences in the theatre and became a huge attraction on records and radio and in films. More than perhaps any other male singer of his generation, he opened the ears of white audiences to the existence of musical forms alien to their previous understanding and experience. While Jolson never sang jazz, his enthusiastic incorporation of ragtime, or more specifically pre-jazz syncopation, helped prepare the way for others who would bring a more realistic and sympathetic touch to black musical traditions. Indeed, so pervasive was the overwhelming Jolson aura that evidence of his influence can be felt in some of the early recordings of Bing Crosby, Ethel Waters and even Louis Armstrong. Recalling the Jolson impact, Bing Crosby said of him, '... his chief attribute was the sort of electricity he generated when he sang. Nobody in those days did that. When he came out and started to sing, he just elevated that audience immediately. Within the first eight bars he had them in the palm of his hand.' Billy Murray, born in Philadelphia, Pennsylvania, was a much more relaxed performer than the non-stop Jolson. He developed a form of singing that remained essentially European in context but which foreshadowed the later casual style of the crooners.

*　*　*

Pinpointing a date for the emergence of the blues as a fully-formed music is impossible, but few would argue with a date somewhere within a decade straddling the turn of the century. Among the early singers to have an impact outside their own narrow communities was Ma Rainey, who claimed to have first heard the blues in Mississippi around 1902. Essentially a tent and vaudeville artist, she gradually incorporated the blues into her act until she eventually dominated the genre. Rainey was not the first singer to record the blues; this honour fell to the black vaudeville entertainer, Mamie Smith. Another vaudevillian, the songwriter and hustler Perry Bradford, persuaded a hesitant Fred Hager of OKeh Records to let Smith sing 'Crazy Blues' in 1920. The recording sold 100,000 copies and suddenly the blues was big business.

The star who eclipsed Rainey as the pre-eminent singer of classic blues was Bessie Smith. Records by Smith vividly show how she towered over all her contemporaries. Her rich, powerful voice, her majestic demeanour and delivery helped win her the justly awarded title, Empress of the Blues. As a singer of the blues Smith was supreme and many of her recordings are required listening and remain examples of immense yet controlled vocal power and majesty. Heartfelt emotions and soaring rhythmic swing combine to weld together the traditions of black folk music, vaudeville and the modern inflections of 1920s jazz. Socialite and writer Carl Van Vechten described her singing as '... a woman cutting her heart open with a knife until it is exposed for all of us to see'. Black audiences loved and idolized Smith. She could be mesmeric; legend has it that in performance she could trance individuals at will. 'I'm gonna walk me one,' she would sometimes declare. If the blues was the major factor in Smith's career, also important were vaudeville songs and popular material. Many of her records of these songs are equally magnificent examples of her work, filled as they are with imaginative vitality and raw swing. They are true jazz performances. Sixty years on, jazz singers revere her memory and still listen to her records and marvel in her power and authority.

In style, Ethel Waters was the antithesis of Bessie Smith. With a light-toned voice, in performance she was cheerful and bright where Smith was dark and brooding. Overcoming an appalling childhood, by the time she was twenty-one she had become a headline attraction in black vaudeville. Billed as 'Sweet Mama Stringbean', she sang the blues but was always alert to the possibilities of using material from outside this field, readily intro-ducing popular songs and white vaudeville numbers into her repertoire. Encouraged by Earl Dancer, her then-stage partner, she was eventually persuaded to perform in white theatres and was soon on the way to the kind of high-profile career denied to Bessie Smith.

Waters was strong-willed in everything and had clear ideas on how to handle her repertoire. Auditioning to replace Florence Mills in the Plantation Club on Broadway, Waters was asked by songwriters Harry Akst and Joe Howard to sing one of their songs. Waters recalled: '... they sang it them-selves for me, doing it fast and corny. "Is that the way you want me to sing it?" I asked. Akst and Howard looked at each other. "Why not sing it your own way?" Now I've always had a strict rule about this. I'll do any new number the way I'm asked to sing it. But once you say, "Do it your way, kid", I sing it my way and won't try any other style that is second guessed on me.' The number was 'Dinah', her first major hit. By the 1930s she was widely known to the mainstream audience. Her records sold well and in 1929 she made her first film, *On With the Show*, in which she sang 'Am I Blue?' In 1931 she sang at New York's Cotton Club where she introduced another song destined to become a standard. Writer Ned E. Williams recalled the occasion: 'There was the unforgettable night when Ethel Waters stood in the spotlight, with the Ellington band pulsating behind her, and sang, for the first time in public, a song by Harold Arlen and Ted Koehler called "Stormy Weather".'

Waters enjoyed singing in Harlem, taking inspiration from the musi-cians who worked with her; men like James P. Johnson, Willie 'The Lion' Smith and Charlie Johnson. They 'could make you sing until your tonsils fell out. Because you wanted to sing. They stirred you into joy and wild ecstasy. They could make you cry. And you'd do anything and work until you dropped for such musicians.' Musicians reciprocated, Jimmy McPart-land recalling being taken by Bix Beiderbecke to hear her sing in 1927: 'We were enthralled by her. We liked Bessie Smith very much, too, but Waters had more polish, I guess you'd say. She phrased so wonderfully, the natural quality of her voice was so fine, and she sang the way she felt – that knocked me out always with an artist.'

In essence McPartland arrives here at the reasons for the impact Waters had upon other singers. She helped create – indeed, was largely responsible for – a style of artistic, jazz-influenced singing that laid out markers subsequently followed and developed by singers as diverse as Ivie Anderson, Connee Boswell, Lee Wiley, Mildred Bailey, Ella Fitzgerald, Frank Sinatra and Peggy Lee. Entertainer Bobby Short stretched still further the bounds of her influence: 'She was the source, I think, in America. She was inspiration for more singers than anyone can possibly think of.' Blues shouter Joe Turner pointed out that she was 'the only singer I absolutely adored...' Turner described how the first record he was ever enthused about was Ethel Waters's version of 'Shoo Shoo Boogie Boo', '... whenever my mother wanted to get me out of bed, she'd put that record on. I'd wake up when I heard that music, and I'd get right up without any trouble.'

Some singers who were inspired by Waters have themselves inspired so many others that a list of those who owe something to her must run into many thousands. Sad to reflect that many never appreciated the fact that much of what they did started with her. Today, some might not even have heard of her.

*   *   *

The first great jazz soloist was Louis Armstrong. A phenomenon, Armstrong was famed for his breathtakingly innovative and dazzling trumpet technique. He was the first real jazz genius – and he began as a singer. Born into poverty, as a child Armstrong was a member of an informal urchin group singing on the streets of New Orleans for nickels and dimes, and throughout his career singing remained integral to his performance, an inherent part of his greatness. Indeed, his trumpet playing and his singing were extensions of one another. The beautiful solos performed on his horn, he continued in his vocalizing; the fractured phrases he sang, he extended to his trumpet playing. If seen in classical singing terms, his vocal deficiencies would never have been accepted in any other musical form but jazz. He created his own concept, his was the first truly great and total jazz voice. He led the way.

Bessie Smith, Ethel Waters and others pre-dated Armstrong, certainly as far as recordings are concerned. But whereas Smith is identified as *the* great blues singer and Waters as establishing the basis of modern, jazz- and blues-*influenced* popular singing, Armstrong was pure jazz gold. Jazz was never to be the same after his initial impact, and neither was singing. Popular singers as well as jazz singers took inspiration, albeit often subconsciously, from his unique and personal phrasing, his projection and his happy persona.

Among singing contemporaries who immediately took on board the rhythmic implications proposed by Armstrong were, importantly, Ethel Waters and a young lyric baritone, Bing Crosby, both innovators in their

31

own right. Extrovert performers such as Cab Calloway were also to adopt obvious but rather superficial elements of Armstrong's performing style.

Armstrong first appeared on record as a vocalist in New York with the Fletcher Henderson Orchestra in 1925, having already recorded in Chicago as a member of King Oliver's band, but it was not until he returned to Chicago and began his ground-breaking Hot Five and Seven recordings that it became obvious that here was something new and exciting, not just in instrumental terms but in singing too. Today the fact of that vocal impact is perhaps dulled, due mainly to the passing of time and because attention is still drawn inevitably to the scintillating magic of his revolutionary trumpet work of that period. But in the 1930s singers like Crosby, Waters, Mildred Bailey, Connee Boswell and, later, Billie Holiday took inspiration in terms of rhythm, phrasing, feeling, fluency and inner truth. Interestingly, this inspiration of singers came not just from his singing but also from his horn playing. The two were thoroughly interchangeable and equally influential.

The first Hot Five track on which Armstrong sings is 'Georgia Grind', in which he takes part in a typical, if lightweight, piece of cabaret hokum in duo performance with his then-wife Lil. As with her piano playing, Lil Hardin Armstrong's singing ability was modest and yet, like her husband, she was always able to project an engaging charm into everything she did. Writer Chris Albertson said of her that she was, 'without doubt, the most vivacious jazz performer' he had ever met. Certainly her vocal recordings during the 1930s are a delight. On 'Georgia Grind', her first vocal side, she provides apt support to Armstrong's extrovert vocal.

Next came 'Heebie Jeebies', an early best seller for Armstrong and probably his most famous scat performance. Whether or not, as he later insisted, he accidently dropped the words of the song onto the studio floor and had to improvise the scat chorus is irrelevant. What is important is that from here there developed generations of singers who have since used scat – sometimes for better, often for worse. Scat, or the use of non-words in singing, pre-dated Armstrong by a long way in both black and white music traditions; but it is from his first recorded use of the medium that modern scat surely evolved. In place of the lyrics he scat-sings phrases that he might just as easily have played on his horn. He merges the lyric with the scat, moving between the two and making it all seem amazingly natural and totally unselfconscious – something not all scat singers are able to do, even today. Importantly, although it is generally accepted that Armstrong created jazz scat singing, he never subscribed to the notion of employing it as an entity in itself. He used it at almost every performance but he seldom completely ignored the lyric. Usually there remained some vestige of the original words. For Armstrong, scat remained a vocal tool to be used sparingly to enhance an interpretation and create something special and identifiably his own. Throughout his career the words of a song meant something within his performance; scat merely added a further dimension to complement both lyric and tune. He never allowed it to take over completely.

It has often been suggested that Hoagy Carmichael composed 'Stardust' by creating a melodic line similar in construction to something that cornettist Bix Beiderbecke might have played. Listening to Carmichael's own oblique vocal approach to the tune suggests that the idea is well founded. Put the song in the hands of Nat King Cole and the idea disappears into the flow of the singer's beautiful legato style. When Louis Armstrong first recorded 'Stardust' in Chicago in 1931, he left little doubt that the structure of the piece is an ideal vehicle for an explorative trumpet solo. At first his pungent lead keeps relatively close to the melody; he continues with a vocal chorus that simply fragments both the melody and the lyric in a quite glorious fashion. Punching out the words with horn-like precision, he cuts through the melody line as if playing his trumpet. He demonstrates clearly how to do what so many jazz singers have since said that they want to do; phrase like a horn. Unlike so many others, however, he does it naturally and without forethought. There then follows a splendidly climactic instrumental ending, the whole performance becoming a perfect example of his genius as instrumentalist and singer.

It was during his tenure at the Sunset Café in Chicago around 1927 that Armstrong began to gain experience as a vocal entertainer. At first he was an embarrassed and rather unwilling stooge for popular Chicago performer May Alix. Knowing he was shy, Alix would throw her arms around his neck and sing 'I Want a Big Butter and Egg Man'. To the delight and glee of both the audience and his fellow musicians, young Armstrong would 'stand and melt'. It was not long, however, before he was taking it all in his stride, quickly becoming confident and exuberant. When he returned to New York in 1929, would-be manager Tommy Rockwell suggested to him that he could gain great commercial success as a solo performer of popular material with a band used simply as a backdrop. Armstrong was not averse to the idea. Many jazz purists have suggested this was a disaster for jazz, contaminating the form and destroying Armstrong's validity as a jazz artist, but as trumpeter Jimmy Maxwell later pointed out, 'Pop material? Louis had to get into it. Where else was there to go? And what he did with it!' Rockwell must be credited for moving Armstrong towards popular material rather than remaining with jazz originals. It was an important and inevitable move not just for Armstrong but for jazz itself. Not only did it present him on a much broader stage but it was to benefit jazz performers as a whole in moving the music away from a collective concept to one of solo performance. With large bands used as a showcase for both his playing and singing, Armstrong's records became juke-box hits. Popular songs such as 'Ain't Misbehavin'', 'Body and Soul', 'I'm Confessin'', 'Just a Gigolo' and 'If I Could Be With You (One Hour Tonight)', became standard jazz vehicles which were successful on a national and international level.

In the early 1930s Armstrong was the uncrowned king of black American music, but his influence was becoming far more pervasive. Eventually it was to stretch around the globe and conquer the world. The importance of his contribution to jazz and to jazz singing cannot be over-stressed. It is a valid argument to suggest that without Louis Armstrong and without his cross-over to popular song, jazz music might have ended as a mere footnote to the 1920s. To a great extent it was his success, innovative brilliance, phenomenal technique, stature and influence that directed jazz on into the swing era. It was his rhythmic innovations that informed the arranging skills of Don Redman and Fletcher Henderson and indirectly popular music as a whole. These ideas also provided food for thought for future jazz instrumental soloists including giants such as Coleman Hawkins, Roy Eldridge, Benny Carter and Lester Young.

From 1929, Armstrong's singing took on equal status to his trumpet playing. There are some who still lament that fact, but for popular singing it was of great significance. Over the next decade he recorded hundreds of popular songs, some being the first recorded versions and many becoming standard jazz vehicles including 'Exactly Like You', 'I Got Rhythm', 'Memories of You', 'Sunny Side of the Street', 'Rockin' Chair', 'Them There Eyes', 'Lazy River', 'Wrap Your Troubles in Dreams'. Additionally, it seemed that due to his example instrumentalists of all kinds just had to sing. By the late 1930s many young trumpet players, whose first inspiration was Armstrong, were beginning to make names for themselves and it is not surprising that some felt the urge to sing: Roy Eldridge, Oran 'Hot Lips' Page, Jonah Jones, Rex Stewart, Louis Prima, Wingy Manone, Bunny Berigan, Ray Nance, Charlie Shavers. Even the morose Cootie Williams had a crack at it. Many other instrumentalists followed Armstrong's lead in developing into singers with their own identifiable voice and style, trombonist Jack Teagarden being one such example. Unfortunately, over the years the idea that every instrumentalist must vocalize has become tiresome as hundreds of professional and semi-pro trumpet players feel obliged to growl out often embarrassing and unmusical vocal choruses, *à la* Louis. Jimmy Rushing acknowledged Armstrong's influence: 'What a jazz singer ... you know ... if I ever get stuck when I'm singing I drop right back on Pops's style – it's the basic way of jazz singing and you can't get away from it. He's the boss and it's inescapable.'

In the last two decades of his working life Louis Armstrong became a household name, recognized and loved throughout the world. It was ironic that in this Indian summer of a long career it was his singing rather than his trumpet playing that brought about his belated generalized fame. In these final years his public appearances, even the mention of his name, could bring a smile to even the most downcast face. This might appear unimportant, even irrelevant, in regard to his stature as an innovatory figure but it was important in bringing about a higher profile for, and a general awareness of, jazz music.

* * *

Among the many pre-electric recording artists of the early 1920s who still retain nostalgic significance are Sophie Tucker, Irving Kaufman, Marion Harris, Cliff 'Ukelele Ike' Edwards, Nora Bayes, Frank Crumit and Blossom

Seeley. They introduced many examples of the new popular songs and so too did a new breed of singers who were not of the vaudeville tradition and unused to projecting their voices in theatres. They were also as yet uncertain of the technique required for the newly invented microphone. Among these new vocalists were Whispering Jack Smith, Rudy Vallee, Chick Bullock, Gene Austin, Scrappy Lambert and many more, most of whom failed miserably to convey even a hint of sincerity. One exception, Russ Colombo, showed potential but sadly died too soon, killed in a shooting accident. Only one male singer of this time proved to be of real and lasting consequence – Bing Crosby.

Crosby took an interest in jazz while still in his teens, singing and playing drums with a high school 'jass' band. At university he teamed up with a pal, Al Rinker, and after some hard times the duo was eventually heard and hired by Paul Whiteman who added Harry Barris to form the Rhythm Boys vocal trio. When first introduced to Whiteman the brash young Crosby cautioned, 'We don't sing any of that vo-de-o-do stuff. We do a brand new thing called the hotcha-cha.' Hit recordings such as 'Mississippi Mud' and 'I'm Coming Virginia' eventually helped convince Crosby that he could make it on his own. During his time with Whiteman, he had worked with many fine jazzmen employed by the bandleader in his jazz-age juggernaut: among them, Tommy and Jimmy Dorsey, Joe Venuti and Bix Beiderbecke. Perhaps more important than his Whiteman colleagues, Crosby listened to and was enthralled by Louis Armstrong. He appreciated and assimilated the momentous rhythmic changes that Armstrong was imposing upon popular singing. A competing crooner, the lugubrious Rudy Vallee, later described Crosby's own initial impact. He had witnessed an early appearance of the Rhythm Boys at the Coconut Grove in Hollywood. They were having difficulty in being heard, '... since they didn't have any amplification ... and didn't use megaphones, nobody paid the slightest attention to them'. Crosby, realizing this, left the stage and headed towards the audience. 'Suddenly the room was as quiet as a grave. Out in the middle of the floor was one of the trio, singing. The crowd was quiet, very quiet, and when he finished the place went into ecstasy ... this young man walked right off the floor with no expression whatsoever on his face. No triumph! No elation! No conquest! It was as though he were deaf like Beethoven and couldn't hear the audience had liked what he did.'

Crosby's voice at this time was described as 'having a glowing depth', his vocal solos as 'having a cry in them'. Artie Shaw, then an unknown young musician, recalled that 'there was something special about him. He was doing something that hadn't been done before.' But perhaps the most significant aspect of Crosby's career was the fact that he coincided with the important advances then being made in the techniques of broadcasting and recording. The invention of new, sensitive microphones meant that it was no longer necessary for a singer to sing loudly in order to be heard. Now, as Crosby discovered, it was possible to sing softly and intimately, to croon gently into the mike and still be heard clearly by the listener. This new confidential singing style had an immediate effect on other young singers, male and female, white and black. Even Armstrong listened and incorporated some of Crosby's vocal devices into his own singing, thus neatly closing a circle of mutual professional admiration. From 1930, the year he began his solo career, until he was overtaken by Frank Sinatra, Crosby was the pre-eminent popular singer in America. His conversational approach to song lyrics, allied as they were to a highly relaxed yet rhythmic delivery, took much from black music but offered it in a manner that was entirely his own. He could put over hot jazz or sweet romance. Although massively popular, his new intimate style came under considerable attack. Boston's Cardinal O'Connell declared his 'revolting disgust at a man whining a degenerate song, which is unworthy of any American man'. Just what the cardinal thought in later years when Crosby won an Oscar for his portrayal of a Catholic priest in a Hollywood movie hardly bears imagining.

During the 1930s, most male singers of popular songs in America – and overseas – took note of what Crosby was doing and adopted elements of his style. Thus, gradually and much diluted, Crosby's incorporation of jazz and black style slipped into the maelstrom of change through which American popular song was then passing. Through his example and followers, Crosby opened still wider the avenue through which jazz would influence popular music. He did have failings, most notably his sometimes inadequate interpretation of lyrics, but for the most part this was hidden by the sincerity and warmth of his delivery. The manner in which he told the story of the songs he sang was truly an extension of simple talking, and had the confidentiality of an old friend. But the words seldom carried the weight of utmost conviction. This development in popular singing was left to others.

*   *   *

If most white male singers in the 1920s lacked conviction, a few of their female counterparts conveyed total involvement with the material they sang. They were singers who had the necessary qualities of sincerity and warmth, plus rhythmic and interpretative skills, required for the more sophisticated lyrics being written mainly by writers who were familiar with ragtime, jazz and blues. Importantly, these singers made better and more effective use of microphone techniques than most of their male counterparts. They included Marion Harris, Annette Hanshaw, Connee Boswell, Lee Wiley and Mildred Bailey.

Other singers of the period who still retain some vestige of critical acclaim are those who showed a semblance of cross-over cultural awareness. Nevertheless, while Helen Morgan, Lillian Roth, Libby Holman and Ruth Etting may have retained their place with nostalgia buffs, in terms of vocal credibility they are clearly outshone by Harris and Hanshaw.

Helen Morgan will be forever associated with the term 'torch singer' and best remembered for introducing the Jerome Kern–P. G. Wodehouse song, 'Bill', which she sang in *Showboat* in 1927. Lillian Roth is remembered more for a hedonistic lifestyle than for her vocal abilities. Libby Holman made a specialty of singing doom-laden songs, like 'Moanin' Low' and 'Am I Blue?', and her sensual stage presence allowed the audience to overlook her lack of vocal prowess. Ruth Etting became a Broadway and Hollywood star and her singing of ballads, such as Irving Berlin's 'Shakin' the Blues Away', Walter Donaldson's and Gus Kahn's 'Love Me or Leave Me', and Rodgers's and Hart's 'Ten Cents a Dance', made her into a leading recording artist. Often accompanying her on record were the Dorsey brothers, Joe Venuti and Eddie Lang. Of the four, Etting was the superior singer but it is towards the, by then, well-established Marion Harris and the unassuming Annette Hanshaw that we must look for real vocal quality.

Marion Harris was one of the first white singers to incorporate the blues into her repertoire. An excellent cabaret performer, she was a top recording star of the 1920s, predominantly singing lowdown drags and peppy mid-tempo novelty songs. Much of the material she used was also performed by black artists of the day. Her recording career began in 1916, and although displaying the same boisterous zest of other American pre-electric recording artists such as Jolson, Blossom Seeley, Eddie Cantor and Esther Walker, she was also able to provide a degree of subtlety in her performance which carried her through to the 1930s. This was an era which demanded charm, finesse and swing in vocal performance. She starred in London's West End in the 1930s along with bandleader Roy Fox who said of her, 'You had to see Marion Harris on the cabaret floor or on the stage to appreciate the fact that her artistry was something to marvel at both as a singer and in the way she put over a song.' She recorded while in London, and contemporary reports suggest that she took the West End by storm as royalty and society flocked to see her. Fox went on to say that Harris was 'one of the greatest singers I have ever heard'. She continued to perform throughout the 1930s but died tragically in a hotel blaze.

Annette Hanshaw did not have a cabaret and vaudeville background. After starting out as a song demonstrator in her own music shop, she became exclusively a radio and recording artist. She sang with a delicately poignant voice which appealed to a broad section of the public, and although now sounding rather dated her records remain attractive and have a certain period charm. On many of these recordings there is the added attraction of accompaniment by young jazz stars of the day including Eddie Lang, Red Nichols, Adrian Rollini and the Dorseys. Her releases sold well but conflicted with Columbia's major female star, Ruth Etting, and she was shuffled over to cheaper subsidiary labels, her recordings often issued under pseudonyms. Dubbed the 'Personality Girl', many of her earlier recordings ended with her catch-phrase, 'That's all!', a legacy from her first test pressing when, as a nervous fifteen-year-old, she spontaneously ended with those words. Herman Rose, who was to become her manager and later her husband, liked the ending and asked that she retain it. She would often write extra choruses to fill out the performance and on many of her early recordings she accompanies herself either on piano or ukelele. Her recording of 'Lovable and Sweet' is as fine a performance of its kind as any of that era. In it Hanshaw shows just how, even in 1929, she could swing. Little wonder that Tommy Dorsey described her as 'the musicians' singer' and that John Hammond Jnr said of her, 'I don't think she realizes how good she is.' Care must be taken when seeking recorded examples of Hanshaw because some of her records feature her purposely mimicking her close friend Helen Kane, 'The Boop-oop-a-doop Girl'. Although excellent impersonations, they are hardly a good introduction to Hanshaw's talent as a singer. Never really caring for show-business, she retired when she was in her mid-twenties. In the 1980s Maria Muldaur re-recorded a popular Hanshaw song, 'Cookin' Breakfast for the One I Love', with more than a hint of an affectionate look back at the original version.

*   *   *

As the 1920s evolved into the early 1930s, singers began to appear who clearly had learned the lessons of the earlier decade and taken note of the rhythmic advances of Louis Armstrong and the melodic grace of Ethel Waters while, in some cases, retaining something of the forceful drive of Bessie Smith.

Despite physical handicap brought on by childhood poliomyelitis, resulting in her being permanently wheelchair-bound, Connee Boswell was ebullient by nature and became an extremely influential singer of those years. Born in Kansas City but raised in New Orleans, she and her sisters became proficient singers and instrumentalists. As children, they heard a great deal of black music and began to incorporate elements of it in their own work. Some of the singers they heard were domestic servants. 'We weren't wealthy,' Connee remembered, 'but we could afford help so I guess we all grew up listening to blues and spirituals...' The Boswell sisters began singing locally and were soon on radio but had little idea how to adapt to microphones. Their breakthrough with modern technology came about by accident, as Connee recalled: 'We were going to cut our [radio] transcription one week and I had a terrible cold and couldn't hit the high notes strongly and clearly enough, so Martha covered the piano with burlap, I dropped all the songs ... an octave or two and the three of us got very close around the mike and sang, sweet and low, into it. Of course, we had no idea what we sounded like, but the next week we heard the playback and knew we were on to something that no one else was doing.'

What the Boswells had done was inadvertently revolutionize close harmony singing. Early vocal groups, such as the Keller Sisters and Lynch, the Brox Sisters, the Ponce Sisters, and the Trix Sisters, were separate voices singing together; the Boswells were three voices singing as one, three musical brains acting and interacting with one another. Their success developed when they were featured on the coast-to-coast Chesterfield Show that was aired six times a week, alternating with Bing Crosby, Arthur Tracy the 'Street Singer', and Ruth Etting. Although some later groups would cling to older conceptions, most succeeding vocal groups, male as well as female, owe their musical shape to the pattern laid down by the Boswell Sisters.

For all the group influence, however, the effect of Connee Boswell on individual singers was even greater. In the early 1930s all three sisters married and only Connee continued with her singing career. Although from the very first she had sometimes recorded without her sisters, in 1935 she went solo. Even as part of the group her solo choruses had made an impact, often spontaneously improvised as they were within the strictures of a carefully arranged and well-rehearsed performance. In her solo work it was apparent that her timing, her easy sense of swing, allied to a warmly personal style and great interpretative gifts, made her a model for others. No other white singer at this time was doing exactly what she did. Not only did succeeding singers take note, even established singers listened and adapted their own styles, Mildred Bailey and Crosby among them.

Boswell's casual-sounding style broke away from the more formal on-the-beat style currently in vogue. She took liberties with her phrasing which, along with her sure sense of time, gave her performances an appealing freshness. 'I never did anything the same way twice. I never really thought about what I was doing while I was doing it.'

Reputedly, the popular swing bandleader Chick Webb observed that until he could find someone who sounded the way Boswell did he would not hire a singer. True or not, when Webb did hire a female singer it was Ella Fitzgerald who was unequivocal in her admiration of Boswell: 'There was only one singer who influenced me. I tried to sing like her all the time because everything she did made sense musically... When I was a little girl I listened to records by all the singers white and black and I knew that Connee Boswell was doing things that no one else was doing at the time.'

Boswell continued her singing career into the 1950s. A 1956 album recorded with the Original Memphis Five showed that she had lost none of her vitality and swing, and she clearly revelled in working with jazzmen again, just as in her earlier years she had sung with the Dorsey brothers, Bunny Berigan and Miff Mole (the latter re-joining her on the 1956 session).

Along with Bing Crosby and Connee Boswell were two other distinctive and distinguished artists who were indisputably influential singers: Mildred Bailey and Lee Wiley.

Heavily built but featherlight in voice, Mildred Bailey was the sister of Al Rinker, Bing Crosby's partner in the Rhythm Boys, and from 1929 she too sang with Paul Whiteman's band. She was one of the first non-black singers fully to digest black music, in particular that of the southern blues singers, and re-create it in her own personal style. In no way did she merely impersonate this material, and such was her talent and integrity that she not only won the approval of blacks but also appealed to white audiences at a time when black music was still a long way from being a wholly acceptable part of the popular canon. She sang in an easy, natural and unaffected manner but with unmistakable musicianly gifts. Her recording career included early sessions with Eddie Lang and Frankie Trumbauer and bands as diverse as the Casa Loma Orchestra and one led by Jimmy Noone. It is interesting to note that the blues-aware Bailey recorded with Noone just a few months after a popular 1930s blues star, Georgia White, cut her first-ever recording with the same Noone group singing, surprisingly, not a blues but a popular song.

Bailey's popular appeal resulted in many record dates and various billings, including the 'Princess of Rhythm', and in later years, during her marriage to Red Norvo, she was half of 'Mr and Mrs Swing'. Most famously, however, when she had a huge hit with Hoagy Carmichael's song 'Rockin' Chair', she became known ever afterwards as the 'Rockin' Chair Lady'. Bailey was not one to sit still either with her style or her ideas about inter-pretation. After hearing Connee Boswell she adapted some of her tech-niques, becoming more aggressive and musically daring. Later still, when Fitzgerald, Billie Holiday and Helen Humes came along, she listened to them, too. Unusually, as she developed so her singing became higher. She also applied a more subtle touch to her vibrato.

Bailey's interpretations of songs were filled with emotion, drawn not from emotionalism but from technique and inner feeling. And she had the much-needed knack of re-creating anew every song each time she sang it. Composer Alec Wilder observed this in practice, seeing Bailey sing a song with which she was very familiar but which nevertheless caused her tears to flow. 'Although she had sung the song a great many times, it was the first time; and I suddenly realized that everybody, when they do anything that they have done many times before, should forget the habit and not take it for granted, and make it all new immediately. There are those I have heard who sounded as though they had sung it a hundred times, she never did.' Count Basie's drummer Jo Jones recalled: 'Mildred and the Boswells, they were the white chicks who knew what was going on. They went to the clubs and listened to the black musicians, and it rubbed off on their work.'

In striking contrast to Connee Boswell and Mildred Bailey, who each made hundreds of records in the 1930s, Lee Wiley made only a handful during that same period. As so often happens in the jazz world, this is not a measure of respective qualities but a denunciation of the foibles of recording companies. Lee Wiley began her career singing on local radio somewhere in Oklahoma. Her first claim to fame was singing with the Leo Reisman Orchestra on radio: 'I just used to sing maybe two vocal choruses in the thirty minute programme', but later, 'I started doing those little "playlets" as we called them, and each of them led into a song, you know. I had never acted, but it was either you act or you lose your job.' Later she had her own radio programme and featured on record with the Casa Loma Orchestra and the Dorsey brothers. During these successful years her career was carefully scripted by composer Victor Young. Wiley delighted in singing the verses to popular songs and built each performance with a conscious but non-stagy sense of theatre. Perhaps due to her association with Young and to her own endeavours as a songwriter, she usually adhered fairly closely to the songs as set down by composers and lyricists, although she did sometimes gently amend a lyric to make it easier for her range. She sang with deceptive simplicity, bringing a sense of controlled passion to her readings of the great standards. An extremely vulnerable singer, she sang without deceit and in consequence when she erred she tended to err badly. She also had a tendency to fudge the end of a phrase and sometimes pronounce certain words oddly, for example, strangulating the first two words in the first phrase of 'You Do Something to Me'.

She worked with many different kinds of bands, including, in the 1940s, a big band led by her then-husband, pianist Jess Stacy. Possibly her finest hour came with sessions she recorded mainly in the 1940s singing the works of Cole Porter, Harold Arlen, George and Ira Gershwin, and Rodgers and Hart, perhaps the first-ever example of 'songbook' albums. The low-key intimacy of her interpretations, delivered as they were in a fragile, sometimes wistful voice, and accompanied by small jazz groups, produced many fine performances that might be termed definitive: 'I've Got a Crush on You', 'How Long Has This Been Going On?', 'Baby's Awake Now', 'I've Got the World on a String'.

Wiley acknowledged her debt to Ethel Waters, observing that she had heard her records back home in Oklahoma but was later pressed by Tommy Dorsey to renew her listening: 'I loved to hear her and adapted her style and softened it, made it more ladylike'. Whilst usually maintaining the demeanour of a 'lady', Wiley could when necessary be extremely raunchy.

Musicians have always recognized that hers was a very special talent but, possibly because of the fragility that made it so appealing, it was all too easily overlooked when set against other more assertive singers. Perhaps aware of this, Wiley once remarked, 'Had I been a fella, I believe I'd have played the trumpet.'

During the years that Wiley was singing to small but appreciative audiences and gaining plaudits from jazz musicians, and Bailey and Boswell were carving out successful careers in broadcasting, the worlds of jazz and popular song moved closer together than at any time in the past, a confluence that also had enormous commercial ramifications. Singers such as Wiley, Bailey, Boswell, Crosby and Waters attracted followings, although for the general audience their appeal, and that of Hanshaw, has more to do with a love of style than any awareness of the role played by jazz in their performances. Their sincere, highly musical delivery set standards of excellence and created paradigms of performance that were to echo down the years but, other than Mildred Bailey, they were not a part of this confluence of jazz and popular music – a confluence that was to become known as the swing era.

THREE
YOU DON'T LEARN THAT IN SCHOOL

Singing is the easy part. Trying to make a living out of it,
that's the hard part. The audience doesn't know what you have to
go through just to get the gig. — *Chris Connor*

'We had a band bus for a number of years, it was very old – we called it the "shed on wheels". The heating system was always breaking down in wintertime. On one trip ... we had thick ice on the inside of the windows and the windscreen wipers failed in the middle of a blizzard.'

For anyone brought up in the atmosphere of the swing era, when band buses traversed the USA on a seemingly endless series of one-night stands, these words will surely evoke memories, perhaps even the warm glow of nostalgia. In fact, the speaker is not a long-forgotten American band singer of the 1930s; he is Mark Porter, a young British singer, recalling his time in the late 1980s and early 1990s spent with the New Squadronaires Orchestra.

'Ten years with a band is a lot of time on the road,' Porter continues. 'I think I've visited almost every town in Britain that has a theatre or dance hall – or at least it seems that way.' The band bus was not his only means of travel. 'Before I could drive a car, most of my journeys were made by train... When you go on stage the audience thinks it's glamorous, what they don't see are the hours of changing trains, traffic jams and other hold-ups. I remember one gig in Norfolk where I was stuck behind a tractor. The first show was at 5 p.m., I arrived at the theatre at 4.55. I left the car engine running for the stage-door man to park and had four minutes to get my stage clothes on. I must say I am proud of the way I managed it; as I ran up the stairs my intro music was being played and I breezed on stage hopefully looking as if nothing had happened.'

But however important it is to present a professional, unflappable face to the public, it is another kind of learning that comes from experiences like this. 'As far as I am concerned,' Porter explains, 'I believe that singing with a big band is the best training a singer of my type can get. You learn discipline and also to work with all types of musicians. I consider myself fortunate... Many young singers I know have sadly never had the opportunity to work with professional live musicians. They know nothing else but backing tapes. No matter how good these tapes may be – and some are excellently produced – I think a "performance" is limited and lacks the spontaneity you get with live music.'

Singing to backing tapes! Jo Stafford or Dick Haymes would surely cringe at this crass reality for today's would-be singing stars. But, of course, the opportunities for singers to work with a big band are exceedingly rare today. Once upon a time it was commonplace; indeed, it was almost the only place a singer could learn his trade. And in many ways it was the best school of all.

'Working in a band was an important part of growing up, musically and as a human being,' Frank Sinatra said. 'It was a career builder, a seat of learning, a sort of cross country college that taught you about collaboration, brotherhood and sharing rough times. There is no teacher like experience. And singing in a band is like lifting weights. You're conditioning yourself... When it comes to professional experience, there's nothing to beat those one-night tours when you rotate between five places around the clock – the bus, your hotel room, the greasy spoon restaurant, the dressing room, if any, and the bandstand. Then back on the bus and the next night's gig, maybe four hundred miles away or more.'

Jo Stafford, who shared Sinatra's experiences with the Tommy Dorsey band, took a characteristically wryly humorous view of another aspect of life on the road: 'We travelled a lot by bus and, well, a band bus is arranged like a bandstand. On a bandstand if you have strings, the strings are in front, and they're fairly calm people who behave themselves. Next are the saxophones who get a little rowdy – but not too much. Next come the trombones, who get a little raunchy, and then the trumpet players, who are out of control. And that's the way the bus worked. Starting in front it's fairly calm, but as you worked your way back, you came to the sax players, then the trombone players, then the trumpet section. All the way in back was the rhythm section. They were the worst; they were real evil. That's where Frank usually sat. So did I.'

Rosemary Clooney's recollections were similar, except that she divided the bus not into instrumental sections but by habits, all of them bad. 'There would be the booze section, and then there would be the grass section. And then a couple of times we had some that stayed way at the back – and I think they were on everything but roller skates.'

The sudden burst of popularity of a jazz-based kind of music that was the swing era caught the music industry by surprise. As the commercial possibilities became apparent, bands mushroomed. There were literally hundreds of bands, needing thousands of musicians, but despite the jazz base only a minority were truly jazz musicians. And every band, it seemed, had a singer, probably two – a boy and a girl. Somehow, singers were found to fill these suddenly created job opportunities. But the available workforce was anything but experienced. Singers were often hired on the strength of a recommendation or an audition of only one song. In the case of Ray Eberle, he was hired because Glenn Miller assumed that if his brother Bob Eberly [sic] could sing well then so could he. He couldn't. Mostly, however, singers were hired because they showed promise, looked good, and could learn on the job. This was no formal academy. Singing night after night in venues ranging from palatial ballrooms and plush hotel lounges to barren school gymnasiums and draughty country barns, they learned their trade. Using sound systems that ranged from 1930s state-of-the-art to none at all, they discovered their own shortcomings and struggled to correct or at least to conceal them. Slowly, their trade was turned into a craft.

That it worked, this cross-country college, is never questioned. Ernestine Anderson, who went out on the road with Russell Jacquet's band when she was thirteen and had to have a chaperone, remarked of the life: 'No money but good training. Big bands are always good training as I found out when I went with Lionel Hampton.' That she had needed to learn is evident from an even earlier experience: 'A piano player told me I was a jazz singer when I was twelve when I was singing in a talent contest. I told them the wrong key and had to sing around the melody, improvising.'

In an interview in *Crescendo International* Betty Bennett agreed that big bands provided invaluable lessons: 'My two years with Alvino Rey was what led me to myself. Though he didn't have the hippest band in the world, he let me figure out what I wanted to do vocally. And I got some invaluable training on that band. Even if I was largely discovering the things I did not want to do. I was trying to sing like girl band vocalists are supposed to sing. And that wasn't me at all. My mother told me to be myself. I started to sing songs like I thought they should be sung. That's what I've been doing ever since... I remember sometimes we'd have ten one-day theatres in a row to do – three shows a day. The first show was something like 11 or 12 a.m. After the job we'd drive 500 miles, in order to do the same thing next day. There was never a question of checking in. I'd just take a sleeping pill, curl up on the seat and do the best I could. But singing in all kinds of weather, so to speak, sick and well, hoarse with good or bad microphones – I really believe that a kind of consistency comes from it. I date whatever consistency I have from that time.'

The price of education on the road could be high. Physical and emotional exhaustion was not uncommon. Maxine Sullivan said, 'I often wondered how Ella and Helen Humes and the other singers could do the one-night-stand thing, year after year. I did it once with Benny Carter and when I got back to New York I kissed the ground.'

It could be even worse. 'I was really sickened and exhausted by one-nighters,' Chris Connor remembered. 'Two or three hundred mile hops, grab a hamburger, sort out a gown at every gig, two or three hours at the job, then back on the bus again and travel all night. It was a rough life. It did me in. I was physically exhausted.'

But all that was yesterday and, rare exceptions such as Mark Porter's experiences apart, yesterday has gone. Today, instead of one-night stands, the would-be singer can go to a real college. A place of bricks and mortar with courses and teachers and diplomas at the end of it all. In many respects this has to be seen as an improvement, but the on-the-road academy taught valuable lessons that need to be known but which can never be fully replicated in a classroom. Sometimes with the right kind of teacher, some of the lessons can be passed on. Los Angeles-based Mike Campbell, who learned partly in a classroom and now teaches in one, believes in the values – but he takes care to add important cautionary comments: 'I had formal training on guitar, I could always sing, and it helped my ear tremendously. I studied voice privately with Lee and Sally Sweetland, my gurus, for one and a half years. I teach now and use their method of vocal technique. Lee was with the Metropolitan Opera and Sally is a legendary studio singer with forty years' experience and also was the girl singer with the Sauter-Finegan band. They are still teaching. And I went to college and studied. Always studying something – arranging, piano, guitar, sight-singing – knowledge is power. The more you know about your craft, the better you can approach it.' Campbell grew up in a musical family in Hollywood and as a young man joined the Doodletown Pipers vocal group, eventually becoming lead singer. Later, he formed a Las Vegas show band but the lure of jazz was too strong and he returned to Los Angeles and a career as a jazz singer. He also started teaching and in 1983 began a nine-year stint at the Grove School of Music. In the mid-1990s he was Vocal Program Director at Musicians Institute in Hollywood and a busy clinician in the USA and Europe. For all his deep involvement in teaching, Campbell is aware that this alone does not make a jazz musician. 'You can be a technical wizard and not make any music. There are plenty out there today, guys who give you thousands of notes per bar and you sit there and say, "who cares?" Then you have guys like Jimmy Rowles, Tom Harrell, Phil Woods, they'll give you four notes and they are absolutely phenomenal. Training is important, but technique as an end to itself doesn't work for me. I've got to have that emotion, got to have the passion.'

The view taken of training varies enormously from singer to singer; for some the external imposition of disciplines has been essential, to others it has brought a better understanding of their instrument, some have benefited physically by learning how to care for their voices. As for their teachers, they include the purely academic, the craftsman-singer-turned-teacher, and instrumentalists. For the classical-style teacher, certain aspects of the jazz singer's world are foreign – for example, establishing the right tempo and finding the right note in an intro. Instrumentalists can help a singer with these and also with phrasing, rhythmic understanding and intonation by example. When the young Chicago-based singer Jackie Allen attended the University of Wisconsin at Madison, she was uncertain in her ambitions until she encountered the teachers: 'I didn't know whether to major in musical drama or in classical music French horn but as soon as I got there, the jazz department (which included master jazz bassist Richard Davis and avant-garde pianist John Wildman) just pulled me in. Richard Davis took me under his wing, but everyone on the faculty had a different, unique style and outlook, and each one had something to give me.'

Among other singers finding help from instrumentalists as an ideal form of tuition is Stacey Kent. After receiving a degree in comparative literature in the USA she decided to visit England, 'just to get away. I ended up doing a one-year post-graduate jazz course, just for the fun of it. Soon I was meeting musicians and making contacts and the work started to flow in.' She had always sung but never thought that this would become her life: 'I had no idea this would happen! I planned on returning to New York, but with all the offers I was getting, I stayed. So my career started without me ever having to make a decision to start it.' As a child, she had studied classical piano, 'but then in my own spare time, I would work things out for myself. For example, I would go to a movie and the music would stick in my head and so I'd go home and try to work it out on the piano. I guess from an early stage, I was conducting my own ear-training course. So I think this has played a big part in my development. I'm not a good piano player but I do have a good pair of ears that I worked on before I even realized it. As a girl, I just played what I heard because it seemed the natural thing to do. When I began to study, I realized how vital that was, and is.

'I didn't really have vocal training. Again, it was just something that I could do naturally. I practise and work it out for myself. I've seen a couple of coaches over the past couple of years, to ask specific questions and work out specific things. But as far as jazz goes, no one taught me about "jazz singing", I just listened a lot.'

The benefits Kent gained by being able to play an instrument are underlined by Carmen McRae: 'As an improviser what helped me was my five years with the piano, and I did work at being a pianist and a singer combined. I believe that all singers should have a little bit of piano, knowing that when you hit a note, that it is in tune and not sharp or flat. It's just that if I am improvising I know the structure of the chord – I know my limitations. If you're being accompanied by just chords you only hit notes that will be right for that particular chord that's being played – or the next chord that it leads into.'

Sue Kibbey admits to playing piano 'badly', and just chords: 'I use it to teach myself new songs. I had formal training at London's Guildhall School of Music and Drama in 1987 – jazz and rock studies. I find it useful to know about arrangements, it gives you a language to speak to musicians with. They tend to respect you if you know what you're talking about. But I had no formal training for voice. My music teacher was instrumental in teaching me about breathing, phrasing, dynamics, tone, etc.'

Academies are not for everyone, of course. Helen Merrill was inspired to become a singer by listening to her mother singing around the house: 'I was unable to afford to study music and singing. In retrospect this is probably just as well as training might have got in the way.' However, as Kitty Margolis explains when speaking of her training which had covered vocal technique, musical theory, ear-training and improvisation: 'It sharpened what I knew instinctively.'

Chris McNulty, a New York-based Australian, is another singer who questions the validity of formal training for a jazz singer. Speaking of her own work with guitarist Peter Leitch, she considers the problems of teaching abstractions: 'We have a very intuitive sense of pitching and placement between the guitar and the voice – not academic at all, just a real union with the sound that is something special. I don't know how you could teach that, but it's extremely important as a singer.' Generalizing, McNulty continues, 'You need to know how to control your voice, but the more intuitive you are as a singer the better singer you are going to be. I have never got into training. I never hear a trained voice I like. You can train yourself, that's fine. But how can someone train you to do this? God, I don't know! Of course, there may be moments in your career when you need to go and see somebody. There may be certain changes taking place physically that might require it – as long as you use it and it doesn't use you. But training a voice is not the way I want to go. Young singers have to find their own voice.'

But plunging in at the deep end, without knowing anything about the technicalities of singing or even something as basic as which key to use, can be daunting and can also set a singer off on the wrong foot with other musicians. Susannah McCorkle recognized early on in her career that musicians playing with her might harbour resentment: 'Although I was younger and less experienced than they, I was the front person. I got a lot of bitterness and hostility from some musicians who had been playing twenty or thirty years and were basically envious of singers.' Playing with new musicians can be a problem for a singer but, as Marguerite Juenemann has discovered, it can be a spur: 'I enjoy playing with different musicians as they bring something new to some of the same material you might have done for what could seem like too often.' But she warns, 'Being able to express what you need to have in some arrangements is extremely important. Know the music and the arrangements. A performance has a better chance of being strong and your players will have a stronger lead to follow. Respecting musicianship and the artform in this way adds to the quality of the performance.'

The uneasiness felt by some instrumentalists towards singers can be justified, as Norma Winstone acknowledges: 'If you don't know what speed you want to do the thing at, you don't know how many bars intro, and you don't know what key, they can't take you seriously, can they?' The other side of this particular coin is expressed by Dave Frishberg, recalling his days as an accompanist: 'What I hated was the singer imposing on me his or her insecurities about music and depositing it all in my lap.' But then, as pianist Sal Mosca remarks wryly, 'If I walked on a bandstand and didn't really know what was going on I'd be insecure too.'

A problem for some jazz musicians is an inability to understand the importance of the words of a song, the stories they tell, the emotional content, and the sound the singer wants to develop. They are more likely to note that a singer has dropped a beat than that she has captured the tone of the lyric. 'It takes a long time to learn a song,' Abbey Lincoln says, 'and to understand the song.' This is something a musician might well understand if he is the soloist, but when he is an accompanist it is a very different matter. Being an accompanist is a vocation; he needs to be sensitive to a singer's needs and not be simply involved in technique. He must respect the singer's phrasing, inflections, shading and time. As Weslia Whitfield says of her accompanist, husband Mike Greensill, 'He watches me breathe in order to accompany what I'm doing, and I stay aware of what he's playing so as to not step on anything inadvertently. I also try to clearly convey to him anything I'm going to do so as not to sabotage his musical ideas.'

Ethel Waters built a close musical relationship with pianist Pearl Wright in the 1920s: 'Pearl and I had worked together through a sort of telepathy. I never had to tell her what I wanted. She understood my every mood and musical desire. She could interpret a number exactly as I wanted it played. A clue to this instinctive co-operation lies in Pearl being a singer herself. An accompanist who can sing knows the effects you seek, and you can feel understanding and help coming out through her fingers, through the piano, to you.' Seventy years on, and Barbara Paris found similar response from the qualities of accompaniment given by pianist-singer Ellyn Rucker: 'She interprets from a real jazz perspective.' Jimmy Rowles was a rare example of a consummate jazz pianist who was also a masterly accompanist. Shortly after Rowles's death in 1996, Norma Winstone recalled a collaboration with him on *Well Kept Secret*: 'I'll never forget him, or the way he worked. When we did "Where or When" he just dropped into this tempo after the intro that was so *right*, even though we hadn't discussed it beforehand or anything, that I just found myself smiling as I sang it. It was beautiful to sing with him.'

Collaborations like these are both laudable and enviable, but it is sometimes difficult when the musician charged with the role of accompanist is himself creative. Mark Murphy addresses this point: 'Look, some of them can do it, some of them can't. I have a repertoire for jazz musicians who can't read music. A lot of them are not good readers because some have the improvisational talent which blocks the left side of the brain which reads... I don't even know if I've got a left-hand side to my brain because my creative gift is so dominant.'

Because a musician can't read, or is creative, does not automatically mean that rapport with a singer is impossible, although the prospect of working with musicians such as these can cause pre-gig apprehension. Mike Campbell remembers an occasion in New York when he had a date with three very famous musicians: 'We had a rehearsal in the bass player's apartment and these legendary players couldn't read! They couldn't even read chord charts. So we didn't even get through five songs and we were playing at a famous club that night. I walked out of the rehearsal stunned and shaken. "I'm gonna make a fool of myself tonight." I went to the gig early, concerned at how they would play but they were burning the place down. I said to a friend, "I hope they play like that for me." When I went up and counted off the first tune they did, they just burned those charts. Lots of mistakes but no total crashes. It was incredibly inspiring, they just burned them. So that's a thrill.'

The mutual respect, earned on this occasion the hard way, is obviously important but it is a state of mind that is sometimes hard to achieve. An instrumentalist who has accompanied many of the best singers jazz has ever known takes a dryly resigned view: 'All singers are bitches to work with,' he says, almost seriously. 'I'm married to a singer but that doesn't change anything.' After a reflective pause he amends this universal condemnation. 'No, Peggy Lee is a doll. You would ask her what she wanted you to play and she'd tell you, "Just play whatever you think is right." Oh, and Helen Humes was just the same, but the rest of them are bitches.'

Maxine Sullivan, surely another exception to this blanket bitch rule, offered a comment for the defence: 'Look, there are such things as lousy musicians.'

Apart from the often much-needed sense of humour that jazz people possess, they are also usually tolerant people, as Barbara Lashley discovered when, at almost forty, she made her first venture into professional performance. She had been singing in the Berkeley Community Chorus after taking a degree in Afro-American Studies at the University of California at Berkeley. The director of the chorus, noting her interest and recognizing her potential, suggested that she should take singing lessons and also that she might like to go down to Solomon Grundy's, a club on San Francisco's waterfront, to listen to jazz. She did, and one day learned of a jam session run by a pianist named Bill Bell who invited her down: 'And I said to myself, "Well, why not? I mean, what have I got to lose?" So I went down to this place and I had this song on my mind, "Tenderly", and of course I didn't know that much about playing with musicians and jazz – that was all to come later – but I just did this on a whim. Of course, when I got up on the little bandstand they had there, Bill says, "Now what key do you think you sing that in?" And I said, "Key?" I don't know. Ah, let's see, "The evening breeze..." "Oh, okay, that's about a G", and I said, "Oh, fine", and he started the intro and it was so natural to just start singing it. So afterwards he said, "I think you have the right idea but get some singing lessons so you have some technique behind you."' Later, Billy Cayou, one of the house musicians at Solomon Grundy's, offered to coach Lashley how to phrase and to give her ideas on how to approach her songs: 'Bill was a good teacher. He's a bass player and bass players are noted for having the knowledge of phrasing down to a science and the best way that they show that knowledge is by working with you. They encourage you to consider what the message of the song is all about, how you want to say it, and to whom you want to say it.'

The deep-end approach to entering the singing business can be much less comfortable than Lashley's experience. Indeed, as Terry Blaine discovered, it can be positively harmful. Blaine had studied classical music at school in America, playing piano, clarinet and flute: 'I had natural ability but not the patience, I couldn't always focus.' She had always loved singing and at home sang to pop records. After leaving college, she abruptly dropped everything and went on the road as a singer with a rock band. The intentions were good but the result was almost catastrophic: 'It was a good experience, going out on the road, meeting new people, broadening your world. Ultimately, experience is a greater teacher. You can have all the formal training in the world but at some point you have to let it back out again in a way which is not only pleasing to an audience but also to yourself. But singing is not like playing the piano; if a C is written, you hit a C. With your voice, you have to develop it, pamper it, take care of it and learn about it. It's part of you, so it's affected by everything you do. That was all lost on me until later on.

'I often joke that I left my first voice up at this rock 'n' roll club up in White Plains, New York. Years later a good friend was up at that club and I asked her, "Did you happen to see my voice there? I know I left it there, what with screaming over a rock group at the time, doing five or six sets a night, six nights a week." That's a rude awakening for someone who had a measure of classical training. But this is the reality of Top 40 work. I lost my voice early on in my career. Then, when I started to study voice that was a turning point. For the first time I was saying, "Yes, I think I want to do this", but wasn't quite sure what I wanted to do but knew I needed to get a handle on it. I had to learn how to balance better the amount of energy that was going out, how to hear on stage, how to hold something back and not give it all out in the first set of the first night and not have anything left for the rest of the week – tons of lessons to be learned.'

Jan Ponsford's deep end was auditioning with a British jazz-rock fusion band, and mutual misunderstandings led to an amicable and ultimately beneficial experience: 'The band was called Big Chief and had saxophonist Dick Heckstall-Smith in it. The group's material was eclectic, with a heavy jazz bias. The first song I rehearsed with them was "Twisted". I knew Joni Mitchell's version, the band knew Wardell Gray's version! I was nervous and forgot the lyrics, so I scatted until I remembered the words again. When I finished the band was bowled over by it. They thought I had scatted on purpose. I got the job.' Of course, the deep-end approach is not for everyone. Indeed, it takes a degree of tough-mindedness to survive such a fierce baptism. Fortunately, Ponsford is determined and has a clear-eyed view of the life of the jazz singer. As a young girl she first heard live jazz at the Reading Jazz and Blues Festival. Until then, like all teenagers growing up in the 1960s and early 1970s, the music to which she was exposed was rock and pop although she had earlier listened to Ella Fitzgerald, Frank Sinatra and classical music [to which she would improvise words and counter melodies] while all her friends were listening to the Beatles. Instinctively, she began to absorb the music of black and black-influenced pop artists such as Jimi Hendrix and The Cream and especially blues-based bands, which is what took her to Reading: 'I was listening to some macho heavy metal, lying there on the grass when suddenly George Melly and John Chilton's Feetwarmers came on. It sounded so happy and alive and acoustic – there's something warm, wonderful and earthy about acoustic, so different after the other turgid, deafening stuff. I was diverted to another plane.' Once re-directed, Ponsford found her métier although for a time she did sing folk music: 'Actually, I sing anything, anywhere, anytime. But I do think of myself as a jazz singer because I improvise. I can't actually sing straight. If somebody gives me a song as written I'll take liberties with it and make it mine, mould it to me and do what I want to do with it. So I guess I'm a jazzer!'

Ponsford continued to draw on multiple influences; in particular, once she was on a jazz track, the singing of Sheila Jordan and Helen Merrill – but preferred to teach herself rather than be formally trained, 'as at that time in the UK I couldn't find a teacher approving of or with an understanding of the essence of jazz singing'.

Nevertheless, many singers do gain from the undoubted benefits that emerge from a classical education. The New York singer Dominique Eade sampled many aspects of formal tuition: 'I chose jazz gradually. I sang and wrote folk-pop music in high school, but I got interested in jazz through my parents' record collection, and a Billie Holiday record that came out around the same time as the movie, *Lady Sings the Blues*, and Thelonious Monk's *Criss Cross* that my brother brought home as a gift for my mother. I began to sing jazz more often in college. I sang with a jazz group at Vassar, where I was an English major. After two years, I left Vassar to attend Berklee College of Music in Boston where I studied and performed jazz exclusively. I ended up in music school, the New England Conservatory, where I got my bachelor's degree and an Artist Diploma. I'm glad that I established a direction before music school, but studying had a big impact on my musicianship. In my studies and listening, I've always been interested in many kinds of music. At NEC I had the chance to study classical theory and composition, ethnic or world musics, and jazz. All of that music has influenced me as a composer and improviser. The combination of rigorous ear-training and theory helped me develop my abilities as an improviser, which was very important to me.'

Eade's educational background, then, covers voice, ear-training, classical and jazz theory, composition, music history and ensembles. She also studied privately with Stanley Cowell, Bob Moses, Ran Blake and Dave Holland: 'With all these teachers, I worked on aspects of musicianship in the same way that they would work with an instrumentalist. Because I've always been interested in exploring the voice as an instrument, I have also studied vocal technique with different voice teachers. For myself and my students I've always tried to find ways to apply that technique to singing jazz.'

Norwegian singer Magni Wentzel also received extensive formal training: 'It meant a lot to me in my development.' It was some years before she became committed to jazz, in the meantime working successfully in other musical genres: 'I am classically trained and I have also sung on the classical stage. I have performed in opera...' Among other singers who took aspects of classical training into their work was Teddi King who told *Crescendo International*, 'I studied classical singing as a girl but never used the higher range of my voice when I went into the jazz and commercial field.' Weslia Whitfield also studied classical music and takes her studying very seriously: 'Formal training

51

was a very big deal for me. I have a degree in music and studied privately for almost twenty years. I don't know where I'd be without it... I would not be even half the singer or musician without it. I learned to sing, but more importantly I learned to *hear*... I studied piano from age seven to thirteen and began voice lessons at fourteen. That was when I became brave enough to tell someone that I wanted to study singing. I studied the classical or bel canto method of singing and did a lot of opera work in college. I sang as a salaried chorister for four seasons with the San Francisco Opera and for many years before and after that as a professional church soloist and chorister... I have been assisted by every teacher I ever studied with. In recent years I've received much help from Michael Feinstein, Margaret Whiting, Eileen Farrell, Orrin Keepnews and, most of all, from Mike Greensill!'

Regardless of the nature of the singing that is to be done, clearly there are aspects of the teaching process that are beneficial, especially those that relate to voice care and such all-important matters as breathing. While still a high school student, Lucy Reed was fortunate in having a teacher who inculcated the basics: 'Her name was Celeste Burns. She formed a girls' quartet with my friends and me and taught us how to write our own arrangements and secured an audition for us at radio station KSTP in St Paul, Minnesota, where we performed on a weekly show for two years. The four probably most important things she taught me were, one, in regard to pitch. She taught us to be very conscious of singing high enough to reach the correct pitch. And, two, we dissected each song by reading the lyric like poetry and marking with pencil where we would take a breath at the end of a sentence or at a comma. And, three, she taught us how to breathe to accomplish that. By holding the abdomen in, the diaphragm out, the chest up during the entire song. It produces a posture which is itself effective in performance and allows you to sneak in little breaths without the shoulders moving up and down. It also enables you to sing long phrases without gasping. After a little practice this comes naturally and you can learn to sight-read a song and breathe in the correct places. And, number four, to phrase a song like you would if you were reading it as poetry because sometimes if the music is written by one person and the lyric by another the accent in the music is not in the place it should be to accent a certain word.' Reed later sang with a popular dance band in Michigan, married the drummer and started a family. Two years later, her husband was killed during World War Two, and a couple of years after that she returned to singing. She worked with Woody Herman and Charlie Ventura, eventually settling down in Chicago where she built a solid reputation and a highly successful career. It was in New York, however, that she recorded with Bill Evans in the mid-1950s. There were no more records until 1992 when Audiophile realized that Chicago's gain was the rest of the world's loss and put right that particularly glaring omission.

Reed's remarks on breathing reflect those made by Frank Sinatra when he talked about his on-the-job learning with Tommy Dorsey: 'The thing that influenced me most was the way Tommy played his trombone. He would take a musical phrase and play it all the way through seemingly without breathing for eight, ten, maybe sixteen bars. How the hell did he do that? I used to sit behind him on the bandstand and watch, trying to see him sneak a breath. But I never saw the bellows move in his back. His jacket didn't even move. So I edged my chair around to the side a little and peeked around to watch him. Finally, after a while, I discovered that he had a "sneak pinhole" in the corner of his mouth – not an actual hole but a tiny place he left open where he was breathing... I decided to make my voice work in the same way as a trombone or violin – not sounding like them but "playing" the voice like those instruments.'

Sinatra developed his breath control by swimming underwater thinking song lyrics, until he was able to sing long phrases without taking a visible or audible breath: 'That gave the melody a flowing unbroken quality and that's what made me sound different. When I started singing that way people began taking notice.'

Mark Murphy had neither the advantage of singing with a big band, nor that of formal training, although he did try this for a while: 'My father started me out and then I went to voice teachers who gave me half-ass opera training as it was the only way they knew how to teach.' Remembering that, when Murphy began his own career as a teacher, he made sure he didn't fall into the same mistakes: 'What I've done really with my own teaching technique is to adapt classical technique to the needs of jazz.' Murphy is conscious, too, of the problems faced by singers getting started: 'I had a hard time at the beginning because wheezy singers were considered jazz singers even though they didn't improvise or play around with the harmonies – people I called the sometimes-jazz singers! But I'm getting my own back now because I'm spawning a whole new generation of singers who learned from me and who have voices and use them.' Murphy's impact in the 1950s was substantial. Quite clearly jazz had a new and important voice and the fact that he was rooted in bebop made him wholly contemporary in sound, style, repertoire and approach. Unwilling to compromise, Murphy never took the steps that might have brought widespread recognition, preferring to work within the necessarily close limits of the musical form he loved, and still loves. This refusal to bend from the path led him at times to be neglected even by the jazz public. He expanded his concept and honed it to a fine edge: 'It began to mature in me in the early 1960s, but I had to put it away while the other musical events of the 60s happened. I could not comply at all. Artistically, it was a very strange time.' But Murphy stuck to his guns, continuing to refine his art and eventually seeing a kind of reward in the development of his activities as a teacher even if the wide audience remains out of reach for someone so determined to avoid compromise.

Quite clearly, Murphy has become the kind of teacher he might have longed to meet when he was coming up but who did not then exist. Understandably he remains cautious about teaching jazz, aware that an inferior teacher can cause serious damage to prospective talent; not necessarily through bad teaching technique but through a failure to understand that voice and personality are inextricably interwoven, a factor that is of a special importance in jazz singing.

Jan Ponsford is also slightly suspicious of teachers: 'Jazz is an aural tradition, handed down the generations with love and devotion. Teachers on the whole are classically based, nothing to do with jazz. No dedication, no message... Some try to intimidate jazzers but in fact are themselves intimidated. Some jazzers confronted by such teachers think that because they are classically trained they must be good. But you mustn't let them get away with it. A good teacher turns you on to finding out things for yourself by awakening curiosity, not teaching parrot fashion. Some teachers who are now in an educational environment which accepts jazz come to me and ask, "What is the secret?" When I tell them that I don't know, that I just get inside the chords and open my mind, they don't like it. They have learned by rote. They do not understand that jazz is intuitive. If you don't feel it you'll never learn to do it let alone teach it. Often these people are failed classical singers who have got into teaching not from vocation but as a job.'

The old establishment teachers to whom Ponsford refers are slowly being replaced. As the American singer-teacher Marguerite Juenemann observes: '... the adage "those who can't do, teach" holds no value. Those of us who are working in this way have been asked to teach because of our performer experience.' Ponsford herself is now similarly employed: 'I love teaching, although it can be very tiring and I need a break from it from time to time, but I have had some amazing breakthroughs with students although they don't always know what the breakthrough is – but eventually cotton on. I want to impart the joy. Open their ears to the joy and inspiration.'

When that happens it can inspire and bring joy to the teacher. For part of each year Mark Murphy teaches at a school in Graz, Austria: 'You should hear my singers there. My God, the last night of the last season I did there it was so exciting. These young kids, getting up there and just putting up their dreams of stardom on that stage. It's a joy.'

*   *   *

Other things were learned on the road; it was not just music all the way. In the 1930s and well beyond, black artists ran real risks in some parts of the Deep South and one-night stands could become harsh lessons in the reality of being black in white America. Some black women added to the everyday problems by accepting jobs with otherwise all-white bands: June Richmond with Jimmy Dorsey in 1938, Billie Holiday with Artie Shaw, also in 1938, and Lena Horne with Charlie Barnet in 1940. Horne recalled the difficulties pioneering ladies such as these endured over racist taunts and discrimination: 'Many times when I was singing with Charlie Barnet I wanted to quit. I might have, too, had it not been for the wonderful support I always got in every way from Charlie and the boys in the band.' In the early 1960s things hadn't improved that much. Signed by the prestigious Joe Glaser agency, which had handled Louis Armstrong for many years, Shirley Horn went out on tour expecting anything but what she faced: 'I had been working in Washington, DC, since I was a teenager, and always imagined that going on the road would be exciting and glamorous but it wasn't. We had a four-week gig at a Holiday Inn in Valparaiso, Indiana. When we arrived there, somebody told me it was the home of the Ku Klux Klan. The hotel bartender was a fan, but the audience wasn't prepared for my music. There hadn't been much jazz in Valparaiso before. The third week, I asked the hotel manager why I hadn't seen any Negro faces in the club. He smiled and said, "That's because we ran them all out of here."'

Another thirty years after that, the correspondence columns of the magazine *JazzTimes* were awash with letters prompted by an article on racism in jazz. The article cited the example of singer Vanessa Rubin who had been badly treated at a private club, being asked to eat in a screened-off section of the kitchen and also being questioned about the suitability of her material. Rubin took the view that this was all because she was black. After the storm of letters had abated, she herself wrote to the magazine, pointing out that after fifteen years in the business and a lifetime of being black, she was well qualified to judge what was a result of her colour and what was not. She had felt obliged to write because of the intervening letters that told tales of musicians, jazz and otherwise, white as well as black, being treated badly in such clubs, looked on as hired help – musicians who never got to eat anywhere, let alone in the kitchen, and who were regularly insulted by members of the public with neither knowledge of nor interest in the artists' craft.

'I'd like to see musicians respected for what they do,' Jan Ponsford says. 'I'd like to see it looked upon as work and not just some kind of hobby not needing payment. I'd like to see musicians getting a good rate of pay. Good conditions in the work place, like you do in other forms of labour. Health and safety measures in the workplace. Proper breaks and toilet facilities, instead of, in some situations, being treated as somehow sub-human!' Even in the superior setting of London's Savoy Hotel, Cleo Laine encountered an inevitable barrier. At first delighted to find she had been given a dressing room suite, she then spotted a notice on the door, 'politely requesting artistes not to fraternize with guests in the Showroom before or after the show'.

Of course, telling the artist not to fraternize with the guests is one thing, persuading the guests not to interfere with the artists is another matter entirely. Norma Winstone remarks, 'I've even had people come up and start a conversation when I was on the stand and someone was soloing.' Even worse was an early experience of Jan Ponsford's: 'I would do three numbers with the band and wait sitting in the audience where I would often find myself in trouble. One night the band were putting away their instruments and I was getting strangled by a drunken punter.' To get out of these situations she suggested that she should remain on stage but rather than just sit there she wanted to play an instrument, unwittingly encountering another work problem: 'The drummer had some congas and I asked if I could come around his place to learn to play them. His answer was, "No way, I'm not gonna be on stage with some chick singer cosmetically playing congas." "Girls" were not supposed to play instruments!... This was (is?) a common attitude. Women sang. Men played. In fact, the bandleader of the first band I was in had a favourite adage, "A bit of crumpet on stage covers up a multitude of sins", referring to the inability of the male musicians to play their instruments properly. It distracts the audience by giving them something nice to look at!'

Considering that club and hotel work is the other great learning academy, and has continued throughout the days of the one-night stand era and into the formal college period, it is enough to make an outsider wonder if some form of mild insanity drives singers to enter into the kind of world that brings them into contact with the people and places they describe.

Of course, all singers have an ideal environment in which they would like to work, but all accept that reality is usually much harsher. Not that creating an ideal venue is especially demanding of promoter, club owner or manager. Laila Dalseth would settle for 'any place where people try to listen to jazz'. As Chris Connor says, 'The way a place presents you can make a big difference to the way the audience feels about you.' Terry Blaine underlines the contribution a thoughtful management can make: 'They can help by announcing before the set that as a courtesy to the performers the audience should please refrain from blowing cigar smoke up into the singer's face or talking loud during the set. That would reinforce the right kind of relationship for people who are there to appreciate the music. I feel very strongly about non-artistic environments – you've just got to do the best you can and reach out to the audience. Outdoors – wet seats, monitor blown, wind – you have to remember that there are people out there who have come to see you do the very best you can; keep it positive no matter what.' Ideally, Blaine would choose to work 'anyplace where the musicians and audience are open to an exchange, the audience wants to hear you. Mark Shane [pianist, accompanist] always says, "Up there you're the doctor, go out and administer the medicine."'

For Mark Murphy the ideal venues are just certain clubs, 'Like Yoshi's in Oakland and another, Scullers, in Boston where I can call them with conditions. A place in Sydney, Australia, Kinsella's, where I went on a two-week run with a five-piece band. It's a club where you feel that all the staff are behind you. They serve meals quietly, everything runs smoothly. All that matters, knowing the staff are with you. It's hard to achieve but when you get optimum conditions you can grow so much in one night that you are not the same singer you were the day before. As for singing in noisy, smoky, non-artistic environments. Me!? Seriously, in the 1960s and 1970s I thought I was losing my voice and I had to stop playing those clubs. But, really, when it's noisy, you're not doing your work right. You control the noise. Communicate! If you're not communicating, you've got a problem. But sometimes it's hard and I get nervous. Like those awful afternoon gigs at outdoor jazz festivals when you have to deal with wind and no chance of a sound check and I know if you get 40,000 people out there only 300 of them know who I am, because I'm still so specialized. That's when I'm nervous.'

Most singers would agree with Kitty Margolis's succinct and well-reasoned definition of the ideal venue: 'I like an audience that is open and fairly quiet. Jazz clubs are the most relaxed, concerts with great sound systems are wonderful. Festivals are fun because you see lots of your musician friends.'

A positive attitude of mind can certainly help overcome problems encountered on the road, in clubs or any other location. 'There are certain stresses and strains in this life,' Stacey Kent declares, 'but aren't there stresses and strains in any life? I'm very happy to be fortunate enough to work at what I love. People go to work every day, bored with their job, hating their job – I love my job and I'm lucky enough to be working a lot, so I try not to complain too much about the problems.'

Venues large and small, grand and seedy, all have their own hazards. The same artist can find himself in very different settings on successive nights. Mark Porter says, 'One minute I can be working at the Royal Albert Hall in London with a twenty-six-piece orchestra supporting Bob Hope, then the following night I'm in Pontypool Working Men's Club singing with backing tapes. It's enough to drive someone insane but at the same time I suppose it keeps your feet on the ground.'

The challenge of having to play in a wide variety of settings also comes into Susannah McCorkle's thoughts on performing. The award-winning Concord recording artist says, 'I love the performance part of it. I always have my pride and dignity and integrity about every job. I'm always there to sing my very best and reach the audience. I don't care where I play and I'm glad I feel this way. To have a career in this kind of music, you've got to be able to play all kinds of rooms. I know now that it is not always the fanciest room where you have the best time; it can be the grittiest little jazz club as long as the sound system is good and the people are into it and you are being treated well.' McCorkle chose the jazz life only when she had already built a career as a linguist, translating and interpreting in four languages. She was also painting and writing but had always loved singing: 'As a teenager I sang in choral groups and high school variety shows and did some summer stock musicals.' But it was not until she was working in Paris that she turned to jazz: 'I discovered Billie Holiday and thought she was absolutely the most wonderful singer I'd heard and I still do think that. She's my inspiration and the reason I became a jazz singer and a singer of standards.' Having made her decision, McCorkle went to London where, in the early 1970s, she began to build her new career which would eventually lead to great success back home in America. Playing at the Algonquin in

New York or the Smithsonian in Washington, DC, and on television is a far cry from the London club and pub circuit on which she began her jazz life, but in a sense it is all one to her: 'I have a good time wherever I work and I love singing to people not especially into jazz but being strong enough to reach them with my music, getting them laughing, thinking and moving. It's a challenge, it's a battle but it's a great way to spend your life, I think.'

Stacey Kent echoes this sentiment: 'There are some clubs that are blessed with perfect audiences. And sometimes they're in unlikely places – these are very special nights, when the whole room is silent and seems mesmerized. That's when I drive home beaming.' Recalling an engagement at Ronnie Scott's in Birmingham, England, she remembers, 'Just as I was announcing the last number of the night, a young woman stood up and said, "Can I just say something? I brought a table of sixteen people here tonight who wanted to go to TGI Friday's for a good time. Instead, I forced them to come here. They didn't like jazz and they didn't want to come but they did and now they're completely converted. The whole table loves your music. Thank you!" This made me so happy. I know how wonderful this music is and how accessible it is and almost anyone who hears it will love it – when it is played with simple, melodic, swinging conviction.'

Nevertheless there is still smoke and there is still noise, the twin banes of the singer's existence. For a singer just starting out, the threat of long-term damage might not be apparent. Nicki Leighton-Thomas, a young British singer, takes an optimistic view: 'The ideal venue is the one where people come to listen rather than have you to punctuate the silences in their conversation. Also where the piano and PA are good. A smoky atmosphere doesn't really bother me and even a non-artistic environment doesn't – don't they become artistic the moment you start to play?' La Velle, an American singer based in Geneva, Switzerland, is herself a smoker and, while she finds cigar smoke especially troublesome, takes a philosophical view of cigarette smoking and how a singer should respond: 'I think a lot of vocalists make a mountain out of a mole hill. They see people smoking cigarettes and say, "I can't possibly sing in this smoke-filled room." Listen, people that smoke cigarettes buy your records too, kid.'

Susannah McCorkle, who is active with the American Lung Association's drive against smoking, consciously draws upon technique only when she is working under adverse conditions and forced to breathe in smoke: 'Smoke gives me so much hassle I'm not even attempting to sing in European jazz clubs because I just can't stand it. I have a much better singing technique than I used to have because I'm healthier and more physically strong but when I get smoke in my throat I choke and sing bad notes because I breathed smoke. A bad enemy.' Magni Wentzel agrees: 'Smoke is very bad... Sometimes I'm desperate.' She also picks up on the companion problem: 'Noise is very hard but only seldom occurs because I usually have good audiences. If it happens, I just concentrate on what I'm doing and do the best I can to gain one more musical experience.'

'Noise,' Mike Campbell says, 'sucks the life right out of you.' But he recognizes that it is a problem to be confronted: 'It goes with the territory, goes with the job. It happens with the non-artistic audience and can be really tough. You ask yourself, "Why am I here?" But you've got to be professional. An ideal venue would be a hip audience, maybe a 400–500-seat theatre or an intimate room. A warm audience is wonderful.' Jan Ponsford pursues this line of thought: 'It would be ideal to work in a non-smoking environment, particularly as a singer – but people have no idea. I hate noisy places where you can't hear your own voice. It's a total waste of time and no joy; the tendency is to overblow and thereby damage your voice.' As to how to bring a noisy audience under control, Ponsford suggests what is often the most effective way: 'If you withdraw and sing a slow, spacious ballad it can sometimes gradually silence a room – quite a feat.' Shirley Horn agrees: 'It works to get softer and softer, if you can maintain your cool that long.' Carol Kidd concurs: 'I mean, the louder you sing, the louder they're going to talk.' Stacey Kent adds, 'Sure, people can be noisy in certain venues, but there's always someone listening.'

Any singer can be driven to distraction by an unresponsive or noisy audience of smokers. While it might be small consolation to the young and inexperienced, these are problems even the greatest can suffer – and overcome. Chris McNulty remembers hearing Carmen McRae handle an audience late in her career when her health (she was an asthmatic) was far from good: 'I went to hear Carmen at the Blue Note in New York and she made me weep. She was having a hard time this night. The audience was really obnoxious – talking. She really knows how to use a microphone and she had a beautiful sound system down by her side. She had it set so it would pick up her voice however faint and she pulled away from the microphone at this particular moment in the song and it had an extraordinary effect, it was so soft, so beautiful. The whole room just shut up.'

Perhaps the subconscious thought that each night will bring one of these magical moments is a hidden persuader that keeps jazz singers in the business: the hope for an experience such as that of Stacey Kent at Ronnie Scott's or Carmen McRae at the Blue Note. And happen they do. Mel Tormé remarks, 'Standing ovations don't impress me. I can sing badly and get one. When that happens I can walk off stage in a depth of depression that may last several days. Other times I get apathetic reactions when I know I have been great. Once in a while, though, that strange silver chord that goes between me and the audience grows taut and it's – well, exhilarating.'

And as Mark Murphy says, 'You are an artist and every artist is based on technique. Finally the technique becomes your tool. You, the artist, really use it and control it. When I sing I am conscious of technique. I'm conscious of everything. But there comes a point when those who can do it go like a car into overdrive. It becomes magic and those are the nights when I trance the audience.'

FOUR
FINE AND MELLOW

Every girl singer should get down on her knees and
thank God there was a Billie Holiday. — *Annie Ross*

For a fan, the chance to see one of his idols in the intimate setting of a nightclub or hotel lounge, perhaps in a piano bar or a neighbourhood pub, can be a moment to treasure. For the artist, these magic moments are not merely seen from another perspective, they are often dramatically different. What appears to be a happy and fulfilling performance may be just another mundane gig; the experience may have been unsettling or distressing, perhaps even traumatic. However accustomed they might be to the rigours of working the hotel and club circuits, or touring the world on one-night stands, at times events can be soul-destroying. Every touring singer has tales to tell about the frustrations, the uncertainties, and the crushing put-downs. Insensitivity and no-win situations are commonplace. The pianist-singer Ellyn Rucker was playing a hotel lounge when she was approached by the manager. 'I have a request from the near table,' he told her. Delighted, Rucker asked, 'What would they like to hear?' 'They'd like to hear you keep the noise down,' he said. 'They can't hear themselves talk.'

Nightclubs and the hazards of smoke and noise, lounges and the chattering classes, unresponsive audiences, unfeeling management, out-of-tune – if sometimes freshly painted – pianos, inadequate sound systems, the recurring irritations and crises of extended tours, are just some of the problems a jazz singer has to confront. The bleaker side was experienced by Chris McNulty during her first UK tour when, typically, she had to perform two one-hour sets nightly with musicians she had neither rehearsed with nor even met before. Welcomed profusely at the start of one date by the club owner, she coped extremely well and ended the session to well-earned applause. The club officials, so pleased to see her arrive on time (promoters are notorious for operating to a different set of values), were quickly off the scene at the end of the gig. McNulty was alone in an almost deserted club with only the bar staff left to help her find a taxi, a small task to perform but one in which they were markedly disinterested. She didn't know where her hotel was and was faced with the prospect of being ejected onto an unfriendly street late at night in an unsavoury part of a strange town. Luckily she was rescued by a member of the audience who delivered her safely to her hotel.

It would be nice to think that the root of the problem facing this particular young singer – being fêted at first then dropped like yesterday's news when the job is done – will disappear as her international stature increases. Sadly, that is not necessarily the case.

In her old age Adelaide Hall had difficulty getting about. At one out-of-town concert she had a badly sprained ankle and could barely walk, but once her music started she moved majestically and with such grace that no one in the audience was aware of her pain. At the concert's end, praise was lavished on her by fans, friends and organizers alike. It was a wonderful occasion – in her eighties, she was still a star. Next morning, however, she was just another old lady on her own with a bad ankle, a train to catch, and luggage she was unable to carry. Tearful and distraught, she wondered how she would cope but, fortunately, and again by a chance encounter, she too was rescued and made her train connection.

Mike Campbell realistically accepts the sometimes difficult business side of a singer's life: 'It's just as cut-throat and greedy as most businesses are but in showbiz it's so personal – so much of yourself is attached to what you do it becomes extremely difficult to deal with hard facts. Fighting for your money is very tough. They tell you they're going to pay you so much then at the end of the night they say something different because there's only three people in. I worked one very famous club where the guy was always scratching for money. We had a good night and he said he would be back at the end to pay us. We waited till 2 a.m., 3 a.m., 4 a.m., then rang him up. He says he'll come in. Never turned up. Had to go in the next day to see him. He was very apologetic and gave us a cheque. The cheque bounced. Eventually he did pay us. Okay, he's a likeable guy but it isn't the right way to treat an artist.'

Although low moments may be counteracted by the occasional highs that come from moments of inspired music-making and heart-warming rapport, they inevitably colour a singer's view of the life. Yet, however low the lows, and however infrequent the highs, it is the life the singer has chosen – unless, of course, you subscribe to Mark Murphy's view: 'It's as if you're chosen. You are given a gift and you do it.' That young singers continue to enter the life is not for want of warnings from the past. Unpleasant incidents have occurred as long as clubs and bars have hired musicians to play jazz. The problems faced by singers in the 1990s in clubs all around the world have always existed but then, as now, the singers kept on singing.

In the 1920s and 1930s, every major city in America had its clubs, often clustered in areas that sometimes passed into legend, occasionally into immortality through songs. Los Angeles had Central Avenue, Chicago had State Street, Kansas City had 18th and Vine, and New York had 52nd Street.

Even if the fundamental purpose of a club was something other than to provide musical entertainment, music was often an added attraction. The size of the club and its degree of splendour or squalor made little differ-ence. Of course, the bigger clubs could take larger musical ensembles and stage lavish floor shows, although smaller places might sometimes squeeze in a big band. Naturally, the grander venues charged their customers more and were thus able to afford top line bands and acts. In some of the lower dives musicians might be barely tolerated and perform for tips alone. And then there were the after-hours joints, the places where musicians gathered to wind down after a dreary night spent playing stock arrangements with some society band or to regenerate their enthusiasm after many soul-destroying weeks out on the road. Some of New York's clubs became legendary as launching pads for new stars – Billie Holiday, for example, at Pod's and Jerry's.

In Los Angeles in 1943, after years of scuffling as a jazz pianist in second-rate rooms along Central Avenue, Nat King Cole broke onto the Harlem Hit Parade with 'That Ain't Right'. Later, this hit for Cole and his trio was consolidated by the popularity of 'Straighten Up and Fly Right'. Vocal hits such as these and his first major cross-over success, 'For Sentimental Reasons', ensured that Cole moved on to better venues. His jazz trio days were virtually over and suddenly a major popular voice was discovered.

The jazz club scene in Kansas City made giants of instrumentalists such as Ben Webster, Lester Young and Count Basie and also advanced the careers of singers like Jimmy Rushing, Julia Lee and Joe Turner, and lesser lights such as blues shouter Walter Brown and Pha Terrell, whose falsetto singing style briefly became popular when he was with Andy Kirk's band. Drummer Jo Jones remembered jam sessions in Kansas City when Terrell 'would come right out of the audience and sing right in the middle of a number, and he knew exactly where to start'.

Future movie actress Martha Raye also sang in Kansas City when she was a teenager. Mary Lou Williams remembers: 'She stayed close on to two weeks, and was down at the clubs digging the music and singing like mad, night after night.' Raye, whose singing style carries clear echoes of early Anita O'Day, also sang in New York. Ed Kirkeby, Fats Waller's manager, recalled sessions at a New York club operated by bass saxophonist Adrian Rollini: 'A great attraction at the Tap Room was a series of song battles between Martha Raye and Ella Logan [singer-actress and aunt of Annie Ross], two up-and-coming singers who would take turns against each other just for the hell of it.'

New York was not only a major centre for clubs, it also had important dance halls and hotel entertainment and was the national centre for recording studios. Countless singers recorded in New York in the 1930s, often as mere appendages to famous bands but sometimes as stars. Billie Holiday, Ethel Waters, Mildred Bailey and Lee Wiley are among the most noted names and they and others were often backed by leading jazz instrumentalists.

There were many singers whose light burned only briefly, however bright it might have been at the time. Disenchantment, weariness, a desire for a 'normal' life, were commonplace reasons for their departure from the scene. Teddy Grace comes to mind as an example of a remarkably good singer whose career was strikingly uncommon. Also unusual was her singing style; although she was white and middle-class, she had a surprising affinity for the blues. She recorded with Jack Teagarden, Bob Crosby and Bud Freeman and was with Mal Hallett's popular dance band. In 1940 Grace quit in despair over her treatment by Decca. After losing her voice while working on recruitment and bond-selling drives during World War Two, she never sang again. Often regarded as the stylistic link between Connee Boswell and Kay Starr, she has also been described as a female vocal equivalent to Jack Teagarden.

Teagarden had a casual delivery and an easy way with both the blues and popular song. Writer Charles Fox described Teagarden's lazy way of singing as 'blues sentimentality', an apt description of the great trombonist's gentle vocal style. Hoagy Carmichael said of him, 'A warm and honest talent like Jack's is a rare thing indeed.' Teagarden sang the blues with sad conviction and in later years developed into an excellent interpreter of popular ballads. His vocal collaborations with Louis Armstrong remain delightfully unique moments in jazz history.

*   *   *

Harlem's Cotton Club holds a revered place in the story of New York's nightlife. Most notable of the bands which played there were those of Duke Ellington and Cab Calloway. Ellington's choice of sidemen was flawless, and some of his vocalists were also excellent, if occasionally and predictably overshadowed by instrumental giants. Fine examples would include Adelaide Hall in 1927 with 'Creole Love Call', Betty Roché in 1955 on 'Take the "A" Train', and later Alice Babs for his sacred works. Over the years there were others of note including Joya Sherrill and Kay Davis, Herb Jeffries and Al Hibbler, and especially singing sideman Ray Nance. But best of all and forever an integral part of the Ellington legend was Ivie Anderson. A sensitive and musicianly singer, Anderson had a fragility about her which complemented, and in turn was enhanced by, the inimitable Ellington sound. Few band singers of the era had such a varied and demanding repertoire: 'I Got It Bad and That Ain't Good', 'It Don't Mean a Thing (If It Ain't Got That Swing)', 'Ebony Rhapsody', 'My Old Flame', 'Kissin' My Baby Goodnight', 'I'm Checkin' Out – Go'om Bye', 'A Lonely Co-ed', 'Solitude'. Anderson more than coped with the demands, she handled the songs magnificently, bringing to each of them an air of delicate charm. Her fine interpretative abilities and lithe, relaxed swing were sadly missed when illhealth forced her to leave the band while she was still a young woman.

Cab Calloway had a career that lasted for over seventy years. With an outrageously extrovert stage presence, he performed his songs in a style that owed much to the vaudeville tradition and was dotted with touches of Louis Armstrong and the exuberance of his elder sister, Blanche Calloway, a noted vaudevillian and band leader. There were also occasional startling hints of the Jewish cantorial style about Calloway's delivery which contrasted strikingly with the song content. He enjoyed great success with songs that dealt with taboo subjects, deftly disguised in 'jive-talk' and thus slipping by recording company and radio self-censorship. He told tales of drugs in 'Minnie the Moocher', 'Reefer Man' and 'Kickin' the Gong Around'; of sex in 'Trickeration'; and he even sneaked in songs about race, 'Yaller'.

Jive-talk abounded: 'The Scat Song', 'Zaz Zuh Zaz', and his anthem, 'Hi-De-Ho'. The popularity of these songs and numerous sequels has tended to colour the judgment of jazz critics who complain that Calloway's extended vocals hide the talents of the many fine jazz soloists in the backing ensembles. In fact, Calloway was a much better singer than most critics are prepared to acknowledge. His repertoire was not exclusively given over to jive and risqué material and amidst them are several splendid interpretations of popular songs, including 'Between the Devil and the Deep Blue Sea' and 'I'll Be Around'.

Of all the big bands of the 1930s, Count Basie's is one with singers whose jazz credentials are unquestioned. Jimmy Rushing and Helen Humes were not only among the finest singers in jazz but were also gifted exponents of the blues.

Humes began her career at a very early age, making her first records when she was only fourteen years old. In 1937, when she was in her early twenties, Basie heard her and offered her a job but Humes thought the money inadequate and declined. Basie hired Billie Holiday instead, but the following year he renewed his offer to Humes and this time she accepted. Her first successful record with Basie was a fine performance of 'Blame It on My Last Affair', arranged by Jimmy Mundy, imbuing the lyric with wistful tenderness. From commercial necessity, much of the material she recorded with Basie was aimed at the popular audience, some being direct attempts to cash-in on successes by other bands: 'Moonlight Serenade', 'And the Angels Sing'. When she was allowed to sing songs she wanted to perform, Humes was always interesting and often outstanding.

She left Basie in 1941, later telling Whitney Balliett, 'I was tired and my health was getting bad. I was nervous with all that bus travel, so I went home to ... sit around and rest.' She did not remain idle for long and in 1942 began carving out a career as a single, increasingly working in the burgeoning r&b market where she had a number of hit records. In the late 1950s and early 1960s she recorded some of her finest jazz albums, mostly for Contemporary Records, but as tastes changed she decided to retire. In 1973, persuaded by writer Stanley Dance, she returned to appear with Basie at the Newport Jazz Festival; remarkably, her voice was still in excellent shape, having lost none of its delicate and youthful charm. She continued to work and record excellent albums until shortly before her death in 1981.

Humes was an exceptionally gifted blues singer, her light, clear voice ringing with conviction and unforced emotion. She had a penchant for *double entendre*, slyly subverting her own 'Million Dollar Secret' with a delicious wickedness that had audiences shouting for more. She would innocently proclaim, 'I just like to sing... I don't know what you'd call 'em – little cute blues, I don't know, little fun blues – something to make people laugh.' Primarily, Humes preferred to sing ballads: 'But people have usually associated me with the blues and as a swing or a jazz singer. However, I guess, I just love singing, period. I'm just a singer.'

Also 'just a singer' was Humes's singing companion in the Basie band, Jimmy Rushing. He had sung and played various instruments in the mid-west and on the west coast before returning home to Oklahoma City in 1927 to join Walter Page's Blue Devils. At the time Rushing's forte was not yet the blues. Recalling those days, Ralph Ellison, the distinguished writer and educator, who grew up in Oklahoma City, described how Rushing began as a ballad singer and brought sincerity and feeling to banal lyrics, charging them with the same 'mysterious potentiality of meaning which haunts the blues'. Ellison went on to draw attention to the reverse effect that Rushing generated, how his blues singing also is transformed by his 'imposition of a romantic lyricism upon the blues tradition'.

After singing with the Blue Devils, Rushing moved on to Bennie Moten's band with Bill Basie. Eventually, he became a major attraction with Basie's own band and stayed with him until 1950. Rushing was a light tenor but projected such power and accuracy that singing in front of a wailing big band was never a problem. Many of his recordings in the 1930s and 1940s were outstanding: 'Blues in the Dark', 'Sent for You Yesterday', 'I Left My Baby', 'Goin' to Chicago' and 'Harvard Blues', the lyric of which, by George Frazier, he sang soulfully and with conviction but probably without much understanding of this undergraduate tale of campus life. Rushing's post-Basie recordings are a recurring joy. Albums such as *Goin' to Chicago*, *The Essential Jimmy Rushing*, *The Jazz Odyssey of James Rushing Esq* and *Little Jimmy Rushing and the Big Brass* are all fine examples of the singer in full flow.

Even in the twilight of his career he managed to make his deliberately restricted repertoire sound fresh and interesting. On his last formal recording date he was persuaded by the pianist-arranger for the session, Dave Frishberg, to try some songs that were new to him: 'I felt it was a shame that most people thought of him merely as a blues singer. I think he's one of the strongest interpreters of pop songs I ever heard.' The result of Frishberg's persuasion, an album entitled *The You and Me That Used to Be*, was a fitting epilogue to Rushing's remarkable singing career. Certainly his voice is frayed; in place of the finely honed rapier was a rusting replica. But he contrived to fashion moving and very personal interpretations of songs such as 'When I Grow Too Old to Dream', 'More Than You Know', 'Thanks a Million' and 'I Surrender Dear'.

Although Rushing and the Basie band played New York clubs in the late 1930s, notably the Famous Door, such places were not ideal showcases for big bands. Most clubs more easily accommodated small groups or solo pianists or singers. Many were seedy dives where, as ragtime pianist-turned-comic Jimmy Durante remarked, 'the only fresh air was what we took in on our clothes'. Several band leaders met audience expectations of hearing a vocal by singing themselves. Many were trumpet-playing disciples of Louis Armstrong and some had hit records, like Wingy Manone with 'Isle of Capri' and Bunny Berigan's 'I Can't Get Started'. Henry 'Red' Allen was a highly original trumpet player, initially inspired by King Oliver but very soon impressed by Armstrong's virtuosity as soloist. An emotional player with natural exuberance, Allen's style owed a lot to Armstrong but he was enough of an individualist to develop his own flexible and very personal approach. His use of long melodic lines with unexpected intervals is also evident in his singing. His 1935 recording of 'Body and Soul', a song that Armstrong had recorded in 1930, clearly illustrates Allen's individuality both as a trumpet stylist and as a singer. In the Armstrong version the trumpet solo builds slowly and majestically over an arrangement which sticks closely to the melody. Allen also builds, but busily and urgently, with short-phrased asides to his own main solo thrust, as if commenting upon it. His vocal duplicates the same urgency. Jonah Jones was another vocalist-trumpet player who worked regularly on 52nd Street. He was resident for a long time at the Onyx Club with his partner, swing violinist Stuff Smith, with whom he recorded the popular 'You'se a Viper'.

Singer Marietta Williams was booked into the Onyx Club as an intermission act. She changed her name to Maxine Sullivan and in 1937 had a hit record with 'Loch Lomond'. Sullivan carved herself a comfortable but ultimately restrictive niche singing similar Scottish folk ditties, such as 'Annie Laurie' and 'Comin' Through the Rye'. In the wake of these successes came a mild furore when Scottish-born Ella Logan accused Sullivan of stealing her idea of swinging old folk classics. Sullivan described in *down beat* how she created her individual style: 'The characteristics which I consider most important in singing are the way in which I hit notes – softly and without effort; a relaxed feeling at all times; and a feeling for what I am singing. Most of all, I like to take sad numbers with a simple melody, changing the notes to fit the soft, straight manner – strict tempo vocalizing and without jive.'

Self-effacing and down-to-earth, Sullivan once observed: 'I never thought of myself as a great singer, or a great anything. But when I listen to things like "Gone with the Wind", and especially "Stop, You're Breaking My Heart", I think I was a pretty good singer. I didn't dare think that way in those days, because in my estimation Ella Fitzgerald and Billie were on the throne, so I would just consider myself one of the lucky people in show business that had a break.'

When Sullivan returned to singing in the 1970s after a lengthy retirement, her vocal style was largely unchanged. She was by now a tiny grey-haired figure but still with a warm open smile. She was singing better than ever, her voice remaining relaxed and assured with the same pure articulation of her youth but with a richer, more gutsy, quality. In these later years she recorded numerous albums and those where she is accompanied by saxophonists Scott Hamilton or Bob Wilber are especially remarkable testimonials to the durability of this elegant and charming singer.

Not surprisingly, pianists proliferated in the clubs of New York. Some played alone or led trios, some accompanied singers and others sang to their own accompaniment. Doyen of them all was Fats Waller: pianist, organist, composer, singer. If Waller had contented himself with composing songs such as 'Squeeze Me', '(What Did I Do to Be So) Black and Blue', 'Ain't Misbehavin'', 'Honeysuckle Rose', 'Blue Turning Grey Over You', it would be easy to grant him the accolade of greatness. It is even easier if some of the songs he is believed to have composed but promptly sold for the price of a gallon of whiskey are added: 'I Can't Give You Anything but Love', 'On the Sunny Side of the Street'. Some of his songs were dashed off in taxis *en route* to recording sessions, others simply improvised at the piano in the studio with apparent spontaneity. His qualities as an instrumentalist are similarly exceptional but it is his singing that most actively demonstrates the musical conflicts in the man and his work. All too often Waller took his singing lightly, especially if the material in hand was inferior – which it often was. On occasion, Waller simply demolished songs he did not care for. Listening to 'Let's Sing Again', 'Sugar Blues', 'Swingin' Them Jingle Bells', you hear a parodist, a comedian, a subversive. Yet, even at his most destructive, his sheer musicality refuses to be completely overcome. Beneath the falsetto shrieks that forever consign 'Jingle Bells', whoever might sing it, to comedy corner, the piano-playing strides majestically. Even when he liked the songs – his own music with lyrics by long-time collaborator Andy Razaf, for example – humour is never far away. A gentler humour certainly, but it suggests that here is a man who doesn't care to be taken too seriously too much of the time.

Waller's legendary capacity for good times, his drinking, eating and womanizing, comes through his singing not just in his extensive use of innuendo and his sly asides, but in the happy-go-lucky sound of his voice. He sounds infectiously good-humoured, carefree, undemanding. It is hard to be unhappy when Waller is singing. Interestingly, as an instrumentalist he can also generate the same happy response with his joyful exuberance. He created definitive performances of some songs, including 'Honeysuckle Rose', 'Ain't Misbehavin'', 'Your Feets Too Big', 'When Somebody Thinks You're Wonderful', 'My Very Good Friend the Milkman' and 'I'm Crazy 'Bout My Baby'.

Undoubtedly, Waller's style was original and spontaneous and he had a ready ability to reshape a song. Not surprisingly, he set an example others tried to follow and during his lifetime two obvious vocal imitators come to mind, Putney Dandridge and Bob Howard. More than fifty years after his death, a number of singers paid homage to 'The Harmful Little Armful', including Marty Grosz, whose unabashed admiration for Waller is always evident in the joyful verve he projects at each performance, and George Melly, who occasionally introduces elements of Waller into his own extensive repertoire. Without resorting to imitation, both Grosz and Melly demonstrate the same light-heartedness and irreverence that was inherent in Waller's work. The attraction was explained by Grosz: 'I never set out to consciously imitate him, but I was drawn to his records because they had that feeling that a party was going on.'

Shortly after Waller's early death, Louis Armstrong said, 'Fats is gone now ... but to me he's still here with us. His very good spirit will keep him with us for ages. Right now, every time someone mentions Fats Waller's name, why you can see the grins on all the faces, as if to say, "Yeah, yeah, yeah, yeah, Fats is a solid sender, ain't he?" '

A contemporary of Waller was Una Mae Carlisle who was persuaded to team up with him. Her piano playing was much influenced by Waller but her singing style was very different. She favoured soulful ballads for which her lazy delivery was admirably suited. Another popular entertainer of the 1930s was Cleo Patra Brown. An excellent boogie-woogie pianist, Brown has been cited by Nellie Lutcher as a trend-setter for female piano players and vocalists who emphasize somewhat risqué humour and hard-swinging piano playing. Discovered in 1932 by the legendary club owner Texas Guinan, who signed her to an exclusive contract, Brown began making regular radio appearances. Her renditions of Pinetop Smith's 'Boogie Woogie' and 'You're a Heavenly Thing', recorded for Decca in 1935, became very popular, the former helping spark off the boogie-woogie craze. Those who followed Brown's trend and gained considerable success include Lutcher herself, Rose Murphy, Julia Lee, Hazel Scott and Hadda Brooks. Scott had a classical piano background and sang and played in a more sophisticated manner than most of the others. Her popularity peaked in the early 1940s just before Brooks, another classically trained pianist, appeared on the scene and helped put the small independent Modern Records in business.

The nightclubs of New York and other cities in the 1930s and 1940s were not, of course, the exclusive haunts of jazz singers. Just as piano-playing singers like Lutcher, Brooks and Scott edged sideways into r&b or jazz-influenced popular music, so there were others who made their reputations on or over the edge of jazz. The fundamental nature of nightclubs, places where people go to have fun, inevitably leads to an element of light-heartedness in the repertoires of some singers. To the general public, Fats Waller might be the best known jester in jazz but he was certainly not alone. Perhaps the most interesting of those singers who use humour to colour their work is Leo Watson, without question a man out of his time – if not, in the eyes of some of his audiences, out of his mind. Although much of his material can be loosely termed novelty songs, he possessed remarkable jazz qualities. Now frequently overlooked, he delivered impromptu lyrics which might be about anything that sprang into his inventive mind. Slim Gaillard described how Watson would 'start singing about the walls, the rug, the table, ashtrays – he'd just sing ... he was a trombone player and drummer and a great singer. He'd sing anything that came into his mind but he drank wine and then got into dope.'

Watson first made his name on 52nd Street with the Spirits of Rhythm in which he imitated instrumental style by using nonsense words in a strangely humorous manner. Lawrence Koch aptly described Watson's performance as 'a kind of stream-of-consciousness singing' by which he pre-empted some of Gaillard's more way-out complexities. Watson, along with Slim and Slam (Gaillard and his partner, bassist Slam Stewart) and Harry 'The Hipster' Gibson, were the high-profile representatives of the crazy side of the 52nd Street jazz scene. Later, Watson teamed up with Gaillard and his then-partner, Bam Brown, in California, thus causing much confusion and not a little joy on the west coast. Mel Tormé recalled Watson with enthusiasm. 'Leo Watson was in a class by himself! Ella, Sarah, myself – we're all jazz-influenced, jazz-oriented singers – but Leo Watson was the first and only guy who really was a jazz singer.' Watson's commitment was total; his high energy level, unflagging swing and erratic use of scat were important factors in the progress of scat singing and it is necessary to move ahead a generation, to Bobby McFerrin, to find someone with comparable, if different, technical virtuosity.

*   *   *

For all the inadequacies of many clubs, then and now, singers today cannot fail to be aware that it was in New York's clubland that there arose in the 1930s a genius of jazz singing. Just as Louis Armstrong and Ethel Waters had overcome staggeringly disadvantaged childhoods to become stars, so Billie Holiday emerged from the harshest of circumstances to light a beacon which has ever since illuminated jazz singing.

Hearing her small voice for the first time, the narrow range, the scant regard for melodic orthodoxy, the sometimes pinched sound, the often alarmingly delayed entries, many first-time listeners might wonder just why Billie Holiday is so often regarded as the greatest of all jazz singers. If that first encounter should be with her records from the 1940s, when there was a sometimes wilful melancholy in the air – 'Strange Fruit', 'Gloomy Sunday', etc – the newcomer might wonder at the absence of the joyousness that pervades so much of jazz. If initial exposure should be to her late recordings, when her voice had deteriorated into a fragmented and distorted reflection of its earlier limited self, when her pitch was decidedly suspect, when at times she appeared merely to talk lethargically to musical accompaniment rather than sing, then an unprepared listener might well be forgiven for doubting the wisdom of the mass of critical and peer approval. And yet, however adverse that first reaction, almost everyone in jazz comes in time to agree with this particular instance of received wisdom – to acknowledge that what they are hearing is an artist of great stature, a true original, and a figure of enormous influence.

Ella Fitzgerald explained that influence when speaking to Clancy Sigal in 1990: 'I idolized Billie and her songs. But Billie wasn't like what people say. She was like that because of her songs, not the other way around. She was the first really modern singer to my way of thinking. We all wanted to be like her.' Holiday was an influence not only upon singers in jazz but also upon singers in many other areas of popular music; indeed, an influence not only upon performing artists but also upon the art they perform. If all this were not enough, there is also the Billie Holiday legend, a self-sustaining, ever-increasing catalogue which began during her lifetime but later grew beyond her wildest imaginings – and which has served only to cloud the issue. The effect of all this was summed up by Stuart Nicholson in his biography of Billie Holiday: 'Today she has been so consumed by her image that it has rendered her a victim at the expense of her music, the one thing that made her unique.'

Billie Holiday was born on 7 April 1915 at Philadelphia General Hospital. Her mother, Sarah Julia Harris, known as Sadie, named her child Eleanora (spelled Elinore when the birth was registered). Eleanora most often used the surname Holiday because her mother told her that her father was the guitarist Clarence Holiday, although the truth of this is uncertain.

Psychologically damaged by domestic uncertainties, she was eventually placed into care at Baltimore's House of the Good Shepherd for Colored Girls – this before she was ten years old. Within two more years, she had become a victim of rape – and was committed this time to the care of the Catholic Sisters of the Good Shepherd. Already, enough had happened to the little girl to provide latter-day writers and journalists with the material for building a legend; and more was to happen before she first ventured onto the public stage as a singer.

She and her mother moved to New York where both were arrested on prostitution charges; she served time after conviction and she was still only fourteen. But she had begun to take an interest in singing, listening to records by Louis Armstrong, Sophie Tucker, Bessie Smith and Ethel Waters. Her own efforts were heard by a neighbour, saxophonist Kenneth Hollon, who took her with him to a New York club where she made her initial public appearance and earned her first money as a singer. It was around this time that she decided that while the surname Holiday suited her projected image, another first name was needed. She chose that of a popular screen actress of the day, Billie Dove. During 1930 and 1931 her reputation gradually spread through the musicial underworld of Harlem. Musicians admired her singing and moreover they liked her. For her part, she enjoyed their company, listening and learning as they played, and happily sharing their after-hours sessions that included music, booze and pot. By the time Billie was seventeen, the legend-makers had an embarrassment of potentially sensational, if misleading, riches. In fact, what she was doing was not really so extraordinary given the time and the place, the company she was keeping and the air of intense musical excitement. As guitarist Danny Barker remarked of the attitude of the younger set: 'Who the hell wants to sleep? You might miss something.'

In 1932, Harlem's hot musicians were virtually unanimous in their admiration for the young singer. By no stretch of the imagination was she simply a singer who sang with jazzmen, she was as much a jazz musician as they were.

The following year, Holiday was deputizing for Monette Moore at Covan's, a club close to the Lafayette Theater, when John Hammond Jnr, a rich jazz-loving young man-about-town and a fan of Moore's, came in. He was expecting to hear the pleasant orthodoxies of Moore, a likeable if unexceptional entertainer. Originally a blues-singing cabaret artist, she happened to be understudying Ethel Waters on Broadway. Hammond was bowled over by Holiday's completely original singing style. Later, when his instant judgment was backed by that of a friend, singer Mildred Bailey ('This girl can sing!'), he began to promote her, first with articles published in *Melody Maker* in England, and tried unavailingly to persuade a record company to take an interest in her. Hammond, who was just five years older than Holiday, revelled in black music and was an early advocate for racial equality. He had an excellent ear and would in time play a significant role in furthering the careers of Benny Goodman and Count Basie (and many years later those of George Benson, Aretha Franklin and Bruce Springsteen). In 1933, Hammond had only recently begun what would be a distinguished career as a record producer. He had already brought out some sides for English Columbia, using top-flight New York jazzmen, including Goodman, Benny Carter and Fletcher Henderson, and it was to Goodman he turned to provide the backing group when he eventually arranged Holiday's first recording date. In fact, during a few days in late November Hammond was responsible for a quite remarkable confluence of female jazz singing at Columbia. On 24 November, he produced Bessie Smith's return to the recording studio after a long absence (which also turned out to be her final date); three days later he recorded Ethel Waters, currently a major recording artist; and on the same date and in the same studio, he recorded Billie Holiday for the first time. In Stuart Nicholson's words, it was 'a unique distillation of the past, present and future of female vernacular singing'.

Holiday recorded one song, 'Your Mother's Son-in-Law', finding the entire process nerve-wracking, difficult and in a sense rather unsatisfactory. Neither key nor tempo was right for her – already she was sufficiently self-aware to know what worked for her and what did not – and the presence in the studio of the mature, successful and supremely confident Waters did nothing to ease her tension. Apparently Waters was unimpressed, reportedly declaring that the newcomer sang as if her shoes were too tight.

A week later, Holiday came back to the studio to record the second side and, significantly, it was a tune written expressly for the occasion and with her alone in mind as its performer. 'Riffin' the Scotch', despite its title, is a song of unrequited love, a subject that would become a theme of Holiday's repertoire and that in time, inevitably perhaps, became inextricably entwined with her private life and liaisons. Nevertheless, the session was unsuccessful and the result went unreleased; two weeks on and a further session produced the version of this song needed to make up her first release. At the time the record was not deemed to be especially remarkable. Critical observations referred to her small range, acid attack, her inability to correctly phrase a popular melody. In short, she did not meet contemporary conceptions of the cute songstress. As the years passed and she became famous, this first attempt was often dismissed as merely an academically interesting example of a young singer's as yet unformed style. In fact, most of the features that distinguish Holiday's work are clearly in place, especially on the second song which benefits from a slower tempo.

At the time, however, there was insufficient public response to justify Hammond's faith in Holiday's ability. Consequently, two years would pass before she recorded again. During this time she continued to work in Harlem clubs, appeared at the Apollo Theater, without lighting any fires, and with Duke Ellington was featured in a short film, *Symphony in Black*, singing 'Blues', a vocal version of Ellington's instrumental, 'Saddest Tale'. Also in this period she made the acquaintance of Lester Young who was to remain a close friend for many years and with whom she had a platonic yet real and deeply felt love affair, in which consummation was restricted to their joint appearances on records.

Holiday's return to the studios found her teamed with another of Hammond's protégés, pianist Teddy Wilson. With him she also found a remarkably empathetic relationship, even though Wilson would observe in later years that he 'was not a Billie Holiday fan'. Nevertheless, the pick-up bands he hired for his dates with the singer and his arrangements, often 'heads', show a truly remarkable understanding of her needs. From the start, everything that they did together had about it an air of being absolutely right. The first session, on 2 July 1935, which produced four sides, was notable. Despite any equivocation Wilson might have felt about the singer, he had no doubts about the results of that date, declaring, 'That session was never, never surpassed. It may have been equalled, but never surpassed.' In the band was Goodman again, playing exceptionally well, Roy Eldridge, trumpet, and Ben Webster, tenor saxophone, and an excellent rhythm team of Wilson, John Trueheart, guitarist with the Chick Webb band, John Kirby, bass, and Cozy Cole, drums.

Of the four songs, 'I Wished on the Moon', 'What a Little Moonlight Can Do', 'Miss Brown to You', and 'A Sunbonnet Blue', two, 'Moonlight' and 'Miss Brown', fully merit Wilson's claim. Indeed, they not only became staples of the singer's repertoire but 'Moonlight' has been one of the most discussed and analysed of her many recordings.

Despite Wilson's later praise for this particular session and Hammond's unwavering support for the singer, even these records were not especially well received or reviewed at the time. With the benefit of hindsight, it is possible to see that the occasion was of great significance, not only as an important milestone in the singer's career but also as a great step forward in the development of jazz singing. Here was a singer of subtlety with no pretence to be anything other than a jazz singer and, although having rehearsed with Wilson, displaying the freewheeling impression of an impromptu performance. Before this, Louis Armstrong's and Mildred Bailey's work notwithstanding, jazz singing was usually an adjunct to a jazz instrumental performance, frequently dismissed or misunderstood. Here the jazz singer was an integral part of the jazz group. It would be a long time before what happened on this date became an accepted manner in which to record a singer in jazz, but a start had been made. During the next few years, Holiday would build upon this foundation with a succession of fine record dates, many of which, especially those on which she was joined by Lester Young, passed into musical legend alongside the personal legend that was also gradually making its presence felt.

Often with Wilson and Young, the singer made many fine sides. She explained to Leonard Feather in a *Metronome* Blindfold Test in 1948: 'You know, the only ones who can take a solo while I'm singing and still not interfere with me are Lester Young and Teddy.' Her material, selected by Wilson when he was on a date, drew mainly from popular songs of the day, frequently newly written material which she was therefore introducing to the public. Teddy Wilson explained to Don DeMichael that in those days the publishers made the hits: 'They had what they called number one, number two and number three plugs', which were the songs they thought would be hits. 'We never got into the plug tunes. We had the choice of the rest...' Although Holiday's style had been substantially in place since her 1933 recording début, she would still try new things from time to time and was unafraid to test herself with songs that pushed against her limited range. Masterpieces, minor and major, and always interesting performances, appear with startling regularity and seemingly insouciant ease: 'Billie's Blues', a rare instance of her singing in the blues form, from 10 July 1936, and 'He Ain't Got Rhythm', 'This Year's Kisses' and 'I Must Have That Man', from 25 January 1937, the first recording date which brought Holiday together with Young.

Shortly after this session Holiday's putative father, Clarence Holiday, died. It was around this time that she joined the Count Basie band. The first of two spells with a big band, the experience with Basie was not especially happy for Holiday. It was followed by an equally unsatisfactory period with Artie Shaw which ended in November 1938. She was beset by a combination of unsuitable material with Basie and racist incidents while with Shaw. Insofar as her material was concerned, she knew what was best for her, as Basie later attested: 'It was really just a matter of getting her tunes like she wanted them. Because she knew how she wanted to sound and you couldn't tell her what to do.' While with Shaw, an otherwise all-white band, Holiday had to face racist taunts and behaviour. Not only did this happen in the Deep South but also in New York where she was obliged to use the service elevator at the hotel in which the band was appearing.

The tiny number of recordings from this period, all but one being airshots, are interesting without being exceptional examples of an unusual big band singer in an era when ordinariness was often the norm. During this same period, however, Holiday was continuing to make records with small groups, many of them outstanding. Among the songs she recorded between May 1937 and January 1938 were 'I'll Get By', 'Foolin' Myself', 'Me, Myself and I', 'Sailboat in the Moonlight', 'Getting Some Fun out of Life', 'He's Funny That Way', 'When You're Smiling' and 'Back in Your Own Backyard', all with Young and all with moments that transcend anything that other singers, and saxophonists, were doing at this time. Throughout this period, Holiday confidently recast songs in her own image, reworking them not for effect but because it was clearly the way in which she heard them inside her head, and was capable of bringing her ideas into aural reality and sharing them with her audience then and ever afterwards.

The musical partnership of Holiday and Young was remarkable. It was Young, a habitual bestower of nicknames, who called her 'Lady Day' and she responded by naming him 'Pres' (for President). Their bond was of minds, hearts and emotions. There have been many such relationships in jazz, but they have been between two instrumentalists: Louis Armstrong with Earl Hines and with Jack Teagarden, Dizzy Gillespie and Charlie Parker, Goodman and Wilson, Gerry Mulligan and Chet Baker, Kenny Davern and Bob Wilber, Joe Venuti and Eddie Lang, etc. There are few, if any, comparable blendings of singer and instrumentalist; even when Armstrong and Teagarden worked together, it was either as an instrumental team or as a vocal duo, not as instrumentalist and singer. Of course, occasional inspired teamings have occurred, either live or on record, but a sustained period of interaction at such a remarkably high level leaves the stage uncluttered by any serious contenders. Individually, Holiday and Young were unique; together, they comfortably subordinated themselves to the partnership and miraculously retained their individuality; and as a pair they were similarly unique in the annals of jazz.

Although Holiday's status with the American Record Corporation underwent changes during the late 1930s, she continued to record with Young. Her recordings for ARC's Brunswick label were with Teddy Wilson; from mid-1936 she also began recording for Vocalion, another ARC label, under the supervision of Bernie Hanighen, a songwriter ('If the Moon Turned Green', 'When a Woman Loves a Man'). Holiday had known Hanighen for some years and she would later regard him as an important figure in her career, mainly it seems because he was responsible for recording her as Billie Holiday and Her Orchestra. When Hanighen was replaced by Morty Palitz, Holiday was moved onto the parent label which eventually became known as Columbia. The change to being billed under her own name gradually had an effect upon the format of her recordings. The shift away from the concept of the singer as an integral part of a jazz group towards the singer as featured artist with jazz accompaniment was slight but significant. There were still opportunities for solos by instrumentalists and many remarkable examples occurred, especially by Young, as detailed above, but in time the instrumentalists were edged into the background.

Before that change was fully effected, a final handful of very good recordings were made, among them the last Holiday-Young teaming for many years. This came on 21 March 1941 and included an exceptional performance of 'All of Me', the best take of which was not released until the advent of the long-playing record era because it was too long for one side of a 78 rpm record. Stuart Nicholson observes that this particular performance 'stands as a fitting climax to a unique partnership in jazz' with both artists 'achieving a level of creativity that at the time neither realized they would never exceed. It was a poignant climax to an astonishing musical relationship.'

Prior to this there had been another event of significance to Holiday's career. On 20 April 1939 she recorded 'Strange Fruit' for Milt Gabler's Commodore label. Gabler recalled that Holiday 'came in with a long face. She was unhappy. She had just started to sing a song called "Strange Fruit" which was the first protest song, an anti-lynching song she'd been singing at the downtown Café Society. She said to me, "Columbia won't record it because they're afraid of the content of the song." They were worried about the Southern record dealers, the adverse publicity. They also didn't think it was a pop hit ... so I said, "Billie ask them if they'll give you permission to do a record for me. I'm just a little record store, one of their good customers. What do they have to lose?"'

Holiday had been singing the song during an engagement at Barney Josephson's club for a few weeks. Even she had not liked it at first, but the effect upon the club's patrons convinced her that this was something special. Indeed it was. A protest song long before the era when protest songs became a standard part of an 'aware' singer's repertoire, 'Strange Fruit' evokes with chilling imagery the lynching of blacks. Abel Meeropol (Lewis Allen) wrote the song at a time when lynchings were still a fairly common if conveniently overlooked facet of life in some parts of the United States. But it is the singer's manner of dealing with the song's imagery that would eventually redirect her style and the presentation of much of her subsequent work, regardless of the subject matter. She presents 'Strange Fruit' not so much as a singer but as an actress, creating through her words and the emotional intensity with which she delivers them, an atmosphere that is brooding, stark and grimly real. The carefree manner in which she handled the melodic and harmonic structures of other songs is completely absent; indeed, she pays scant regard at all to these aspects of performance.

In a sense 'Strange Fruit' became 'her' song. Folk singer Josh White recorded it not long afterwards but subsequently hardly anyone else ever did so, although Cassandra Wilson included the song on a 1996 album. 'Strange Fruit' marked a change in how Holiday was perceived by audiences and how she perceived herself. The effect was not immediate; as we have seen, she continued to record the kind of song with which hitherto she had been associated. Apart from those songs already mentioned there were the light-hearted lyrics and performances of 'Them There Eyes', 'Laughing at

75

Life' and 'Let's Do It', but by 1941 the spotlight was very firmly upon the singer as artist. This was how her audience appeared to want her and she was more than content to respond. Throughout much of her life she harboured hopeless dreams of becoming an actress; now the desire slowly emerged in her manner of presentation. In mid-1941 other songs were recorded which became hallmarks of her repertoire: 'God Bless the Child', 'Am I Blue?', and, in August of that year, 'Gloomy Sunday'. This song, issued on OKeh, a Columbia subsidiary, came cloaked with a reputation for eastern European despondency; indeed, the original issue's label bore the subtitle, 'The Hungarian Suicide Song'. It was a sure indication that the unexpected success of 'Strange Fruit' had not gone unnoticed at Columbia.

Apparent at this time is a marked slowing down in tempo of many of the ballads she sang. A growing number of her songs now became almost dirge-like in tempo and are couched in the wronged/deserted/lonely/mistreated/misunderstood woman vein, thus helping to formalize the impression of a living legend. Songs like 'My Old Flame', 'I'll Be Seeing You' and 'Lover Come Back to Me', all for Commodore, were matched by the record company she now joined, Decca (where she was produced by Commodore's Milt Gabler). 'Lover Man', 'Don't Explain' and 'Good Morning, Heartache' continued the development of a repertoire and a reputation at odds with that which had surrounded her earliest period. Gone is the joy, the optimism, the verve and enthusiasm. In its place is pervading and occasionally dominant self-conscious gloom.

Curiously enough, whereas for jazz fans the earlier period is a wondrous storehouse of musical excellence, many are now tending to single out the Decca years as the time when the singer was at her peak. True, her voice was in excellent shape, perhaps the best it ever was, but the nature of her performance, the staginess, the repertoire with its restricted nature and pessimism, all conspired to diminish Holiday's true genius and stature as a *jazz* artist. Of course, there are many fine performances within this zone of marled twilight; she had not suddenly become an inferior singer. She was still great; but her nonchalant genius was less evident as she consciously sought to establish herself as a 'serious' artist.

A singer whose performances influenced Holiday into taking this path was Mabel Mercer, a club entertainer little known outside New York, who was barely a singer at all. She spoke her lyrics rather than sang them, especially late in her career, but she delivered them in a way that imposed upon the material a distinctive stamp that made them definitively her own. Sylvia Syms said of her: 'Mabel was not a great singer but she had a way with words and phrases that was unique.' Syms, herself a fine singer who was taken by Holiday to hear Mercer, said that 'Billie had an animal instinct about Mabel and enjoyed bringing people to listen to her'. Another singer Holiday took to hear Mercer was Frank Sinatra who later was to say of Mercer that more than anyone she taught him how to handle a lyric. He also said of Holiday that she 'remains the greatest single musical influence on me'.

To Mercer, who was born in England, must go at least partial responsibility for the change in Holiday's approach to songs. An authoritative and sophisticated performer, Mercer could hold an audience spellbound with her supper club soliloquies. Pianist Billy Taylor recalled the first occasion he heard her: 'I was just about to leave when an elderly-looking lady came out, perched herself on the stool, and began to sing or recite. She had an absolutely unique style, not jazz but really beautiful. Her material was as personal as her approach.' Many other singers responded to Mercer's impeccable taste and ability to move an audience, including Margaret Whiting, Peggy Lee and Sarah Vaughan, all marvelling at her ability to illuminate every syllable with remarkable enunciation. Little wonder that Holiday was so impressed and became so stylistically self-aware during this period. Incidentally, it is strange that, unlike her speaking voice, when Holiday was singing her diction was usually good.

Holiday continued to work with leading jazz musicians of the day and in the mid-1940s began working with Norman Granz's Jazz At The Philharmonic, but mostly she clung to her new diminished repertoire of studiedly introspective songs. She also made her first feature film, thus coming as close as she ever would to achieving one of her ambitions. But in *New Orleans* (1946) she was cast as a maid, a sad if typical reflection of how Hollywood saw blacks at this time.

When Holiday's mother, Sadie, died in 1945 the effect upon the singer was severe. She had long been a heavy drinker and a user of narcotics; both addictions now accelerated and she became depressed and heavily dependent upon others, mostly men with few redeeming features. She was mistreated, and in many cases physically abused.

In 1947 she was charged with narcotics offences and in a strange and ultimately damaging decision, seemingly pressed upon her by her manager, Joe Glaser, she not only pleaded guilty but also rejected legal representation. She was sent to prison where she was treated for her addiction. In March 1948 she appeared at Carnegie Hall with huge success and followed up with another Standing Room Only concert there in April. It should have been the start of a new and triumphant period in the singer's life but it wasn't. The fact that she now had a prison record meant that she no longer qualified for a New York Cabaret Card, a document she needed if she was to be allowed to perform in licensed premises. She could and did appear in concert halls and in theatres and continued to make records, but the mainstay of her professional life, New York's clubland, was prohibited. And the mainstays of her private life, her dependency upon alcohol, shady men and narcotics, resumed their importance. Indeed, they began to gain ground as her professional life suffered. Not that these reverses were immediately apparent. Wherever she did appear she was greeted enthusiastically. Just how many among her growing audience of admirers were there because of her acquired notoriety can only be surmised. What seems irrefutable is that her new audience was not especially interested in Billie Holiday the Jazz

Singer but in Billie Holiday the Tragic Woman. More and more, the songs that she sang – even though in most cases she had been singing them for years – were thought of as personal statements about the indignities heaped upon her. As Nicholson puts it, 'her real-life story had become the source of meaningfulness in her voice'.

Her private life continued in disarray; there were more drugs charges, more hospitalization. Despite such setbacks there were also some record dates and she even appeared on television – something which, if nothing else, exposes the hypocrisy of the withdrawal of her New York Cabaret Card.

Although at odds with the authorities, she remained popular with the jazz audience and in a 1948 *Metronome* Blindfold Test was asked to comment upon some of her contemporaries. She proved to be forthright in her opinions: 'I always loved Peggy [Lee]...'; 'I just do not like [Ruth Brown]...'; 'You know, on "The Man I Love" [Sarah Vaughan] goes so far out, it stinks ... but this one ["Make Believe"] is worth three stars'; '[Jackie Cain and Roy Kral] should be able to work in any good hotel, any theatre – anywhere they're the best'.

Her recording contract with Decca had not been renewed in March 1950 and in the spring of 1952 she signed with Norman Granz's Clef label and thus began her third and last period as a recording artist. The period quickly came to rank favourably with her earlier sessions with Teddy Wilson and Lester Young. Among the artists Granz used to accompany her were Oscar Peterson, Barney Kessel, Ray Brown, Ben Webster, Harry Edison, Jimmy Rowles and Benny Carter. Significantly, Granz insisted upon a substantial number of songs that were new to her.

The results were usually good, sometimes outstanding. Of course the voice was different and in most respects inferior to what it had been, especially during her Decca period. Yet it has qualities that urge themselves upon the listener, qualities that jazz critic and poet Philip Larkin referred to as 'at once charred and scorching'. Listening to her records from these final years, it is hard to achieve detached critical consideration. It is tempting even for the confirmed jazz lover to side with those who entwine the singer's life with her art and read into her interpretations some elements of the life she had led and which had damaged her psychologically, emotionally and physically. There is no doubt that she touches many as she echoes world-weary resignation, helpless vulnerability, and the occasional brushing of the bottom of an all-but-dried-up emotional well.

There were highlights still to come in her life outside the recording studio. A visit to Europe which began in January 1954 brought her to Britain and a concert at London's Royal Albert Hall before 6000 ecstatic fans. Back in America, an even bigger audience attended the 1954 Newport Jazz Festival at which Holiday was joined on stage by Lester Young. Late in the year and early in 1955 she again recorded for Granz, achieving notable success with songs such as 'Too Marvellous for Words', 'P. S. I Love You', 'Ain't Misbehavin'' and 'I've Got My Love to Keep Me Warm'. These recordings clearly demonstrate that she had managed to cling onto some of the enthusiasm and vigour of her youth even though there is a constant *frisson* that at any moment everything might come apart at the seams.

In 1956 she made a number of concert appearances promoting her autobiography, *Lady Sings the Blues*, co-authored with William Dufty. The book contained a number of recollections that were arbitrarily dismissed as exaggerations or inventions but that years later have been found to be substantially accurate. She also made a number of television appearances, including one, on 8 December 1957, which brought her once more into musical contact with Lester Young. *The Sound of Jazz* has Holiday singing 'Fine and Mellow' with an all-star band including Roy Eldridge, Coleman Hawkins and Ben Webster, but it is Young's solo that most catches the attention with its poignant echoing of a once-mighty talent reaching out for one last attempt at musical consummation with his partner of long ago.

By this time, Holiday's addiction had taken an irreversible grip and her public appearances were fraught with the tensions of getting her on stage and keeping her there. In October 1958 she sang at the Monterey Jazz Festival where she had to be physically supported on stage by accompanists Gerry Mulligan and Buddy DeFranco. The following month she made a short disastrous tour of Europe. Early in 1959 she visited London for a television appearance, then returned to the USA to make an album with an orchestra directed by Ray Ellis. Aware that in the past she had let people down and that opportunities to record were few, she said to Columbia's Irving Townsend, 'Now I know I'm the one that talked you into making this session, and I won't let you down. I won't goof.' Recorded over five days in early March, it is perhaps the occasion where Holiday the Singer, the Artist, and the Tragic Woman become most intermingled. Broken in health, desperately weary, barely aware of what was happening to and around her, she turned this last formal recording date into a moving valedictory to a career and life gone so catastrophically wrong. Cushioned by strings, she delivers careworn performances of a selection of songs, the titles and lyrics of which seem to paraphrase her declining life: 'Just One More Chance', 'You Took Advantage of Me', 'All the Way', 'I'll Never Smile Again', 'Don't Worry 'Bout Me'.

Four days after Holiday completed this session, Lester Young died. She attended his funeral on 19 March, wanting to sing but was told that she could not do so. The rejection was devastating. During the next few weeks she made a number of appearances at out-of-town clubs and also at a New York theatre. That she was aware of the manner in which her legend weighed heavily upon her as an artist is apparent from a newspaper interview she gave at this time: 'Every time I do a show I'm up against everything that's ever been written about me. I have to fight the whole scene to get people to listen to their own ears and believe in me again.'

But time had run out. Late in May she was hospitalized again. Even then the fates pursued her as she was harried by the police and by yet another shady character, a lawyer, who persuaded her to sign various documents most of which were more advantageous to him than to her. Drugs were found at her hospital bedside and she was charged, fingerprinted and photographed, and placed under police guard. While the lawyer and others did deals linked to her estate, her spirit finally gave way and she died on 17 July 1959.

But although Billie Holiday was dead, the legend was still in full flight and showed no signs of weakening. Indeed, it grew in strength as the years passed. The appearance in 1972 of a feature film, *Lady Sings the Blues*, encouraged legend at the expense of truth. And there were books and articles and an unending programme of reissues of her recordings.

It is probably the legendary nature of her life and career that most confuses latter-day audiences for her records. And to some extent it also affects opinions expressed by other singers. It has become almost *de rigueur* for singers in jazz to cite Holiday as an influence, even when there is little reflection of her style in their work. So how influential was she? In some ways a case might be made for isolating Holiday from all singers, not just after her lifetime but also before and during it. Despite her claims to have listened to and admired the singing of Louis Armstrong and Bessie Smith, it was inspiration rather than style assimilation she got from them. From Smith she developed her rhythmic delivery and subtle use of vocal techniques, a direct simplicity of approach, and sparing use of embellishment and vibrato. She spoke about the latter to Max Jones: 'When I got into show business you had to have that shake. If you didn't, you was dead. I didn't have that kind of vibrato and when I sang people used to say, "What's she putting down?" I always did try to sing like a tenor, or some horn. That big vibrato fits a few voices, but those that have it usually have too much. I just don't like it. You have to use it sparingly. You know, the hard thing is *not* to sing with that shake.'

From Armstrong came skill in improvising, the bending of words, the relaxed sense of swing. Stuart Nicholson suggests that an additional area of influence may lie in Holiday's childhood experiences in an institution run by the Catholic church. In Maryland the church was strict and true to Rome and the Gregorian chants were in stark contrast to the holy-rolling of the sanctified churches which produced singers such as Dinah Washington and Aretha Franklin. In the churches she attended, Holiday would have experienced songs sung undemonstratively and with a minimum of melodic movement. It is interesting at this point to note that Ethel Waters was also raised in the Catholic church and, like Holiday, had none of the characteristics displayed by the gospel singers.

Whatever the source of inspiration, where other singers might present a song, Holiday creates one. Take, for example, three performances of one song, 'My Last Affair', by Helen Humes, Mildred Bailey and Holiday, each one in its way a perfect example of the singers' art. Recording in 1958, Humes sings in an easy mid-tempo. Using slightly dragged-out phrasing, she provides a delightful, if conventional, typically sunny performance, building finally to a rousing rideout chorus. It is an excellent example of straight ahead swinging. Bailey, recording in 1937, uses a slow to medium tempo and provides a light and lilting vocal style, warm but with a hint of melancholy about it. This is another delightful and perfect performance. Holiday also recorded her version in 1937 but in terms of innovation and improvisation she is light years ahead of her two contemporaries. Indeed, she is in a class of her own. The slow rocking intro is followed by a vocal chorus quite unlike those of Humes and Bailey. She literally reinvents the melody and the song's rhythms without resort to any over-ornamentation. Her phrasing is trumpet-like and simple – a typically instrumental concep-tion. There is no adherence to the original melodic line, yet the sense of the lyric is miraculously retained, totally and convincingly; in fact it is enhanced in every sense. This is where Holiday's genius lies. This is what so delighted musicians about her performances; not just her musicianship but the brilliance of her musicianship. A musician may play with dazzling virtuosity – that tells you he knows his instrument. But he need play only a simple phrase to melt every heart in the room – if he has the talent to choose the right phrase. Billie Holiday had that talent.

In conversation with *Jazz Journal*'s Sinclair Traill, singer Babs Gonzales concentrated upon a sometimes overlooked aspect of Holiday's work, '... even before Ella Fitzgerald knew how to run those changes, Billie Holiday was running those chord changes when I was in grammar school. She was doing that a long time before anyone else. And it's really funny that people don't think of that aspect of Billie's work, they always think of the feeling she gave her songs, the soul and despair she possessed in her voice, but they never think of how she was running changes even before Ella.'

Charles Fox remarked that for the blues singer 'the poetry was already there but for Billie, she had to create it'. Create it she surely did. Holiday rarely sang the blues yet there is a constant awareness of the blues in all that she does. As Max Kaminsky observed: 'Her voice *was* the blues.'

If the links with singers for whom Holiday expressed admiration are tenuous, there is the unmistakable fact that her first recording date in 1933 does not show an uninformed singer. This is a singer who already knows what she wants to do and how she wants to do it. Still only eighteen years old, she certainly had much to learn but there is no doubt that she was already started along the road that she followed unerringly for the next decade. Most of what Holiday brought to her art was formed within herself. Tracing stylistic forbears, in the case of, say, Louis Armstrong or Lester Young is beset by the difficulty of finding any progenitor who stands up to more than a cursory inspection. These musicians were not taught in the accepted sense of this word. Of course trumpet playing can be taught; the saxophone can be taught; singing can be taught. With a capable and willing pupil, good teachers can, with time, help produce excellent, even great, musicians. But however capable and willing the pupil, even the finest teachers in the world with infinite time at their disposal cannot produce a

81

Louis Armstrong or a Lester Young. This is because, whatever teaching can do – and it can do much – it cannot create genius. That is what Armstrong was, what Young was, and what Holiday was.

As we have seen, there came a point in her life where her genius was infiltrated by an overly self-aware desire to be an artist. But she still continued to delight and attract as she built a different kind of musical life upon the foundations that her genius had created. For a time it was less the work of a creative jazz mind and more an extension of her perceived public persona. Comments which, coincidently, might be made just as readily about Armstrong.

When singers who admired Holiday began to develop their own careers, they found little scope in simply imitating her style. Most of them saw within the framework of what she did a basis for development of their own ideas. Because there was diversity in her influence, the results were often very different – not only from what she had done but from one another. Among those directly influenced were Jerry Kruger, Marilyn Moore, Carmen McRae and Abbey Lincoln. Also singers as different from one another as Peggy Lee and Anita O'Day can be seen to have sprung from concepts set down by Holiday.

Holiday's intimate exploration of the emotional content of the lyrics she sang, and the expressing of that emotion through both the lyric and the mood she set, were most obviously targeted by Peggy Lee. As Abbey Lincoln remarked, 'Peggy Lee wouldn't have known what to do if it hadn't been for Billie.' Like Holiday, Lee delved deeply into the lyric and the lyrical mood of the songs she sang, and by the late 1940s and the start of her solo career she had refined this aspect of Holiday's art into finely spun gold. In doing so, Lee moved gradually away from a jazz context, unconsciously setting markers for an entire generation of singers whose work developed aspects of popular singing which Holiday almost certainly glimpsed – witness the stylistic approach to *Lady in Satin* – but probably failed to realize was an extension of her own work a decade or more before.

In striking contrast to Lee's elegant examination of the lyric content of songs, Anita O'Day pursued instead the harmonic variations Holiday used and especially the audacious rhythmic experiments. Thus, where Lee might be seen as a precursor of a generation of sophisticated song stylists, O'Day was a founder of a line of latter-day hipsters, but she never over-looked Holiday's depth of feeling. Discussing Holiday's recording of 'My Man', O'Day said to Don Gold, 'Only someone who has lived the way she does, who has lived such experiences, could interpret "My Man" as she does – so beautifully, so grand, so sincere.'

However indirectly it might be, the vast majority of singers who have emerged since the late 1940s and were still emerging in the late 1990s owe some debt to Billie Holiday. In many instances the links are slender, with newcomers modelling themselves upon singers several times removed from the fountainhead. Yet most claims to having been affected by Holiday are not only truthful but are also founded upon careful consideration. In 1996 *JazzTimes* interviewed several singers on the continuing impact Holiday has on jazz. Diana Krall spoke for most when she said, '... it was her artistry which was so important ... she really makes you feel', and Dianne Reeves wisely saw the way to handle inspirators of such magnitude: 'You listen to them and you get inspired by them, but you can never be them...'

At various times in her life, Carmen McRae (who wrote the song 'Dream of Life', which Holiday recorded in 1939) commented upon the effect her exposure to Holiday had upon her own career. 'Oh yes!', she declared to Barbara Gardner in a *down beat* interview in 1962, 'When I was seventeen or eighteen years old, I not only sang like her, I tried to do everything she did. I had her down pat, even to her gestures.' To Arthur Taylor, in 1970, she said that to her young eyes Holiday had 'seemed so utterly perfect ... that I felt anything after her would be anticlimactic'. As time passed, of course, McRae developed her own style and was able to set behind her any slavishness and feelings of inadequacy, but she never failed to acknowledge the debt. 'She is my only influence,' she emphasized in another *down beat* interview, this time in 1991. Yet McRae was neither blind nor deaf to the imperfections of her idol, observing that sometimes she listened to Holiday and thought that she was through, 'then the next night she sings her ass off...' Nevertheless McRae was emphatic about Holiday's integrity: '... she sings the way she is'.

This ability to see and hear flaws in Holiday's work and to separate the good from the not so good is rare. Apart from McRae, the British singer and teacher Jan Ponsford is one who has commented that while Holiday's 'phrasing and ideas are great, I don't personally enjoy her sound'. Singer-teacher Nanette Natal agrees: 'A lot of people might even find her sound offensive, it was raw and it was underdeveloped and wasn't polished but it was so real and so moving and so deep that it hit the very core of you. It was really truth.' Pianist Jimmy Rowles who often accompanied Holiday on record commented, 'Billie didn't have a real voice – she just had a sound. Yeah, it was something that came naturally out of her personality.' Most often singers overlook the flaws, pay their respects, acknowledge their debt – be it real or imagined, strong or nebulous – and help the legend live on. Even Ella Fitzgerald was in awe of her, declaring herself afraid to sing 'Lover Man' after hearing Holiday's definitive version. And Billy Eckstine stated, 'She can do no wrong to me... I can't think of anyone with more soul than Lady Day.'

Meanwhile, record company reissues continue to offer a constant reminder of what Holiday did during the three stages of her career. Just what she would have thought about it all is speculative, but a mixture of frustration, bewilderment and wry amusement is as good a guess as any. Her own view was simple: 'I don't think I'm singing. I feel like I am playing a horn. I try to improvise like Lester Young, like Louis Armstrong, or someone else I admire. What comes out is what I feel. I hate straight singing. I have to change a tune to my way of doing it. That's all I know.'

FIVE
LET THE GOOD TIMES ROLL

When anyone sings they ought to let the soul
come out - just let it flow out. — Dinah Washington

The fact that the first true jazz singer, Louis Armstrong, and the next major innovator, Billie Holiday, were black is no mere coincidence. Neither is it by chance that the two great superstars who appeared later, Ella Fitzgerald and Sarah Vaughan, were also black. Most of the main threads in jazz singing have emerged from black culture: the blues, gospel, r&b, soul and, of course, jazz itself. Even the principal exception, the 32-bar popular song, for decades a significant factor and dominated from the start by white composers, was always interactive with black musical developments and thought. Latterly, this thread is showing some signs of diminution as good melodists grow fewer and more and more singers choose to write their own material. Even so, black influence is never far away. Young white jazz singers of the 1990s grew up in the atmosphere of rock and are thus but one step removed from black sources.

Nevertheless, it is inescapable that a strikingly large proportion of the recent upsurge in the numbers of singers in jazz is white. Soul music and its derivatives, however, presents an opposite view. Certainly there are white soul singers and there exists the diluted form termed 'blue-eyed soul', but for the most part this is an area of popular music that is dominated by black artists and which has most psychological and emotional appeal for black singers. There are two obvious reasons for this. One is that just as for white singers rock is a more lucrative and prominent area than jazz in which to work, so too for blacks is soul a possible route to the top in popular music. The other reason is much more complex and has to do with racial identity, pride and self-awareness.

A thorough exploration of this subject requires considerably more space than is available here and is, anyway, outside the scope of this book. However, some generalized thoughts on the historical patterns of black musical development in America do have a bearing upon any discussion of jazz singing.

*   *   *

In many respects, the blues can be seen to be the most pervasive form of black music, inasmuch as it has influenced and become an integral part of jazz, r&b and soul. However, it was not the first distinctly black music to appear in North America and have an impact upon white audiences. A century and more before the blues emerged, a vitalized form of hymn singing had countless devotees all across the Deep South. This was labelled first as spirituals but in time became known as gospel.

The origins of gospel music lie in the evolving need for spirituality among blacks in North America during their centuries of servitude. From the beginning, slaves were in need of any kind of spiritual uplift and with so many things actively proscribed by their masters they clutched at whatever was allowed. When English missionaries began working in North America at the beginning of the eighteenth century they saw no reason to exclude blacks from those whose souls they sought to save. The music used by the early propagators of the gospel were lively hymn tunes composed by men such as Isaac Watts, perhaps the most influential religious songwriter of his times; John Newton, a former slave-ship captain who saw the light and, incidentally, wrote 'Amazing Grace'; and Richard Allen, a freed slave who founded the African Methodist Episcopal Church. Interestingly, John Wesley, who would later found the Methodist Church, assembled his first collection of hymns while he was minister of Christ Church in Savannah, Georgia, in 1736. White churchgoers in Savannah met regularly for hymn singing and the extent to which blacks later responded readily to Methodist hymns in their churches might indicate a measure of recognition of a form with which they were already familiar or perhaps which itself owed something to black music. During the 'Great Awakening' in the 1730s and the 'Second Awakening', which began in the 1780s and lasted through the first quarter of the next century, more and more blacks turned to Christianity. Integral to the Second Awakening were evangelical tent shows, known as 'camp meetings', which were hugely popular with slaves. The camp meetings saw a re-emergence into black music of some old and near-forgotten concepts, such as ring shouts. This blending of English hymns and revived African chants created a distinctive form of religious song and the so-called negro spiritual became the first identifiably black contribution to American music.

By 1865 and the ending of the Civil War, the spiritual was already integral to black culture and within twenty years had spread through the reunited states and as far as Europe, thanks in large part to a group of singers from Fisk, a desperately poor black college at Nashville, Tennessee. In 1871 the singers embarked upon a fund-raising tour that took the world of music by storm. At least, it proved hugely popular with whites because the Fisk Jubilee Singers, like their emulators and successors, appear often to have changed their music into a form more readily acceptable to their predominantly white audiences. Black and white attitudes towards spirituals differed. While whites might see them as purely religious, some black writers considered them to be social statements reflecting the conditions of servitude and aspirations to freedom, justice and survival. The reality is more likely to be a complex mingling of many things, central to which is the African-American sense of 'at-homeness with one's self', a physiological and psychical expression summed up in one word – soul.

Fifty years on and closer to the black impulse within spirituals than were the Fisk Jubilee Singers comes Thomas A. Dorsey, whose rich and varied career was of enormous importance to gospel music or, as it was then called, jubilee singing. Attracted both by the sacred music of the church and the decidedly less godly music of the streets and back country, Dorsey vacillated between gospel and the blues during the early 1920s. Eventually, he threw off his blues persona, 'Georgia Tom', and settled into the church to write and perform. He was also instrumental in furthering the careers of many future gospel stars, including Sallie Martin, Willie Mae Ford Smith and Mahalia Jackson. The music Dorsey wrote for the church in the 1930s typifies the style of gospel singing around that period and includes his most famous composition, 'Precious Lord, Take My Hand', which harkened back to the core of black religious music, eschewing the some-what laundered version that was still widely accepted as negro spirituals. Mahalia Jackson told Nat Hentoff: 'We've had gospel songs as far back as I can remember, although years ago they used to call it jubilee singing, and the Fisk Jubilee Singers used to go all over the world singing those songs with just a little bounce – not as much bounce as now, though, in gospel singing. Most of the gospel songs came out of our Baptist hymnbook that's published by our National Baptist Convention.' Joe Bostic, who used to promote Jackson's Carnegie Hall concerts, further identified the change, explaining, 'Gospel music began to concern itself more than the jubilee had with tonal qualities and music stylings ... and emotionally, it was even more uninhibited than jubilee singing ... it was as if God walked on the street and you could talk to him.'

This brighter, more rhythmic music emanating from the likes of Tom Dorsey contained more than a hint of the blues. Importantly, Dorsey shifted the balance to create an affirmative tone which said that however bad things might look – this was the time of the Great Depression (although for many blacks things could not get much worse) – there was still cause to be joyful. Dorsey's gospel music carried with it an overt explication of a factor central to evangelical Christianity: Good News.

Mahalia Jackson was perhaps the most famous gospel singer of them all, especially to the world outside America. Sometimes carried away by her fervour and sheer delight in singing, she was banned by some of the more conservative churches. Frequently invited to enter the secular side of black music, she turned down all offers although she did not always express dislike for earthier sounds. As she told writer and broadcaster Studs Terkel, when reminiscing about her childhood: 'When the old people weren't home, I'd turn on a Bessie Smith record. And play it over and over... Her music haunted you even when she stopped singing.'

Jackson's performances often showed improvisational similarities to those of jazz or blues artists. Her programme notes often warned: 'Miss Jackson will choose selections from her repertoire on the spur of the moment'. Jackson explained, 'A lot of times I change my programming because I change my feeling. And I don't sing the same song the same way twice.' She went on to describe why she felt the need to change a performance: 'There's something the public reaches into me for, and there seems to be something in each audience that I can feel. I can feel whether there's a low spirit. Some places I go, uptempo songs don't go, and other places, sad songs aren't right.' Among her recordings with which jazz enthusiasts would most associate are: 'Jesus', 'Walk Over God's Heaven', 'Didn't It Rain' and 'When the Saints Go Marching In' (which at least on this occasion is given a proper spiritual rendition). In time, Jackson, too, became steadily more attuned to white audiences and to some extent was alienated from the black. John Hammond Jnr stated that she 'was only interested in money...' but the singer herself contended, 'I don't work for money. I sing because I love to sing.' Gloria Lynne, who sang with the choir of the Mother African Methodist Episcopal Zion Church as a child in the late 1930s, admired Jackson for her soul and sound: 'She has such a feeling and such depth, and she sings gospel music which I would like to sing too.' Helen Humes remembered hearing gospel music from the North Street Baptist Church in Louisville, Kentucky, next door to the house where she grew up. The kids 'would start to sing as soon as they could carry a tune. We'd go from church to church singing and into outlying towns.' For Carrie Smith there was a blending of sacred and secular: 'I ... started singing in the Baptist Church in Union, New Jersey, where we moved when I was seven. I was singing spiri-tuals and my mom and dad had Bessie Smith records and some Ethel Waters from the 1920s and I used to listen to them.' For a while Smith, who in later years appeared internationally as a jazz and blues singer, sang in Mahalia Jackson's gospel troupe.

The list of black singers who first sang in church is unending, ranging from early classic blues singers like Lucille Hegamin, who sang in various choirs in the first decade of the twentieth century, through later blues singers such as Big Miller and Jimmy Witherspoon, and jazz-informed singers like Ernestine Anderson and Della Reese, to Kevin Mahogany, popular in the last decade of the century.

Through the years, soloists of gospel music made their marks. Apart from Mahalia Jackson there were Clara Ward, Marion Williams, Shirley Caesar, Albertina Walker, Madeleine Bell, Marie Knight, and the remarkable Sister Rosetta Tharpe. Like Tom Dorsey, Tharpe was able to fluidly move between sacred and secular music. She began recording in 1938, becoming an instant gospel star, but she also attracted wider attention by singing and sometimes recording with popular bands of the day including Cab Calloway in 1938 and Lucky Millinder in 1941/2 after coming to prominence in a Cotton Club revue. A jazz singer whose medium happens to be religious music, Tharpe accepted her dual role with equanimity: 'It doesn't bother me when people say I'm a jazz singer. I regard it as quite a compliment, knowing it is meant as such.' On her early recordings she used only her own steel-bodied guitar to create a rocking, pulsating rhythm. Later she teamed up with Marie Knight, the duo recording with accompaniment by pianist, Sam Price, with whom she had also worked at the Café Society. Among her most popular recordings are: 'Look Away in the Heavenly Land', 'Up Above My Head, I Hear Music in the Air', 'Milky White Way' and 'Strange Things Happen Every Day'. In performance Tharpe was uproarious and swinging and made dynamic use of her acute sense of rhythm. Her European tours in the 1960s attracted large and enthusiastic audiences.

Although the pioneers of gospel were the great solo singers, there were also groups, commonly quartets, which began to make an impact in the 1930s. Their open-hearted, full-throated, emotionally intense and joyous style found emulators in popular music. Even in the restrained stylings of the popular singing group, the Mills Brothers, lie hints of an awareness of gospel.

The popularity of gospel music, and the volume sales of records did not escape the attention of promoters and record producers. During the 1940s and through the following decade, gospel singers were tempted across the ever-narrowing gulf between their own music, with all its emotional, religious, spiritual and racial profundity, and popular forms which retained the joyousness and emotional qualities but which dealt increasingly with decidedly secular, if not actually sacrilegious, subjects. The gospel groups, which continued to flourish during the two decades after the ending of World War Two, also provided a learning vehicle for many young men and women who would later find success in r&b and soul.

In the early 1950s gospel music infiltrated even further into jazz in an unlikely alliance when some hard bop instrumentalists, such as Horace Silver, Art Blakey and Cannonball Adderley, began to incorporate the emotional urgency of gospel into their music. This, together with briefly popular funky organ-led trios, turned jazz in a direction which would eventually bring others to jazz-soul.

Just what effect the gospel singers of earlier generations had upon early jazzmen is open to speculation, although one veteran New Orleans trumpeter, Papa Mutt Carey, had no doubts: 'Hell, that music was swinging all the way back in [Buddy] Bolden's time, and before him in the Holy Roller churches he got it from.'

*   *   *

The blues is a seminal thread in the fabric of African-American music, linking field holler and worksong through jazz to soul, rap and other forms of black music. The flatted third and seventh of the blues was as common in black churches as in the fields, streets and workplace. The blues had evolved from slavery days, a time as Jimmy Rushing once said with remarkable understatement, '... when those people weren't treated right'. The blues is more than just music, commonly of a simple 12- or 8-bar structure; it is about feelings, about inner hurt, and sorrow. Yet the blues format can also be used to convey happiness, heartfelt joy and humour. It is also about a vocal technique of blue notes, sliding notes, vocal buzzes, glottal sounds, cries and moans. Techniques such as these have been used by generations of blues and jazz singers, not just for singing a blues but also incorporated into vaudeville numbers, Broadway and Tin Pan Alley tunes, helping to make both song and performance believable, honest and personal. These techniques are as visible in the work of contemporary singers such as Kevin Mahogany and Cassandra Wilson as they are in the 1920s recordings of, say, Blind Lemon Jefferson or Victoria Spivey. Technique, in this sense, is not a matter of vocal skill or virtuosity. Indeed, it is possible for an effective blues singer to work with only a mediocre voice while a singer with perfect vocal equipment can miss completely the spirit of the blues.

Despite surface changes as the blues matured from its earliest rough and ready days to the sophisticated urban sounds that eventually emerged, in its essence it has remained largely unaltered. As T-Bone Walker stated unequivocally, 'You know there's only one blues... That's the regular 12-bar pattern and then you interpret over that. Just write new words or improvise different and you've got a new blues. Now, you take a piece like "St Louis Blues". That's a pretty tune and it has a kind of a bluesy tone, but that's not the blues. You can't dress up the blues. The only blues is the kind I sing and the kind that Jimmy Rushing sings... I'm not saying that "St Louis Blues" isn't fine music, you understand. But it just isn't blues... Blues is all by itself.'

Jimmy Rushing concurred, declaring to *Jazz Journal*'s Sinclair Traill, 'You can't add to the blues, because if you try to augment the blues, then they become something else ... the old time blues cannot be added to, or they ain't blues any longer.'

Rushing should know. He was not only a blues singer but he was also a truly creative artist. The limitations of the blues, insofar as his need to be creative was concerned, must have presented him with problems surmountable only by his ability to convincingly sing other kinds of material.

Clarinettist Buster Bailey had no doubts that Bessie Smith was also a highly creative artist. 'Bessie was the Louis Armstrong of the blues singers. She had more original ideas for blues and things than the others did.' The qualities of her singing voice were somewhat restricted, but any limitations in her range were overcome by her commanding delivery. Additionally, she showed by her ability to get inside her material that the blues were not merely songs, they were statements of life. Smith's art took her beyond restrictions of voice and material and into the hearts and souls of her audience. Billy Eckstine remembered her in performance and being struck by her stagecraft: 'She would come out after she'd maybe sung a fast blues – she'd go off the stage and then come back for her big song, a real slow blues, you know, the real drag blues. She'd step out of the wing and start singing the song very slowly, and as she finished each chorus she'd just take a slight step towards stage left. And each chorus she would take another step, so by the time she had finished like that she would be on the other side of the stage and off into the wing... And between one side of the stage and the other she sang about twenty choruses of the greatest blues you ever listened to.'

Smith displayed great integrity towards the blues she sang and which were so much a part of her. And while this was a strength, it was also a factor in her decline from the peak of public adulation. As they will, times changed and so too did musical tastes, but she did not. True, she sang vaudeville material and popular songs, just as she had always done, but she imbued them with the essence of the blues and in her case this was essayed in a manner that often suggested deepest unhappiness. While Ethel Waters could and did comfortably adapt to change, and could and did lighten the mood she evoked in her listeners, Bessie Smith allied despondency to her majesty and chose not to adopt the sophistication of her contemporaries and successors. The public, as is its wont, preferred the new to the old and turned to other, almost by definition lesser, singers and Smith's day was done. Reportedly, she was starting to make changes and hoping to claw her way back when her life ended abruptly at the age of thirty-seven following a car accident, on the road to another engagement.

Alberta Hunter was another singer with the gift for imbuing all kinds of material with the true spirit of the blues. She began her career as a child, beginning to write a song, 'Down Hearted Blues', when she was ten years old, just before she ran away from home: 'Later on I recorded it for Paramount Records and it was a tremendous hit.' It was an even bigger hit for Bessie Smith; her recording of Hunter's song resulted in sales of over three-quarters of a million copies.

Hunter's career not only started early, it also ended late. Indeed, she had more than one career, in and outside music. As a child she began singing blues, popular songs and jazz in some of Chicago's most famous – and notorious – venues, ranging from Dago Frank's whorehouse to Hugh Hoskins's club, from the Panama Club to the Dreamland Café: 'It was at the Panama that I introduced the "St Louis Blues". Oh, yes, I was there a long time and people like Bert Williams and Al Jolson would come to hear me sing ... blues and popular numbers... But it was at the Dreamland that I really went to town. It was there that I introduced "Loveless Love", which W. C. Handy brought to me on a little piece of paper – not even on manuscript. It was at the Dreamland that I also introduced "A Good Man Is Hard to Find"... Sophie Tucker heard about (this song) and sent over her maid to tell me she wanted to see me. I knew she wanted the song, and so I didn't go. So do you know how she got it? She sent over her piano player ... to listen to it and learn it, and got somebody to take down the words. But when she sang the song she always gave me credit.'

Hunter's career drifted a little in the 1960s and she retired to take up nursing until 1977 when her employers realized that diminutive Nurse Hunter was eighty-two years old and compulsorily retired her. Soon afterwards, she started singing again, enrapturing audiences some not yet born when she was thinking about her first retirement. As British jazz and blues singer Christine Tyrrell commented: 'Alberta Hunter when she was old was better at phrasing than when she was a young singer. She talked it, but the phrasing was perfect.'

The toughness of spirit which sustained Alberta Hunter was reflected in the case of Joe Turner although there was nothing frail about him. Tall and powerfully built, Turner was a blues singer of the old school, described by Philip Larkin as a 'knotty-voiced shouter'. Turner, whose early life was spent in Kansas City, had a strong sense of the origins of the music he personified in the course of a long career. 'The blues was here before I got here,' he told *Crescendo International*. 'They had a lot of blues singers before my time, see. That's where I learned it from – listening to records and people singing. We had a lot of records of Bessie Smith, Leroy Carr, Lonnie Johnson.' Musing on his style, Turner continued, 'I didn't like to sing them blues slow. I had an idea I could swing 'em – kinda pick it up and get 'em in a good mood.'

Like Alberta Hunter, Turner's career had its stages. In the 1930s he was mostly to be heard singing in the bars and clubs of Kansas City, especially the Reno and Sunset clubs on 12th Street. Turner first worked at the Sunset as a singing bartender, which is where pianist-arranger Mary Lou Williams remembered him: '... while Joe was serving drinks he would suddenly pick up a cue for a blues and sing it right where he stood, with Pete [Johnson] playing piano for him. I don't think I'll ever forget the thrill of listening to big Joe Turner shouting and sending everybody, night after night, while mixing drinks.'

The hectic nature of Kansas City's wide-open clubland might be inferred from a remark Turner made: 'Everybody wants to know about the good old days... I was there... I never saw them.' But he certainly saw the nights. Jo Jones recalls first meeting Turner at the Sunset: 'I remember we used to play behind Joe there. There was a place close by called the Lone Star. Joe Turner would start to sing the blues at the Sunset, and then he'd go across the street and sing the blues at the Lone Star, and we were still playing all this time. Joe would socialize there for a while and stop in front and have breakfast and then he'd come back into the Sunset, go up to the microphone, and sing some more blues, and we'd have been playing all the time.'

The high-living nights of his youth and the later tiring years of touring eventually laid Turner low and he lost his health and his spirit. On the occasion of Turner's seventieth birthday a special party was arranged at his home in Los Angeles with some fifty or sixty friends in attendance. German boogie-woogie pianist Axel Zwingenberger was there, having arranged to record the proceedings. Also present was r&b performer Roy Milton to play drums and, for good measure, blues shouter and alto saxophonist, Eddie 'Cleanhead' Vinson. Zwingenberger recalls that Joe was down, not having sung since his illness: 'He had it in his head that his voice was gone and that he would never sing again. He was very depressed, refused to join in the celebrations and disappeared into his bedroom. Roy and I started to play anyway, and soon we got into one of those rocking grooves that Joe loved. Suddenly, from the bedroom there came an almighty roar.' The blues spirit had re-entered the tired body of Big Joe Turner and he came out and sang for the rest of the day. The resulting album is a pure delight with a joyful Turner really letting those good times roll. He was back in business once more, singing almost as well as ever.

Turner had evolved through the blues of the 1930s into r&b in the 1940s and then on to rock 'n' roll in the 1950s without ever changing his style or his material. From the late 1950s until his death Turner sang mostly with jazz accompaniment, producing some of his most exciting work, in particular *Boss of the Blues*, a classic album.

Other early bluesmen who survived through into the years of rock were Lonnie Johnson and T-Bone Walker. Johnson, a versatile guitarist, became very much a part of the early jazz recording scene in the 1920s, making records with notables such as Joe 'King' Oliver, Louis Armstrong, Duke Ellington and Eddie Lang. As a singer of soulful blues and bitter-sweet blues ballads, he was a major star wielding tremendous influence on later blues performers. In the 1940s he became popular in the r&b field, changing to electric guitar and making many recordings for King Records ranging from the bawdy to the sweetly sentimental and had four big hits, 'Tomorrow Night', 'Pleasing You', 'So Tired' and 'Confused'. His career continued sporadically into the 1970s when he was knocked down by a hit-and-run driver.

Like Johnson and Turner, Walker was a singer who worked comfortably in a jazz context when the spirit moved him without ever losing his deep-seated affinity with the blues. After experience playing guitar in various territory bands in the 1930s, and eagerly experimenting with electrical amplification, he developed a distinctive way of singing that was conversational in style, and he fitted in well with jazz groups and in particular with top-flight modernists. In 1973 he recorded an album, *Very Rare*, which included guest soloists Dizzy Gillespie, Gerry Mulligan, Zoot Sims and Al Cohn. As Walker explained to Max Jones: 'I worked with Billie Holiday, Nat Cole, Joe Guy on some of Norman Granz's earliest Jazz At The Philharmonic concerts... As for backing: I don't want no r&b backing. I'd much rather play with Dizzy Gillespie... I've always worked with jazz musicians, used to sing with big bands all the time... One time I did a week with Duke Ellington and I didn't have a band on one package and Basie's band worked with me... I'd rather have a big band behind me with an arrangement.' Walker's preference for working with big bands is mirrored by other blues artists including Eddie 'Cleanhead' Vinson, who made some of his finest recordings in the 1940s, and also by B. B. King who sang on into the 1990s.

The blues has proved to be remarkably durable, and despite surface changes has remained close to its original form, retaining a predominantly black feeling. Latter-day international audiences, however, appear to be largely white. Talking of this to writer W. Royal Stokes, blues singer Jimmy Witherspoon conceded the difficulties inherent in the subject: 'The blues is hard to define. A lot of ridiculous stories have been written about the blues. That you have to be poor and black to be authentic. Kay Starr and Jack Teagarden can sing the blues, Mose Allison can sing the blues. Everyone has the blues sometime or other. Blues is not played on the radio and so young blacks are unaware and so I get more white kids at my concerts. They don't read up on black culture – young whites at college have turned some young blacks on to the blues.'

The potential of the blues for crossing racial divides is not isolated. Other musical forms that were originally black had similar qualities, although for many years record companies remained unaware, even deliberately categorizing their releases into racial subdivisions.

*   *   *

Throughout the 1920s and 1930s, most major record companies and a host of minors issued records aimed primarily at the black audience. They were known then as 'race records'. It is believed to have been Ralph J. Peer, recording director of OKeh Records, who originally coined the term when he called the company's series of blues recordings 'The Original Race Records'. Vocalion took up the challenge, saying that their series was 'Better and Cleaner Race Records'. J. Mayo Williams, recording director at Paramount, joined in with 'The Popular Race Record' series. It was on these and dozens of similarly orientated small independent labels that black music – blues, jazz, vaudeville – appeared in the 1920s and continued to a lesser degree throughout the 1930s. Similarly, after the end of World War Two, jump music, which was played mostly by small groups, was marketed through a host of independents.

By then the 'classic' blues of the 1920s was long gone. In the 1930s a diminished blues record scene was dominated by male singers, mainly country and urban artists, with only four female blues singers recording prolifically during the decade. They were Memphis Minnie on Columbia, Merline Johnson and Lil Johnson for ARC, and Georgia White on Decca. Of the four, doe-eyed Georgia White was by far the most jazz orientated. According to Big Bill Broonzy, she was 'a real nice looking gal ... very easy to get along with, good hearted and real friendly'. White was at ease with the blues and with popular material which she sang with rare wit and honesty. Her delivery was direct with no attempt at ornamentation. Born in Georgia, she worked in Chicago in the 1920s singing at the Apex Club with Jimmie Noone's band. An accomplished musician, she probably also played piano on many of her early recordings. The variety of material she recorded included blues from the 1920s such as 'Moonshine Blues' and 'Trouble in Mind', *double entendre* songs like 'I'll Keep Sitting on It' and 'Hot Nuts', and popular songs such as 'Someday Sweetheart'. Among the ninety-odd sides she recorded were a handful featuring the hot jazz trumpet of Jonah Jones.

Another Chicago-based singer, Lil Green, came to the fore briefly in the early 1940s. Although described as a blues singer, like many so-called blues singers she sang mostly blues-based ballads and popular songs written, in many cases, by Big Bill Broonzy and Joe McCoy, with some titles credited to herself. For a few short years the tall and attractive figure of Lil Green was a regular sight in black theatres where she proved to be extremely popular, although she remained almost totally unknown to white audiences. Her high-pitched and appealing delivery was unique. Records like 'If I Didn't Love You', 'Give Your Mama One Smile' and 'What's the Matter with Love?' were pleasant and unpretentious songs which proved to be popular with black servicemen during the war years. On the other hand, her major hit, 'Romance in the Dark', was sexually explicit and later became a jazz standard with recordings by singers as diverse as Mary Ann McCall, Dinah Washington and Cassandra Wilson. It was Green's version of 'Why Don't You Do Right?' that attracted Peggy Lee to the song, providing her with her first big hit with the Benny Goodman band.

* * *

To a great extent jump music, energetic, swinging, riff-based, was instrumental rather than vocal although Louis Jordan, formerly an alto saxophonist with Chick Webb's band, presented an engaging line in novelty vocals. T-Bone Walker remarked that he 'plays good blues and he sings them like they were originally sung, too'. The music which was the versatile Jordan's forte, and which attracted an audience that ranged far beyond the customary bounds for black music, was built knowingly upon aspects of the dying traditions of the swing era and the all-pervading blues. 'With my little band,' he declared, 'I did everything they did with a big band. I made the blues jump.' He also had a storehouse of good-natured, slyly humorous songs: 'Saturday Night Fish Fry', 'Is You Is, or Is You Ain't (Ma Baby)?', 'Ain't Nobody Here but Us Chickens' and 'Let the Good Times Roll'. The runaway success of Jordan and his band, the Tympany Five, persuaded others that this was the way to fame and possibly fortune and during the late 1940s and early 1950s he had many emulators. Indeed, among black musicians of the period working in r&b it is hard to find many who do not owe some debt to him: and the debt owed by white musicians is incalculable. At the dawn of the 1950s Jordan was being given a close run for his place in the r&b charts. He decided that the way to fight off the likes of Wynonie Harris and Roy Brown was to form a big band. Ignoring the obvious signs of what was happening to the few surviving big bands at this time, and against the specific advice of Milt Gabler, his producer at Decca who was nurturing white groups along similar lines, Jordan went ahead and in due course failed with the new venture. His health suffered and he quit Decca. This was in 1954, the year that Gabler unleashed upon a soon-to-be awestruck world, a white band, Bill Haley and the Comets. Gabler recalls, 'I'd sing Jordan riffs to the group that would be picked up by the electric guitars and the tenor sax of Rudy Pompelli. They got a sound that had the drive of the Tympany Five and the colour of country and western.' The similarities between the style adopted by Haley and his own style cannot have been unobserved by Jordan, nor the irony of Haley's subsequent international fame and fortune. What he thought of the eventual outcome was told to Arnold Shaw: 'Rock 'n' roll was not a marriage of r&b and country and western. Rock 'n' roll was just a white imitation, a white adaptation of Negro r&b.' Joe Turner concurred: 'I was doing rock and roll music before it was called rock 'n' roll.'

Jordan died in 1975 but the world hadn't heard the last of him. In 1990 a musical show, *Five Guys Named Moe* – actually an almost non-stop parade of Jordan's songs strung together on a virtually non-existent story-line – was vibrantly staged, became a long-running surprise smash and continued to barrel around the world to the manic tune of cash registers for several years, demonstrating that in music there's no business like old business.

During the period when jump music was popular, most of the black swing bands carried a blues shouter as well as a balladeer. Eddie 'Clean-head' Vinson started out with the Milt Larkins band; Walter Brown, Big Miller and Jimmy Witherspoon all learned their craft with Jay McShann; and Wynonie Harris first recorded with the Lucky Millinder band.

Vinson, who first moved to New York in 1942 to work with Cootie Williams, explained how his career developed: 'Then I organized a big band myself', but 'I had to break down to a seven-piece combination, because you couldn't carry a big band around – it was getting kinda rough then for big bands.' He had big hits with 'Kidney Stew Blues' and 'Wake Up, Old Maid', but as times got tougher he had to go out as a single. As a singer Vinson admitted to being influenced by Jordan: 'Louis Jordan, now – that was my man.' Nevertheless, Vinson had a rough and declamatory delivery that was all his own.

Walter Brown had a hit in 1941 with the Jay McShann band and their recording of 'Confessin' the Blues'. Brown had a rather nasal delivery and although quite popular at the time his chief claim to latter-day fame is that some of his recordings with McShann feature the alto saxophone of the young Charlie Parker.

Clarence Horatio 'Big' Miller was a big man with a big voice. A blues singer who improvised, Miller learned his trade singing with the bands of Lionel Hampton, Jay McShann and briefly with Duke Ellington, although his early influence was the church. Black poet Langston Hughes wrote a series of blues songs for Miller who also collaborated with Jon Hendricks in *The Evolution of the Blues Song*, a presentation that was twice performed at Carnegie Hall. In the late 1960s Miller settled in Canada where as well as performing he became a respected teacher. In 1985 Miller expressed his feelings about singing jazz: 'I live and breathe music. I dream about it. It gets pretty overpowering.' In 1996 Jon Hendricks revived *The Evolution of the Blues Song* at the Monterey Jazz Festival, this time accompanied by Joe Williams and Dianne Reeves.

Jimmy Witherspoon, a major figure in the blues and blues-ballad lineage, states: 'Most of the songs ... I've really lived ... if I can relate to a lyric, then I can feel the song and express the true meaning of the blues.' With a well-rounded and melodious voice, Witherspoon always gives the impression that he has a wealth of vocal power in reserve. Although he sang from early childhood, Witherspoon did not sing the blues until he was an adult and far from home, as he told W. Royal Stokes: 'I was singing spirituals in church when I was five. When World War Two came I was in Calcutta, India, in the US Merchant Marine. I sang with Teddy Weatherford's band there. Before that I was singing ballads. Most black singers were trying to lose their identity and I was no exception. Blues wasn't hardly allowed in no house. My parents were very religious. Not until I was feeling lonesome for home in India that I started singing the blues.' After a few successes in r&b he scuffled for a number of years before being featured at the 1959 Monterey Jazz Festival. He made an enormous impact with the audience and his career blossomed from then on with a number of excellent recordings which featured jazz stars such as Ben Webster and Gerry Mulligan. After winning battles with ill health he was still touring in the mid-1990s.

One r&b star who was unable to carry his success through to a wider audience was Wynonie Harris. A performer with tremendous energy, he was often described as having vocal chords of steel. His hit records began with 'Who Threw the Whiskey in the Well?' when singing with the Lucky Millinder band and later came 'Good Rockin' Tonight', 'Good Morning, Judge' and 'Bloodshot Eyes'. Harris had a happy shouting style but could when required handle a ballad with the best. Melvin Moore, who followed Harris into the Millinder band, said of him, 'Wynonie was a mess, man, all he wanted to do was rock 'em and roll 'em.'

Following World War Two, blues-orientated and other black forms of music became very popular, especially on America's west coast where there was a boom in job opportunities for blacks in defence industry plants. Artists like Charles Brown, Nat King Cole, Roy Milton and Joe Liggins suddenly began to make names for themselves. At the same time a new term was manufactured to replace the word 'race' which was by then considered too derogatory. The new tag, originated by *Billboard* magazine, was 'Blues & Rhythm' which quickly evolved into 'rhythm and blues' – later shortened to 'r&b'.

Other than the already popular Louis Jordan, a performer instrumental in starting off the post-war blues explosion was Cecil Gant. Still in uniform, singer-pianist Gant was advertised as the 'The G. I. Sing-sation'. Discovered at a street-corner Treasury Bond rally in Los Angeles, Gant's initial recording, 'I Wonder', a slow and poignant blues-ballad, although poorly recorded, unexpectedly reached the Top Five of the Harlem Hit Parade.

Whereas Gant's fame was short-lived, Charles Brown, who also began recording in the 1940s, survived into the 1990s. Brown developed his soft but expressive style in the clubs of Los Angeles in the years after the war. His reflective voice was influential and he had many hits in the r&b ratings. Piano trios were then very popular, the most famous being the Nat King Cole Trio, and Brown initially came to the fore as part of Johnny Moore's Three Blazers. His many hits included 'Drifting Blues' and 'Merry Christmas, Baby'. Brown's roots can be found in the work of Pha Terrell, the high-voiced balladeer with the Andy Kirk band, whom he idolized. Brown described himself as 'more of a blues ballad singer, not a blues singer'. He once declared that he did not like to sing 'raunchy blues where people talk about killing their old lady if they find her with somebody else. I don't want to kill her. I want her to come back to me.' His vocal style could be deeply sad, echoing the disillusion then prevalent among blacks still treated as second-class citizens despite war service.

There were women, too, in r&b in its early days but often they sang as singles or to their own accompaniment. Ebullient Nellie Lutcher learned to play jazz piano by listening to records by Teddy Wilson and Earl Hines. In Los Angeles she teamed up for a while with Wilbur and Douglas Daniels, formerly with the Spirits of Rhythm. Lutcher recalls them as being 'marvellous entertainers' but because a club owner considered them to be trouble makers she was asked to take over as leader: 'What a great job. Dexter Gordon worked with me and Lee Young played drums. I finally began to concentrate on my singing and wrote a few songs... One night, Frank Bull gave me a good spot performing live on a benefit show.' This was in 1947 and Dave Dexter Jnr, an executive at Capitol Records, heard the broadcast of the show. He had also heard demo records that Lutcher's brother Joe had sent in and decided to take a chance. The result was the million-selling 'Hurry On Down' (her own composition but based closely on Julia Lee's 'Come On Over to My House'). Within a year Lutcher had two more big hits with 'He's a Real Gone Guy' and 'Fine Brown Frame'. Lutcher's chief asset was communication, her wild and exaggerated vocal style contrasting with her unique and subtle piano accompaniment. Lutcher explained, 'I really owe my singing to the public. They made me sing... I kept begging off... I just couldn't convince them... And they kept saying, "I know you can sing something for us". I finally sang a song or two.'

Her popularity did not last. Although she continued to work into the mid-1960s, the writing was on the wall. She recalled to Leonard Feather the occasion when she knew it was over: 'I was booked into a room outside Montreal, a club that had established itself through rock. All the owners knew was, if you had a name they would book you. It was the worst possible situation; people were talking louder than I was singing. So I told my agent to just forget me.' Lutcher left performing and for a while worked outside music, no doubt enjoying the respite. As she had once remarked, 'You build a nice house and what happens? You're never home to enjoy it because you're always on the road.' The quiet life eventually palled a little and meanwhile the musical world turned and in the early 1970s her career was rejuvenated and she returned with much of her old vitality still intact.

Another singer-pianist Dave Dexter Jnr recorded for Capitol was Julia Lee. A product of the same Kansas City nightlife that produced Joe Turner, Lee's most successful period came in the 1940s. At the core of Lee's popular repertoire on Capitol were bouncy, ribald *double entendre* songs like 'King Size Papa', 'My Man Stands Out', 'Don't Come Too Soon' and 'Don't Save It Too Long'. But she also recorded many haunting blues and sensitive blues ballads such as 'Since I've Been with You', 'Living Backstreet for You', 'Breeze', 'Lotus Blossom', 'Decent Woman Blues' and 'Bleeding Hearted Blues', and swinging mid-tempo gems like 'My Sin' and 'Wise Guys'. Warm and easy-going, Lee's fame rested mainly with black audiences. Among singers who expressed admiration for her were Monette Moore and Mildred Bailey. That Lee never received the international acclaim accorded Lutcher rests to some extent in her desire to remain resident in Kansas City surrounded by her friends.

*　*　*

For all their successes, even after allowing for the ups and downs of their careers, r&b singers such as Jordan and Lutcher never achieved the status of role models for aspiring young blacks. This was something they had in common with jazz musicians. Only rarely in the early part of the twentieth century, and even less in the second half, have musicians in jazz been idolized. Indeed, there are many instances of the reverse being the case; of jazz musicians being cited as the kind of person a young striver should not seek to emulate. At times, even Louis Armstrong was roundly condemned for appearing to pander to white preconceptions of the jolly black entertainer. If anything, r&b went even further down that particular road. As for gospel, as we have seen, there was a suspicion that even this form of black music had been diluted to white norms. And, anyway, there was no financial goal worth chasing after; for every Mahalia Jackson there were hundreds of fine singers who never made a cent from singing in church.

But soul was something else. Soul was a way to the top, to financial rewards beyond dreams but within reach. Deeply rooted in gospel and the blues, and with the fervour and intensity of both, soul became the banner-carrying form of black musical expression for the last quarter of the twentieth century. And it certainly has its stars and millionaires; although two of its most notable exponents, Ray Charles and Dinah Washington, both resolutely defy pigeon-holing due to their astonishing versatility.

Early in his career, Ray Charles modelled his singing style upon the relaxed sophistication of Charles Brown and Nat King Cole and he also sang r&b. He skirted the edges of gospel, often sounding more like a gospel singer than a real gospel singer, but never actually entering into the religious frame of mind the form demands of its true exponents. He played piano and sang well in a jazz setting and has even sung country and western music. His eclecticism makes him hard to categorize without severely limiting his true value, but whatever he does, he brings to his music a deep emotional commitment that offers a secular echo to one of the principal tenets of gospel. Yet it is all overlaid with a feeling for the blues and performed with the urgent rhythmic drive of r&b. In describing Charles, what emerges is a definition of what makes a soul singer, albeit one with great originality and utmost conviction.

If Ray Charles can be fairly described as the greatest gospel star that never was, then Dinah Washington might be said to be the greatest soul singer that never was. In her case, it was death that robbed her of the title.

As a child, growing up in Chicago, where she had lived from the age of three, she sang in church where she was heard by gospel singer Sallie Martin, one-time partner of Thomas A. Dorsey. 'She could really sing,' Martin attested, 'but, shoot, she'd catch the eye of some man and she'd be out the church before the minister finished off the doxology.' Hired by Martin as a member of her backing group, Washington, then still called by her real name, Ruth Jones, was admired by Lil Hardin Armstrong: 'I heard them once or twice but all I can remember is that girl's voice.'

As her career developed, Washington, who was given her new name when she was hired by Lionel Hampton, cut a swathe through black show business. Forever associated with the blues, Washington told friend and writer Max Jones, 'People who call me a blues singer don't understand what I do. I used to specialize in blues with Hamp's band, and I still sing 'em. But I'm not restricted to one thing. I think of myself as just a singer.' Clearly she regarded herself as a singer of popular songs and identified just what kinds of material she liked best and what she didn't like: 'I like to sing, and I'll sing ballads, church songs, blues anything... Rock 'n' roll you can have, but I like real blues. You can break loose on those.' Of Bessie Smith she said, 'I listen to her now and don't hear nothin' wrong'. Billie Holiday was her original inspiration: 'I love her.'

Dinah Washington lived high, spending her substantial earnings on jewels, alcohol, drugs and men. She had a powerful personality; even Betty Carter, no shrinking violet herself, remarked, 'She was strong willed, her personality was such that whenever she was around, performing or not, you knew it.' Perhaps she needed to maintain a confrontational stance to fend off the pressures of the business she was in. Tenor saxophonist Eddie Chamblee, one of her nine husbands ('I change husbands before they change me'), knew both sides of her personality: 'Dinah had the ego of an ox, but Ruth Jones was a sweet little girl.'

Her way with a song was always committed and extremely personal. She sang with such vibrant passion that even the superficial romanticism of the string backings which sometimes accompanied her on records was sliced away by her resolutely soulful voice. As jazz historian Dan Morgenstern said, she '... fought bad material with jazz weapons'. And she affected her listeners deeply, be they ticket- and record-buying members of the public, or other musicians. 'Dinah taught me her exquisite phrasing,' pianist Patti Bown remembers, 'to create something original with an already written melody that enhanced it and yet never lost the original melody. She wasn't analytical, but she sharply focused on the tune. Sometimes after a record date, she'd have a few drinks and cry, listening to her own records and reminiscing. She was a "one-take" singer who would focus right in on what is necessary to make a song work.'

Comfortably moving between r&b and ballads, the blues and jazz, Washington constantly displayed a high measure of musical integrity. Yet another product of the big bands, Washington said of that part of her career, 'Lionel [Hampton] taught me the value of showmanship. With his band I learned what this business is about.' Full-voiced with a wholly distinctive, elegantly fractured quality that implied without ever fully expressing a tear, she gave depth and meaning to mediocre material, and to songs of quality she brought iridescence and profundity. What she would have done with soul music in the fullness of time can only be imagined because, in 1963, as soul was taking off, she died, probably accidentally, after too much drink and too many sleeping pills.

Perhaps the most gifted and certainly one of the most successful soul singers to come out of the gospel tradition is Aretha Franklin. Raised in a gospel-drenched family, regular visitors and friends of her preacher father included Mahalia Jackson, Clara Ward, Marion Williams, Sam Cooke and James Cleveland. With such exemplars as this it is hardly surprising that she brings to her singing all the integrity and vibrancy of the greatest gospel singers and her exultant, soaring voice brings to soul the essence of the word's literal meaning.

Franklin was eighteen when she made her first popular recordings. John Hammond Jnr, who produced the session, later described it as one of the three or four most exciting recording sessions of his life. He recalled: 'She had all the passion of a gospel veteran, along with humour and a natural vocal technique almost unknown in a jazz singer.' Of the first song recorded at the session, Curtis Lewis's 'Today I Sing the Blues', Hammond said, 'I sometimes wonder if she ever made a better record.' Intended as a jazz-orientated session, Franklin certainly never again came quite so close to jazz improvisation as she did on these first twelve songs where she is backed by musicians like Ray Bryant, Al Sears, Tyree Glenn and Milt Hinton. It was jazz with a soul turn-of-phrase. Other singers responded to Franklin. In 1970 Carol Sloane told Fred Bouchard, 'Aretha's one of my favourite singers ... she deserves to be on top. She worked long and hard to get there. To me, she sounds just the way she did on her first record date... She just sat at the piano and played for herself real good, right from the beginning... Aretha's honesty will sustain her. She's not jiving anybody – she's just out there singing.'

The enormous popularity of soul and its potential for fame and fortune has turned the music into a billion-dollar branch of popular music and its star performers into pop icons. Inevitably, it has affected other areas of popular music, including jazz which accepted soul in the 1960s in instrumental form. Elements of soul coloured the work of many jazz singers from the 1960s onwards. In the 1990s soul is still evident, for example in the work of prominent singers such as Cassandra Wilson and Rachelle Ferrell. Essentially, however, soul steers a course that only occasionally intersects with that of jazz. In a very real sense soul has always been more in harmony with gospel music. As blues singer Big Miller put it: 'You find soul from being in church – people show their emotions. That's where the soulful feeling comes from.'

SIX

HOW DO THEY DO IT THAT WAY?

Basically technique in itself is useless – unless you are
going to do something artistic with it. — Tina May

Black Americans had dominated jazz and jazz-related music until the
swing era. Even then, although they did not generally enjoy similar financial rewards, musically their domination was not affected. In jazz singing
this was a period which saw Billie Holiday's rise and Ella Fitzgerald also
begin her career, and as the 1930s gave way to the 1940s there were other
black singers who began to make their marks: Nat King Cole, Louis Jordan,
Billy Eckstine, Sarah Vaughan and others. But just as jazz was fast
becoming a musical form that acknowledged few boundaries of nationality
and race, so too was jazz singing and its derivatives starting to throw off
such shackles. As for popular music, beginning in the early 1940s and
continuing into the following decade, enormous changes took place in
America which, in time, affected music worldwide. In the vanguard of
change came the singers. The 1930s stars, the leaders and instrumentalists
from the big bands, were swept aside as the public turned to the new stars,
many of whom had once occupied a possibly begrudged place on the band-
stands of the swing era.

The reasons for the change – a massive decline in the fortunes and
numbers of big bands and a corresponding surge to stardom of scores of
singers – are many and complex. Living patterns; the ageing of the fans;
suburban sprawl; decline in public transportation systems; changes in
public taste; the cost of keeping a big band together – all these and other
factors have been blamed, singly or in combination. Complicating the
matter still further is the American Federation of Musicians' recording ban
of 1941/2 which prohibited union members, essentially all instrumentalists
in America, from recording, but which had no effect on singers who were
either members of a different union or not unionized at all. Arranger Paul
Weston and bandleader Alvino Rey went on record as stating unambigu-
ously, if a little too narrowly, that the singers killed the big bands. The
reality lies in the combining during a short period of time of all these many
causes, but at its heart lies the simple fact that like so many other areas of
popular culture, popular music is subject to change for its own sake – and
often imposed by the industries which depend upon change to uphold
profits. Built-in obsolescence is a valuable facet of many industries and
showbiz is no exception. If the commercial successes of the swing era were
to be continued there had to be something new.

The fact that the singers already existed and had begun developing
followings of their own pointed at them as being the obvious choice. In
particular, Frank Sinatra's ecstatic juvenile fans cannot have escaped
anyone's notice. He could do no wrong, his recordings sold in millions and

his decision to embark upon a solo career in 1942 showed timing as perfect as that which he brought to his singing.

In no time at all other singers were following in his footsteps, some prompted by their own observation of the scene, some urged into solo careers by offers of lucrative recording contracts. Sinatra was with Columbia and soon RCA Victor had Perry Como and Decca had Dick Haymes. But Sinatra was the one who had the most effect upon other singers, then and later, who heard in his approach to songs an emphasis quite different from that of Bing Crosby who continued to record successfully and was seemingly impervious to the changes taking place around him.

Nevertheless, the changes were significant, not least in style. As Mike Campbell observes: 'Sinatra was possibly the first true story teller outside the blues singers and Louis Armstrong. The first guy to take those great standards and turn them into emotional experiences. You are in that bar with him; no one really did that before Sinatra.'

It was not only the manner of interpretation of songs that underwent change. The manner of presentation was also altered. Hitherto, singers had customarily sung a chorus within a band arrangement, having to make what impact they could within a framework not necessarily designed to show-case them. Indeed, many band singers learned the hard way that for all the undoubted skills of many big band arrangers, some did not have much interest in the needs of singers.

Singers coming out of the bands to be marketed as independent names sometimes chose songs suitable as star vehicles, imposing star status on the song. Others, like Sinatra, displayed more respect and chose to inhabit the songs. It therefore became extremely important to these latter singers that the songs they chose to sing were high in quality and, most importantly, suited them. The best of this new wave of popular singers, along with the majority of jazz and jazz-influenced singers, always put the song first. Fortunately, the available material was awash with great songs which, in their structure, melodies and lyrics, had all the qualities necessary to make them desirable to singers and audiences and durable enough to survive and prove to be of interest to singers generations ahead.

At the end of the twentieth century, young singers are discovering that there is an audience willing to listen to the older songs. Part of this audience consists of young people seeking, perhaps subconsciously, something different from that with which they are surrounded. There is also an older element in the audience that remembers the old songs and singers and regrets the manner in which record companies and radio and television programme planners are failing to take their tastes into account. Song-writer and arranger Billy VerPlanck notes: 'The older generation was brought up with quality songs in the romantic era and they still want to hear this kind of music. I think that the record companies have not recognized the market – forty-five to death!'

In the 1940s and early 1950s, VerPlanck played in and wrote arrangements for the bands of Jess Stacy, Charlie Spivak, Jimmy Dorsey, Billy May, Charlie Barnet, Claude Thornhill and Tommy Dorsey. Later, he continued to write the arrangements that played such an important part in the career of his wife, Marlene VerPlanck. After a lifetime immersed in music, VerPlanck's enthusiasm remains undimmed and he has clear ideas about the music he loves. Referring to composer George Gershwin, VerPlanck continues: 'His "Porgy", "There's a Boat Dat's Leaving Soon for New York"; Brahms never wrote a tune as lovely as that. Not that he wasn't a terrific musician, he was. But on concept of melody? You are talking here of something absolutely astounding. Irving Berlin's "The Best Thing for You Will Be Me" starts on a downward chord completely out of the key and yet it's perfectly natural, just a marvellous thing. When you think of the modulations in Jerome Kern's "All the Things You Are". A marvellous, breathtaking piece of material. A work of art. "I Got Rhythm", it's a panatonic scale yet absolutely a work of art, the permutations of the rhythm in the thing are remarkable... Think of Rodgers's and Hart's "My Funny Valentine", "Manhattan", "The Lady Is a Tramp", these are remarkable songs, think of the joy you get from all of them and think of the starting point you get for improvisation.'

With the wealth of songs available to them, the singers of the late 1940s and early 1950s could choose, if they cared to, those that best suited their vocal and emotional needs. Regrettably, many accepted the advice of commercially orientated hit-makers which gave them hits but damaged their artistic status. For others, the emotional content of the songs became increasingly important in the wake of Billie Holiday. Singers such as Peggy Lee, Teddi King, Betty Bennett and Jackie Paris began an exploration of the emotional value of songs. In Lee's case, over the years it directed her on a course away from the jazz mainstream, but she never lost touch with the jazz foundations of her style. Although Lee's direction was signposted by Holiday, her influences were many and varied and included Lee Wiley, Mildred Bailey and Maxine Sullivan. She was also conscious of blues singers and listened to many black artists, sometimes covering their 'race' record hits with even more successful versions of her own: Lil Green's 'Why Don't You Do Right?', Little Willie John's 'Fever', Joe Williams's 'Well All Right, Okay, You Win', Ray Charles's 'Hallelujah but I Love Her So'. Although covers were sometimes produced as a matter of exploitative expediency, in Lee's case they seem to have been done out of a genuine sense of admiration for the artists concerned and a love for these particular songs. Indeed, long after her fame was assured, Lee continued this practice, adding to her repertoire songs from the new mainstream of pop in the 1960s and after, songs by the Beatles and others. For all the diversity of her repertoire, Lee found and maintained her own approach. As Mike Campbell says, 'She sang so simply and she sang just to you.'

Campbell also stresses the attraction of a simple, direct approach he found in the singing of another major artist who emerged in the 1940s, but not in his case from a big band background: 'I loved Nat King Cole's simplicity and just how comfortable he was with himself. He didn't try to be anything he wasn't and I loved that. He was just magic.' The need to be comfortable with one's self and with one's material is of great importance to singers and this emerges from the manner in which they select their material, and with many this material is drawn from that same great stock of superior popular songs used by Sinatra and Lee and Cole. But having found the song, the singer still needs to find a way to inhabit it.

Stacey Kent explains her approach: 'I'm constantly finding new-old songs that I didn't know. Or I'll find a book and look for verses to songs I already know. I'm doing this constantly and the repertoire continues to grow... I'm not sure that I have a tangible answer to what attracts me to a song... If I love the feel or the melody of a song it might not matter what the lyric is. Of course, the lyric *matters* but I almost feel that I can make any lyric work for myself. There is rarely a song that I can't sing because of a lyric – because if it's a silly "throw away" lyric, like "Fine and Dandy" for example, then I can sing it in a carefree sort of way. I don't always have to take the song so desperately seriously. Sometimes, of course, there are songs with an exquisite lyric that tells such a true story and with such poetry that I'm moved every time I hear it. I feel this way particularly about Johnny Mercer – he's got magic in his lyrics.' Turning to the need to enter fully into the song, Kent continues: 'The thing I love about jazz and singing this repertoire is that I can be myself and not have to put on an act at all. And yet, for the amount of time that a song lasts I can take on the particular persona or situation of *any* particular song ... and mean the lyric even if it isn't true to me personally. In other words, I can sing "Polka Dots and Moonbeams" earnestly and honestly without even bothering to think that I myself might not ask a "pug-nosed dream", dressed in polka-dots, to dance. For those four of five minutes during the song, I am that person, regardless of gender; because the lyric doesn't have to be taken literally to have meaning. The situation is a metaphor for so many other situations which would apply to me and my own story. For me, this is an extremely important point and one of the main reasons why I love this music – to be able to express myself honestly, without disguise, through and with a perfect music. Standards are a perfect blend of poetry and melody and music and I can sing them, feel them, deliver them my own way, being myself and telling someone else's story, and/or my own story, at the same time.'

Essentially the same repertoire, then, is finding adherents in the 1990s as it did in the 1940s and 1950s although the manner in which it is being used has certain differences, sometimes subtle, other times overt, which reflect the changes that have taken place in both pop and jazz in the intervening years.

In the wake of Frank Sinatra and Peggy Lee and others of their generation, such as Haymes and Como, Jo Stafford and Dinah Shore, came a host of singers eager to enter the same flourishing marketplace: Rosemary Clooney, Vic Damone, Doris Day, Johnny Hartman, Tony Bennett and Nancy Wilson, and later, Harry Connick Jnr. The extent to which these singers developed the jazz influence varied enormously not only from one to another but also within each singer's work at different times in his or her career.

In the cases of Bennett and Clooney, their place is seen in different ways by others and a measure of conflict appears in the opinions expressed. In conversation with Val Wilmer, Ernestine Anderson said, 'Singers I like are Ella, Sarah, Anita, Billie and Rosemary Clooney – she has a beautiful quality, but who'd call her a jazz singer?' Clooney herself explained her role: 'I am a conduit, I interpret. I look for words that mean something to me.' In 1995 ASCAP acknowledged where her gifts lie with the Pied Piper Award, inscribing it with the tribute that she was 'an American Musical Treasure and one of the best friends a song ever had'. Frank Sinatra holds a similar view: 'Rosemary Clooney has that great talent which exudes warmth and feeling in every song she sings. She's a symbol of good modern American music.'

Just as Clooney has attracted deserved praise when her true role is understood but has sometimes been sidelined for the wrong reasons, so has Tony Bennett received a mixed response from the jazz world. Carmen McRae, in an interview with *down beat* in 1991, expressed the view that a clear understanding of the concept of jazz singing has been lost, as evidenced by the Grammy awards which found Harry Connick beating singers such as Jon Hendricks and Tony Bennett. 'I like Harry,' McRae said. 'He's a nice kid and everything, but over Tony Bennett, no way.' What McRae did not expound upon was whether or not either of them, Connick or Bennett, should be considered as jazz singers. That Bennett is a superior singer of the popular repertoire appears unchallengeable, especially as, with maturity, his diction, sometimes suspect in his younger days, has improved and he is an able interpreter of lyrics. Singer Salena Jones says, 'I listen to how he holds a note and I hear the cry in the word. It's not what he's delivering on the surface, but 'way below. It's what he's doing underneath. Who cares if he cracks a note?' Mike Campbell homes onto Bennett's phrasing in deciding his place in the scheme of things: 'On a musical level, phrasing is important. Jon Hendricks, Ella, Tormé, Mark Murphy – their phrasing is so distinctive, like instrumental-orientated. Sinatra and Tony Bennett never sound like an instrument.' Carol Sloane also looks at phrasing, and in 1970 delivered a slightly different verdict on Bennett's credentials in jazz in conversation with Fred Bouchard: 'If good phrasing makes a jazz singer, that's Billie. That also makes Frank Sinatra a jazz singer. And Carmen McRae. And it's beginning to make Tony Bennett a jazz singer.' Furthermore, listening closely to Bennett's phrasing on, say, 'You Don't Know What Love Is', it is clear that he is aware of Billie Holiday.

Bennett had an album leading the jazz charts for several months in 1995 but to what extent that is the result of canny marketing is open to question, although certainly not to objection. For a singer to make money is not something to be decried unless, of course, the singer has no talent. In Bennett's case, he has talent and he has durability and, since the mid-1960s, has worked often with very good jazz accompaniment, notably the Ralph Sharon Trio. His growth in stature must serve as encouragement to those still in there pitching – although for those just starting out, the knowledge that they might have to wait half a lifetime for their day in the sun may well be rather daunting.

*   *   *

In the mid-1950s certain differences gradually became apparent in the manner in which some popular singers were singing. Ever since Bing Crosby, Connee Boswell and their emulators had discovered the way how to use microphones, many had turned away from the full-throated style of Al Jolson. They no longer needed to sing loud; the microphone did all that was needed and an unforced intimacy was possible. But by the 1950s other changes occurred. The crooning style, which Sinatra had taken to its limits in his work with Tommy Dorsey and as a single in the 1940s, was becoming *passé.* Sinatra and others began to feel a need to sing in a more open manner. Allied with this was the growth of technical expertise in recording studios and the quality of recordings. Sinatra had, in fact, begun to lose his popularity. Times were changing and his bobby-soxed fans of a decade ago were now in their twenties and were also feeling a need for something a little more mature. Their successors, the new pre-teen and early teen audience, were, as always, looking for something completely different and which, in their case, turned out to be rock 'n' roll.

Sinatra changed companies, signing with Capitol Records, a move that brought him into the fold of a company which, then at least, placed musical excellence ahead of commercial considerations. The company, formed by songwriter-film producer Buddy DeSylva, lyricist Johnny Mercer and businessman Glenn Wallichs, had started up in 1942, done an immediate deal with the striking AF of M, and signed Nat King Cole as one of its first artists. Over the next few years the company, often in the person of Dave Dexter Jnr, added the cream of popular singers, headed by Jo Stafford, Peggy Lee and Sinatra, and Julia Lee and Nellie Lutcher, and gave them all understanding, empathy and musical settings that were unsurpassed in commercial record company annals before or since.

Sinatra's well thought-out 'concept' albums for Capitol – the long-playing record having also come into extensive use in the early 1950s – showed that his intonation, phrasing and interpretative skills had toughened up and improved. Also, he was now singing in a non-crooning manner and even the intimate ballads had a more direct and distinctly more mature sound. His choice of tunes and tempo was still exemplary and he once again set the standards by which his kind of singer would continue to be judged down the years. Sinatra's care with and affection for his material – which in his later years was sometimes slightly slipshod due to an acquired habit of trying to add a pseudo-hipness to lyrics that really didn't need it – is matched by most of the jazz-influenced popular singers who followed.

It is a quality that repeatedly turns up in the thinking of jazz singers. The song's story, whether taken literally or metaphorically, is an important element in creating a viable whole. Although many, if not most, jazz singers sought and continue to seek variety in their repertoires, there is often an unspoken, unacknowledged or even unconsciously formed theme to their selections. The theme might be nothing more than a simple, yet invaluable, thread of excellence; or it might be the facility each song has to provide a solid foundation upon which to build their own improvisations. In their search, singers today have ever-widening boundaries which have resulted in repertoires of hundreds of songs. It wasn't always so, as Susannah McCorkle points out: 'Some famous singers had just thirty songs and travelled all over the world doing them. I think my favourite American pop singers tend to stay within a narrow range of songs that they do. I'm thinking in terms of Nat King Cole, one of my favourite singers especially in the trio days, or Frank Sinatra or Tony Bennett or Peggy Lee. They wouldn't do a very wide range of songs the way a Brazilian pop singer would. I guess that's why I'm a little different. I like doing Brazilian songs and Portuguese songs and singing very softly or doing a tribute to Bessie Smith and belting – within my own vocal limits of course – and doing Dave Frishberg songs, or doing contemporary songs, or 1920s songs. I really like being a singer of all types of good songs. And I love all my songs. It's hard to know what to leave out when I plan a programme.'

Planning a programme takes time and care and for many singers there is the added need of having to hunt down sheet music, once a commonplace task but now not always easy. Until the 1950s sheet music was readily available and was bought in huge quantities either to play or simply to learn the lyrics. From this time onwards it became steadily less available, to the disadvantage of singers. 'A new song is a treasure to me,' Lucy Reed says. 'And I look for good stories to tell, like my current new interests, one being "Alone Too Long", by Arthur Schwartz and Dorothy Fields. I heard it on an old Mark Murphy album and wasn't able to purchase the sheet music. It was out of print in Chicago. A friend of mine called ASCAP in New York and they sent it to me.' Reed's reason for the search is explained: 'I always like to learn a song the way the composers wrote it, not from someone else's conception of it.' Weslia Whitfield agrees with this approach: 'I try to get the original sheet music, complete with the verse and teach it to myself, sing it over and over, think about the song and then form my own interpretation of it.' The problems arising from the difficulties encountered in obtaining sheet music are self-evident. Without it, a singer must perforce learn a song from a record which means that, like it or not, they are hearing someone else's interpretation of a song they might otherwise approach very differently. British traditional singer Christine Tyrrell is unusual in having her repertoire chosen for her: 'I don't read music and when I used to plan my own programmes I found that often I would chose something in the same key as the song I had just done. This tends to become boring and samey for the audience, so now I rely on the boys and especially [bandleader] Phil Mason to choose my songs for me. I learn any new songs singing them to myself around the house until I've got them the way I want them.' Weslia Whitfield, once she has a song the way she wants it, consciously avoids singing it other than on stage: 'I rarely do any actual singing of those songs outside of performance. I spend most of my time *thinking* through them, and any singing during that time is of songs *not* in the show – maybe they'll be part of the show to come.'

Lucy Reed is also careful in how she imposes her personality onto a song: 'My training to read a lyric like poetry is so deeply ingrained in me that I must tell a story. [However] I don't like to change the melody first time through out of respect to the composer but taking some liberties after that is acceptable and expected in jazz.' Carmen McRae concurs but stresses the need to remain aware of the expectations of others: 'I'd rather not improvise continuously, rather pick a tune and sing it straight occasionally for those people in the audience who want to hear it that way.'

Impressing one's own identity onto material is a part of the development of a personal style, something that all jazz singers strive to achieve. As La Velle puts it: 'I always want to be me.' Achieving this is approached in different ways, not only as an effect of different personalities but also as something that can change within one singer's work as she matures. At first, a singer's approach to her material might be almost entirely instinctive. As time goes by, instinct remains but an intellectual approach can be added and one coloured by experience. Inevitably, young singers often use exemplars – not necessarily copying but using the guidelines of older or past, and sometimes forgotten, talents. Ernestine Anderson told Val Wilmer that she would 'try to use all the different qualities of the singers I like; for example, Ella, who always sings true notes, I try to take all these notes and convert them to my own style of singing, but I never consciously try to copy anyone'.

Johnny Mercer was a frequent visitor to the house of fellow songwriter Richard Whiting, as were Harry Warren and Jerome Kern. Whiting's daughter, Margaret, remembers, 'they were either singing or writing their songs. But I thought that went on at everybody's house.' When she declared her intention of becoming a singer, Mercer offered some advice: '... find a style that's your own. Who are your favourite singers?' Whiting told him, 'Judy Garland, Ethel Waters, Frances Langford, Mildred Bailey'. Mercer said,

'Fine. Listen to them. Copy them for a while, if you want. Find out what makes them different, and that way you'll find your own style.'

Finding a style for Barbara Lashley was hard, even though she was raised in a music-filled home. Her parents had grown up in Harlem and danced at the Savoy Ballroom, and music by swing bands and r&b singers was always being played in the house. But Lashley grew up through that and into the rock era and beyond, not starting to sing until she was approaching forty and with no specific style appealing to her: 'I thought, "What kind of style do I like?" I grew up with so many different kinds of styles.' That this presented her with a problem is apparent from the reactions of people who hear her sing: 'I've had people tell me I can sing classical music ... that I can sing like Sarah Vaughan and I've had people say, "Oh, you sound like Billie Holiday". It's hard to put a finger on the kind of style that I enjoy the best. I'm a romantic, so I like a lot of romantic songs. I like the melody, [but] I like to scat every now and then... I don't like to do it all the time, but like to feel natural doing it... I like the blues, but like to feel natural doing that, too. It has to be right. I just cannot get up and start shouting the blues. It's just not a part of me, I'm black and all that but I just can't do it at the drop of a hat.'

To feel that a song is right, to feel natural singing it, is clearly essential to Lashley and is a sentiment that must surely be echoed by all good singers. The days when a singer had to sing unsuitable material for commercial reasons are largely gone. The young British singer, Nicki Leighton-Thomas, offers an aesthetic view of unsuitable material: 'There is nothing worse than hearing a bored singer singing a tired song, though if you're doing a restaurant/bar gig, there is always a request from someone to do one of "those" songs, which you've either got to enjoy totally, or just say that you're not going to do it! If you know that Ella Fitzgerald, Shirley Horn, Sarah Vaughan or Billie Holiday all did a great version of that song, it gets a little difficult believing that this particular version you are going to do will go down in musical history as an important step forward! And if you don't believe it, no one else will.'

Nevertheless, some contemporary singers in jazz and jazz-influenced music voluntarily choose not to abandon the accumulated repository of popular songs in favour of current Top 40 material or original compositions. As Chris McNulty says: 'I like to do originals but the 1930s and 1940s was an extraordinary time in music in the USA when it all came together. It was so exciting – all the movies in Hollywood, the blues, European classical traditions – all came together and you got those songs. It's never going to happen like that again. Nothing comes close, it was a point in our evolution when the black and white experiences were mixed. I'll never stop going back to those tunes. Originals can be beautiful but they haven't got the everlasting power of those tunes.'

Stacey Kent agrees with these sentiments: 'I know there is a future for this music – different fads and approaches to the music might come and go but the foundations will always be there, i.e. the American songbook. This period in history is too important and too rich for it to simply disappear. Of course, it will shift as the generations of those who grew up with this music pass away; but it can't be replaced. There are no Jerome Kerns, Johnny Mercers, etc, today. This music is timeless and so I believe there will always be a place for it.'

It is hard to argue with these comments and yet there has always been and always must be an element of change in jazz. Ever since its first stirrings the music has absorbed, reflected, reinterpreted, donated to and interacted with most other areas of music – and not just popular music. In a literal sense, jazz has always been fusion music and if it is to survive it will continue to fuse with other forms and original material will be needed. How this will affect the singers of jazz is open to speculation. Indeed, there might be almost as many answers to that as there are singers.

Jan Ponsford favours originals for good reasons but understands also the need for touchstones: 'Now I sing a lot of my own compositions, after years of interpreting standards. I became fed up with people saying "that sounded like so-and-so". There is less chance of them saying that if I'm doing my own material. But I recognize that people need to pigeon-hole you to explain to others what you sound like.'

Having sung pop and rock before she turned to jazz, Terry Blaine is aware of the possibilities in a repertoire that extends the boundaries: 'I think as a singer you have a place where you start from. I've come out of a pop style much more than a jazz style. Before ten years ago I had a lot of different influences. Maybe that's what people find interesting in my style. I have a good sense of time and swing but then I have a lot of pop qualities in my singing.'

Mark Murphy, too, seeks to extend the repertoire but knows that it is far from easy: 'I get new songs sent to me all the time and I do some writing myself. But it's not as if we're in a golden age. You've got to look for the new Johnny Mandel song or the new Stephen Sondheim song, and they're not writing songs like that anymore.' Sometimes a new song drops into a singer's lap. 'My ears are always out,' Murphy remarks, 'I just hear something and it moves me. A classic example – a lyric I wrote in 1995 with a musician at the school in Austria where I teach. I was teaching in one room and I had to go into my own office to get some books and he was playing something that caught me right by the short and curlies, if you'll pardon the expression. That's what it does, something just gets to you. I just have to have that, you know. I guess it's a mixture of things – call it "conscious intuitiveness". But you have to be alert, always listening.'

Stretching the repertoire, and the manner in which the singer approaches the songs, can be delicate ground for someone trying to build a following. The American singer-teacher Marguerite Juenemann, who trained as a classical instrumentalist before singing jazz, empathises with singers who know their instrument and work 'from an educated, extended-vocal-technique point of view... The likes of Jay Clayton, Joan LaBarbera, Urszula Dudziak for example. They are stretching the capacity of this instrument and may be less accepted by the general public because of how much risk, instrumentally (and traditionally), they are willing to take to expand their instruments' use. But then, the opinions and likes of the general public may be less consideration than those artists' reasons for performance. Creating movement in any artform, expressing from your own point of view, expanding and expounding upon that which has come before, seems to be an especially difficult although desirable path to follow. I am grateful for people who push back boundaries...' Since the late 1980s Juenemann has taught at the University of Massachusetts, also performing in concerts with leading contemporary jazz musicians. Her early experience in jazz-related singing came when in 1978 she helped form the vocal group Rare Silk which toured with Benny Goodman.

Another singer with forthright views on the direction taken by singers of jazz in the 1990s is Tom Lellis, who 'graduated to jazz from rock 'n' roll' and takes a pessimistic view of the material available to today's singers. He recalls that back in the 1970s, 'I heard Ella doing Beatles tunes and Stevie Wonder tunes. There was no one writing for singers like Ella and Sarah, so they were relegated to singing pop music of the day which in my estimation was beneath them. What is more, they were not able to accomplish it as well as they might because it was out of their genre and time frame. In historical context there was a great songwriting era heard through those singers; songwriters like Cole Porter, George Gershwin, Frank Loesser, etc, and an abundance of material. Then, by the 1960s, it had dried up. I think the compositional direction was lost in favour of rock 'n' roll and the golden era of American music was over.'

When considering material for his own repertoire, Lellis feels that the next wave of good songwriters was in Brazil. However, they were 'writing for those who were well known, they're not going to be writing for me. So I turned to composing and writing lyrics to tunes that struck me', music by the likes of jazzmen McCoy Tyner and Keith Jarrett. 'That began my direction, writing lyrics for previously unsung material – compositions by wonderful instrumentalists.'

Lellis is not alone in displaying a liking for Brazilian music, nor for turning to contemporary jazz musicians for inspiration. There are many others with similar ideas but he is unhappy with some aspects of the musical base of the new generation of jazz singers. 'Current trends are not to my liking,' Lellis continues, 'especially this turn back to classical forms of jazz à la bebop. After singing rock 'n' roll I was influenced by post-bop and modal playing and I feel bebop to be an anachronism. When I started singing, Dixieland was fifty years old and now bebop is fifty years old and I equate them to each other in their anachronisms. Dixieland sounds old and Charlie Parker-bebop sounds old to me. I much prefer post-bop such as

Wayne Shorter and Herbie Hancock. From *Milestones* in 1959 onwards defines the post-bop era. That's the music that brought me in.'

Lellis started learning the piano at twenty-four. He explains, 'I heard Chick Corea, McCoy Tyner, Bill Evans, Herbie Hancock, Keith Jarrett... I wanted to sing with them so badly and knew I couldn't so I began to play, to try and compensate by playing in a style that somehow mirrored them... I have been playing ever since and at that point I stopped looking to singers and piano became a vehicle that was to take me deeper into the music. I began to listen to players more and began to appreciate that their linear approach was so much further ahead of the singers that it was someplace to aspire to whereas the singers were stuck in a rut at that point.' An alternative view is expressed by Jackie Allen who grew up around a lot of instrumentalists so that when she started singing she felt that she needed to please them, her musical peers: 'And only in the past couple of years, as I've moved toward the cabaret style, can I see how that fact influenced my style. I began to respect the vocalist more to realize that she *is* different, that she doesn't have to scat all the time, to blow like a horn player on every song. I began to realize that I don't have to prove myself to the instrumentalists.'

Kurt Elling, however, echoed Lellis's sentiments when speaking to Greg Robinson: 'Singers are just way in the backwater, as far as the musical development in the genre... No one has gone the way that the heavies in instrumental jazz have gone.' Something of a hot property, Elling's first album was released on Blue Note in 1996. He lists key influences as instrumentalists Tony Williams, Wayne Shorter and Keith Jarrett, echoing some of the preferences of Tom Lellis. His favourite singers include Jon Hendricks, Eddie Jefferson and, especially, Mark Murphy (who along with Hendricks is a guru to many aspiring singers). Elling feels that most new singers are not exploring too deeply into the rhythmic and harmonic freedoms of today's top instrumentalists. As he explains: '... everybody's attention was so focused on people like Ella Fitzgerald and Mel Tormé ... everybody wanted to sound just like them. Somebody like Mark Murphy, who I think took heavy strides in the direction of freedom, was kind of left out a bit.' Mike Campbell is another singer eager to express his respect for Murphy: 'He was a real influence on me and still is today. He has been very supportive. Although I don't sing like him at all, I'm amazed by his stamina. When he counts off the downbeat he becomes twenty-five years old again. It's amazing, his energy, his integrity, his love of the music. He's so courageous, always in for new things. Probably the guy today of all the singers who inspires me most.'

Despite Campbell's praise, there is little doubt that Elling's comment is valid. Murphy and many other true jazz singers have been left out. After forty years on the road Murphy is still touring the world and still dedicating himself to teaching whenever he can. Viewed from the late 1990s, his long-term ambition is to '... make a little bread and find a seat in some school so

I can semi-retire, I'm sort of tired out'. That a singer as distinguished as Murphy, who is striving to project his craft into a new generation of singers, should feel moved to speak in this way casts a shadow upon the future. The new college-based learning arena is flourishing but if Murphy can become so discouraged, then newcomers might consider this to be a warning.

* * *

What is encouraging about recent developments in jazz singing is that singers like Murphy are increasingly to be found teaching in universities and colleges and conducting clinics at which they can pass on their hard-earned knowledge. Among the results of this has been a steady rise in the numbers of trained singers, culminating in the great surge of the 1990s. Newcomers can now learn vocal technique, physical care of the voice, and a host of other things. If they choose to do so, that is. Singing jazz is hard work; learning to sing correctly is also hard work and not everyone is able to accept this. There are, after all, many who still believe the old canards about jazz, among which is the assumption that untutored musicians simply make it up as they go along. Marguerite Juenemann, has encountered this: 'As an educator, I have found that some voice "students" are very disinclined to learn how to be good musicians. I think this lowers the standard of the artform since nearly all of those we listen to in order to learn from were at some point studying in a traditional way. There simply are things to know that don't just drop out of the air. From a performer's perspective, I find that not enough singers use as much of their instrument as is expected of other players. Nor do they put forward as much music as the artform commands.'

Nanette Natal, another excellent singer who is also a distinguished teacher, had already enjoyed success in the commercial end of the music business but chafed against the absence of creative freedom: 'Jazz was a place where I could improvise and try lots of different types of music and rhythms... Jazz is a very complicated music, there has to be a certain level of skill that you develop, a certain sense of personal empowerment, a sense of yourself that you have to have to really let go and to improvise in the way that's demanded in that type of music. You really have to grow into that. It takes a certain amount of years as well as experience.'

The qualities of jazz that attracted Natal, and which serve as a welcoming beacon to young people - notably the opportunities for improvisation - are underlined by Juenemann: 'I chose to work in jazz because all the classic training in the past was directly applicable to this format and served as a great aid in performing, arranging and rehearsing with knowledge and education providing a firm base; an infinitely more comfortable place to be in. With all that education to call on, improvisation was the added attraction that jazz requires and I found immediate "soul food" in that aspect of the music. Release; getting out on a limb and trusting innate and/or acquired senses to hold on to while dangling by a thread of spon-

114

taneous inspiration. Learning to trust that which you abandon yourself to is a very freeing, growth-producing experience.'

It was the style of jazz singing that attracted Weslia Whitfield: 'I chose to move toward jazz because of all the "club" or "saloon" singing going on in this century it is the least plagued by affectation, sentimentality or overwrought dramatization. Of them all, it is the medium that is most focused on and concerned with the "music" and not necessarily the performer.' These views echo those of Carol Sloane despite the fact that she had no formal training. She chose jazz because she 'found it more challenging, more interesting than any other music'. Sloane is not alone in being untrained – in the formal sense – indeed, some other outstanding singers such as Mark Murphy, Susannah McCorkle, Helen Merrill and Chris McNulty have achieved success without it.

Nevertheless, most singers need some guidance at some time. 'I had no formal training at all in voice,' McCorkle says, 'but when I lived in Italy an Italian trumpet player gave me a breathing exercise which is very good for strengthening the diaphragm.' In many singers, however, the impulse to avoid constrictive training is strong. As already suggested, young people experiencing the desire to sing incline towards using instinct; an intellectual response is more likely to come with maturity. Also, we know that jazz singers do not necessarily require a trained voice although ear training and a rudimentary knowledge of harmony help, as does the ability to establish and set a tempo. As for the use of rubato – singing or playing freed from strict adherence to the beat – this is often beyond even those singers who habitually work in a jazz context. This risk-taking element in jazz is one of the music's unique qualities. Add the desirability of, if not the actual need for, experimentation into melodic content, development of intonation, and, of course, improvisation (which *can* be taught) and the value of suitable training is clear. But all the training colleges in the world cannot fully explain how Ella Fitzgerald came to possess such a naturally acute ear or, as critic Benny Green has asked, how she is 'able to ride the twin horses of musical invention and lyrical coherence'.

An important aspect of singing that can be taught is vocal care. Young singers need to know how to take care of their voices and should be taught not to abuse them, and also how to protect the non-singing parts of their bodies. Mike Campbell talks sense when he says, 'Don't scream at ball games, don't smoke or drink, stay away from coffee, ice-cream, dairy produce. I try to speak like I sing, to use the voice properly. When I was younger I did five or six warm-up exercises, and would sing certain sections of songs. Now that I'm teaching so much I have no time to practise. Of course, I practise when something comes up in order to get my muscles back into singing shape and to help me focus on what I'm doing and concentrate.'

Most important of all aspects of a young singer's studies is the acquisition of technique. In addition to her teaching, Nanette Natal also contributes a series of articles to *The Music Paper* in which she stresses certain key areas, breathing, resonation, placement: 'The most important aspect of vocal technique is breath control. Without it, all the concepts that you learn cannot be truly manifested. To be able to use your instrument fully and creatively, the body and mind must work together. There is nothing more frustrating than having an idea in your head and not being able to execute it physically. Without the proper breath support, the untrained singer will eventually reach a creative impasse because it is, in fact, breath support that turns ideas into sound... The resonation of all sound must begin outside the body. It is only when the sound originates this way that you can have true control over the quality of your sound. Pulling back in any fashion by placing tones in the head or any other part of the facial mask will only result in unbalanced and incomplete sounds. You must let go, both physically and emotionally, to truly learn to control your tone...'

Of course, the acquisition of technique alone does not a singer make – it is what the singer does with her technique that matters. As Natal demonstrates vividly in performance, possession of technique need not lead to a constricted by-rote singing style. Quite the opposite in fact, because she is one of the most interesting and exciting singers working in jazz today. As she says, 'Having a strong technique will give you confidence and the skill to take real chances in your music. When you have control over your sound, you can push yourself to the limits.' But technique does not concern itself with a significant factor in jazz, emotional involvement. As Natal stresses, 'If you are all technique and no feel, it doesn't mean anything. Feel outweighs a lot of technique. There are an awful lot of people who can be very technically controlled but are not really saying anything. Being a good singer means that you say something. Very often it is technique that frees people so that they can say something or say more of what they want to say. When I sing, I'm not at all conscious of technique because at this point, and this is what it really should be, you *own* the technique and you're free then to express yourself. I'm not thinking when I'm performing, I'm really just being in the moment, and trusting my technique. I know where to breathe, I don't think about where I'm going to inflect a change; certainly when I work on a tune I have a sense of the structure of it and the basic interpretation, but when I'm performing the tune it always has a different feeling. It's always somewhat different, it's never exactly the same and there's no thinking process anymore when you're performing the music. You're really one with the music and you just let go.'

Most singers agree with Natal's expression of the need to subordinate technique, once learned, to the special non-technical needs of a jazz performance. 'Basically technique in itself is useless,' Tina May says, 'unless you are going to do something artistic with it. You don't want to be thinking about technique when you are singing other than knowing that when you go for a high note you have already taken care of it in your preparation. It is important to learn breathing techniques because it is going to help your phrasing and let you be yourself. It allows you to express yourself.' Nicki Leighton-Thomas agrees with this: 'Taking music and singing lessons is important from the technical side of things. It's all very well to have a good voice and natural performance skills but these can always be improved.' However, she also points to the potential problems generated by classical training methods: 'I had some classical training which proved very useful, but also a slight hindrance with jazz. I don't regret having done it but I find myself undoing much of what I worked hard at during that time.' Mike Campbell passes on to his students not only the techniques of singing but also qualifying wisdom: 'My teacher said, "You learn technique so you can forget technique – it's about making music." Technique is just a way to protect your instrument – it's not an end, then it becomes stiff. You need technique, but that's not what it's about. While you are thinking about it, the song is over. It's about purity, about passion.'

Before he entered jazz, Kurt Elling had learned technique as a chorister, singing the classical repertoire. Self-taught in jazz style, he explained to Myrna Daniels of the LA Jazz Times: 'I have voice teachers for technique, but what I do is a little different, so I have to learn it on the gig, from the musicians around me... I already know how to [breathe], I did all that choral work. At this point I know my voice. I take an occasional lesson but I've figured out a practice routine for myself. It's knowing how to practise to improve what you do... I'm developing technique so that I can do what I want to do in total freedom.'

The concept of freedom is something that crops up often when singers speak of the application of technique. 'I'm not at all conscious of technique,' says Susannah McCorkle. 'I never think about phrasing or breath control or the lyrics. I've got to know the song so well that it's second nature to me; and I have to be in such good physical condition that I'm not worried about breathing and I don't want to intellectualize the song. I just want to throw myself into it and be that song from the inside when I do it.' Similarly, for Jan Ponsford technique is something to set aside once the moment of performance has arrived: 'If you practise then your machine should be warmed up so that when you make music you don't need to be thinking of technique. I don't want to spend time when I'm trying to interpret the song thinking, "Okay, I should have breathed there, now I should do this, that or the other". Sometimes, when things are not working right or the sound system is out or I'm getting cramp in my foot from standing incorrectly, then I'll check through my body, my machinery, in the same way a sax player might check their reed or the pads, asking myself why the intonation is not quite right. But not because I'm actually conscious of technique. When someone is flying with the music, the reason the music is coming out that way is because the technique has been honed in practice. You don't want to hear an exercise in technique in performance. You just want to hear the music flow. I don't want to be thinking about technique, it will just get in the way.' As a teacher she is cautious in her approach to her students: 'When teaching technique I'm trying to get the best out of their voices for what they're physically, emotionally and spontaneously able to do without hurting themselves. Bad singing is when you're not being honest and when you're hurting yourself. Good singing is when you are touching the heart of someone and yourself. I try to stop excessive vibrato, nasal whining, shouting, tightening of the throat. I'd rather someone just sing sweetly and softly. I'm into quality rather than quantity. I'm impressed by amazing vocal ranges and dexterity, but I'd rather hear an octave that is beautiful than someone screeching on four octaves that sounds dreadful. I don't dislike mannerisms but what I don't like is that overblown, theatrical presentation of a song which threatens to infiltrate jazz.'

To some extent it is also desirable that in addition to technique singers should have some knowledge of their physical being in order to exercise the necessary control over those parts of the body that produce vocal sound. In a sense, the vocal fold mass is not designed to produce singing – or for that matter any sound; its main purpose is to prevent food or liquid entering the air passages leading to the lungs. Thus, an understanding of the interaction of the palate, pharynx, larynx, etc, is at least useful. For singers intent on developing interesting or original vocal patterns without damaging themselves, it can be vital knowledge.

For many reasons, academic training is clearly invaluable. But it would be wrong to assume that it is all that a would-be singer needs. Academies cannot teach a singer how to become emotionally involved with a song, neither can they teach a singer the means of personalizing a song. Personality is a quality that lifted some of the untrained jazz singers of the past above the crowd. There was no way that Louis Armstrong or Sarah Vaughan or Betty Carter could ever have been mistaken for one of the crowd. If there is a danger inherent in the growth of academy-based training it is that of cloning – one of the most serious flaws in latter-day pop music.

Fortunately, many of the singer-teachers presently working with new singers in jazz are aware of the dangers of too much instruction at the expense of hands-on experience. In recalling the early 1980s, Jan Ponsford says, 'There were no jazz singing classes when I was coming up. In fact, jazz was a dirty word within education. No course existed. Eventually, educationalists realized that there was a whole market out there that while not listening to the classics was nevertheless interested in music. There was no understanding within the establishment so they had to bring in people like myself to do workshops. People who had learned by doing it. To a great extent it was tokenism, but the music did gain some respect and that's increasing. But you have to be careful with young singers. I know that if I'd had to learn in that environment, it might have knocked it all out of me. I know that it is important, but in some areas I would have needed to be left to my own devices and just listened and listened. That is what I did and that way I never stopped learning. I listened to Parker, to Monk. I just soaked it all up, chatted to musicians, listened to what they had to say, read about the history of it all – because I was interested. But in the end there is nothing like getting out there and doing it.' Once out there, there are still dangers: 'I don't know anyone who committed themselves to an artform that is about being true and honest who hasn't been knocked about in one way or another.'

All this talk of training as a significant feature of the jazz singing scene of recent years should not be taken as an implication that singers in the past were unknowledgeable in matters of technique. They were not, although much was learned on the job or learned an even harder way, by error and serious misuse of vocal equipment. Mark Murphy came up in the 1950s, teaching himself as he went along and learning the lessons he later taught safely in the classroom: 'A dangerous habit is to keep singing in the throat area. If you can't alleviate the strain around your vocal chords you're gonna have trouble. Ninety-five per cent of people starting to sing haven't a clue what goes on in the physical process of it and none of them knows how to breathe. The breathing is the bottom line. Everyone should learn it or not sing. Jazz singing and grand opera may be the opposite ends of the spectrum but they are the two most difficult kinds of singing and take the biggest amount of time to learn. That's because you have to put not only enormous amounts of technique into it, but also your life. It isn't a music you can fool around with. You can't go into a song with no preparation and think you're going to get away with it.' Earlier still, when Lena Horne went to Hollywood in 1940 to make *Cabin in the Sky*, she was coached by movie do-it-all Kay Thompson, singer, songwriter, arranger, conductor, actress, comedienne: 'The most important thing she taught me was breath control. She had a very easy way of showing you how to use your breath, which is really the whole trick about popular singing. I hadn't realized some of the power I had till she worked with me and showed me how to utilize it. I had a ball with her... I was hitting notes I didn't know I could.' And Lee Wiley, too, received tuition: 'The way I was taught to sing, you can sing if you're seventy-five. Mostly I had good training and learnt to breathe, and that's about all there is to singing other than your own notes, or what you do with your mind. And phrasing and all that, but breathing is certainly important.'

For all the encouragement to study and the opportunities to learn, there remains for newcomers the temptation embodied in the fact that many of the greatest names in jazz singing – Louis Armstrong, Billie Holiday, Ella Fitzgerald, Sarah Vaughan, Carmen McRae, Betty Carter, Carol Sloane, Mark Murphy, Helen Merrill, Sheila Jordan – had either no formal training or at best very little. Added to this is the fact that the tyro singer can point to recent self-taught examples, such as Susannah McCorkle, Chris McNulty and Jan Ponsford, which tends to reinforce any argument they might proffer for going it alone. While no one would want to dissuade a young singer from simply going out there and doing it, the possible harm this might do to hopes of a long career cannot be overlooked. A balanced approach might be best for those who fear restriction through formal studying – study at least enough to protect the instrument. After all, the voice might be a passport to fame, if not fortune. Most important of all, however, is that the would-be singer lets nothing stand in his or her way.

Fully trained or not, ready or not, talented or not, once launched into the arena, most singers will find that the going gets tougher. Even the hardiest souls often find themselves beset by common enemies such as indifference, misunderstanding and changes in the public's tastes for jazz and popular music. Not that any of this is new. It was ever thus, and nowhere was it more difficult than during the era of bebop when singers seeking to sing jazz were increasingly marginalized. It was during this period that scat became one of the most prominent aspects of jazz singing. It also became one of the least understood and most overused of styles, the ramifications of which echo to the present day.

SEVEN

HOW HIGH THE MOON

Mind you, I think a little scat goes a long way. — *Mel Tormé*

Changes in public taste, in living patterns, etc, and the subsequent commercial decisions taken by the moguls of the music industry during the 1940s, led to a change in fortunes both for big bands and singers. The bands declined but the status of the singers blossomed. Far broader opportunities opened for many of them in the jazz-influenced popular field than had been possible as mere band singers. For others there were opportunities in r&b. But popular singing, whether slanted towards ballads and the standard repertoire, or the blues-based jive of r&b, wasn't for everyone. For every Jo Stafford, Peggy Lee, Nat Cole or Frank Sinatra and for every Helen Humes, Nellie Lutcher, Louis Jordan or Wynonie Harris, there were singers who wanted to remain close to the central core of jazz. But that core was itself undergoing radical change and that meant that the singers' role became more defined.

As jazz shifted, so too did perceptions of the singer. Before the 1940s singers were considered simply as singers. They were either hot or sweet, hip or corny. Jazz fans and jazz musicians kept clear of the sweet and corny kind but enjoyed listening to or accompanying those that were hip and could swing. They were the ones who tended to come high in the polls during the early years of the swing era. In 1937, for instance, Ella Fitzgerald topped both the American *down beat* poll and the British *Melody Maker* poll, with Mildred Bailey coming second and Billie Holiday third. *Down beat* came up with the same result in 1940 but in 1941, as popular singing became more dominant and the commercial aspects of the industry shifted into higher gear, Helen O'Connell topped the *down beat* poll on the basis of three hits, 'Amapola', 'Green Eyes' and 'Tangerine', all made with the Jimmy Dorsey band. Her poll success emphasized the fact that definitions of singing styles were imprecise. By 1941 it was not particularly strange that O'Connell should feature in the poll and from 1943 through to the end of the decade singers like Helen Forrest, Jo Stafford and June Christy dominated the polls with Billie Holiday consistently a runner-up. Polls in the early 1950s were dominated by Sarah Vaughan, then aiming her recordings at the popular market. Kay Starr, then making it big in the popular field, explained, 'You can't make enough money as a jazz singer.' But by 1959, close to the end of what was subsequently seen to be a golden era for singers, the defining lines were again clearly drawn. *Down beat* now termed its annual listing the 'International Jazz Critics Poll' and the 'Female Singers' section was limited to jazz-based singers, with Ella Fitzgerald again heading the list, Billie Holiday second, Sarah Vaughan third. The only possible controversy was the appearance of Mahalia Jackson and Peggy Lee, not that this caused too much concern. The most controversial name in the male listing was that of Frank Sinatra who came fifth following Jimmy Rushing, Louis Armstrong, Ray Charles and Joe Turner.

Part of the problem in arriving at clear definitions lay in the fact that jazz had fragmented into post-swing, traditional and bebop, none of which seemed to have a clear role for singers. Under the blanket of swing there had been an infinite variety of forms, including the blues-based styles of Jimmy Rushing and Helen Humes, the swing style of Ella Fitzgerald and Maxine Sullivan, and the popular vocalizing of Helen O'Connell, Jo Stafford and Frank Sinatra. Now, those singers who wished to remain in jazz and develop as artists found that they had little choice but to adopt a more contemporary approach.

One of the new lines of jazz singing which emerged was firmly connected to the dying big band tradition. The most prominent representatives of this line were two singers who, although sharing some similarities in lineage, were themselves quite dissimilar: Anita O'Day and June Christy.

Another of the new lines was bebop. Whether or not a musician played it, liked it, or even understood it, bebop made an impact that was both confrontational in its immediacy and insidious in its gradual influence. Today, the bebop line of jazz singing continues uninterrupted even if occasionally the link has seemed tenuous.

*   *   *

The early years of Anita O'Day's career were turbulent, at times downright erratic. But despite the ups and downs, the alarmingly casual manner in which she risked livelihood and life itself, she possessed certain important strengths – of mind, body and character – which eventually pulled her through.

She was born Anita Colton and as a teenager scraped a living in Depression-hit America as a marathon-dancing contestant, where a frequent fellow participant was Frankie Laine. It was at one 'Walkathon' contest that she was given an opportunity to sing with Erskine Tate's band, a longtime resident at Chicago's Savoy Ballroom. Anita, who changed her name to O'Day (pig-Latin for 'dough', a slang predecessor of 'bread'), enjoyed the experience and figured that whatever hardships a singer's life might hold, they couldn't possibly be any worse than those of a marathon dancer and before she was out of her teens was singing for her supper. At a Chicago club she was heard by Gene Krupa who told her that if ever a slot appeared in his band he would call her. In the meantime she auditioned for Benny Goodman who rejected her because she strayed too far from the melody (he hired Helen Forrest) but not long afterwards Krupa's singer, Irene Daye, quit and he kept his word and hired O'Day.

The impact of O'Day's arrival on the Krupa bandstand, which came within a few weeks of the arrival of Roy Eldridge, was sensational. Until then Krupa's band had been sound but average, although moderately successful due largely to the leader's charisma and personal popularity.

The addition of O'Day and Eldridge lifted the band way above the average; Eldridge's fiery trumpet playing gave the band a superb ensemble spark and a front-rank jazz soloist and he also had an engaging and energetic line in vocals. O'Day had an uneasy start; no one had thought it necessary to write arrangements for the new arrival and she was expected to sing Daye's songs in her style and key. Soon, however, O'Day proved to be a quirky, dynamic asset. Her popularity must have surprised almost everyone, geared as conceptions were to the pretty canary warbling moon-in-June songs in front of many big bands. For one thing she didn't dress right! Not for O'Day the flowing evening gown; she wore a tailored suit which matched those worn by the rest of the band. More important than appearances, she sang songs with bite and a refreshing lack of sentimentality, and she swung. A string of popular recordings followed: 'Alreet', 'Kick It', 'Bolero at the Savoy', 'Massachusetts' and 'Let Me Off Uptown' (on which she was teamed with Eldridge).

The strong personalities and independent natures of O'Day and Eldridge, important factors in their popularity and success, were also divisive. They caused sparks between one another and in time O'Day decided that she had had enough and quit to join Stan Kenton, who said of her: 'Anita O'Day is the most uninhibited singer I've ever known. She sings without fear, and that is what makes her so dynamic.' She had more hits, 'And Her Tears Flowed Like Wine' and 'The Lady in Red', then went back to a re-formed Krupa band, in 1945, before going out as a single. This career choice was inevitable for a singer of her single-mindedness and independence. From then onwards, for the next forty-plus years, she toured and recorded, battled with and eventually won out over problems with alcohol and drugs, recounted unflinchingly in her autobiography, *High Times, Hard Times*, and secured for herself a lasting place in the pantheon of undiluted jazz singers.

O'Day's conception of singing emerges from a crystal-clear awareness of the essence of Billie Holiday's singing style but couched in a musical language that is very much her own: 'Everyone would say, "Gee, you're great. You sound just like Billie Holiday". The only drawback was that nobody ever remembered my name. Consequently, I stopped listening to other singers and started playing the recordings of instrumentalists. So instead of thinking how Billie did it, I'd work out phrasing, emphasis, whatever, that took off from Stan Getz, Buddy DeFranco, or Zoot Sims. Maybe I'd use a nasal approach with an open throat to get onto a different form, emphasize an unexpected word until I developed a style of my own.'

A little-known singer named Jerry Kruger who had also sung with Krupa's band also admired Holiday. The aspects of Holiday's style which Kruger adopted (she was no mere imitator) were the absence of vibrato and an unadorned vocal line, concepts which O'Day took even further. Gunther Schuller suggests that Kruger is a link between Holiday and O'Day but it is unclear if O'Day was influenced by or even heard her. O'Day's deliberate avoidance of sentimentality and her detached, coolly appraising view of the love songs she sang, came as a jolt to the expectations of fans. Just as she had chosen to present herself physically in a rather austere fashion, as one of the band, so her vocal lines were unpretentious, direct and instrumental. She was typically off-handed in her view of herself: 'I've always had a nothing voice.' O'Day could also be forthright in her opinions of other singers: '... Carmen [McRae] is a wonderful singer. This chick has a lot of voice, a lot of chops, she can sing a lot of things. But, in my opinion, she can't sing a fast tune and really get on time. Take another great, Sarah Vaughan. Sarah's got great chops, a big neck, a good sound, but on a fast tune she runs behind the beat. That's why Ella is, more or less, first. In later days, she's into something other than improvising, but whatever her approach she can sing a ballad, an uptune, a novelty, almost anything. But nobody has it all. Like me, Ella doesn't have a real good voice.'

O'Day's discarding of vibrato was not so much a matter of choice but was dictated by her physique. In conversation with Brian Priestley she compared physical dimensions with Sarah Vaughan who had a wide neck and hence had an 'ultra-wide vibrato' while 'I have got the smallest neck in the world which is why I sing staccato 'cos I don't have any hold tones... The doctor cut off my oesophagus, [an] accident when they took out my tonsils. So that could be why I blow... I put the air past that, and I use the upper part, the back part of my throat. That's how I get my tone.'

O'Day acknowledges that her early listening to singers was eclectic, listing Holiday, Ella Fitzgerald and Mildred Bailey ('she sang her consonants – didn't sing her vowels'). She also admired Martha Raye: 'I went to a movie and saw Martha Raye do "Mr Paganini", and thought, "that's the way to do it".' O'Day's liking for the singing movie actress-comedienne is far from unique. Rosemary Clooney thought Raye 'one of the best singers that ever lived'. For her time, Raye's vocal style was unusual, cool, vibrato-free and verging on flat; factors which make clearer the admiration she attracted from singers seeking a different approach to songs. Jon Hendricks also considered Raye to be 'one of the all-time great unrecognized jazz singers'.

Perhaps as a result of her time with the Krupa band, perhaps instinctively, O'Day tied her singing more closely to the drummer in any group with which she sang than to any other instrumentalist. In her conversation with Priestley, she was unequivocal about the importance to her: 'I always carry a drummer. You can always turn the piano mike off and I can still do my job. But you got a poor drummer back there – you're in trouble.' Chris McNulty, while herself preferring the bass player as the musician to listen to, 'to really know where you are', understands O'Day's preference: 'The drummer is really important to me too and I can understand Anita saying that with her style.'

Although totally immersed in jazz, O'Day does admit to liking other kinds of singers: 'There are a lot of pop singers I've admired – soloists backed by a band. Helen Forrest and Helen O'Connell are two. Helen Forrest was a good lead singer, a very together lady, who was one of the best. Helen O'Connell was a natural of her kind... Most of her songs are ballads. I'd imagine she learns the melody and stays with it, which is okay as long as it doesn't bore her.' She went on to speak of other contemporaries: 'Georgia Gibbs, Jo Stafford, Dinah Shore, Patti Page and Rosemary Clooney have worked a variety of ways. Peggy Lee is a good example of this. She began as a band singer, married a guitar player and got into songwriting. She had individuality, magnetism and beauty. She changed with the times and stayed on top for many years. But she didn't improvise.'

When O'Day moved on, her place in the Kenton band was taken by June Christy, six years O'Day's junior, and also seeking a different approach to the popular repertoire. Like O'Day, she had a minimal vibrato although in her case it appeared to be more a matter of deliberate control than of physical chance. She sang with a dead tone, occasionally came dangerously close to singing flat, and often appeared deliberately to avoid emotional involvement in the songs she sang.

While O'Day had been one of the first hip singers in an era that was still un-cool, Christy was more consciously hip, which is, in a sense, a contradiction in terms. At the time, a cultural shift was taking place in America. The Beat Generation heralded changes soon to take place in attitudes towards just about everything. Later manifestations of change such as Make Love Not War, flower power, hippies, rock, were too organized, too consciously anti-establishment, too square, too desperately attempting to be hip. It didn't fool the Beats who were hip before anyone else knew that hipness existed. It was not hip to try to be hip. Bop was hip. It was not hip to develop a conscious variation on a bop theme; a variation that was often more in the minds of listeners than in the sound and style of the music or in the intentions of its practitioners. Yet the variation on a bop theme practised in California – and which brought to the fore a succession of gifted musicians such as Shorty Rogers, Shelly Manne, Art Pepper, Bud Shank, Jimmy Giuffre, Lennie Niehaus, Bill Perkins and Bob Cooper, many of them at one time or another members of the Kenton band – became the epitome of hipness. Not surprisingly, a label was slapped on them (even if labelling was just about as un-hip as it was possible to be); they became the west coast school of cool jazz. Christy fitted smoothly into this laid-back atmosphere of sometimes studied calm.

Her first recording with Kenton was 'Tampico'. Years later she told Stan Woolley of *Jazz Journal International*: 'I remember being terribly disappointed because I felt that this is the ultimate in jazz being with the Kenton band and I didn't think that "Tampico" was a jazz song. Which it wasn't. But, in the meantime, it was an immediate best seller which was the nicest thing that could happen and it established me right away.' She soon followed this with her version of the beboppers' anthem, 'How High the Moon', and by the end of the 1940s she had become one of the band's main attractions. When she had first joined the band her particular needs had not been addressed. Arranger Gene Roland told Woolley: 'When June arrived she was more or less an Anita O'Day impersonator. She had Anita's style and even looked a little like her. At first she did Anita's material and then Stan developed a style for her and we gradually got away from the Anita O'Day thing.' Importantly for her continued success, Kenton and his principal arranger, Pete Rugolo, later designed their arrangements for Christy with care and attention to the special needs of her voice. Mood and moodiness, allied to the strange passion of the day for appearing passion-less, created many interesting effects including 'June Christy', one of a series of Rugolo compositions written and titled for band members to allow them to display their special talents. Performing the song presented Christy with certain problems: 'I was very self-conscious about that recording and got Stan to promise me that I wouldn't have to sing it in front of the band, so when we did it they hid me away in a booth. I was afraid of it, to say the least, and whenever we performed it in public I always sang it off-stage.'

After Christy left Kenton, she pursued a successful career as a single with a series of very popular albums for Capitol Records, most notably a Rugolo-arranged set, the title of which, *Something Cool*, perfectly summed up Christy and her west coast musical surroundings. Although Christy broke much less stylistic new ground than O'Day, she was much more readily accessible and hence influenced more singers. Lucy Reed, at the time already an accomplished singer although she had yet to make her first records, remembers the impact of Christy: 'When Stan Kenton introduced June Christy with her wonderful husky straight tone in the 1940s I think it became the "in" sound to sing with no vibrato. She was unique and made me realize that one should try to develop his or her own perception and sound.'

When Christy left Kenton, among her successors was a singer more audibly influenced by O'Day than almost any other singer in jazz and jazz-influenced popular music. Chris Connor had an unassuming view of her own status, *vis-à-vis* the older singer: 'Anita is much more of a jazz singer than I am, because she does a lot of scatting and the instrumental things that a horn does. I know she listens to instrumentalists and gets very influenced by musicians' phrasings, the saxophone lines and things like that.' Connor had started singing while still in school and later joined the Snowflakes, the vocal group with Claude Thornhill's band. After Kenton, Connor developed a steady if unspectacular career as a single, working on into the 1990s when she could be heard in the USA and Europe singing in clubs and at festivals. An aspect of audience perceptions is revealed by the fact that Connor's complete disregard for appearances sometimes disturbed people who disliked the facial contortions she unconsciously displayed when singing. The old feeling that a singer's main duty was to stand in front of the band and look pretty was not easily killed off.

Another singer of the period who also owed a stylistic debt to Billie Holiday was Mary Ann McCall. A few months older than O'Day, she sang with several swing era bands including Tommy Dorsey and Woody Herman, adhering to the party line and making few waves. However, a second spell with Herman's band which began in 1946 saw striking changes taking place in her style and by the time that she left the band, four years later, she had matured into a fine jazz singer. In the year she left Herman, 1950, she was voted best female singer in polls in several jazz magazines. McCall's ability was underlined by Herman: 'Mary Ann was singing like no one ever, then ... with the Four Brothers band, she won the *down beat* poll, and she deserved it.' Partly through musical inclination, perhaps abetted by her first marriage, to tenor saxophonist Al Cohn, she inclined towards bebop away from the post-big band direction taken by most singers.

Although McCall continued to sing throughout the rest of her life, for a time she succumbed to addiction. At one stage, she declared later, 'I spent four or five hundred dollars a week for the stuff.' She was not alone. O'Day observed that 'a business like ours can make us easy marks'. In her case the habit she developed came alarmingly close to killing her. Christy and Connor, too, had battles to fight; in their cases with alcohol. Clearly the pressures on singers in the late 1940s and 1950s were no less than in the 1930s but were of a different order. The solutions – if that's what they were – could be far more damaging than the problems they sought to alleviate.

Among the musical problems facing singers as bebop began to gain ground was that it was not especially popular in the commercial sense of the word. At first, the role that singers who wanted to work in bebop were obliged to create was not as a featured performer. Instead, they were integrated into the bop ensemble. More than at any other time, the singer now had consciously to consider herself as an instrumentalist. It must have seemed an intimidating task although the recollections of many singers suggest that the most needed characteristic was the courage to get up and do it.

Helen Merrill, who started out in New York in the 1940s, remarked on how inspirational the music was: 'But I didn't appreciate at the time that it was all so special,' she told Don Waterhouse of *Jazz Journal International*, 'I just thought that musicians everywhere were as good as Charlie Parker, Dizzy Gillespie, Al Haig, George Wallington. Bop was the music of the times. Those times had to do with personal expression. You had to find your own voice, feeling, a way of describing those feelings. You created your own sound, your own way of projecting and performing a song. If you didn't do that, if you copied other people, even with great fervour, you were not taken as seriously as those who did have their own conception of music.'

Merrill was among a handful of singers who managed to make a small niche for themselves within the bebop groups of the day. The ebullient Joe Carroll, who worked with small groups of the period, was another. At the end of the 1940s he began a stint with Dizzy Gillespie's big band. A comic element was central in the work of many bebop singers and in Carroll's case it often bordered on self-parody – something which Gillespie was happy to encourage, the pair of them composing 'Oo-Shoo-Be-Do-Be'.

Babs Gonzales was another energetic performer and self-promoter who first came to serious attention as a member of a vocal trio in which his partners were Pee Wee Tinney and Tadd Dameron. Babs's Three Bips and a Bop highlighted Dameron's role as an arranger, and an early record success, in 1947, was a Gonzales composition, 'Oop-pop-a-da'. Like Carroll and Gillespie (who had a hit with this song), Gonzales could not refrain for long from taking a light-hearted view of his limited singing abilities even if some fans took the comedic beboppers a little too seriously. Dave Frishberg commented: 'I was intrigued by the bebop singers. I thought it was funny. And it is. They were entertainers, of course; I don't think any of them said, "Listen to how creative I am". But to try to pass that off as some kind of profound jazz expression doesn't cut any ice with me.' Mike Campbell states: 'I do not do bebop tunes because, lyrically they are very lame.' But some singers were looking into bebop in the hope of finding a means of very serious expression of their desire to sing jazz without having to cling to a momentarily outmoded style.

Betty Roché, singing with Duke Ellington's band in the mid-1940s and again in the early 1950s, was deeply influenced by bebop and her recordings show an intriguing confluence of sometimes opposing musical concepts as her bop inflections contrast strikingly with the post-swing era patterns through which Ellington's music was passing at the time. Ellington himself remarked of her, 'Betty Roché was thirty years ahead of her time. She never imitated anybody and she never sounded like anybody but Betty Roché.' Waxing lyrical in his praise, Ellington stated: 'She had a soul inflection in a bop state of intrigue, and it was presented to the listener in a most believable manner as by a little girl with an adult delivery.'

Sarah Vaughan, with Billy Eckstine's bebop big band, considered herself very much a part of the movement: 'We tried to educate the people. We used to play dances, and there were just a very few who understood who would be in a corner, jitterbugging forever, while the rest just stood staring at us.'

Charlie Ventura's Bop for the People band had Jackie Cain and Roy Kral. The arrangements Ventura used harmonized the voices of Cain and Kral with saxophones, thus creating a distinctive and saleable 'voice-instrument' sound. The vocal duo was followed by Betty Bennett who recalled for *Crescendo International*: 'The thing I liked best about singing with the Ventura band was that you didn't sit on the bandstand with a fixed grin on your face, as do most girl singers. But every couple of tunes, if I didn't sing a solo, I sang a part. In fact, there were very few things that I wasn't featured in somehow. It was very enjoyable. In those days the words meant nothing to me. They were just a way to swoop up and down to get from one jazz note to another jazz note.'

Sheila Jordan also recalled the use or absence of words when singing in a bebop environment, thinking specifically of the emergence of scat as a prominent form of jazz singing: 'It all arose because everyone wanted to do bebop music. And there weren't words enough for it. And singing all the bebop changes is the most fun, it's a challenge.'

Jordan, like Helen Merrill, had drifted into singing with bebop musicians simply because they were there. She was about fourteen years old and took it for granted that the musicians she was seeing and hearing locally, in Detroit, were nothing different from musicians everywhere. Thus, her mentors and early influences and associates were men like Tommy Flanagan, Barry Harris and Kenny Burrell. Although impressed by Billie Holiday, Jordan could state that '... basically I listened more to instrumentalists... It was Bird made you want to do it.' Jordan had little formal musical education, a few piano lessons only, and never had any voice training. Nevertheless, she later studied under Lennie Tristano who used scat as a training method for improvisation. Jordan continued to move with the times, recording and performing live with leading figures of the jazz avant-garde such as George Russell, Steve Kuhn and Steve Swallow. Her own lack of formal musical education did not prevent her from becoming a respected teacher and clinician in the USA and Europe. Thanks to her experience, she brings to her classes a clear-sighted view of the importance of the relationship between theory and practice. Her comments pre-echo those of later teachers: 'There weren't (jazz) courses when I was coming up. You could not learn the way kids can today. My course is a performance course. I feel you have to get up there and do it.'

Jordan is a highly distinctive singer of jazz; when she works with only bass accompaniment, as in her duets with Harvie Swartz, there is an unmistakable feeling that the listener is experiencing a unique meeting of minds. Jordan confirmed this to Peter Gamble in *Jazz FM*: '...the spontaneity is unbelievable – like one voice'. But she adds, 'It's like a wonderful way to sing but it demands concentration.' A full-time singer and teacher only since the mid-1980s, Jordan is quietly self-deprecating about her abilities: 'I never expected to make a living out of music – it was just something I loved to do.'

*   *   *

Perhaps the most striking aspect of much bebop and post-bop singing is the use of scat; or, as some might argue, its overuse. During the 1930s a handful of singers used scat, notably Cab Calloway and Leo Watson. These singers approached the form in different ways. Calloway formulated a mode of scat which reflected his whimsical development of a cast of characters for his songs, notably the drug-takers who inhabited songs such as 'Minnie the Moocher'. Watson's use of scat, which was way ahead of its time, heralded the bebop scatters of the following decade. In Watson's case, the staccato nature of his vocal lines were intended to replicate a trombone solo. Another singer of the same period was George 'Bon Bon' Tunnell. A fine balladeer, Tunnell's scatting shows a greater sense of structure than Watson's and a more deliberate approach to the 'lyric'.

Scat came into its own with bebop but often divided audiences, critics and singers. Writer-critic Leonard Feather declared that 'scat singing with only a couple of exceptions – should be banned'. Contrary to that opinion, Jon Hendricks, a foremost user of the idiom says, 'One can never say that in order to be a jazz singer you have to scat... What one *can* say is that it helps.' Nevertheless, Jay Clayton warns, 'I think some people are scatting too soon – before they understand the song.'

Scat singing has never been an unreservedly accepted mode of expression in jazz circles. A singer like Betty Carter, although ingenious when scatting, can be much more convincing when stretching and contorting a lyric, however convoluted she might be, rather than expressing her thoughts by scat. Many singers who use scat often deliver cliché-ridden phrases, while pop singers who occasionally use scat in an attempt to prove how hip they are, usually end up showing just how sad they are. There was a time when 'to scat' conveyed to an audience a sense of irreverence and fun. Too often, today's scat is as serious as your life. Contemporary scat singers often appear to stifle the fun, replacing it with earnest and intense virtuosity. Watson was joyously irreverent and some of his frivolity would not go amiss in the work of many latter-day scatters. The reason for scatting – and it should have a reason – can be serious. Carla White explained her obsession with the form to Deni Kasrel: 'What the jazz singer did was stand up, do 32 bars, sit down, and maybe come back at the end and do another 32 bars. The instrumentalists had all the fun, taking all those extended solos... I said, "Something has to give. I want to have fun too!" So I started focusing on scat singing.' However, she admitted, 'It got out of hand. You can go for so long that the music gets dissipated.' Now, she prefers more tunes per hour than her hour-long performances of the 1980s. 'You can tell more stories that way and take your audience on more journeys.'

A good scat singer, uninhibited in her virtuosity, can carry off what a pop singer cannot, simply because she knows what she is doing; cutting across octaves, perhaps at first soaring skywards then descending in a flurry of scattered notes. At its worst this is something that can sound pretentious, at its best it can be an awe-inspiring cascade of sound. But it should have a purpose.

Working in the context of bebop, singers found scat an ideal way – sometimes the only way – to participate in the music being played. 'The music was so exciting,' said Annie Ross, 'everyone wanted to do it. And singers wanted to extend the whole business of singing a song.'

Some singers find themselves equivocal over scat. Terry Blaine acknowledges that she is a 'great admirer of people who can scat. I could never do it.' But she continues with a cautionary note: 'I can only listen to it in certain contexts – some can turn me on, others put me to sleep.' Weslia Whitfield is equally thoughtful in her consideration of scat: 'I do not believe that scat or no-scat is the way by which a jazz singer is identified – Billie Holiday did not ever scat. I don't either – but that's because I don't do it very well, and I can easily compare my lack of ability in this area to people who do scat wonderfully, such as Madeline Eastman.' Laila Dalseth takes a similar line: 'I'm not much of a scat singer myself. I think the words are an important part of a song, and only a few singers are in my opinion capable of good scatting – Mel Tormé, Sarah Vaughan and a few others.'

Tormé would agree with this assessment: 'Truth of the matter is that scat singing is the toughest kind of singing... I'm talking about how your mouth is stretched out of shape; I'm talking about taking a specific chord pattern and, with never knowing what you're gonna sing at that moment, to indeed sing.' He adds, 'There's very few people that can sing scat. There's me and Ella and Sarah and Carmen. And that's really it... Mind you, I think a little scat goes a long way.'

Once again a cautionary note and one that young singers, who sometimes think that scat is an obligatory part of a jazz singer's arsenal, might consider. The fact that few of the early jazz singers used scat and masters of the art such as Tormé can express reservations, suggests that forethought might bring about a more balanced judgment on scat. First understand the song, then decide if scat has a place in its performance. Helen Merrill is another with cautious views: 'Scat has nothing to do with jazz singing. It has to do with a display of "Look, Ma, I'm dancing".' She was also less sure of the qualities of some of the acknowledged scatters: 'Ella does it beautifully but I don't think that Sarah did it very well.' And Merrill offered a further caution: 'If you're going to scat you'd better be able to play as good as any of the jazz musicians, that's all.' Betty Carter sees the distinction that lies between straight lyric singing and scat: 'If you're singing a song with lyrics, that's when the voice comes into play because it's the tone of it that makes the thing work. But scatting is another artform altogether.'

Perhaps in no other singer is the artform of scat most clearly evident than in the work of Ella Fitzgerald. During the decade and a half that began in the mid-1950s, the period when she was making the great Songbook series, many critics mooted that her search for pure vocal sound was detrimental to the meaning of the lyrics. She was also criticized for her occasional forays into the blues. Where no one could find fault – and which effectively demolished any doubts about her status as a jazz singer – was in her use of scat. For Fitzgerald, scat excursions, often at breakneck tempos, were a means of delivering breathtaking performances to round off an evening's entertainment. In their turn they also created permanent parallels by which to judge performances by other singers of jazz standards like 'How High the Moon', 'Oh, Lady, Be Good!' and 'Air Mail Special'. Her scatting was not always a display of vocal pyrotechnics. Witness for instance her performance with the Duke Ellington orchestra of 'In a Mellowtone' in which she uses her voice to create an impressionistic sound image. Fitzgerald had taken to bebop with ease and eagerness: 'These bop musicians have stimulated me more than I can say. I've been inspired by them and I want the world to know it. Bop musicians have more to say than any other musicians playing today.'

For Anita O'Day, another leading exponent, scat was a means of developing an intimate musical byplay with instrumentalists that would rarely work well if the singer remained glued to a lyric. When singing with a piano-bass-drums trio, O'Day is aware of the limitations of trading with piano and bass. All night long, she observed, it's just the piano or the bass: 'So I take a scat chorus, then I split it with the drummer. It doesn't come in first, but the idea is to improvise on the chord structure of the song with riffs that fit... Scat has its place, I think.'

There is an undoubted freedom of expression for some singers which makes itself felt when they scat. Just as Ella Fitzgerald sounded joyous, so too are possibilities opened up for others. Lucy Reed, usually thought of as an exquisite balladeer, explains this aspect of scatting: 'What I do enjoy, musically, is scatting with an instrumentalist or another singer for many choruses. It can be improvisational, both harmonically and rhythmically, with no distraction or concern about destroying the lyric. Excitement builds up with this kind of jamming that's very contagious. I love it.'

Alongside scat but not a part of it, in the 1950s there was a rise of interest in vocalese. Essentially, vocalese is the setting of words to a previously improvised instrumental solo or ensemble passage. Notwithstanding the fact that it often places great demands upon a singer's deftness and fluidity, especially when the instrumental solo is fast and note-heavy, the fact that the improvisation already exists and the vocalese is built upon it suggests that the form contains within it something that is the very antithesis of jazz. The precise origins of vocalese are somewhat speculative but it was in the 1950s that it made a splash in jazz circles and also, perhaps surprisingly, caused a few ripples in the world of popular music.

During the previous decade Eddie Jefferson had sung lyrics he had written in this manner, notably a vocalized version of James Moody's improvised saxophone solo on 'I'm in the Mood for Love'. In 1952 Jefferson's version of Moody's original, retitled 'Moody's Mood for Love', was recorded by another singer, Clarence 'King Pleasure' Beeks, coupled with Beeks's vocalized setting of Charlie Parker's 'Parker's Mood'. This record sold very well and other singers sat up and took notice. Among them was a group of singers who habitually gathered to talk, sing and improvise, including Dave Lambert (who, with Buddy Stewart, had recorded an early bebop vocal, 'What's This?', with Gene Krupa's band in 1945). Lambert and Jon Hendricks were both admirers of Charlie Parker. Lambert had broadcast with Parker in 1949 and later recorded with him. Hendricks had abandoned his plans for a career in law due to Parker's urging him to 'come to New York and sing jazz'. Lambert and Hendricks teamed up in 1955 to make a record and two years later added Annie Ross to become one of the most famous vocal trios in jazz. An album by the trio used overdubbing to create a denser ensemble sound and was based upon classic recordings by

132

the Count Basie band. *Sing a Song of Basie* led to a successful period of concerts and recordings of which some were vocalese and others real improvisations. Reactions to Lambert, Hendricks and Ross were mixed. Babs Gonzales had no doubts about their abilities and limitations: 'Lambert and Hendricks are very good friends of mine, and good musicians, but to my ear they don't swing.' Carol Sloane, on the other hand, thinks: 'There aren't enough good words in the dictionary for what Lambert, Hendricks and Ross did during the time they were doing it.'

Audiences have mixed views on scat, their opinions being unpredictable in that they are not divided by stylistic preferences or even by whether or not they are jazz fans. Indeed, the non-jazz fan is often likely to assume that someone singing scat must be a jazz singer while the jazz fan might well be less easily convinced. There is a possible subdivision within jazz fans suggested by Mark Murphy: 'People are used to songs being an unchanging line of storytelling... Scatting or improvising... It makes an audience work harder.'

*   *   *

There is a third use in jazz of the human voice to produce sounds other than words. Unlike scat and vocalese, however, this is less easy to define and pigeon-hole.

Just as many early jazzmen used instruments to create a sound akin to that of the human voice, or at least as an extension thereof, so some singers have found that using the voice in imitation of an instrument meets their needs in certain situations. An early example, from 1928, would be Gladys Bentley singing 'How Much of That Stuff', each chorus of which ends with an imitation of a moaning cornet. Perhaps most famous of all early examples of wordless vocalizing that is not really scat, even though she describes it as such, is Adelaide Hall's subtle and delightful singing on Duke Ellington's 1927 recording of 'Creole Love Call'. Like so many instances of good music in jazz, it happened by chance. As Hall recalled: 'I was in a travelling show, I closed the first half and Duke Ellington opened the second half. One night I was standing in the wings – 'cause I was always a big Ellington fan, watching and listening and the boys swung into "Creole Love Call". They were playing so well and that melody got into me so I began to improvise a wordless sort of vocal – I suppose you would call it a kind of scatting. Anyway, I was kind of moaning away, Ellington rushed into the wings and said, "Hey, that's great, Addie, would you record that with me?" I told him that I was just humming and didn't know just what it was I had done, and he said, "That's all right, you'll be able to recreate something like it at the session."' And so she did, the result being a timeless moment of jazz recording.

An advantage of wordless singing to non-English speaking singers is that it allows them to communicate in a way that overcomes linguistic boundaries by simply ignoring them. The Brazilian singer, Flora Purim, has sung in English and in her native Portuguese, but finds wordless singing has its advantages: 'Words are good when they are explicit, but when they are not, words can become sounds. You are better off putting your emotion into humming the song than singing the words to it.' Urszula Dudziak, from Poland, states: 'I found that you can reach people without words.'

The British singer Norma Winstone, while not hampered by having to sing in a foreign language, nevertheless found wordless singing of value to her. For one thing, 'it can mean whatever the listener wants it to mean'. Winstone learned to play piano as a child but was interested in singers and by the time she was in her mid-teens, the late 1950s, had begun to sing professionally. She first admired popular singers including Frank Sinatra and Lena Horne but also heard Ella Fitzgerald and was particularly taken by her scat singing. She did not try this for herself, however, and it was not until she had begun to team up with pianist-composer Michael Garrick that an opportunity presented itself to improvise wordlessly in an instrumental number. A band member left and she was invited to sing his tenor saxophone part; she found that not only did she have a facility for this form of singing but that fellow musicians and audiences also enjoyed it and persuaded her to continue. She then began listening to earlier practitioners, including some of Ellington's singers, Hall, Joya Sherrill and Kay Davis. This musical mood of the moment kept her working in this form for some time although she would later return to the standard songbook in a decisive manner, becoming one of the most potent singers in jazz during the 1990s. Winstone also writes lyrics, mainly impressionistic, displaying a flair for colorations that blend well with the musicians with whom she is most closely associated, including Tony Coe, Kenny Wheeler and John Taylor.

In less able hands than those of singers like Dudziak and Winstone, a tendency towards blandness can creep into wordless singing, edging it away from what might reasonably be labelled jazz towards the remote and shadowy reaches of 'world music' – a curious catch-all phrase that often seems to owe more to a marketing man's desperate strategy than a truly meaningful definition. It is sometimes easy to understand such desperation. For example, how can singers such as Al Jarreau and Bobby McFerrin be categorized without doing either the singers or the music they sing a disservice?

Jarreau moved very slowly into full-time singing and it was not until the late 1970s that he was an internationally recognized name. Born in 1940, Jarreau's jazz listening was inevitably post-bop and his interest in jazz singing evolved out of the work of Dave Lambert and Jon Hendricks. The period of his adolescence also saw the rise in popularity of soul music and Jarreau happily incorporated elements of this in his work alongside jazz-rock fusion and later, as he gained in confidence, many vocal sounds that owe their origins to Oriental, Arabic and African music. He also sings a form of scat that is identifiably from the same stable as that used by his mentors and by the likes of Fitzgerald and O'Day.

Even more expansive in the manner in which he welcomes into his musical fold vocal forms from other lands and genres is Bobby McFerrin. Born into a highly musical family – his parents were opera singers – McFerrin trained as a classical pianist at Juilliard and later at Sacramento State before taking up a musical career as an accompanist. He appeared as a singer in tandem with Jon Hendricks but it was a 1981 appearance at the Kool Jazz Festival in New York that first alerted the jazz world that a truly original talent had dropped into its midst. His unaccompanied performance at the festival created a sensation and within two years he had firmly established his place as a major innovator and an improviser of enormous skill and ingenuity. His eclectic use of vocal sounds from all parts of the world which are built into a collage of musical snippets from jazz, pop and numerous folk and ethnic musics, results in a remarkable whole. In addition to producing a wide range of vocal sounds, including clicks and pops, McFerrin also accompanies himself by using his body as a sound-box, generating drumming sounds by beating noises out of his slender frame. The result can lead some listeners into thinking that what they are hearing is not really a vocal performance, and McFerrin acknowledges that some might find his style a little inaccessible: 'I've been accused sometimes of not really thinking what songs are about. Because I've always been into the sounds of words rather than the words themselves.' On the other hand, melody, he considers, is the essence of music, 'the thing I can hook up on'.

By the mid-1990s, McFerrin's musical horizons were becoming too restricted for someone with his adventurous spirit. He had started to draw upon his classical background and was holder of the post of Creative Chair with the Saint Paul Chamber Orchestra and was working with symphony orchestras, including the London Philharmonic, with concerts at prestigious venues such as London's Royal Festival Hall. He was also writing an opera and, on the album *Paper Music*, was singing wordless vocal lines to the solo parts of concertos by Bach and Vivaldi. To the world of classical music he has brought some of the atmosphere of the unexpected that forever hovers on the edges of jazz performance: 'I'll be on the podium and decide I want something to happen. So, instead of holding a pause for two seconds, I'll hold it for ten. The orchestra will think, "What's he up to?" Suddenly, everything becomes charged with that mysterious energy.'

What such things mean to the world of jazz singing, if indeed they mean anything, is debatable. Nevertheless, McFerrin's appearance on the platforms of some of the world's great concert halls means that jazz-based wordless singing has travelled far from the concepts demonstrated by Louis Armstrong, Gladys Bentley, Cab Calloway, Anita O'Day and Leo Watson. Like it or not, modern scat singing is a valid and fast-increasing area of jazz singing, freeing many singers from what they see as the restriction of a lyric and allowing their musical imaginations to stretch far beyond what would be possible in any other form of music.

EIGHT
STAIRWAY TO THE STARS

Before Ella and Sarah you had to sing the melody straight. They opened it up for others to follow individual styles of their own. — *Betty Carter*

When asked to nominate early influences, the majority of jazz singers list Billie Holiday and Ella Fitzgerald and Sarah Vaughan. To a lesser extent, Carmen McRae is named while Betty Carter is rarely mentioned, perhaps because her time is too close for her to be fully acknowledged. In the eyes of the jazz public the first three have real status yet all five rank among the very finest exponents of jazz singing.

Singers from jazz who have captured and enraptured the general audience are few. Among the men might be numbered Louis Armstrong and Fats Waller; among the women there might be Fitzgerald, Vaughan and, perhaps, Peggy Lee. Not even Holiday could accurately be included in such a list and, as for Lee, she is admired largely for her post-jazz career.

By far the favourite among the ladies is Fitzgerald. The reason why she has attracted such widespread admiration and affection is located in the early months of 1956 when the singer began recording for Norman Granz on his Verve label. Her career had been managed by Granz for some time but with his benign influence now also exerted over her recordings, a major shift took place. For Verve, she began a series of recordings, several of which were in the Songbook series, while others were kin in terms of material, arrangements, accompaniment and concept. The albums were clearly aimed at a far wider audience than that of jazz. Witness the unsigned sleeve blurb on her album, *like someone in love.*

'This is it - if you're in love, if you've ever loved, if you're about to fall in love; in short, if you're a member of the human race, then these sounds are for you: Ella's feeling and the beauty of songs about people in love -'

Heady PR prose indeed, not usually found on jazz albums. The Songbooks, in which Fitzgerald sang the songs of several great American composers and lyricists, found with unerring accuracy that rare niche wherein jazz and popular music - and the jazz and popular music audience - meet with utmost felicity. Carmen McRae best described the essence of Fitzgerald at this time: '... the epitome of jazz feeling and the popular song wedded together. With her, the transition from jazz to the commercial context wasn't only smooth, it was artistic.' But they needed that extra promotional push that almost no jazz albums then received, and certainly do not get today. Granz understood that and attended to it.

The manner in which Fitzgerald sang these songs raises that least precise of the constituents which form the definition of what makes a jazz singer: public taste and perception. What Fitzgerald achieved with the recordings made during the late 1950s and early 1960s was a joyful symbiosis of those elements of jazz that can be appreciated and enjoyed by the non-jazz audience, and those elements of pop that are acceptable to jazz fans. Fitzgerald explained to record company executive Joe Smith how her change of direction was deliberately conceived: 'In the 1950s I started singing with a different kind of style. That came about because Norman Granz felt that there was something else to my voice besides just singing. Basin Street and Birdland had closed down, and I was wondering where I was going to work. All the bop/jazz clubs were gone. So we tried this new style, picking out songwriters and singing their songs... People who never heard me suddenly heard songs which surprised them because they didn't think I could sing them. People always figure you could only do one thing ... it opened up another whole level of audience for me.' Marty Paich, who worked on some of her albums at this time, described how they attained the end product: 'We have a lot of fun. When we're trying to figure out a final chorus for instance, I'll sit at the piano and play some wild chords, and she'll improvise lyrics as only Ella can. Then I'll go home, write down and develop what has evolved, and take it back to her and remind her of what she'd shown me.'

It must be acknowledged in passing that some jazz fans felt that Granz took Fitzgerald too far away from the jazz core in making the Song-books and similar albums, a criticism which conveniently overlooks the fact that, simultaneously, he was starring her in live and recorded performances with his Jazz At The Philharmonic musicians, in which she was unmistak-ably in a jazz groove. The singer was, in fact, fully capable of taking care of both audiences – what these records did was to separate the two strands and allow her to concentrate upon each without constantly looking over her musical shoulder. Nevertheless, even when singing the most commercially popular songs – for example, 'Ev'ry Time We Say Goodbye' from the *Cole Porter Songbook* – she swings. Conversely, even when tearing up the place on breakneck performances of 'How High the Moon' or 'Oh, Lady, Be Good!' she is always melodious.

In addition to Porter, in 1956, the Songbooks included Rodgers and Hart (also 1956), Duke Ellington (1957), Irving Berlin (1958), George and Ira Gershwin (1959), Harold Arlen (1961), Jerome Kern (1963) and Johnny Mercer (1964). After the Songbooks the general public, even those who hated jazz, accepted Fitzgerald. The chief factor in the turnaround was, of course, the repertoire. The great standards from the cream of America's popular songsmiths were known to all, familiar to the extent that almost all could feel comfortable with them. Nothing strange was being sung and, importantly, they were being sung in a relatively straightforward manner without the distraction of overt improvisation. And, just as important, the voice was warm and clear, the diction near-perfect, the pitch true. Frequently, the arrangements were bland and, given the quality of the arrangers, it must be assumed that this was deliberate. On display here were singer and songs and nothing was allowed to come between the concept and the listener.

When the spell is broken, as it is briefly on the Harold Arlen set by Billy May's lively arrangements, the listener's attention is distracted from the central point – Fitzgerald's voice delivering the lyricist's words. If, as has been claimed with a measure of justification, the singer sometimes did not imbue the lyrics with the emotional depth and thoughtful interpretation of, say, Carmen McRae, then it was a small price to pay. Assuming that they noticed it at all, because this new audience for Fitzgerald was one which had grown accustomed to a style of performing very different from that which McRae and her kin chose to follow. Indeed, Fitzgerald herself had changed over the two decades her career had run before the move to Verve and the start of her classic period.

Born in Newport News, Virginia, on 25 April 1917, she never knew her father. She was taken to New York by her mother and grew up wanting to be a dancer although she also took piano lessons, preferring to listen to her teacher rather than to play herself or study seriously. She also displayed an early interest in singing. Taking her cue from her mother, she listened and responded to the singing on records of the Boswell Sisters and especially Connee Boswell. Prompted by her mother, she entered an Apollo Theater amateur night contest, as a dancer. Stricken with stage fright, something she would never completely overcome, she couldn't dance a step. Instead, she sang a song, 'Judy', written by Hoagy Carmichael and Sammy Lerner, which she had heard the Boswells sing. The audience liked it and she sang another song, 'The Object of My Affection', written by Pinky Tomlin and Horace Coy Poe, and won first prize. She tried other amateur contests at other theatres including the Lafayette and the Harlem Opera House, failing and winning respectively, and was heard by several people with an ear for good new singing talent. Over the years many claimed responsibility for this particular piece of talent spotting, among them Benny Carter, Charles Linton and Bardu Ali, all three of whom were connected with Chick Webb (Carter as sometime sideman and arranger, Linton as singer, Ali as front man for the crippled bandleader). After being turned away by Fletcher Henderson – one of the rare instances of a swing era bandleader who chose not to encumber himself with a singer – Fitzgerald was given a try-out by Webb.

During these same months, Fitzgerald's mother died following injuries sustained in a road accident and when she was signed permanently by Webb she was still a minor. Webb became her guardian, and began to feature her more and more prominently. He soon saw the awkward and shy young woman become the band's biggest attraction next only to his own drumming. She was later to recall for Leonard Feather her first recording, 'Love and Kisses': 'I'll never forget it. After we made it the band was in Philadelphia one night when they wouldn't let me in to some beer garden where I wanted to hear it on the piccolo [jukebox]. So I had some fellow who was over twenty-one go in and put a nickel in while I stood outside and listened to my own voice coming out.'

She had several recording successes with Webb, featured sometimes with the full band and on other occasions with only a small group: 'Sing Me a Swing Song', 'Oh, Yes, Take Another Guess', 'The Dipsy Doodle', 'If Dreams Come True', 'A-Tisket, A-Tasket' (a song for which she collaborated on the lyric with Al Feldman) and 'Undecided'. The last of these songs was recorded four months before Webb's untimely death in 1939 but such was Fitzgerald's popularity by this time that she took over as nominal leader of the band which kept afloat for another few years.

She then began her solo career, although many of her recording dates during the 1940s, for Decca, found her teamed with other contracted artists: Louis Armstrong, the Ink Spots, the Delta Rhythm Boys, Louis Jordan, the Mills Brothers, Four Hits and a Miss, the Song Spinners. Despite the unlikeliness of some of these teamings, several of the records were hits: 'You Won't Be Satisfied' with Armstrong, 'Into Each Life Some Rain Must Fall' with the Ink Spots, 'My Happiness' with the Spinners, 'Stone Cold Dead in De Market' with Jordan. Undoubtedly, these popular successes helped establish her name with an audience beyond that for jazz, but the somewhat gimmicky nature of these pairings was incapable of sustained success. For one thing, they couldn't be repeated live. Meanwhile, she continued to appeal to jazz fans although a 1950 album, *Ella Sings Gershwin*, on which she is accompanied only by pianist Ellis Larkins, seemed at the time to fall between two stools. Subsequently, the merits of this particular 'songbook' have been highly praised, frequently rated above the later *George and Ira Gershwin Songbook* for Verve. She also recorded with small groups featuring r&b and jazz musicians such as organist Bill Doggett, bass player Ray Brown (to whom she was married between 1948 and 1952) and pianist Don Abney, and with large studio orchestras, directed by such as Sy Oliver, Benny Carter, Gordon Jenkins and Tutti Camarata.

Nevertheless, despite occasional successes with jazz fans and pop fans, such as 'Lullaby of Birdland' and 'Goody, Goody', something was missing. Decca producer Milt Gabler had a long jazz pedigree but was now working for a major commercial concern and followed the edict instigated by the company's founder, Jack Kapp – novelty above quality. The missing ingredient was sustained, measured, thoughtful and personalized control. Since 1949 some of these necessary elements were exercised by Norman Granz over public performances, following her first appearance with his JATP package in February that year. But her management and recording contracts were still with Moe Gale and Decca respectively and it was not until Granz had complete control that her career attained its full potential.

It had been in the 1940s that Fitzgerald began to assimilate bebop. She was touring with Dizzy Gillespie and his big band and Gillespie would play 'Oh, Lady, Be Good!' and say to her, 'Come on and risk this'. She later explained: 'I learned how to what you call bop. It was quite an experience, and he used to always tell me, "Come on up and do it with the fellas"... That's my education in learning how to really bop... Oh, we would have some real crazy experiences, but to me it's been what you call growing up in the music...'

By the mid-1960s and the completion of the Songbook series for Granz's Verve, Fitzgerald was regularly appearing on television and making concert tours throughout the world. Each of these activities helped her to become universally recognized as a popular singer of the highest standing. Her records sold both to the jazz record-buying public and to the mass audience. The soubriquet which labelled her as America's 'First Lady of Song' was apt. She acknowledged the importance of the change: 'The Song-books were a turning-point in my life – a new beginning for me...'

Wherever she went, Fitzgerald was assured of Standing Room Only engagements by the major concert halls or even larger arenas: Berlin's Deutschlandhalle, Carnegie Hall in New York, the Hollywood Bowl. Her albums sold well, and she even had singles competing in the charts with the flood of rock and pop music. She had arrived at that curiously inviolate status where she could do no wrong.

Countless singers name her as an influence or, at least, as someone whose recordings first attracted them to a career in jazz. The respect and admiration felt for her can be expressed by a handful of comments. Betty Carter observed that when she was starting out, 'How High the Moon' and 'Oh, Lady, Be Good!' were recent releases: 'That's what gave us females permission to dig in and do some improvising ourselves; it was no longer a man's world.' 'She was my mother's favourite singer,' Tony Bennett remem-bers. 'I was at the Paramount when I was a young boy, doing seven shows a day, and I said, "Where do you want to go for your birthday, Mama?" She said, "I want to see Ella Fitzgerald." Well, Ella was at Birdland. I was shocked to bring my mother to Birdland.' That was the first time Bennett heard her live and he remained a fan: 'She's the best singer I ever heard. Absolutely.' Mel Tormé has said, 'When I was looking for somebody to hang my vocal hat on, growing up, she was my number one greatest influence. Ella was the absolute epitome of everything that I've ever believed in or loved as far as popular singing was concerned.' She also captured the affection of many, as Peggy Lee declares: 'The first thing that comes to mind when I think of Ella Fitzgerald is love. That encompasses a lot of things: her love of music, her love of life, and her love of doing her work very professionally... She's one of the dearest people I've ever met. Her voice reflects that, I think. She has a magnificent instrument and she uses it to the best advantage. She's a quiet lady, very shy, but all of that beauty that's inside comes out in her voice.'

But the years pass and take their inevitable toll and eventually Fitzgerald's voice began to lose its assuredness. Curiously enough, however, and happily, she never lost the crystal clarity nor even the slightly girlish touch that had always lightened her voice. Even as she moved into old age, when other singers generally confronted a natural darkening of tone, she still sounded youthful.

Also into old age she retained her 'First Lady' standing in the ears and eyes of *aficionados* of American popular song. Yet throughout she retained her acceptance by jazz fans who universally allowed her far more leeway than they granted many other singers who ventured into the popular marketplace. The affection displayed towards the singer by her fans was reciprocated. As Betty Carter told Stuart Nicholson in 1992: 'It's unreal how she's working so hard, being as ill as she is. You wouldn't be working in a wheelchair if you're not working for people. The woman's doing that now. So what's on her mind? It's not the glamour. She just wants to do what she loves; she wants to hear the applause. It's her life, her reason for living.' The veteran jazz musician Benny Carter, who had first heard her at a Harlem amateur night, reflected on Fitzgerald's performance of 'Oh, Lady, Be Good!' on a 1947 recording which had formed the basis of an arrangement of the song performed at a 1990 tribute concert in New York: 'We played exactly what she had sung. When she goes into her improvisations on that record, everything she does following the opening chorus is composition. It's so exciting, so creative, so wonderfully melodic and swinging. She has such an uncanny sense of hearing; she seems to hear every chord change there is. When she scats she doesn't miss anything, and when she's singing something straight, it's pure. It's fantastic.'

In the last few years before her death in 1996, Fitzgerald was not allowed to enjoy the luxuries her success had brought her. She suffered from diabetes, resulting eventually in the amputation of both legs, and from renal failure; she underwent bypass surgery, and her eyesight, always bad, failed. It seems that the gods chose to extract a high price for the talent they gave her. Nevertheless, as the singer La Velle remarked a few days after Fitzgerald's death: 'She is spiritually still with us.' Mel Tormé recorded a tribute in memory of Fitzgerald entitled *Ella, You Showed Me the Way*, saying, 'It is with a heart full of admiration, devotion and love that I undertake this project in her memory.'

*   *   *

Potential conflict between jazz and commerciality must also be confronted when considering the work of another singer who can be justly regarded as a superstar.

When she was in her late teens, Sarah Vaughan appeared at a talent show at the Apollo Theater; she won a $10 prize, but far more important was the presence among the audience of two headlining singers. One was Ella Fitzgerald, who took the time to congratulate the young singer (Fitzgerald was her senior by some seven years) on her performance that night. But it was the other singer, Billy Eckstine, who was to have a far-reaching effect upon Vaughan's career prospects.

At the time Eckstine was singing with Earl Hines and he hastened to tell his boss that here was an ideal female singer for the band. Eckstine later recalled the day she tried out for Hines: 'Sass took the mike they had in this little recording studio, and started singing ... you could see the guys stop their packing to stare at each other. By the time she had finished, all of them were around the piano – looking at the homely little girl who was singing like this, just wailing. When Earl saw the reaction of all the band she was *in*.' Hines hired her, not only as singer but also as second pianist for when his duties took him away from the piano stool. The coincidence of an Apollo talent contest, Fitzgerald's presence that first night, and being hired by a name bandleader suggest career similarities, but these matters apart there were few other resemblances in the lives and careers of the two singers. Perhaps Dizzy Gillespie identified best the difference between Fitzgerald and Vaughan: 'Ella always played the role of a lady... Sarah Vaughan acted just like one of the boys. She used the same language on the bandstand I used with the guys.'

Sarah Vaughan was born in Newark, New Jersey, on 27 March 1924. Hers was not a musical family but she began singing at Newark's Mount Zion Baptist Church. Before reaching her teens, she had begun playing the organ at the church and she also played piano and studied music for eight years, majoring in music at Arts High School. She was thus a well-rounded musician when she joined the Hines band which was the perfect setting for someone with her evident musicianship and questing musical mind. The Hines band at this time, April 1943, was home to some of the most adventurous young musicians in jazz, among them Charlie Parker and Dizzy Gillespie. A year later, Eckstine quit Hines to form a big band to back his planned career as a single. He lured away several Hines sidemen, including Parker and Gillespie, whom he had recommended to Hines, and the now twenty-year-old singer. Although Vaughan recorded with Eckstine's band, the opportunities were clearly limited; the band was, after all, designed as a support to Eckstine. However, the presence during the four years of its existence of just about everybody who was anybody in bebop is indicative of the leader's open-mindedness and generosity. Bebop was not commercial and the band's style was antithetical to what Eckstine hoped to do with his singing career. Eventually, Eckstine realized the problems which in turn reflected his limitations as a singer in a jazz context: 'The band was into bebop and you can't sing so well with that. I decided to go single and go hear Dizzy for kicks.'

After a year with Eckstine, Vaughan moved on and by 1946 she too had embarked upon a solo career. Her recordings of these years, the late 1940s and 1950s, were mostly aimed at the more commercial market but some, with Parker and Gillespie and other emergent beboppers, display clearly the fact that working in such company had affected her singing style. Indeed, it affected her entire approach to her work, be it jazz or commercial. Gifted with a wide range, she had the ability to sing tunefully and expressively from the deepest contralto growls to magically sparkling high notes. Another quality she displayed from her earliest years was the great joy she clearly had in her voice and her ability to do with it pretty nearly anything she chose.

Almost inevitably, this characteristic of Vaughan's singing led her to adopt an approach to lyrics that was strikingly different from that chosen by her predecessors and peers. This is not to suggest that she was dismissive of the intentions of lyricist and/or composer. Witness her 1947 recording of 'Tenderly', a song which was then quite new and relatively unknown and which she helped turn into a standard (and it remained closely associated with her for the rest of her life). She treats the song with considerable respect and she would always create meaningful versions of songs such as 'Summertime', another regular feature of her repertoire, and 'The Man I Love', however often she might sing them. Nevertheless, she was at her happiest-sounding when she was given free rein to unleash her magnificent instrument on out-and-out jazz performances. Where these two sides of Vaughan were blended with care and appropriate musicality, the results could be both striking and timeless. Her 1962/3 Roulette albums, *The Explosive Side of Sarah Vaughan* and *The Lonely Hours*, for which the arrangements were written and the orchestra directed by Benny Carter, are good examples. She is in complete command of material and voice, bringing a delicately understated emotional vulnerability to the slower tempoed tunes and irrepressible vitality to the swingers. That she is at ease with her surroundings is evident throughout. Also, she is always comfortably within her limits – although it is tempting to suggest that there was no limit to what she could do with her voice. Betty Carter has suggested that of all the singers in jazz, Vaughan is the one with the potential for a very different kind of career: 'With training she could have gone as far as Leontyne Price.' Gunther Schuller went even further, declaring her to be the greatest living singer in the world.

There is no doubt that Vaughan's training as a pianist and organist was helpful to her in developing her singing style. Dan Morgenstern observed of Ella Fitzgerald that 'she thinks like a musician, always able to find the best in any melody'. Not only does Vaughan think like a musician, she also sings like a musician. In her case, like that special kind of musician, the instrumentalist who is not only original of thought and highly creative in execution but is also blessed with a superlative technique. It is this latter quality that has sometimes clouded appreciation of her remarkable talent. There has long been an undercurrent in jazz thinking that is suspicious of technical brilliance. The fear is that technique will cloak an absence of soul. Certainly there are musicians whose technical skills have been used to this end; conversely, there are those whose undoubted depths of feeling for and commitment to jazz have been handicapped by a limited technique. But the list of those with dazzling technique to match their creative outpourings is impressively peppered with major names: Dizzy Gillespie, Charlie Parker, Bud Powell, Oscar Peterson. At her best, and she was rarely less than that, Sarah Vaughan is worthy of inclusion on such a list.

Like the instrumentalists named, improvisation was her forte. In Carmen McRae's opinion, 'she was the best lady improviser'. Vaughan employed her vocal technique in a manner that furthered and enhanced her ability to transmit, through sound and style, the emotional constituents of the songs she sang. Thus, even when the words are not interpreted with a precise reflection of their emotional content, their message is still conveyed to the listener who is prepared to see behind the often ornate facade to the heart of the sound structures she builds. And yet Vaughan refuted the suggestion that she was a jazz singer. She told writer A. James Liska: 'I don't know why people call me a jazz singer, I guess people associate me with jazz because I was raised in it, from way back. I'm not putting jazz down, but I'm not a jazz singer. Betty Bebop (Carter) is a jazz singer, because that's all she does... I've recorded all kinds of music, but (to them) I'm either a jazz singer or a blues singer. I can't sing a blues – just a right-out blues – but I can put the blues in whatever I sing. I might sing "Send In the Clowns" and I might stick a little bluesy part in it, or any song. What I want to do, music-wise, is all kinds of music that I like, and I like all kinds of music...'

At times Vaughan built astonishingly baroque edifices which contrast so dramatically with the spare minimalism of Billie Holiday that they have generated difficulties for some jazz audiences, difficulties that prevented some from taking her fully to their hearts during the central period of her career. Nevertheless, throughout her career there have been countless recorded instances of her skills as a jazz singer. At times, there is a wholly misleading air of ease – as if no effort is involved in creating jewels of musical excellence. For example, in 1961 she recorded some songs for public service radio programmes. Using her regular bass player and drummer of the time, Richard Davis and Percy Brice, with Roland Hanna on piano, she sang with uncontrived relaxation and easy swing, setting down excellent interpretations of several songs including, 'You're Blasé', 'Over the Rainbow' (another of her favourites), 'How Long Has This Been Going On?', 'Poor Butterfly' and, of course, 'Summertime' and 'Tenderly'. Although a one-off occasion, with no expectation that these recordings would ever be heard again after their first broadcast, they are all artistic gems. When rediscovered and issued on CD by Hindsight in the mid-1990s they were proof, if needed, that for any singer of worth there is no such thing as coasting or below par performance.

Discussing Vaughan's professionalism with Leslie Gourse, her biographer, her accompanist in the 1980s, pianist Mike Wofford, said: 'I never heard her complain once about the weather, or about feeling depressed, or about her voice not being quite right. She never apologized to audiences for her having a cold, or if her throat didn't feel good, as so many singers did. She was an old-school professional. She never made excuses. The only things that bothered her were bad lighting or sound systems. She was always on time; she never needed anyone to hold a curtain for her unless something happened beyond her control.'

Back in the late 1950s, alongside her commercially slanted recordings for Mercury, Vaughan had recorded for the label's jazz subsidiary,

EmArcy. There is little doubt that her star was continuing to rise both as a jazz singer and as a hugely popular recording artist. In the latter guise, she had hits duetting with Billy Eckstine, 'Passing Strangers' and 'Broken-hearted Melody'. Among her jazz sides were several with leading jazzmen, including superb sets with Clifford Brown and with Cannonball Adderley, and two outstanding live albums, at Chicago's Mister Kelly's and London House. These and her Roulette recordings of the 1960s demonstrate her effortless mastery. Yet despite her undoubted popularity in both fields, she made very few formal recordings during the late 1960s. Enquiring into rumours that her absence from the recording studios was the result of excessive financial demands by her manager, Leonard Feather asked her, 'Isn't it more logical to assume that you owe your public a few albums? If you just recorded for AFTRA scale, wouldn't that have been better than not being on record at all?' Vaughan replied, 'I believe so. I guess it was a mistake.' However, Vaughan told Feather, 'Negotiations are going on now; I should be back in the studios before the year's out. I can hardly wait to start again. In fact, it'll be like starting all over again.'

Indeed, early in the 1970s she was back in the studios recording for both the pop market and as a jazz singer and was a regular performer at many international jazz festivals. By the 1980s her appearance at any venue, club or concert hall, was, like Fitzgerald, a guarantee of SRO attendance, be it Carnegie Hall or the Hollywood Bowl. There is, however, a strong possibility that the audience was not the same for the two singers. Even at the height of her late popularity, Vaughan was never quite as accessible as Fitzgerald insofar as the mass audience was concerned. Thanks to certain albums where the material is closely related, it is possible to suggest reasons for this. Like Fitzgerald, Vaughan recorded albums dedicated to the music of some of the great songwriters of American popular music – *Sarah Vaughan Sings George Gershwin* (1955), *The Rodgers and Hart Songbook* (1958) and *Duke Ellington Songbook One* (1979), the last for Norman Granz's Pablo label. There is also an album of Irving Berlin songs she recorded in 1957 with Billy Eckstine.

Listening to these albums, it is noticeable that for Vaughan the songs are a point of departure for her talent whereas Fitzgerald bends her talent much more to the demands of the composers. While both approaches are wholly acceptable, it is plain that for the non-jazz listener Fitzgerald's way is more likely to meet with approval. It needs no understanding of the special ways of a jazz improviser, the using of a song as raw material to be shaped into a personal statement. For the jazz audience, it is equally apparent that Vaughan's way is kin to the manner in which an instrumentalist might chose to perform these songs, Fitzgerald's way being correspondingly less original and creative. Of course, these comments must be seen in relation to how the singers, and their producers, chose to direct their performances on these particular occasions. In one sense, Fitzgerald's choice seems to have been the wiser inasmuch as her Songbook recordings not only attracted the popular audience but met with (occasionally grudging) acceptance by jazz fans. Vaughan's albums were relatively overlooked by the pop audience and were also less than enthusiastically received by the jazzers who, perhaps misguided by the album titles, saw them as a deliberately commercial move. Had they listened to them, they would undoubtedly have realized that this was not entirely true.

Vaughan died in 1990 after a short last illness although her health had troubled her for several years during which she often suffered serious breathing difficulties.

*   *   *

For all the marked differences in their approach to their material and the sound of their voices, there are some areas in which Vaughan and Fitzgerald come interestingly close to one another: the blues, scat and star status. For neither singer are the blues an integral part of either style or repertoire. Fitzgerald made an unequivocal declaration on the subject: 'I'm not a blues singer', but she could and occasionally did essay the blues with conviction. Similarly, Vaughan could and sometimes did sing the blues well, but she too was rooted in a different musical culture to which the blues were peripheral. Indeed, in a Leonard Feather Blindfold Test for *Metronome* in 1947, she listened to Bessie Smith's 'Young Woman's Blues', failed to recognize the singer and declared, 'I have absolutely no feeling for this.'

When it comes to scat, both could demonstrate a quite remarkable skill. In most of the songs she sang on record Vaughan used the technique sparingly but with extraordinary facility. For Fitzgerald, when the mood was upon her, scat was an opportunity to display astonishing inventiveness and startlingly agile and sustained vocal technique.

As to their status as stars, although their early years were spent in different musical atmospheres, Fitzgerald a true child of the swing era, Vaughan a child of bebop, both swiftly transcended the implicit limitations of these backgrounds. Their appeal to the wider audience, coming swiftly for Fitzgerald, not so readily for Vaughan, was earned through careful assessment of the potential for their careers based upon intrinsic qualities of voice and technique, and upon the ability to move comfortably between jazz and pop and back again without breaking faith with or testing to breaking point the acceptance of either audience.

What is remarkable about them both is that they achieved superstar status early enough in their lives to enjoy the benefits (although it must be said that Vaughan never had a Norman Granz in her life and instead suffered financially at the hands of a succession of less gifted managers, to some of whom she was married). They emerged from backgrounds that spanned swing era popularity, bebop's birth pangs and the singers' revolution of the 1950s. During this period there was an inbuilt if subconscious acceptance of jazz by audiences and consequently a willingness by the music industry to promote these artists. This willingness no longer exists and in its absence it is hard to see future singers achieving superstardom without being forced to defect from jazz. Given their commitment, today's jazz singers are unlikely to choose stardom.

The fact that Fitzgerald and Vaughan, along with Holiday, are the female singers usually cited as influences is obviously a result of their special skills and talent. Less obvious is why Carmen McRae and Betty Carter are not held in equal regard.

*   *   *

Although similarities are evident in the early careers of Carmen McRae and Betty Carter, the directions they took differed greatly. Through these differences they ranged across the spectrum of jazz singing from McRae's sometimes almost straight ballad singing to Carter's customarily uncompromising jazz improvisation. During their careers, each expressed admiration for the other but, as the years passed, some mutual antipathy emerged.

A measure of uncertainty hangs over their exact dates of birth. At the time of her death, McRae, the elder, was generally stated to have been born in 1920. Carter is usually said to have been born in 1930.

McRae was born in New York City to Jamaican-born parents and was raised in a middle-class community, attending Julia Richman High School in Manhattan where for five years she studied piano. 'I could have been a very good pianist,' she told Barbara Gardner in a 1962 *down beat* interview. But her parents were anxious that she should have a stable life and persuaded her against a career in music. Instead, she took a secretarial course, then worked for the government in Washington, DC, before returning to New York and beginning a double life: secretary by day, club singer and pianist by night.

Carter was born Lillie Mae Jones in Flint, Michigan, into a very religious family. While she was still a child the family moved to Detroit where her father became musical director of the Chapel Hill Baptist Church choir. 'I was an average child in school,' she says, 'but I was never interested in anything besides my music.' She studied piano at the Detroit Conservatory of Music but her listening was mostly to visiting jazz musicians and soon she was singing in Detroit clubs. In 1946 Carter entered and won an amateur talent contest at Detroit's Paradise Theater, singing 'The Man I Love', a song which she later declared she never sang again after that night.

McRae might also have entered a talent contest in New York, possibly at the famous Apollo Theater in 1939. That same year McRae met two important influences on her musical life, Irene Eadie and Billie Holiday.

Eadie was a bandleader in Chicago but gave up her career when she married pianist Teddy Wilson. She helped with Wilson's career and also began writing songs, some of which were written especially for Billie Holiday, among them 'Some Other Spring'. (After her divorce from Wilson she remarried and her music was published under the name Irene Kitchings.) Eadie and writer Helen Oakley Dance introduced Carmen McRae to Holiday, and Eadie might well have lent assistance to the young woman in the writing of a song, 'Dream of Life', which Holiday recorded in 1939. The meeting with Holiday was important to McRae: 'The bud of my ambition to be a singer opened up under Billie's approach – her penchant for taking the ordinary and illuminating it...' Her admiration of Billie led to a period during which she copied her both vocally and physically. In time these imitative characteristics disappeared as her own personality showed through but she always retained Holiday's awareness of and concern for the lyrics of a song. Lyrics, McRae has stated unequivocally, come first because 'you can always improvise on the melody. If the melody ain't too hip, you can always make it hip, if you're a jazz singer.' That she thought of herself as a jazz singer is unquestioned and she never regarded the label as a handicap; indeed she thought it helped establish her role in the eyes of an audience. 'They know when they walk into the club what to expect – I hope – and jazz is it; that's what I do, and that's what I'll always do...'

In 1944 McRae was offered, and accepted, a job with Benny Carter's big band. The following year she sang with Count Basie and Earl Hines and the year after that with Mercer Ellington's band, where she spent eighteen months. Whatever influence these associations might have had, they appear to have been minor. In later years McRae would refer to them only in passing, if she referred to them at all. What was important to her was when she worked for herself and not for another leader. Thus, 1948 became the year her career really got under way when she was hired as a fill-in pianist-singer at Chicago's Archway supper club. She went in for two weeks, borrowing money from the club owner to pay her admission dues to the union and to rent a piano on which she could hastily learn new material. The engagement lasted seventeen weeks and McRae was on her way, singing all over Chicago and in neighbouring towns.

During this same period, the mid-1940s, Carter was also singing in clubs, in her case around Detroit, where she heard and met some major figures of bebop. She was heard by Dizzy Gillespie, who brought his big band to Detroit's El Cino club. On occasion, Carter sang with the band during its engagement; through this she was hired by the club and thus was on hand when the Charlie Parker quintet came into town. She also sang with this band, which included at the time Miles Davis, Duke Jordan and Max Roach. 'That's how I really got started.'

For all her predilection for bebop ('All of us kids were in a bebop groove. We didn't like swing'), Carter then joined Lionel Hampton, a star of the swing era and currently leading an r&b big band. By now she had dropped her given and family names and was known professionally as Lorene Carter. Her stint with Hampton was fraught with conflict. She liked bebop, he did not. He called her 'Betty Bebop' and regularly fired her, often because she insisted on telling him that she preferred Gillespie's band to his. In time, Carter dropped Lorene and kept the first half of the name

Hampton called her. For all their differences, the time she spent with Hampton was valuable in that it allowed her to develop a stage presence and to begin to understand how to relate to an audience. Also, Hampton's lead alto saxophonist, Bobby Plater, taught her how to arrange music.

She left Hampton in 1951 to take a residency at the Apollo Bar in Harlem. It was around this time that Billie Holiday heard her, telling Max Jones, 'I love her. She's really got something. On the slow tunes her diction's bad – that's the onliest fault I've got to find. I think she's crazy – she can scat like Leo Watson... Betty's five years ahead of her time.' During the remainder of the 1950s she worked extensively, sometimes in New York, sometimes on tour, and made her first record albums under her own name: *Betty Carter* in 1955, *Out There* in 1958 and *The Modern Sound of Betty Carter* in 1960. The following year she sang on an album with Ray Charles.

In the 1950s Carmen McRae was also in New York. Her experience gained in Chicago had helped her develop her confidence but at first she could find little work, settling for the job of intermission pianist at Minton's, the club that had been one of the two principal New York venues where bebop emerged in the previous decade. (During the 1940s she had been briefly married to Kenny Clarke, the 'father' of bop drumming.) In 1953, however, she struck out as a solo singer and by the following year was attracting serious critical and public attention. She won *down beat*'s poll as Best New Female Singer and looked all set to make a big break-through. Curiously, she was frequently compared to Sarah Vaughan during these years, usually unfavourably. McRae never made any pretence at not admiring the other singer, but listening to their recordings of those years it is hard to hear any obvious similarities. True, there were some resemblances in their careers and backgrounds (even more than with Carter) but their singing styles have very little in common.

In 1955 McRae appeared at a Carnegie Hall concert (coincidentally singing 'Yardbird Suite' while not far away Charlie Parker collapsed and died that same evening) and was glowingly written up by critics. As a result, she was signed by Joe Glaser's agency and began to record extensively. Her albums for Decca were angled towards the wider public and included some outstanding ballad interpretations. Of particular note are *By Special Request*, *Torchy*, both 1955, *Blue Moon*, 1956, and *Carmen for Cool Ones*, 1957.

Despite the success of their early albums, both McRae and Carter found the going hard from the mid-1960s onwards. The popular music business was in turmoil with the advent of rock-orientated pop and there was little room for singers of their kind. As Carter was to say of the jazz scene to W. Royal Stokes in 1977: '[It] is not what people think it is, because we're putting the jazz tag on a lot of different kinds of music... You can't just go into the studio and do jazz, you gotta do jazz-rock ... or jazz-soul... So the young kids today don't have a real distinctive picture of what jazz really is...' Carter and McRae refused to compromise, preferring to stick to the musical principles by which they had fashioned their careers so far.

Among these principles was the firm belief in the need to be professional, to strive for originality and not settle for copying others. These guidelines were not ideal qualities for gaining commercial success in a period when amateurism was applauded and careers were openly modelled upon stylistic predecessors. Neither singer was unaware of this. As Carter remarked in an interview in *New Republic*, she had resisted the temptations of commercialism even though it was an attitude that helped drive a wedge between herself and her husband of the time. 'I couldn't give up what I was doing to go for the money,' she said.

At the end of the 1960s, Carter had decided that making records for others was no way to progress her career along the lines she wanted. She regarded an album for Atlantic, *Round Midnight*, as the worst thing she had ever done and felt that the company's refusal to allow her to work with arranger Oliver Nelson was a significant contributory factor. After that, she was determined to be her own record producer and in 1971 set up her own label, Bet-Car. She began attracting renewed critical acclaim including excellent notices for her concerts and theatrical performances from critics such as John S. Wilson in the New York *Times* and Mark Jacobson in *Village Voice*. It was to Jacobson that she expressed some of her feelings about popular success and the price it demands from an artist: 'Years back,' Jacobson wrote, 'she realized she would rather play with a combo than stand in front of it. She's wary of the syndrome which makes millionaires of singers and leaves musicians in the pits. She decided it was, for the most part, musicians who are responsible for the creation of jazz, and resolved to take her lumps with them rather than go to Vegas and wear chiffon... In jazz independence has its price and Betty's paying it.'

But by the end of the 1970s Carter's independence was paying off. The 1977 and 1978 Newport In New York jazz festivals earned her acclaim both public and critical and she was mentioned in *Time* and *Newsweek*. From the 1980s onwards she toured extensively, appearing before sell-out audiences all around the world and seeing her self-produced albums garner praise. One, *The Audience with Betty Carter*, received a Grammy nomination and an award from the National Association of Independent Record Distributors. By now, Carter had full control of her artistic life and it showed in her performances. She dominated the stage, whether of club or concert hall, festival or theatre, striding from side to side like a recently caged tiger, manipulating her audiences not for effect but through her artistry. Her control over her environment was impressive. As the young British singer Claire Martin comments, 'From Carter I've learned about taking charge on the stage.'

McRae also exercised control over her audience but she did it differently. Majestically still, demanding attention and respect through her bearing and demeanour, she consistently proved that this attention and respect were well deserved. What she offered her audiences were performances of songs which manage, in the words of *down beat*'s John Tynan, 'to give the constant impression that she's never wrong in the interpretation and delivery of any song'. However firm her control over audiences and material might be, her grip upon the business aspect of her career lacked the same firmness. Helen Merrill reflected on this in conversation with Don Waterhouse: 'In the mid-1970s it was quite normal for people to take advantage of artists. I was sharing a cab with Carmen McRae and I said, "You must be getting nice royalties now." And she said, "Royalties? I never got a royalty in my life; in fact, I just had to hock my ring to pay for my mortgage." Well, that changed for her later in life, as it did for me, but in those days we were accustomed to being ripped off.'

McRae's close relationship with her audience was clear. Although she insisted, 'I have to sing for myself', this was meant in the sense of personal conviction; as she told Arthur Taylor: 'I want to please the people who have taken the time to come and hear me... I sing for the musicians too ... so it's really a combination of musicians, myself and audience.'

In fact McRae could be demanding of her accompanying musicians: 'Accompanying someone cannot be explained by a singer to a pianist. He either knows what to do or he doesn't. An accompanist and a guy who can play the piano are two different things... A guy must really love to do it. He cannot do it because he has nothing else to do.' Carter, too, could be demanding of accompanists as pianist Benny Green recalled in speaking of his time in her band: 'It was a great education for me, she basically took me up from ground level. I had been working but I didn't know much about accompanying a singer. Betty, besides giving me such great on-the-job training, really preached individuality to me, the importance of finding my own sound, and not just becoming a better imitator of my influences.' Green is not the only young musician to serve part of his jazz apprenticeship with Carter. Among pianists alone are Mulgrew Miller, Stephen Scott, Cyrus Chestnut and Jacky Terrasson. What is interesting about Carter's relationship with young musicians is that she doesn't wait for them to come to her, she goes out looking for them. She searches them out at the annual Jazz Educators' Convention and every April hosts the 'Betty Carter Jazz Ahead' gathering at the Majestic Theater in Brooklyn, a week-long cavalcade of would-be jazz musicians eager to hear and be heard by the diva.

Curiously, Carter's assistance to the young appears to stop with accompanists. She seems less prepared to assist and work with young singers. Nevertheless she is aware of the difficulties facing jazz singers: 'Before Ella and Sarah you had to sing the melody straight. They opened it up for others to follow individual styles of their own.' But she warned, 'You have to pay dues, you have to spend some time learning the music. It's a learning craft... Jazz is spontaneous – it's on the job that it happens. It's not something you set up and do each show. You have your theme but every chorus it's different. You try to make it different because this makes you learn. If you are set in one way and you as an individual can't change that then you are not qualified to become a jazz singer – to be a jazz singer – if you can't improvise on the spot under all kinds of circumstances, maybe the piano player goofs, the changes are wrong – you're supposed to handle that without falling apart. Your musicianship is supposed to get you over that little tragedy.'

Over the years both McRae and Carter acquired reputations for being difficult. Certainly both were outspoken and uncompromisingly honest and both knew exactly what was right for them and didn't hesitate to say so. Some promoters, club owners and record producers took such things as personal criticism of their ability to know what was best for the singers. Quite clearly, being 'difficult' was simply another way of describing women who were committed professionals.

This professionalism shows in everything they did and in particular the care they lavished upon recording sessions. When listening to McRae's recordings of ballads, it is instantly apparent that she took to heart that quality she learned from Billie Holiday, that lyrics have enormous value. Many of McRae's interpretations of the great standards are unrivalled by anything that went before or that has come afterwards. Indeed, an argu-ment could be sustained that McRae rather than Ella Fitzgerald might well have been a better choice for the Songbook series. Certainly, there is often much greater emotional depth in McRae's work. On ballads, and especially some of those she recorded for Decca in the mid-1950s, where commercial considerations were obviously in the minds of the producers and for which much of the backing is somewhat overblown, her voice echoes with mature wisdom.

McRae was then in her mid-thirties while Fitzgerald, who began the Songbook cycle in 1956 when she was approaching forty, still retained a girlish timbre in her voice. McRae sings some of those same classic songs with a controlled but unmistakably optimistic vigour. Her phrasing, unde-niably that of a jazz singer, stays close enough to the accepted norm to accommodate the non-jazz listener for whom they were intended while her diction is astonishingly clear. When she sings ballads in the company of jazz musicians, such as on the 1958 *Birds of a Feather*, arranged by Ralph Burns, where her accompanists include guitarist Mundell Lowe and tenor saxophonist Ben Webster, her lyrical interpretation and her elegant phrasing and unhurried swing are at least on par with that of almost any other singer in jazz or popular music. Take an example, the Hoagy Carmichael-Johnny Mercer song, 'Skylark'; her vocal line rarely strays far from the written melody but the few small changes she does make are perfectly placed and clearly demonstrate the extent to which she was attuned to the nuances of jazz. The manner in which she bends a note to launch Webster's solo is worthy of careful study by anyone who seeks to sing jazz. Indeed, this example will serve to enlighten anyone who wishes to understand the difference between a popular singer, however good, and one who is a true jazz singer. The young British singer Tina May expressed her admiration for McRae's artistry: 'I absolutely adore her and I have great admiration for her integrity. I really think that she deserved more exposure. Ella had her hits and Sarah was most successful in combining jazz and commercial work, whereas Carmen did very little commercial work. I don't think she was the type of person who could do that. She was probably a more prickly character. I think she did what she did because that was the way she was. She was wonderful.'

When she sings from the non-ballad portion of her repertoire, McRae still retains an inherent melodiousness, never sacrificing innate stylishness for mere effect. The gentle stretching of phrases across bar lines that marks her ballad singing is extended but is still done without effort. There is never any hint of forcing her material to adopt an unwelcome shape. Here, too, as with her ballads, the lyric is always treated with care and respect, always filled with awareness and understanding. In all her work it is not merely that McRae gives the impression of having experienced personally the stories that unfold, but that she wishes to cloak her listeners with the same emotions they evoke in her. 'I love music only when I can communicate with it,' she said. And in turn she found the way to communicate with her audience whether in public or in private through recordings.

There is communication, too, in the work of Betty Carter but it is of a different order to that of Carmen McRae. Nowhere is this more readily apparent than in Carter's treatment of ballads. Although she has a rich and melodious voice, she often chooses to use it for dramatic effect, disregarding the lyrics, sometimes dispensing with them altogether, and she frequently plays intriguing games with the melody line. On songs that have become a regular feature of her repertoire, such as 'Everything I Have Is Yours', she appears to have first dismantled them before reconstructing them more in keeping with her style. For this reason it is not surprising that Carter writes much of her repertoire, a fact that allows her to develop any particular song without fear of offending the more conservative elements in her audience. Her improvisational skills are much more overt than those of McRae and she will spectacularly perform astonishing lyric-less songs which include scat, vocalese and just sounds. Indeed, 'Sounds' is the title of one such number, which she can sustain seemingly endlessly; performances of this song and of 'Movin' On' can last for twenty-five minutes, during which her inventive flow neither hesitates nor weakens.

Carter's zestful attack on up-tempo songs can be overwhelming to the unprepared, and her re-making of standards can also be disturbing. However, once the listener has accepted that Carter's is an original talent in which integrity is as important as unpredictability, it is not hard to accept that while hers might not be the usual way, it is vibrant with inventiveness. And the relationship between singer and audience is reciprocal: 'You can't get any greater feeling than the one I get when I come off the stage and the audience feels what I have done.' Carter thinks deeply about her craft, never taking anything for granted, always seeking to improve. 'I feel deeply about the music because I lived it,' she told Arthur Taylor. 'I haven't prostituted myself, and I'm really proud of it.'

By the 1980s both Carter and McRae had come far from their early struggles and were now able to enjoy the benefits of many years of hard work. But life on the road takes its toll. Betty Carter's marriage ended in divorce, but she had two sons of whom she was very proud. Carmen McRae's second marriage, to bass player Ike Isaacs, ended in divorce as had her first to Kenny Clarke. In 1987 the two singers worked together on an album, *The Carmen McRae-Betty Carter Duets*, but later McRae would wryly observe: 'Betty is very hard to get along with', and when, in 1990, her album *Carmen Sings Monk* was unjustifiably passed over for a Grammy she was wearily disparaging of the selectors and the winners. 'Those people are not interested in what I do,' she told *down beat*. 'I love Ella Fitzgerald, but Ella's voice is not Ella's voice anymore... They even gave one to Betty Carter, and I know I sing better than her.'

Like Carter, McRae thought constantly of the craft of which she was such a master: 'You have to improvise. You have to have something of your own that has to do with that song. And you have to know where you're going when you improvise... A jazz singer is just like a jazz musician. It's all about improvising. It's something in your heart, and something that is you.'

As the 1990s began, the difference in their ages started to show. Carter was still in full cry, singing as well as ever and continuing to pack in audiences. McRae could still pack them in but she was growing tired and had serious breathing problems. In May 1991 she suffered respiratory failure and made no more public performances, but she continued to make records and in 1992 appeared in a television documentary. In October 1994 she suffered a stroke and died the following month.

Notable among the singers Carmen McRae inspired is Carol Sloane, a friend for many years, and McRae's legacy also lives on in the many timeless, possibly unimprovable versions of songs she recorded in her long career.

But what of Betty Carter's legacy? Certainly there is a body of records – not as extensive as McRae's by any means and not as accessible to the general public nor even to many jazz fans – but there is no discernible following within the community of jazz singers.

In 1972 Carter commented at length upon the absence of new young singers coming along in her wake. It is worth quoting in full this part of her long and revealing conversation with Arthur Taylor: 'After me, there are no more jazz singers. What I mean is that there's nobody scaring me to death. No young woman is giving me any trouble when it comes to singing jazz. I'm not even worried about it, and that's a shame. It's sad that there's nobody stepping on my heels so I can look back and say, "I better get myself together because this little girl is singing her thing off." They're all doing what everybody else is doing, and as I'm not doing what everybody else is doing, I'm not even worried. It's a crime that no little singer is back there sockin' it to me in my field. To keep it going, to keep it alive, because I'm not going to live forever. I'm going to die eventually, and I don't want it to die with me, I want it to keep on.'

Carter is still around, still performing her art, but doing so in a manner that is often intimidating and perhaps it is this that makes her such a hard act to follow. That there are singers around with the ability to take her path must surely be self-evident. That hers is a true jazz course is equally clear but it is not the only course. Others are coming up, but alongside, on parallel if different tracks. At the time, however, her remarks were underscored by the fact that the following decade, the 1980s, was a difficult time for jazz singing. Indeed, it was a lean time for jazz in general.

In a sense it was also a time to reflect upon the qualities of Fitzgerald, Vaughan, McRae and Carter and to realize that their like might never again be seen and heard in jazz if only because the forces that had created them no longer existed.

NINE

NICE WORK IF YOU CAN GET IT

I want to reach people and stir their emotions, make them think
of the poetry in their own lives. — *Susannah McCorkle*

By the start of the 1980s jazz singing had come a long way since the first
blues singers emerged in early twentieth-century America and syncopation
caught the imaginations of singers and songwriters. No one could then have
predicted the innovations of Louis Armstrong, the manner in which jazz
inflections would pervade popular music through the singing of Bing
Crosby and Connee Boswell. No one could have foreseen Billie Holiday, or
the superstardom of Ella Fitzgerald and Sarah Vaughan. And even the most
imaginative seer would never have forecast scat. As for the approach to
jazz singing made by singers such as Betty Carter – to predict her as a
logical descendant of the likes of Bessie Smith or Ethel Waters would have
needed an imagination as unfettered as that of the most questing members
of the avant-garde.

Yet for all the changes, the rich diversity, the many talented singers
around, and the seemingly endless potential, the 1980s were difficult years.
With hindsight it is possible to see that the roots of the malaise lay in
dramatic changes in popular music that had appeared in the 1960s and
1970s.

The rock and pop explosion had greatly affected the music industry.
It was more than just the form, music and the style of performance that
changed. Attitudes of recording company executives, media moguls, and
the record- and ticket-buying public were all affected. Even the way in
which records were produced changed.

The 32-bar popular song, for more than four decades the foundation
upon which so much music was built, was swept aside by rock. In its place,
some groups, such as the Rolling Stones, performed songs in the 12-bar
blues format, but increasingly a great deal of the new music had no regular
structure at all. Groups such as the Beatles, who had had no formal music
training and who chose not to refer back to earlier forms, heard songs in
their heads and performed them in whatever structure they happened to
be. Similarly, time signatures did not conform to a pattern; indeed, the time
signature might change within a single song. Whereas the 32-bar song was
usually written with no particular performer in mind and could be picked
up and sung readily by any singer with an understanding of the formal
structure, the new songs were written often by singers who expected them
to be sung by no one but themselves. An inevitable side effect of this was
that the interlacing of the jazz and popular strands, for so many years a
feature of popular music, all but disappeared. That jazz musicians would
be less amenable to the new music is easy to understand. There were few
ways the jazz improviser could gain inspiration from, and stamp his own

personality upon, a music which jazz pianist Oscar Peterson described as having 'no holes in it'.

The exasperation felt by jazz musicians and others accustomed to replenishing their art from the popular American songbook is explained by pianist-arranger-singer-songwriter Dave Frishberg: 'I feel strongly about what's happened to the pop song, I don't really know how to describe it or explain it except maybe to say that it somehow doesn't seem right. It doesn't seem plausible to me that the American popular song could evolve from Victor Herbert through Jerome Kern through Irving Berlin through George Gershwin through Cole Porter through Johnny Mercer through Harold Arlen through Frank Loesser through Allan Jay Lerner and wind up with Neil Diamond!

'It just doesn't make sense to me. I do understand and accept the fact that music must change and that old music traditions must be allowed to die but I think they should be allowed to die a natural death. I have a feeling that somehow the older musical traditions of previous generations were deliberately kept from the American public at one point and a substitute musical culture was deliberately slipped into the media mainstream and we suddenly found ourselves with a completely new musical culture. It's not to say that great art hasn't arisen and will continue to arise from the new musical culture, but whatever happened to that old tradition of American song writing? All that remains are Johnny Mandel, Alan and Marilyn Bergman, Michel Legrand. But that's really no longer the mainstream of music, is it? And, of course, I must remember too that the group of people that populates the music business today is qualitatively different from the group of people that were in the business when I was attracted to it. A different type of person's attracted to the business today. A typical person who's in today's music business is not only an instrumentalist and a singer but he's also often a songwriter and he's a lyric writer and he's more than likely an expert sound engineer, he's somewhat of a recording executive, he's got some accounting expertise too, I think.'

The problem described by Frishberg has resulted in a static source of material. No longer is the great repository of popular songs replenished, and it is revitalized only by performance. And hardly ever do new popular songs have the necessary qualities of durability. This is not simply because they are disposable elements of a throw-away society – after all, the song-writers of the past were not writing for posterity. They thought that what they did would be forgotten by the time next week's song was published, or next month's show opened on Broadway, or another movie was churned out by Hollywood. Yet their songs did live on. But who today can remember more than a tiny handful of the songs written for the smash-hit musical shows of the past quarter-century? Today's songsmiths seem not to have the same facility or inclination for memorable melodies and lyrics as did their counterparts of the past. Consider, for example, how many songs from 1930s Broadway shows are still sung more than half a century later.

In George and Ira Gershwin's *Girl Crazy* alone there were 'Bidin' My Time', 'But Not for Me', 'Embraceable You' and 'I Got Rhythm'. Or the 1934 show *Anything Goes*, with songs by Cole Porter: 'You're the Top', 'Anything Goes', 'I Get a Kick out of You', 'Blow, Gabriel, Blow' and 'The Gypsy in Me'. It is hard to imagine that more than a handful of songs from all the most successful shows from Broadway and West End musicals of the last twenty-five years put together will still be around in 2065. And almost none of these new songs is constructed in a form that lends itself to harmonic improvisation. Added to which there is a conscious effort by many of today's stage songwriters to keep their material away from anyone seeking to personalize it in a way that conflicts with their original conception.

Just as the form of the music altered, and the business aspects of entertainment changed, so too did performing styles. Not just aurally but also visually, things were radically different. Gone were the tuxedoed and evening-gowned singers decorously presenting songs for listeners; in their place were flamboyantly costumed individuals and groups cavorting across stages already half buried under a mountain of electrical amplification and lighting equipment, cameras and smoke machines, all of which demanded people to look rather than listen. The desire for aural separation and articulation was superseded by a preference for blanket sound. No longer was it possible to understand a lyric by listening to the singer, now it was necessary to print the lyric in the programme notes or on album covers. Mick Jagger told *Rolling Stone* magazine: 'I read an article by Fats Domino which has really influenced me. He said, "You should never sing the lyrics out very clearly."'

It was not only the groups that were different, the new solo stars also adopted a different approach. Dave Frishberg again: 'Many, many singers are more interested in their image than they are in the songs they are singing. They look for things that show off the voice, or display their virtuosity, or their personality. That's the nature of the business. Some of the people it attracts aren't necessarily interested in music. It seems to me that some are entering it as an alternative to another very high-paying jackpot profession. It's almost as if the kid today who contemplates getting into the music business will say, "Well, I think I'll either go to medical school and become a physician, or maybe go into corporate or tax law, or I may become a professional athlete, or maybe I'll become a musician and go into the music business".'

Popular music has never been free of performers who lacked artistic integrity but it had now arrived at a point where the casual camaraderie of classless amateurism begun in the mid-1950s was not merely acceptable as musical entertainment but was actively encouraged. A good voice was no more a necessity than in jazz, but in much of 1980s pop neither was musical merit. This kind of music making could be learned like any other routine assembly-line job and inevitably some found shortcuts, a winning smile or sexy pout sometimes counting for more than know-how. Studio equipment, engineers and professional backing singers can make anyone sound acceptable. Where the singer did have real talent the result could be highly rewarding, musically as well as financially, although, too often, flamboyance was seen as a satisfactory alternative to true worth. There was no shortage of performers offering pale reflections of earlier pop idols such as Elvis Presley, Little Richard and Jimi Hendrix. The vast amount of money generated by rock, good or bad, not only made record companies rich, it also blinded the industry to intrinsic worth, the value of understatement, the subtle potential of emotional involvement – all of which are important elements in good singing.

Audiences seemed not to notice, or if they did, they appeared not to care. The experience of being at a pop concert often had more to do with making a social or political statement than simply to listen to music. To be at Shea Stadium in 1965 or at Woodstock in 1969 or at Wembley Stadium in 1985 was what counted, not the music. Since the 1960s pop music had increasingly become a metaphor of the times. Rock and pop singers were not unaware of the attitude their audiences had towards the music. The Beatles were asked: 'How do you rate your music?' To which they replied, 'We're not good musicians. Just adequate.' This prompted the question: 'Then why are you so popular?' Their answer must have gladdened the hearts of many in the industry: 'Maybe people like adequate music.'

Not that mere adequacy meant it was all easy. Recording sessions in the pop music business could be staggeringly hard work. In the 1930s Bing Crosby might have strolled into the studio and recorded six sides without taking off his hat; a latter-day pop or rock band, however, would commonly take months to prepare an album. Mike Campbell aimed briefly for the wider pop audience and asked Tim Hauser of Manhattan Transfer to produce an album for him: 'Cheryl Bentyne and Janis Siegel sang background, a real pop kind of thing. It was exciting and turned out well and although we didn't get a deal it was great experience to see how Tim worked. It was an excruciatingly difficult experience doing the vocals; I never got to sing the songs through, recording them basically line by line. We did about eight takes of each line and after we did the songs we would sit down at a console with the engineer and commence to put the vocal together. For example, we might like the first two lines from Take 4 and the next four lines from Take 6, next three from Take 1. That's how we compiled the vocal, the guitar solos, the sax solos. It was extraordinarily difficult, time-consuming work and basically the way pop people record. I hated it. The vocals took about three to four hours per song and it is difficult to keep your energy going and your focus together for that length of time. It was physically and mentally exhausting. When I brought the result home my wife said, "Sounds nice, all the notes perfect, but is it the way you want to record for the rest of your life?" I hated that question because I knew I couldn't do it. To me it really wasn't making music. To me, making music means people playing together and communicating.'

More and more young men and women became disposable transients on the music industry's conveyor belt. Unparalleled adulation was poured on those who made it to the top, however brief that stay might be. Of all the characteristics of western society in the last quarter of the twentieth century, the one most inimical to the maintenance of standards has been the need for immediate success and instant gratification. The standards of performance that marked the efforts of earlier popular singing stars such as Jo Stafford, Frank Sinatra and Peggy Lee, were now largely ignored by the music industry. Of course there were, and still are, singers in the rock and pop fields who are skilled and thoroughly trained; Basia and Gino Vannelli are two who come to mind. All too often, however, the industry spawns singers whose pretentiousness in performance attempts to obscure their inadequacies and lack of taste.

Increasingly, what the ears heard was insufficient and soon that blanket sound was supported by the crutch of visuals. Concerts became sound and light spectaculars and Top 40 albums required a high-quality accompanying video if they were to rise in the charts. In some instances the video was more important than the music; poor songs and singers were rescued by imaginative film directors with million-dollar budgets. The art of singing indeed had lost its way.

Meantime, some jazz musicians, viewing what was happening to the music industry, reacted radically and in some cases apparently in desperation. In the late 1960s and 1970s there was a move into free-form jazz which posed new and often insurmountable problems for singers. Reflecting on that period, British jazz singer Tina May observes: 'They hit a bad time in the 1970s when it went free. I think many people who had a little dabble with it at that time are now desperately embarrassed about it. I think we all need some structure. It's okay if you specialize and there are some who are absolutely wonderful at it, such as saxophonist Evan Parker. I could listen to him all day – but it is his specialty. I think it takes a special person to really excel at free form and literally grasp inspiration from the air with no chord sequence beneath it. I'd say free form did jazz a disservice and it's time for that image to be dispelled.'

And so, while pop and jazz, each in its own way, went in search of sound for its own sake rather than music with structure and form, many jazz and jazz-orientated singers languished in comparative obscurity. Record companies dispensed with their services and some went out of the business while massive amounts of record company money were ploughed into promoting hot pop properties. Record sales and corresponding incomes rocketed for the 'star' and talented artists could not fail to be aware of the inequity. 'It can be very hard on singers, very damaging to the ego,' Susannah McCorkle remarks. 'You see terrible singers making tens of millions of dollars and that's sad.'

In time, some younger jazz singers began to adopt and adapt many aspects of rock and pop music, the music of the years in which their musical tastes were formed, but for other singers, whose careers were already under way in the 1960s and early 1970s, it was hard to stay afloat in a world that seemed to be increasingly indifferent to what they were doing. Nevertheless, some of them kept on singing and continued to refine their styles. A tiny handful retained their popularity; Ella Fitzgerald, for instance, was even more successful in these years and in the 1980s had over a hundred different albums available. Others, like Sarah Vaughan, Mel Tormé and Carmen McRae, made a living, but many had to seek alternative means of survival, singing only when an occasional opportunity arose, or maybe singing in a more commercial setting until, they hoped, the bad times would end.

Persistence paid off for Tony Bennett. An exceptional singer of popular standards, over the years Bennett gradually gained credence in some jazz circles. Despite a highly successful first twenty years on the popular scene, he went a long time without a recording contract although continuing to work before capacity crowds. In the 1980s, his style began to be more overtly jazz-influenced than in earlier years although he had declared, 'My biggest influence was Bing Crosby. He was a pop singer who sang jazz. I'm not a jazz singer.' While many jazz singers greatly admire Bennett, this self-judgment is one with which most would agree. Bennett spoke to George Reid of the changes in the industry and in particular how, in the early years of his career, producers took their cue from audience responses: 'Whoever got the most applause was based on talent ... the public knew it, they heard it. Since the mid-1970s, the age of the computer started entering into it, and all of a sudden ... they started saying, "We don't need to ask the public anymore, what we'll do is get the largest group demographically and work on those people and then we'll just programme them and market them." So the performers, even though they look wonderful on television, they are inexperienced performers.'

More than any other male singer, Mel Tormé found the right balance between singing jazz and maintaining a high profile with the wider audience. Tormé first sang professionally when he was four years old, singing two choruses of 'You're Driving Me Crazy' with the popular Coon-Sanders Nighthawks band at the Blackhawk Restaurant in Chicago in 1930. Two years later he was singing and playing piano and drums in vaudeville, and at eight was acting on radio. In the mid-1940s he played drums with the Chico Marx band where he also sang and arranged. In California, he teamed up with a vocal group from Los Angeles City College who asked him to be their lead singer. The group, renamed the Mel-Tones, were so successful that they broadcast and recorded with Artie Shaw's band, making a very successful version of 'What Is This Thing Called Love?' At the age of twenty-one, having already appeared in films and on television, Tormé decided to strike out as a single. He was also writing songs, a notable early success being 'The Christmas Song', recorded by Nat King Cole in 1946.

Tormé's admiration of other singers is wide-ranging although few if any of the singers he cites as favourites appear to have had a direct influence on his own style: 'I admire Bing Crosby and Sinatra and Billie Holiday and Ella and Joe Williams and Ethel Waters. But I also admire Bessie Smith and Leo Watson and Bon Bon Tunnell and Connee Boswell. And Harold Mills of the Mills Brothers and Patti Andrews of the Andrews Sisters. Also, people you don't ordinarily think of as singers, like Buddy Rich and Johnny Mercer and Bobby Sherwood and Woody Herman and Ray Nance. I loved Ivie Anderson and June Richmond... Helen Forrest may have been the best big band singer. And I love Ray Charles and Joe Turner and Helen Humes. And Trummy Young and every horn player who turns to singing. They just never miss.' For all this apparently blanket acceptance of just about all the major singers, Tormé has some surprising reservations. 'I can't say I was crazy about Mildred Bailey. The little voice never seemed to fit such a big woman. And Jack Teagarden's singing bothered me. He had a loose-lipped, going-to-sleep quality. And the later Louis hurt my ears.'

Tormé's own late singing showed how his voice had darkened with age, becoming a rich and fluid baritone. In a succession of concerts and records in the late 1980s and 1990s, many with pianist George Shearing, after a lifetime of singing Tormé not only showed that his star was far from waning but he also continued to uphold the qualities of the great songs of the 1930s and 1940s. He also found personal revitalization from the attitude of audiences in the 1990s: '... it affords me the opportunity to get up every morning and do something that I absolutely love. This is a time in our country where there is a renewed appreciation in music, especially our musical heritage and the standards...'

Another survivor whose career began in the 1940s is Dardanelle. In those days, mostly playing piano and vibes, she led a trio which included guitarist Tal Farlow. She attracted the attention of Lionel Hampton with whom she recorded and she also wrote an arrangement for his band to feature Dinah Washington. Hampton later recalled: 'On one occasion when Dinah was ill, I asked Dardanelle to come out of the audience at the Zanzibar and sing "I Should Care" on the broadcast that evening.' Dardanelle began to feature singing more, although it was not from choice: 'When I became part of the professional music marketplace it seemed that if you were a female you were expected to sing, even if you were proficient on an instrument.'

In fact, Dardanelle was more than merely proficient, having been diverted from a planned career as a concert pianist due to childhood poliomyelitis which left her with a weakened left hand. When she first arrived in New York, she was signed by Joe Glaser who had no qualms at promoting as a singer someone who really wanted to play jazz piano. Dardanelle remembers with amusement that Glaser said to someone, '"She plays fine piano but the girl can't sing!" and he went on to book the trio into the Copacabana for a year, and get us recorded by RCA Victor and

Decca.' Dardanelle was aware that she was living through special times: 'To have lived in the era of great singers – the Golden Age of everything – such as Peggy Lee, Nat Cole, Billie Holiday, Jo Stafford, June Christy and the myriad of singers, male and female, who cared about diction and musicianship, has been a cherished part of my life.'

Having survived the pop-drenched 1980s Dardanelle was still playing and singing to receptive audiences in New York and London in the mid-1990s, and finding time to lecture and broadcast in her home state of Mississippi. It has not escaped her that the kind of music she has lived with throughout her lifetime is no longer the common currency of the world of entertainment: 'When singing became a necessity on my recordings and in the venues where I played, I began thinking "good lyrics" – and growing up in the Golden Age of the great songwriters has been a blessing. But I find their qualities lacking in much current music and so very little of it attracts me.'

Joe Glaser's attitude towards Dardanelle carries hints of a long tradition in jazz thinking (or non-thinking) about a woman's role. In the nineteenth century, performing music in public was deemed decidedly unladylike. Opera singers and actresses in the legitimate theatre might just scrape past scrutineers of moral standards, no one else did. As for playing a musical instrument in public, while a little genteel piano playing in private was acceptable, indeed encouraged in some circles, and possibly a discreet strum on a guitar, any other instrument was frowned upon – especially a saxophone, trumpet or trombone! But singing was a different matter, still not actively encouraged in the nineteenth and early twentieth century, but acceptable. For all the radicalism of jazz music, many of society's mores clung on. Through all the years of early jazz it is hard to find many female instrumentalists apart from pianists, but female singers abound. Even as the years passed, old habits died hard and it was not until the 1980s that female instrumentalists began to make an appreciable impact on jazz, although the percentage remained small. The piano is still the principal instrument and singing the occupation for the majority of women in jazz. It does have its up-side, as Claire Martin remarks: 'I don't feel under pressure specifically because I'm a woman singer. If I was a saxophonist perhaps there would be a greater obligation to prove myself.'

There may be a corresponding yet contrary reason why the number of male singers has not grown appreciably in percentage terms. Men have traditionally concealed their emotions in many areas of life, and music is no exception. The overwhelming majority of song writers is male, setting down their emotional thoughts on paper to be performed by others. And some of the most emotional performances in jazz have come from male instrumentalists using, say, a saxophone as both a means of expression and a protective shield. Women, however, are often presented and usually unreservedly accepted as emotionally vulnerable people who can and do publicly address deeply personal concerns such as those upon which so many popular songs are based: love, longing and loss. Whether or not implicitly sexist distinctions such as these are fair and reasonable is another matter.

It is testimony to the qualities of tenacity as well as skill and talent that so many fine singers emerged over the decades. Indeed, it is that quality of determination to overcome an inherently unfair attitude that helped many surmount the fallow years.

Among other singers of great skill and spirit whose careers began in the 1940s were a few in Europe, notably Alice Babs and Rita Reys. Swedish-born Babs made her first impact in the 1940s and 1950s, but had made records before the outbreak of World War Two. After the war she continued to work in a jazz context, including an appearance at the Paris Jazz Fair in 1949. Audiences at the festival must have been intrigued by the contrast between a sophisticated singer such as Babs and the archaic folk-blues of veteran troubadour Huddie 'Leadbelly' Ledbetter who was also on the bill. Babs's clear, true soprano voice lent itself admirably to other song forms and she achieved success in folk and classical music. In 1963 she recorded with Duke Ellington whose admiration for her is evident from his comment: 'Alice Babs is a composer's dream, for with her he can forget all the limitations and just write his heart out.' By the 1980s Babs had retired to Spain, partly on health grounds, but showed her joy in singing to be undiminished when urged to sing at jazz clubs in Spain and at international Ellington conventions.

The Dutch singer Rita Reys was also highly accomplished and a much admired interpreter of ballads. Although best known for her work in Europe, Reys did visit America, working with Art Blakey, Chico Hamilton and others, and elicited praise from Babs Gonzales, who declared unequivocally, 'She swings.' Although in semi-retirement, she continued to make occasional records and in the mid-1990s was still singing and was booked for the North Sea Jazz Festival.

American singers who began to make their names and build reputations in the latter part of the 1950s and who continued into the 1960s and 1970s included Dakota Staton, Lorez Alexandria, Gloria Lynne, Donna Hightower, Della Reese, Salena Jones and Ernestine Anderson. But during the 1980s many singers were forced to seek non-musical work, among them Carol Sloane who carried the torch lit by Carmen McRae.

Sloane made some critically acclaimed records in the 1960s but was gradually sidelined by changing times and took a job as a legal secretary in Raleigh, North Carolina, singing infrequently, until her time came around again as the 1980s ended. She remains philosophical about her years in the wilderness: 'I lived a different life [in the South], amongst sweet wonderful people, and I spent good, productive years there, even though the rest of the world didn't know it.' For all this hiatus in her career, she could later declare: 'My life has been much more than I expected it to be. One of my goals was to meet people who I admired, and I have had that opportunity and have met a great many of the true geniuses of jazz. That has been a very real side benefit. In fact, most of my friends are in the business of making jazz.'

Although her early influences were broad, Sloane's interest in the work of Carmen McRae has shaped her attitude towards her own singing while remaining stylistically independent: 'My influences are pretty much the same as most jazz singers would cite: Billie, Sarah, Ella and Carmen, but Carmen has been the major influence. As soon as I heard her, I began to focus in on her, although I didn't discard the others.' Countering any reasonable expectations of the adverse effect created by her long years as a secretary, Sloane's work in the late 1980s and early 1990s vividly demonstrates her superbly honed skills as a jazz singer of distinction. Whether singing standards, jazz songs, or the music of latter-day writers such as Dave Frishberg, she brings a fresh and original voice to her interpretations: 'When choosing material I am influenced by my vocal range... I know the extent of my range and I adapt my material, not necessarily to meet my needs but it is important to know what keys are proper for them and not get into areas in the song that are outside my range. If it happens over one or two notes you can get away with it but you certainly wouldn't want to do a whole song in the wrong key. Basically my concept has remained the same. I am not a radical singer, I'm not a Nancy Wilson nor a Betty Carter. I am a very straight ahead, honest singer. I don't like frills and nonsense and pretensions and I hope that's not something that comes across in my singing. It couldn't be, because I'm so simple in a way. I have a great respect for the composer so I don't want to tamper with it terribly much.'

When teamed with jazz instrumentalists of the calibre of alto saxophonist Phil Woods, a man not noted for his eagerness to work with singers, Sloane surpasses even her own high standards to deliver swinging performances filled with startling awareness. Sloane's improvisational skills are exceptional and it is this area of the music that most fascinates her: 'It's why I sing this music because I don't really know what is going to happen in, say, the second chorus. I might not know what is going to happen in the first chorus, but the musicians are playing interesting chords and the second chorus usually is where we stretch out a bit and is more improvisational and I find that is more interesting to me as I never know just what is going to happen.'

It is a pleasing measure of changing times that Sloane, without doubt one of the finest jazz singers active in the 1990s, could perform, record, host her own radio show, in Boston, and reap critical and popular acclaim. But not, of course, earn tens of millions of dollars. Her reward is much more modest. She does receive tribute from other singers. Chris McNulty, for example, says, 'I always have trouble with the opening tune. I have to learn how to do that part better by listening to Carol Sloane. Boy! She's a master. Her repertoire is extraordinary. Just so understated at all times... I have had to learn the art of singing softly and I am glad to have got that one past me. It's a hard thing to do but that's what I like to hear, that's why I like Carol Sloane so much and Carmen McRae; I'm directly out of Carol; and she is out of Carmen.'

Although Lucy Reed never really stopped working, she was obliged to build her career more or less in one place. Fortunately, being cloistered in Chicago appealed to her as a matter of choice but nevertheless kept her talent well hidden from the world outside America's Second City. 'In recent years,' she observed in the mid-1990s, 'I have only performed in small concerts in intimate settings, my favourite kind of situation...' She also returned to recording, teaming up with bassist Ray Brown, guitarist Herb Ellis and pianist Larry Novack for a new album which revealed that her voice had retained all its earlier charm and showed few signs of ageing. Additionally, like so many maturing singers, she brings added resonance to lyrics that have become more meaningful to her – or have perhaps altered their meaning – with the passing years.

The Swedish-born singer Monica Zetterlund had recorded with Bill Evans in 1964. Although this established her on the international scene, she had first become known in the 1950s singing mostly with Scandinavian groups, in particular with her fellow Swede, clarinettist and altoist, Arne Domnérus. She too found her prime vocal years coinciding with the rise of pop and rock.

There were many other talented singers contemporary with Reed and Zetterlund whose careers failed to equate with their talent because of the changing times. Among the best were the pure-sounding Audrey Morris and the unaffected and direct Lurlean Hunter; also there was Beverley Kenney, an imaginative and swinging singer, and Carole Creveling, who had a husky voice and gimmick-free delivery. Yet another was Ruth Price, who grew up in a small Pennsylvania town 'where as far as I knew there was no jazz, not even on the radio'. She went to ballet school and eventually began to work professionally in a Philadelphia ballet company. She told Leonard Feather: 'The way I got to hear popular music was strange. There wasn't much money in dancing, so someone suggested that another little girl and I try to get some work in night clubs. I guess the only reason they hired us in some of those places was that the rest of the show was so blue, they'd put us in to bring it up to a level where the police wouldn't close it.'

Price's real introduction to jazz came when she first heard Charlie Parker. A boyfriend asked her one night to go with him to hear Bird. 'I said, "Bird, what's that?" But when I heard him it was so beautiful. This really opened my ears and it didn't seem strange or difficult. On my way home I started humming and the boy said to me, "You know, you could really sing if you wanted to." That did it. Soon I was making a nuisance of myself asking bands if I could sing with them.' Price was eventually hired by Charlie Ventura and later recorded two albums in New York and appeared for several months at Village Vanguard. She moved to Los Angeles in 1957 and in 1961 recorded her best-remembered album, *Ruth Price with Shelly*

Manne & His Men at the Manne Hole. Sadly, like so many others at that time, her talent remained a well-kept secret although she did record an album in the bleak 1980s.

Although Marlene VerPlanck never stopped singing professionally, in a sense she took a twenty-year sabbatical from the kind of music she really wanted to sing. As Marlene Pampinella she began singing at nineteen after abandoning a prospective career in journalism. After briefly taking singing lessons she was singing in clubs within weeks and soon attended an audition with the Tex Beneke band. 'I did a great audition,' she reflects, adding candidly, 'but fell apart on the job. After two weeks Tex let me go.' Undaunted, and learning fast, she took a job with Charlie Spivak and rapidly progressed to the Tommy Dorsey band. By the time that Dorsey died, in 1956, she had married Billy VerPlanck, trombonist-arranger in the band. The VerPlancks decided to settle in New York and sought work in the studios although for three years she studied every day from 6 a.m. until noon. 'Then I would go off to the commercials studio, the Jingle Mill, and do five commercials an hour, for up to five hours each day.'

Although it was a tough schedule, it gave her hands-on experience of studio singing including the finer points of microphone technique. With Billy VerPlanck writing and arranging in the same sector of the industry, the pair soon became greatly sought after. For well over two decades, conveniently overlapping much of the 1980s, she was one of the most successful studio singers in New York, singing on countless high-profile television commercials and also working as backing singer on recording dates with a wide range of artists including Frank Sinatra and KISS. Tiny in build, VerPlanck has a tenacity of spirit that belies her delicate appearance, and through the years neither she nor her husband lost sight of their objectives. In the late 1960s he had produced two record albums for his wife which led to yet more studio work and also to an appearance on a radio project with pianist-arranger Loonis McGlohon which was based upon Alec Wilder's book, *The American Popular Song.* Gradually, work such as this and dates at New York nightclubs redirected her career until she was able to turn her back on commercials and devote her undimmed energy to the kind of music she and her husband love. Undoubtedly, the long years of singing in anonymity had been well used for, as Leonard Feather observed, she had become 'a peerless performer of quality songs'.

Helen Merrill's years of absence from centre stage were a combination of inexplicable public indifference to her talent and the fact that she was obliged, for professional and personal reasons, to spend many years outside America. Merrill's jazz baptism came in the 1940s. She had been singing in a travelling talent show in New York. As she told Don Waterhouse of *Jazz Journal International*: 'The actual competition was real, but in fact it was rigged, because all the kids were pretty good singers. I was about fifteen years old, and that's how I started to sing. My career was very peculiar, because I didn't sing a great deal professionally; I used to sing with the jazz people around town. They always embraced me; they understood that I had some kind of talent, so they included me very often in their inner circle of musicians. I worked with them, too, and I also did some kind of concerts when I was sixteen or seventeen at the 8:45 Club in the Bronx with Bud Powell and Miles Davis and all those people. I had a very eclectic taste, I still do. I used to like Jo Stafford very much, because she had a kind of a haunting quality and a lovely pitch and straight tones and wonderful musicianship. I liked Billie Holiday. I used to like a woman named Lil Green. Yes, a lot of blues singers I listened to, but mostly I listened to instrumentalists. I liked listening to musicians *play*. Ben Webster, Lester Young – definitely Lester Young – well, all the young musicians that were around me. Remember I was surrounded by the greatest – I didn't realize how great everybody was – but I was surrounded in New York by the greatest musicians.'

By the end of the 1950s, however, dissatisfied and with work hard to find in America, Merrill toured extensively, including trips to Brazil and Italy, where she stayed for three years. Following her second marriage, she went to live in Japan and allowed her career to take second place to that of her new husband although she did record and broadcast there. In the early 1970s she was back in America but did not resume her recording career until 1977 after which her work attracted critical approval, although even in the mid-1990s she was still less well known than was deserved.

Although America and occasionally Europe was home to jazz singers in the 1950s and 1960s, there were some who came from other continents. Sathima Bea Benjamin, who was born in Capetown, South Africa, began her singing career under the distant influence of voices on radio. When she began to sing in clubs, Benjamin incorporated into her repertoire songs sung by her radio and record mentors, Bessie Smith, Billie Holiday and Anita O'Day, and also the music of her homeland, 'Cape Town Rhythm' and 'High Life'. Club work brought her face to face with the discrimination enshrined in law by *apartheid*. When singing in designated 'white' clubs she recalls: 'Between sets we'd sit in the basement or the kitchen. Does it make you feel inferior? Of course it does. You have to fight it very hard.'

So Benjamin began to fight against the injustices. Her marriage to jazz pianist Dollar Brand, who later changed his name to Abdullah Ibrahim, became simultaneously a struggle to be recognized as performers of international quality and distinction and against government policy. Membership of the outlawed African National Congress party led in time to exile, first in Europe. It was in Zurich that Benjamin met another distant hero, Duke Ellington. 'Our rapport was unbelievable,' she remembers. 'He took me to Paris a few days later and recorded us. I recorded with Billy Strayhorn and Ellington himself. [They] took turns accompanying me at the piano.' Later, at Ellington's urging, Benjamin went to America and sang at the 1965 Newport Jazz Festival and in time she and Ibrahim settled in New York City but she never lost her deep emotional ties to her homeland. 'I think the basis of everything I do is Africa,' she told Ed Hazell of *Coda* magazine. 'There's a sense of rhythm, if you listen carefully, in there. I'm really thrilled that I come from Africa, I feel good about it.'

Benjamin's singing voice is clear and true and she sings with almost no vibrato, a trait she shares with one of her early influences, Anita O'Day. Benjamin studied music formally but was never allowed to sing solo at concerts given at the Teachers Training College she attended in South Africa. When she asked why she was excluded, she was told that it was because rather than hitting notes she had a tendency to slide up or down to them. Unwittingly, she had developed a distinctive glissando, a hallmark of her style and a device used by so many other singers in jazz. 'That meant nothing to me at the time,' Benjamin says, 'but it shows, in retrospect, that I was unconsciously trying to phrase like the black American singers I heard on the radio.'

It is not unusual for artists in jazz to gain credence and a following outside their homelands. It happens to Americans just as much as it does to others. In the case of Marion Montgomery, it is not surprising as she married British musician Laurie Holloway and thus became resident in Britain. Before leaving America, Montgomery's big break came by chance: 'I did a demo of a song and it was sent to Peggy Lee. She heard it along with an A&R man from Capitol Records. She said, "Forget the song and sign the singer." He did and I got a contract.' This was in the early 1960s but it was not until she crossed the Atlantic that she was able to fully spread her vocal wings.

Much less affected by the 1980s drought was the British singer Cleo Laine who first came to prominence when she sang with the Johnny Dankworth Seven and big band in the 1950s. Following her marriage to Dankworth in 1958 she turned increasingly towards a solo career, gaining accolades in many areas of music and theatre. With Dankworth as her frequent musical director and accompanist, Laine extended her repertoire beyond jazz into the fields of popular and classical music. Her highly distinctive voice, in terms of diction, musical speech patterns, fluidity and exceptional range, attracted audiences far outside the jazz world.

In her autobiography, Laine explains how her great musical talent had to be teased gently out of her by Dankworth: 'I was starting to understand and love the music that I sat listening to nightly on the stand, realizing at the same time how inadequate my equipment for the job really was. Here I was, a contralto with a very limited range, who would never consider a song with a large span, although John edged me up by doing arrangements of songs in higher keys unbeknown to me, keys I would never have picked for myself at the time. Or he would do a modulation to a higher key within a song which I was able to cope with, proving that it was often mind over matter. If I was told something was difficult, I couldn't do it, so he hid it from me until I did it naturally, not only testing out my range, but my ear, widening my musical knowledge and my musical vocabulary...'

Laine's appeal to the audience outside jazz might be attributable to her stylistic range although she has suggested the breakthrough came with her recording of the Jerome Kern–P. G. Wodehouse song, 'Bill'. The direct, simple approach she takes on this recording has been noted by Terry Blaine as one of creative programming and intelligent use of technique: 'The great singers are not necessarily the ones who have the greatest technique but the ones that say the most, make you feel the most. I always thought that Cleo Laine was a great example of an astounding technique. Listen to her singing "Riding High", she uses all five octaves of her range finishing on some incredible note. The next song is just her with piano, singing "Bill", absolutely straight, no vocal acrobatics whatsoever. That's what I mean, you can wow them with your technique but when you get down to it, what people want, it's important to be able to come from the heart and step away from all that and say, "there it is, the basic truth". The best singers do that.'

Successful ventures into the performance of musical settings to lyrics by literary figures such as T. S. Eliot, Thomas Hardy, W. H. Auden and William Shakespeare have allowed Laine to ride out the stormy changes that adversely affected so many other singers. She also continued to perform in jazz contexts, scoring tremendous success in America. Throughout the 1980s and 1990s she and her husband were deeply involved in jazz education and she still tours to great acclaim.

A British singer who survived changing patterns in jazz without having to work outside music or make compromises is Norma Winstone. Beginning her career in the early 1960s, she first worked with avant-garde groups and subsequently maintained close ties with some of the most forward-thinking musicians in jazz. Nevertheless, she has also regularly redirected her considerable talents into other areas of jazz and jazz-influenced popular song. During the 1970s and 1980s she worked steadily, edging jazz singing forward with her imaginative work. The avant-garde trio Azimuth which she led (the other members being saxophonist Tony Coe and pianist John Taylor) was one of the period's most interesting groups. In the early 1990s she turned to the great American composers of the 1930s and 1940s for a series of highly-acclaimed concerts and in the mid-1990s, with pianist Jimmy Rowles, she recorded an album, *Well Kept Secret*, which successfully blended the standard songbook with contemporary material. Highly musical in all that she does, Winstone is one of the most adventurous of singers and her habit of occasionally re-creating herself in musical terms has helped maintain her status. She is equally at home as a solo performer and in the context of group performance, sometimes singing as part of Jan Ponsford's vital and enterprising jazz choral group, Vocal Chords. Winstone's versatility and interest in a variety of musical forms will most certainly allow her to continue to play a leading role in jazz singing well into the twenty-first century.

Another British singer, Carol Kidd, also survived changing tastes in music. Starting out singing in pop talent contests in the 1960s, she moved into traditional jazz, dropping out for several years when trad was over-taken by rock and pop. She returned in the mid-1980s to ecstatic reviews and SRO business throughout the UK and especially in her native Scotland. Kidd's timing was right. Quality performances by singers were once again beginning to attract attention.

It was during these years that the numbers of non-American singers in jazz increased. This raises the matter of language. Although music is clearly an international language, singing lyrics is not. Almost without exception, jazz singers in Europe and elsewhere draw at least part of their repertoires, lyrics and all, from America and hence are singing in a foreign language. Even the English speakers are, in a sense, using a foreign tongue. Added to this, differences in physiology means that softly spoken English people tend to have problems getting sounds out while Americans have greater ease in really belting out songs. Strictly speaking, of course, the language of the lyrics is not American but English, but it is not only the surface accent that is American; there are many other differences that run deep.

The form of English spoken by Americans has different speech patterns, pronunciations, intonations, inflections and rhythms. This can cause problems even for British singers and others whose native language is English, who sometimes encounter difficulties in bringing the right verbal nuances to their interpretations. Tina May explains: 'I have a sort of purish English-sounding voice and I'm quite proud of that; after all jazz in the 1990s is such a world music. But there is still a certain pressure to have a mid-Atlantic accent. I have been told that in America they don't like the English accent. My dilemma would be – how do you sound between songs? Do you have to have an accent all the way through? Then you become a completely different character. Besides, all my favourite singers, like Ella and Sarah, didn't have broad accents.' Claire Martin, another leading British singer of the 1990s, confirms the dilemma and its resolu-tion: 'Jazz singing is American music and you slip naturally into the accent when singing.'

For all the difficulties of language, over the years the number of singers from non-English-speaking countries grew. Danish singer Karin Krog came to international attention in the mid-1960s. Her reputation spread in large part thanks to engagements and recordings with leading American jazz musicians including Don Ellis, Clare Fischer, Warne Marsh, Dexter Gordon and Archie Shepp. During the following decade she also began a continuing musical association with British saxophonist John Surman. Krog's repertoire is broad, incorporating standards, jazz classics, the witty, sophisticated songs of Dave Frishberg, and elements of African and Eastern music. Perhaps the very things that make Krog's singing so interesting, her adventurous spirit and her enjoyment in working with musicians who are among the best of the avant-garde, are also those that have held back the widespread appreciation which is clearly her due. Nevertheless she continued to explore, admitting: 'After many years singing all sorts of songs, there is still the small voice inside urging experimentation.'

Laila Dalseth, who is Norwegian and has only rarely strayed outside her homeland, has linked her singing style closely to that of Billie Holiday. Dalseth has achieved a remarkable affinity with Holiday's style; her phrasing, timing and a studiedly casual behind-the-beat swing. But she never resorts to simple imitation, managing to impose a personal statement upon the tradition she emulates. Like almost all European singers, Dalseth's early influences came through radio and records: 'I learned many popular songs and evergreens when my sisters and I were singing together at home but my first jazz influence came through radio. I heard all the jazz greats when I was listening to "Voice of America" and some Norwegian jazz programmes in the 1950s.'

Another Norwegian singer who started out at a very early age is Magni Wentzel. It was to be a long haul, however, before she was recorded as a jazz singer and was heard around the world. Unlike Dalseth, who is self-taught, Wentzel undertook extensive vocal and instrumental studies in Norway and also studied classical guitar in Spain and performed and recorded classical guitar music. During her period in Spain she began singing jazz with, among others, pianist Tete Montoliu and saxophonist Pony Poindexter. This was in the mid-1960s and by the end of the decade she was back in Norway, performing on the jazz club circuit. Singing sometimes in Norwegian, Wentzel has an eclectic repertoire that includes r&b. In 1983, when she was thirty-eight years old, she made her first jazz vocal album. Since then, a new album every two years has helped spread her name but, like Dalseth, her undoubted talent remains underappreciated by the international audience.

Urszula Dudziak is another European singer who became interested in jazz singing through hearing records. In Dudziak's case it was Ella Fitzgerald who was her first motivator. By the early 1960s, Dudziak, who was born in Poland in 1943, was singing in jazz clubs and in 1963 decided to study voice in Warsaw. She met the Polish multi-instrumentalist Michal Urbaniak professionally in 1965; two years later they married and thereafter the couple toured extensively, eventually taking up residence in America. Much of Dudziak's work is in scat and other wordless forms, thereby easing the difficulties of accommodating an alien language.

*   *   *

Despite the fact that jazz at the start of the 1980s had advanced dramatically from its origins and regardless of the individual merit of the singers, as we have seen, many artists, American and non-American, active in the 1960s and 1970s found the decade a barren time. This was a contributory factor to the view we adopted at the end of our earlier book, published in 1986. Jazz singing did seem to be in decline with few new albums from established singers and little visible sign of new singers coming into jazz.

In fact, the 1980s were the years in which numerous embryonic singers were learning their craft and preparing to burst upon the scene.

During the late 1980s jazz singers took stock. Obviously, the music industry was not interested in them. Undeterred and bloody-minded, the singers refused to admit defeat. Many began to promote themselves, starting their own record labels, or doing deals with small-time recording operations. Marguerite Juenemann formed Juenetunes, Dominique Eade's first albums came out on Accurate, Madeline Eastman and Kitty Margolis joined forces to create Mad-Kat. The American singer Barbara Morrison appeared on the German independent Mons label owned by jazz musician Thilo Berg. Nanette Natal had formed Benyo in 1980 but despite widespread critical acclaim had not been picked up by a major label. Terry Blaine sang on Jukebox Jazz, Chris McNulty on Discovery and Amosaya, Lisa Thorson appeared on Brownstone, Jackie Allen on Lake Shore Jazz, Ellen Johnson on Nine Winds; Meredith D'Ambrosio was on Sunnyside, the covers of her albums being reproductions of her own watercolours.

A few newcomers managed to reach larger companies: Roseanna Vitro, who had issued a 1982 album on Texas Rose Music, ex-Basie singers Dennis Rowland and Mary Stallings, Karrin Allyson and Eden Atwood, whose first album was self-produced, were all signed by Concord joining an élite group that included Mel Tormé, Ernestine Anderson, Rosemary Clooney, Susannah McCorkle and Carol Sloane. Nnenna Freelon was contracted to Columbia, Kurt Elling, Cassandra Wilson and Rachelle Ferrell joined the prestigious Blue Note, Dee Dee Bridgewater was on Verve and Diana Krall recorded on the GRP Impulse! label. Audiophile continued to do well for singers, bringing out new material and reissues by Dardanelle, Marlene VerPlanck, Barbara Lea, Daryle Ryce, Daryl Sherman, Mike Campbell, Carrie Smith and a host of others. In Britain, small labels were the only companies prepared to take a chance on jazz singers; Claire Martin joined Carol Kidd on Linn while Tina May was with 33 Records, Val Wiseman on Big Bear and Ian Shaw on Ronnie Scott's Jazz House. In 1996 singers such as Stacey Kent and Nicki Leighton-Thomas were planning their first compact discs. Not surprisingly, fans searched for many of these albums in vain in main-street stores. Instead, they had to be bought by mail order, or from one of a few specialist jazz shops. Mostly, however, would-be collectors bought them direct from the singer at a concert or club appearance.

The relationship between record companies and jazz has long been uneasy and in particular with jazz and jazz-influenced singers. The example of Decca's Jack Kapp is one of a benign autocrat. He had launched American Decca with the backing of Edward Lewis who had created English Decca in 1931. One of Kapp's early signings was Bing Crosby whose recording career he carefully guided. Crosby was impressed with Kapp and had faith in his ability to create success: 'He developed a recording programme for me that involved every kind of music. I sang with every kind of band and every kind of vocal group – religious songs, patriotic songs, and even light opera. I thought he was crazy, but I had confidence and went along with his suggestions. He gave me a very expanded repertoire which most other singers at that time hadn't bothered to get into. I just did exactly what he told me to do and it worked.' Dave Kapp confirmed the relationship between his brother and Crosby: 'They never argued at all. He'd say he didn't want to sing this or that kind of song, but he usually did. Bing would say, "I don't know if I should sing this. It's pretty rotten, but if Jack wants it – I'll sing it".'

Lee Wiley also remembered her time at the company: 'Now you know at Decca, they had an Indian over the door, and it says, "Sing the melody".' She added, 'Jack Kapp used to think I couldn't sing straight.' For all the apparent limitations in his thinking in respect of artists who varied his creed, and his autocracy, Kapp was undeniably astute in his commercial perceptiveness. Interestingly, when Kapp died, Decca dropped many of its black artists.

As already recounted, in the 1940s at Capitol Records the autocracy, if that is the word for it, was one of musical excellence created by Johnny Mercer, Buddy DeSylva and Glenn Wallichs and executed in large part by Dave Dexter Jnr who was responsible for signing Peggy Lee, Nat King Cole, Nellie Lutcher, Julia Lee and Stan Kenton among many superior artists then and into the mid-1950s.

When Capitol was sold, the new owners gradually moved the way that all large businesses move, towards accountancy-based practices rather than those of artistic merit. The trend is inevitable because the companies need to do this in order to survive. For example, Nesuhi Ertegun of Atlantic Records was representative of many record company executives of the 1950s and 1960s who got into the business because he loved the music. Unfortunately, as Atlantic grew, Ertegun had to spend more time in administration, thus abandoning the very thing that had first attracted him.

In the 1990s artists were sometimes fortunate to find producers with whom they could work with confidence. Dianne Reeves worked with George Duke on *Quiet After the Storm* for Blue Note and for the same label Cassandra Wilson had Craig Street on *Blue Light 'Til Dawn*. Both men found a harmonious relationship with the singers, a means of helping them draw more deeply from the wellspring of their talent.

Such instances seem rare, however, and in any event the producer's role in major companies in the 1990s was not necessarily one of absolute control. By this time, for the most part, the major record companies were wholly profit-orientated, as were the film and other leisure and entertainment industries. Statistics could be found to back up the neglect displayed by record companies. Record sales in 1995, published by the Recording Association of America, showed jazz at 3 per cent of the total against 33.5 per cent for rock. Interestingly enough, the only form to fall below jazz was classical music with 2.9 per cent. Despite these figures, classical music remains a 'flag-ship' element in the catalogues of many major record companies.

Even those majors which purport to support jazz gauge artists on actuarial terms rather than those of artistic merit. Minimum sales requirements are calculated for each new album and if it fails to meet those sales figures the artist's contract is rarely renewed, regardless of who he is or how good. On the face of it this is perfectly sound fiscal reasoning. But whereas in the pop world that artist and record will be heavily promoted and skilfully marketed (the relationship between pop marketing and pop success should not be overlooked), the jazz album is usually allowed to slip almost unnoticed into record stores and inevitably onto a fast track to deletion from the catalogue. By definition, the small specialist jazz labels do not have the money to sustain jazz properly, and yet it is largely they who keep the music available to record buyers, not only through their own issues but also because their activities force the majors to continue to pay lip service to contemporary jazz by promoting a small number of artists, who represent a tiny percentage of the whole.

Of course, the majors have embarked on (often large) reissue programmes which undoubtedly provide a great service to the jazz public. It cannot be overlooked, however, that it is often cheaper to produce a boxed-set of the complete works of a long-dead artist than to produce a single album by a living musician. Today it seems that no one is prepared to attempt the delicate entrepreneurial balancing act begun by Norman Granz in the 1950s. Of course, when Granz began, the artists with whom he built his labels, Verve, Clef, Norgran and, later, Pablo, were not the names he made them. The extent to which Granz and, say, Ella Fitzgerald and Oscar Peterson were interdependent is impossible to ascertain: would he have been so successful without them, would they have reached their pinnacles if they had been obliged to set up their own labels or were consigned to the clutches of accountants?

If there is an incipient Norman Granz in the offing as we approach the year 2000, someone prepared to take financial risks motivated primarily by love for the music, he is keeping a low profile. As for the budding Ella Fitzgeralds, they are recording on their own labels or with small independents, the often lonely carriers of the flag of jazz singing. Against the odds, many of the new singers have begun to establish their names, however precariously or parochially. As they do so, it has quickly become apparent that not only is there a broad sweep of nationalities among them but also the source of their repertoires was similarly ignoring previous boundaries. As Tina May remarks: 'It doesn't all have to come from America anymore.' Singers with post-bop and post-rock sensibilities, styles and concepts are increasingly commonplace and at the same time there are singers rooted in bop. Perhaps curiously, the long-standing principal staple of the jazz singers' repertoire, the 32-bar song, remains popular. Singers happily seek out and perform material composed thirty and forty years before they were born. While the great song standards are not all that these singers sing, they often provide a substantial part of their repertoires. The inclusion of these songs in concert programmes and on record serves a useful purpose over and above any intended by the singer. Such songs allow listeners to better judge the singer's abilities because comparisons in style, treatment and interpretation are never easy when hearing a previously unheard singer perform an unknown song. Performances of standards help overcome this particular problem and also encourage potential ticket or record buyers uneasy with original material. Some singers, of course, take a different view, balancing their repertoires in the opposite direction in their determination to break new musical ground at the same time as they attempt to break into the club circuit.

Among those who weight their musical output with songs from the great songbooks of the past are Stacey Kent, Mike Campbell, Sue Kibbey, Susannah McCorkle, Sandra King, Chris McNulty, Nicki Leighton-Thomas and Diana Krall.

Stacey Kent's deep understanding of the older songs and singers' styles stemmed from her childhood: 'I grew up listening to and being surrounded by Frank Sinatra, Ella Fitzgerald, Billie Holiday, Louis Armstrong, Anita O'Day, Sarah Vaughan. Their records were everywhere; in shops and restaurants. I was exposed and so had to be influenced! Jazz was a big part of growing up in New York. It wasn't only vocalists, of course, there were a great many instrumentalists too. For example, I knew some of Stan Getz's solos by heart even before I knew what a solo was. I didn't go looking for records by these people. They found me. They were played everywhere. Later, when I went looking, I discovered Mildred Bailey, Maxine Sullivan, Irene Kral, Chet Baker. I guess all of them have influenced me in some way. Anybody you have listened to is an influence – even if you don't like them, you hear where you don't want to go. Today, I don't listen to all that many singers but I do listen to a lot of instrumental music. Lester Young, Stan Getz, Art Tatum, Teddy Wilson, Ben Webster, Charlie Christian. And I love big band music and 1930s swing.'

Nevertheless, Kent's musical taste is not narrow: 'There is no one category of singing that I don't like. I like so many kinds of singing, even if I don't choose to sing them myself. But I don't like to hear singers who lose the meaning of a song through "over souling". There must be respect for your material. Look at Irene Kral and Mildred Bailey – two very different singers who both sing with so much meaning and feeling without ever appearing to do very much at all.'

Kent is not alone in her thinking. When Susannah McCorkle describes what she regards as bad singing she lists: 'Out-of-tune singing, hammy, phony singing; theatricality, giving a little sob to try and make people think you're a little emotional. I hate it. Actressiness, being overtly cute or flirtatious or trying to sound sexy. I like the singers who just are.' Barbara Lea pursues the same topic, remarking that '... some so-called jazz singers seem to have contempt for a song and use it to aggrandize themselves by altering, distorting, scatting – in other words "improving" it.'

Some singers, Lea explained to W. Royal Stokes, 'make you think of them. Others make you think of the song. You don't get up there and try to cry. You get up there and try *not* to cry. Don't stand and try to show how much you are waiting for your man. You stand up and *wait* for your man.'

Mike Campbell likes standards, partly because they 'are not that rangy and there is no need to adjust the material to suit my vocal range. I want a tune to fit like an old friend.'

The British singer Sue Kibbey was influenced in her early years by Billie Holiday but she also listened to Ella Fitzgerald, Sarah Vaughan, Bessie Smith, Helen Humes, Maxine Sullivan and Frank Sinatra. Since then, however, she has matured along her own path: 'I'm not influenced any more by them, not since I found my own style. But perhaps the influence remains in the songs I choose.' Kibbey put aside full-time singing to raise a family but continues to build a reputation for quality and integrity, albeit on a semi-professional basis.

Susannah McCorkle's fascination with songs and lyrics developed out of her appreciation and understanding of the meaning of words: 'I'm a romantic throwback because I'm interested only in singing lyrics. I want to reach people and stir their emotions, make them think of the poetry in their own lives... It's always the lyric that attracts me to a song. I need a good lyric. I really give a lot to the words and they've got to be saying something. After that, both melody and mood are really important to get a rhythmic groove feel on a song. I really stress that with my musicians; I'm going for a feeling on every song. It takes a lot of maturity and depth to strike a mood and stay with it and draw the musicians into it and the audience into it. And that for me is the challenge. Not showing how tricky you can be and what you can do.' And McCorkle is also conscious of the importance of how she presents herself and her music to the audience: '... talk about the songs, talk about the musicians or singers. A lot of people don't know about Billie Holiday or Lester Young and Ethel Waters. And you never know who has just wandered in and is hearing jazz for the first time.'

McCorkle's early career was built on two continents, as was that of Sandra King who began singing at the age of nine in London where she was born in 1950. At sixteen she was heard by Mark Murphy on whose recommendation she was engaged to sing at Ronnie Scott's. Later, she sang with the National Youth Jazz Orchestra, itself a showcase for some of the most notable instrumentalists and singers to appear in Britain since its inception in 1965. King worked mostly in England and elsewhere in Europe but a 1982 visit to America resulted in a remarkable concert performance at the Corcoran Gallery of Art in Washington, DC. Both the concert and the recording of it, released three years later, were greeted with ecstatic praise by critics, notably John S. Wilson in the New York *Times*, who considered her to be 'an interpreter who sees each song in her own terms and creates a distinctive cameo in a voice whose dark textures have a provocative range of shadings'. In this particular case, the repertoire was drawn entirely from the songs of Vernon Duke, the Russian-born composer of some all-American songs: 'Autumn in New York', 'Taking a Chance on Love' and 'I Can't Get Started'. Since the mid-1990s, King has continued to work regularly in America and Europe and to record, gaining many admirers of her approach to music that was not only written years before she was born but was also the product of the culture of a distant land.

Australian Chris McNulty has also found inspiration and a repertoire in the music of American songsmiths of a bygone age, yet her admiration of these songs is qualified by her need to be able to enter fully not only into the mood and feeling of a song but also its meaning: 'The lyric is extremely important and there are some songs I won't do because I can't stand the lyric. Of course, you sometimes change your opinions. Somehow, maybe ten years later, your experience can bring you round to identify with a lyric that previously you didn't like or understand. "Porgy", for instance, is an extraordinary song. I always absolutely adored it but I didn't want to do it for a long time because I was very unsure of the real meaning of the lyric. In fact, I actually misunderstood the lyric. Then someone explained it to me, made it easy for me to lose my discomfort with it. It took another year before I really wanted to do it. That's something I often do with ballads. For example I had "Lost in the Stars" on my list for a long time but I wasn't going to sing it until I was ready to sing it. Now it's a real signature song for me.'

The manner in which young singers who are very much women and men of the present can find emotional links with the past through songs is encouraging to those who see deficiencies in contemporary attitudes, values and culture. But for a young singer, connecting with concepts of an earlier generation can present problems. As Nicki Leighton-Thomas says: 'Building a repertoire can be difficult, getting a good balance between tempo and style and finding material that keeps you and the musicians happy as well as appealing to others. I have been deeply influenced by Dory Previn, whose storytelling in her lyrics reminds me very much of Fran Landesman's.' Previn is a sometimes bitterly ironic poet, songwriter and performer whose material is rarely used by jazz artists. Landesman, also a poet, is best known to jazz audiences for her collaboration with Tommy Wolfe on 'Spring Can Really Hang You Up the Most'. Bob Dorough is also attracted to her work and has recorded an album of Landesman songs. Leighton-Thomas continues, 'I like daring and witty lyrics and sad songs that can be compared to your own strong emotions about particular moments. Dory Previn has been attacked at almost every level on her song writing, and I often get negative responses from people who think her work is too risqué but I've managed to keep a couple of her songs in my sets.' Leighton-Thomas began singing at college, mostly working with pop groups, but gradually extended her repertoire although retaining a clear-sighted view of the kind of singer she is: 'I think of myself as a singer who happens, some of the time, to work within a jazz context. Since meeting

Fran Landesman my work has been more consistently connected to jazz as my repertoire consists of many of Fran's new lyrics with music by Simon Wallace. These are songs that appeal to me very much, mainly as words are important to me and Fran's wonderful, wise, dark and funny lyrics are a joy to sing. I count myself lucky to have a repertoire of such great songs. They also appeal to a non-jazz audience as the poetry is so good – and they appeal to the younger audience as she's quite hip.'

Canadian-born Diana Krall hit the jazz singing world with rather more of a bang than most new singers enjoy, having been picked up by a strong jazz-orientated label. During her formative years she studied classical piano while simultaneously playing jazz piano in a school band. Prompting this departure was her father's record collection: 'I was raised on Fats Waller. My Dad is a record collector, and he must have every Fats Waller recording made... Fats was the first person I heard play piano *and* sing. I started playing his repertoire when I was a kid. I tried to learn all his tunes and to play and sing at the same time.' She began playing professionally at fifteen and after studying at Berklee College of Music in Boston returned to her home in British Columbia. There she played with visiting jazzmen, including Ray Brown, and was encouraged to visit Los Angeles where she studied with pianist Jimmy Rowles, an example of a creative jazz improviser who is also a distinguished accompanist. Rowles inspired her to sing more, although she remains dismissive of her singing: 'I've always been shy about it and I tried to avoid it whenever I could. I got more work because I could sing, but I didn't like doing it in lounges as a single. I didn't feel I had a clear, precise voice – a pretty voice.'

By the time she tried New York, Krall was as much a singer as a pianist, and equally adept in either role. Apart from Ray Brown, she has also worked successfully with John Clayton, Don Thompson and Whit Browne. This cluster of bass players prompted Krall to explain: 'I have many pianistic influences, but I *perform* with bass players in duo and trio settings. They are my left hand. My bass mentors are truly my teachers. They have been the voice of leadership and experience, and I have learned so much music from them.' Krall's singing style is wholly modern but her repertoire is replete with great standards. She sings with an easy swing and her smoky voice enhances the lyrics of all her songs. Add her piano playing, which is strong enough to merit status as a soloist, and it is clear that she is a singer who is here to stay.

*　　*　　*

Jazz has always been subject to constant growth, flux, and interplay with popular and other music. At times some audiences and some musicians have found it difficult to understand the basis on which newcomers come into jazz and what it is that influences and shapes them. As we have seen, among jazz musicians active in the mid-1990s are some born as far back as the 1920s and early 1930s, many from the late 1930s, the 1940s and 1950s,

179

and the early 1960s. There are those who were born as recently as the 1970s and even a handful of precocious *wunderkinds* born in the 1980s. To expect all these people to have similar roots, tastes, ideas, concepts, views and styles is clearly unreasonable.

Most jazz musicians are receptive to the sounds they hear around them, or at least they are aware of them even if they choose not to adopt them into their own work. Even latter-day musical departures such as jazz rap, acid jazz and hip-hop have found acceptance in some quarters, although all three forms have hanging over them some questions. Are they an attempt to fasten together what are essentially incompatible musical elements? And, more importantly to jazz, are they a media invention? In particular, it might be thought that the word jazz is attached to jazz rap and acid jazz as a means of authenticating a form that is itself rootless.

Of the three, jazz rap is the only vocal form (although vocalizing can be found in the others). The sung, or rhythmically spoken, element in jazz rap might include social comment and an indication of political awareness ranging from mildly anti-establishment to violent polemic. Jazz rap does have antecedents, perhaps more strongly located in the world of poetry than music: Beat Generation poets such as Kenneth Rexroth in the late 1940s and early 1950s, Harlem's Last Poets in the 1960s, more recently Gil Scott-Heron, Arrested Development, Dave Bryant. But the extent to which jazz rap can be accepted within the ever-stretching envelope of jazz is a matter for continuing debate. There is an element of non-conformity at the heart of jazz rap and it may well be that hardcore jazz rappers would, anyway, resist being so enfolded.

Acid jazz is largely instrumental music, developing out of young musicians whose own early listening came in discos where, in the 1970s, deejays mixed hard bop, by the likes of Art Blakey and Lee Morgan, into a brew of soul, funk, Latin and pop. Hip-hop was also largely deejay led, with prominent use of electronic (later digital) drumbeat and 'scratching', the repetition of phrases within an album track by physically (at first) stopping and starting a record over and over again at a particularly potent moment. Hip-hop came in time to be an all-purpose term covering not only music but the dance forms which evolved out of it, and also visual elements including graffiti. The status of hip-hop in terms of its relationship with jazz was summed up by Betty Carter in conversation with Stuart Nicholson: 'Hip-hop is the best thing that could have come along for jazz. Because it's so BAD! It's turned so many people off and it's overcrowded the commercial world. It's time for us in jazz to take advantage of it. The kids are indecisive as to what to listen to.'

What was important at times when popular music was besieged by new developments, as indeed it must always be, was that jazz musicians listened to it if only to choose to ignore it afterwards. More and more in the 1990s, jazz singers were chafing at artificial boundaries placed upon them by preconceived ideas of audiences, promoters and record producers. The singers who chose to widen their repertoires were not only the young, they included some who were young only in mind and spirit.

Among many singers for whom the repertoire of popular standards was too restricting were Tom Lellis, Nanette Natal, Claire Martin, Tina May, Dee Dee Bridgewater, Dianne Reeves and Abbey Lincoln – a group whose age range is thirty years.

Tom Lellis has constantly re-assessed himself during his career: 'I used to think of myself as a jazz singer when I was aspiring to learn to improvise. But now I seek beauty more than improvisation. And placement more than gymnastic ability, so less and less I consider myself a jazz singer although I think other people would.' Eclectic in his likes and sources, Lellis seeks to do what jazz singers have always done – to stamp his own personality upon his material and then turn it into a memorable and identifiably individualistic performance: 'I choose tunes that affect my nervous system. I think it was Quincy Jones who said he looks for the chill. If you can't get the chill it's probably not the right tune. That is the criterion for much of my performance and choosing my repertoire. If it can get through to me, it has a chance to get to you. If it's a standard tune I try for an arrangement that is not standard. I try to put some individual mark on a tune rather than playing the same intro that has been played since 1945. Like "All the Things You Are"; every sax player plays that like Charlie Parker did. It was his intro; get a new intro or don't play the tune.'

Not that this means that Lellis seeks to sever the ties that connect each strand of jazz to common sources. Far from it, in fact, because he is deeply concerned to strengthen the ties while simultaneously looking at the music with new eyes: 'The essence of jazz singing is the placement and rhythm value of your performance. The thing that makes Shirley Horn and Ray Charles special is that they have an ability to place things in the quintessential position to maximize effect and interpretation. The biggest detriment to jazz in the last twenty to thirty years is that gymnastic ability has taken over from essence, but essence is irreplaceable and I try to capture that essence more and more. It's the most difficult thing in the idiom to me. To play with a lot of facility is not difficult, it's just the mastering of scales and your instrument, but to play with emotion and depth and interpretative ability is the maturing of an artist. I think that this is the essence and it is one of the last things to come.'

Like an increasing number of jazz singers and instrumentalists, Lellis is interested in and intrigued by the music of Brazil: 'It is not about chops but about results, about musicality, beauty, lyrical melodic content, against the underpinning of rhythm. I think the juxtaposition of sophisticated rhythms and sophisticated changes with a beautiful melody is the counterpoint of jazz's burn. You can have a great solo that is burning, gymnastic and full of facility, and you can have a beautiful, lilting lovely melody over beautiful changes and sophisticated but subtle rhythm and those two have the same heat, the same burn, the same excitement. One takes you to a place that's exhilarating beauty, the other takes you to a place that's exhilarating fire but they are equal in weight. In fact, lately I tend to think the beauty is the stronger more lasting heat.'

Nanette Natal expresses concern at the continuing effect of bebop sensibilities in a world that has moved on. To a great extent she believes that the fault lies with media marketing executives: 'I think that the problem with jazz singing, with jazz musicians, is that when it comes to marketing, everything has to be put in a particular box. A great deal of energy goes behind promoting young jazz instrumentalists, mostly males, but they are playing bebop. It's like they're going to market them as the next Miles Davis; they market them in a way that it looks like it's 1959 at the Black Hawk! Everybody's playing bebop; stuff that's been played and played and played. Jazz was originally music that was always at the cutting edge, in the vanguard of things. It was a political statement as well and I look at the artform in that way and it gives me the freedom to say some of the things I want to say and to keep taking chances and to keep growing. But that's not how jazz music is marketed, either through instrumentalists or through singers. It's all been done before and there isn't really a lot of room for innovation and that's the sad state of it. And certainly when you are dealing with record labels that's the problem.' Natal adds a comment that must echo the thoughts of many: 'It used to be that the music business was run by people who knew about music.'

Most singers in jazz will agree with the need to explore that is explicit in the remarks of Lellis and Natal. It does not follow automatically that the act of exploration will separate the singer from recognizable forms. In seeking to build on something other than bebop and earlier traditions, Lellis and Natal have not placed themselves outside the wide complex world that is jazz. What they have done is to enter into a loose category of questing spirits who seek to stretch the boundaries of style, form and repertoire.

Claire Martin began her singing career in the staid setting of a hotel lounge in Bournemouth on England's south coast. This and a spell singing on cruise liners helped form the basis of her craft but did not prepare her for the plunge into working with avant-garde drummer John Stevens. As she told Kenny Matheson: 'The things I did with John were usually very free and I didn't really know what I was doing. I was just getting my stuff together at that point, and free music isn't really my favourite anyway, so I was really thrown in at the deep end. It was really out there, and it was a great loosening-up experience for me. I'm really glad I did it, even if I didn't find it fully satisfying. There is no right and wrong in free music, every-thing's cool, but I'm a bit of a ring-ting-ting merchant, and I'd be going, "What, no structure?" and John would just be screaming, "Sing!" at me!'

Martin's progression has been rapid, with several highly acclaimed albums on the Linn label to her credit and a great deal of respect in the busi-ness, a result of her awareness of the pitfalls: 'There are jokes about the bubbly blonde who can't count the tune in, but vocalists work hard at their craft. You've got to learn improvisation, chord structures and the changes.' Her repertoire includes r&b, mainstream and standards and also a gradually increasing amount of original material: 'I'm keen to continue writing more of my own songs but it's slow but sure with me, and I don't force them. There are so many great songs out there, and I look for them all the time, but often you come across something by accident which you can bring over into a jazz style. I am a word person and I love stories and melody, but the crucial thing in bringing it over to jazz is down to the harmony, whether the chord changes can stand up to a jazz re-harmonization.'

Another British singer alert to the ways and means of expanding the repertoire for jazz singers is Tina May: 'Jazz is music just to go with. You have to set your own agenda; there are so many things that work.' May is also aware that artificial restrictions still need to be overcome in the 1990s: 'There are those who think that singers should not improvise. I have had reactions from people you really wouldn't expect it from, people who really think singers have their place and that place is singing formally – leave the improvising to the chaps! Now that's not my generation. Jazz has been a sexist area for a long time. But we have moved on.' Freedom of expression for the artist is important to May: 'Jazz is an approach where what the artist says is as important as what she is saying it about. We singers are a grey area. For me, jazz singers need to improvise if they are to be real jazz singers.'

Dee Dee Bridgewater began singing in the 1960s while at university in Illinois. Her family was musical, her father having worked for a while backing Dinah Washington. In New York in the early 1970s she attracted attention singing with the Thad Jones–Mel Lewis big band, then followed Abbey Lincoln into Max Roach's group. She was signed by Atlantic in 1974 but found a jazz-only road hard to follow and branched out, her fusion album, *Just Family*, being highly praised. She also worked in the theatre, appearing in *The Wiz* on Broadway and touring Europe in the leading role in *Lady Day*. In Europe, and especially in France, where she settled, her jazz work was in great demand. Although she returned to America for concert and festival appearances, she began to doubt the validity of what she was doing: 'I can work comfortably in Europe and feel respected there artistically,' she told *JazzTimes*'s Ken Franckling in New York. 'But coming over here, I feel like it becomes this game, that I become a kind of "product". The artistry becomes second to selling this product.'

In France she was able to extend still further her stage career, becoming the first black actress to take the role of Sally Bowles in a version of *Cabaret*. In no way did this impinge upon her standing in jazz circles and she was able to work on a new project very close to her heart, an album of music by Horace Silver: 'I've loved Horace's music ever since I first heard "Song for My Father" on a jukebox when I was fifteen. His music speaks to me. It is rhythmic. It is alive. It is happy. It is groovy. His melodies are simple... His music is so singable – and now he has decided he wants it to be sung.' The resulting album, made in 1994, has a selection of familiar jazz standards by Silver, selected by Bridgewater, all with lyrics written by Silver for the occasion. In seeking out tunes from the jazz repertoire and having words put to them, Bridgewater found inspiration in a niche already explored by a number of singers, including Tom Lellis, Kitty Margolis and Jon Hendricks. 'The jazz composers are the thing for me,' Bridgewater stated. 'Not the popular songwriters. As soon as you put words to it and it is sung, it reaches a much larger audience.'

Bridgewater's desire to expand her repertoire in new directions does not end with the Silver set, although she believes that at least another five albums are possible from the pianist's compositions. She would also like to explore the possibilities of Brazilian music. Her attitude towards her music is also changing and is pointing her more in the direction taken by instrumentalists: 'The older I get, the more I take the approach of the musician. When I hear the music now, I hear it instrumentally. The lyrics become secondary to being able to get these sounds out like a trumpet. There is a lot of stuff out there that one can play around with.'

Dianne Reeves also refuses to be inhibited by boundaries although she retains a love for good lyrics. Her first albums, in the early 1980s, were strongly inclined towards ballads, then she moved more towards jazz, then took a multi-cultural step with *Art & Survival* before turning back to jazz with 1995's *Quiet After the Storm*. This fluctuation in style created some problems for critics and audiences but no one could deny her vitality and inspired enthusiasm in all that she does. She told Willard Jenkins of *JazzTimes* that the only concept for her 1995 album was that it 'would be a jazz record, and that I wanted to do songs that I really loved and discover some new songs and arrange them in a way that made sense to me harmonically and helped me to best deliver the lyrics. So I went about finding songs that I just really enjoy the lyrics; more than anything working on trying to really tell stories.'

Reeves's interests run wide, incorporating African and Caribbean music towards which she has been directed by Harry Belafonte 'whose knowledge of West African and West Indies music led one back full circle to my black American roots'. In fact it is on the 1995 album that she recorded a blues for the first time. She was also impressed early in her life by Cannonball Adderley, 'he always played his roots, you always heard his roots in the music as well as the intrigue'.

Even more deeply committed to her roots, if only by dint of her longer experience, is Abbey Lincoln who, in the 1990s, was still spiritedly extending her repertoire and her audience. In the mid-1950s she had angled her career towards the ballad style of jazz but her musical and personal relationship with Max Roach led her not only deeply into bebop but also into the Civil Rights movement in America in the 1960s. Her work at this time reflected her accentuated political awareness but later she returned to

184

standards with great flair and added maturity. In the mid-1990s her eagerness to extend herself continued unabated and she told Willard Jenkins that it was still exciting '... to find beautiful songs that come out of my life and out of my head and out of my heart'. She was busily writing new material and confidently looking to the future: 'As of now, the well is full of water, it's not at all dried up; I have a brand-new career!'

Quite clearly, the future holds much for Lellis and Natal, Martin and May, Bridgewater and Reeves, with many years of singing ahead of them. Even Lincoln ('1995 will be my sixty-fifth year here on the planet') has many songs left to sing. But will any of them achieve superstardom? Probably not, because the star-making machinery of the entertainment industry shows no signs of losing or even loosening its grip on those singers it chooses to allow into the heady reaches of international megabuck appeal. When those singers who have the qualities the industry feeds upon come from jazz or jazz-related fields, a whiff of compromise can usually be detected. Among those sought-after qualities are several that most jazz singers would discount as irrelevant – physical appearance perhaps, a wide vocal range, and a sense of personal magnetism. Put another way – eye, ear and sex appeal. Of course there have been and still are true jazz singers who happen to be physically attractive (which is, anyway, an entirely subjective matter), who have a multi-octave range, who possess dramatic flair. But these qualities have been incidental to their musical merit. Nevertheless, the image makers still seek individuals who measure up to their imaginary concepts. It might well be that many of those singers who have their own record labels would, if approached, reject a major company's advances out of fear of losing their individuality, independence and integrity.

Among possible candidates for major company build-up who have musical merit and who might, therefore, reach star status are Cassandra Wilson and Rachelle Ferrell. In passing, while mention has been made of the shift towards a non-black majority among latter-day jazz singers – as the music itself has continued to develop as a thoroughly international form – it remains highly probable that present and future innovators and superstars will be black. Certainly those singers attracting most critical and audience acclaim and industry attention and backing are predominantly black Americans.

After a long musical apprenticeship with the avant-garde groups, Steve Coleman & Five Elements and Greg Osby and the M-Base collective, during which she appeared on eight albums, Cassandra Wilson was launched into the bigtime. Signed by Blue Note, her career took a marked upward trajectory with the release of *Blue Light 'Til Dawn*. Born in Mississippi into a musical family, she sang, played guitar and piano, gradually developing an identifiable style which drew upon a plethora of contemporary popular music forms including jazz and blues. Her deep and respectful interest in these forms allied to her acceptance of funk, rap and hip-hop leads towards a style which is many-layered; particularly so as many of the constituent forms are themselves of multiple origins. Wilson has a rich, wide-ranging voice and clearly delights in exploring its potential – a trait she shares with Sarah Vaughan.

She declared to Suzy Marriott of *Jazz on CD* that her involvement with her work is always intuitive: 'I rely a lot on spirituality and on connecting with what I do. It's rarely contrived – always about opening up and allowing the music to lead me rather than me leading the music.' Although her audience appears to accept her unquestioningly, her fellow musicians have sometimes expressed reservations, some clearly believing that her links to the pop scene are too strong. Others accept her work; multi-instrumentalist Henry Threadgill, speaking of a specific recording of one of his compositions, declared: 'She has the ability to deliver not just the words but also the mood and feeling and the whole scenario of a lyric. Virtuoso singers are not necessarily musical. Cassandra is, as you can hear by the way she phrases and blends with the instruments.' Sheila Jordan is also impressed by her, hearing a distinctiveness some others missed: 'Contrary to what other, established, singers have said about her, I think she sounds like Cassandra Wilson and nobody else. She's unique and I like very much what she's doing.' And what Wilson is doing is constantly seeking new boundaries to cross, new fields to conquer: 'I'm always into moving into the unknown.'

It would not be difficult for singers as skilled as most jazz singers are to adapt to the musical needs of pop superstardom, and Wilson clearly has that ability if she chooses to go that way. Similarly, the vocal gap between jazz singer Rachelle Ferrell and, say, pop superstar Whitney Houston is quite narrow. It is easy to imagine Ferrell stepping sideways into the other camp and not impossible to imagine Houston making the opposite move. Financially, of course, it would be disastrous for Houston. Rachelle Ferrell first attracted attention in Philadelphia singing jazz standards in a highly creative manner, accompanying herself well on piano. She worked as a session singer and also as a teacher's teacher at music colleges in New Jersey. In 1991, when she was thirty, record companies recognized the possibilities offered by her astonishing multi-octave range, a voice that is clearly able to accomplish any task she might set it. She built a following in jazz circles in the 1990s, but surprised many by making an r&b album. A contract with and a new album for Blue Note brought her back into the jazz world and her profile was heightened by an appearance at the 1991 North Sea Jazz Festival. Drawing early inspiration from Ella Fitzgerald, Billie Holiday, Abbey Lincoln and Anita Baker, she constantly pushes outwards her stylistic boundaries. Although she continues to favour an orthodox repertoire in her jazz performances, the manner in which she presents it is always adventurous. Her pop and r&b work is also excitingly inventive, as are her arrangements. Consciously striving to avoid pigeon-holing, she is aware of the dangers: 'The American music industry is driven more by marketing than it is by creativity. If you get caught up in a label, sometimes you never get out of there.'

Ferrell's vocal prowess is such that she can clearly do anything she wants; her coolly appraising view of the business end of the music industry suggests that she will not allow herself to be sidetracked from whatever course she sets for herself. Whether or not she decides upon a jazz-only course is another question. This might prove to be uncomfortably restricting for someone with such enormous potential, and in many ways it would be unreasonable for the jazz audience to expect it of her. The attention she has received has sometimes come close to diverting her: 'It's been difficult to keep to my schedule of practice. If you don't keep a handle on it you can forget to open your mouth and sing. I can sit around all day doing interviews, but sooner or later I've got to get on stage and make it all mean something.'

What will be difficult for Ferrell, and for Wilson, will be to achieve cross-over success – if they should seek it – without too much compromise. An aspect of superstardom in the story of jazz singing is the need for the artist to have broad appeal, to be able to cross and recross the line that divides audiences into jazz and non-jazz without offending either group. Louis Armstrong did it; so, too, Ella Fitzgerald and Mel Tormé managed the delicate balancing act – although it must be said that they did so in an entirely unforced manner, the division between jazz and popular success being then not so wide. Indeed, there is a strong case to suggest that few of those who did achieve stardom in jazz either sought or expected it. When it came, it was an unexpected bonus to a lifetime's dedication to their craftsmanship. Recompense in part, perhaps, for the lost hours of travel, the sleepless nights, bad food, damaged health and relationships.

Whether singers such as Cassandra Wilson and Rachelle Ferrell have the desire for cross-over success is a matter for conjecture. That they have the necessary qualities to achieve it is readily apparent. However, there is no sign whatsoever that the music industry's moguls of the 1990s have any more knowledge and understanding of or empathy with jazz than had their predecessors at any time in the past. If the singers should choose to take the step they will need to be careful.

With the uncertainties of the past and present to work from, all that can be said of what the future might hold for them – and for all the other women and men singing jazz in the 1990s – is that it's anyone's guess. Nevertheless, it is an interesting topic for speculation.

TEN
A HUNDRED YEARS FROM TODAY

Perhaps we will end up in some jazz archive somewhere. — *Carol Sloane*

What directions might jazz singing take in the future? What new concepts will emerge, which of the accepted forms that are around today will survive and which will be discarded? Will the fundamental elements of the classic blues remain? Will the love songs of the great composers and lyricists of the 1930s and 1940s be around a hundred years from today? Or will the computerized playing – and writing – of music that is prevalent in pop and has already infiltrated jazz take over? Can jazz ever again produce world-famous artists such as Ella Fitzgerald and Sarah Vaughan in a milieu in which singing superstars are man-made creations of a multi-billion-dollar industry? Will innovative geniuses comparable to Louis Armstrong and Billie Holiday appear to change the form of jazz singing? Indeed, does jazz singing – in whatever form it might take – have a future?

Perhaps the nature of the jazz singer's repertoire will have an effect upon the extent to which the music will prevail. The traditional repertoire – 32-bar popular songs, some blues, giving way to bop and post-bop concepts – is under constant pressure from industry and audience attitudes and from technology. Helen Merrill picks up this last aspect when she declares, '... high technology is not for our kind of music – my kind of music'.

As for the changing repertoire, this is something that concerns many singers. Magni Wentzel qualifies her general optimism: 'Yes, there is a future for jazz singing. But we need great melodies and we don't seem to be getting them from composers today.' Indeed we are not. Even among the younger singers the failure of latter-day composers to produce songs with the inherent qualities that made their predecessors so durable and suitable for jazz improvisation is a serious and justified cause for concern.

In an age of increasing cynicism, the subject matter of the majority of popular songs of the past – innocent love, unrequited love, sentimental love – might well be a candidate for early dismissal in the twenty-first century.

Among the inevitabilities that lie in the future is the fact that the background of the singers, which has already undergone considerable change, will be strikingly different. Educational establishments of the USA, Britain and some other European countries are increasingly including jazz in their syllabuses and for the moment there is nothing to suggest that this trend will be reversed. But educational establishments need money to operate and this is something that needs careful consideration before anyone grows too sanguine. Like it or not, and many do not, money is a key factor in the future of jazz. Inevitably, many creative artists, perhaps naturally, are unable to throw off disdain for bottom-line thinking. Businessmen are equally unwilling to accept the – to them – unlikely premise that innovation comes from the heart and mind, not from the chequebook.

Unfortunately, it is not only in the music industry that, even after a hundred years of its existence, jazz is still widely ignored and misunderstood. The broadcasting media is similarly often resistant to jazz. In Britain at least, jazz on radio is frequently ill-conceived, while jazz on television is almost non-existent. Compounding the problem, decision makers in arts-funding bodies have for years been prejudiced against jazz. In Britain, where they are now being forced to acknowledge its existence and needs, they remain largely ignorant and mistrustful of jazz. Statistics gleaned from the Arts Council's own review of jazz in the 1990s and widely publicized by Jazz Services Limited and the Association of British Jazz Musicians offers conclusive evidence that approximately the same number of people, three million, attend live jazz events each year as attend opera, yet jazz receives only 1 per cent of the funding given to opera. Perhaps fund controllers have fallen into a double trap: on one hand the class prejudice which, in Britain at least, hangs uneasily over opera and classical music; and on the other hand the marketing hype that has of late surrounded certain opera singers. The Arts Council's declared intention to publish early and firm recommendations was somehow delayed. In the months before the announcement rumours abounded, among them that any additional funding might perhaps be incorporated within the general fund allocation on an 'it's all music, isn't it' principle. Cynics thought that this was little more than an advance warning that jazz was once again about to be short-changed. Meanwhile, realists (who sometimes inhabit the same corporeal – if not corporate – body as cynics) knew that what was needed was a well funded, substantial, well-planned, and knowledgeably-operated infrastructure for jazz.

In 1996, the Arts Council, back pedalling furiously, cast doubt on their original findings intimating that interest in jazz might be on the decline. Anything it would seem was preferable than to fund jazz fairly to the detriment of other areas of music. Eventually a jazz policy was produced – identifying the real priorities but still fudging the issue of funding. The vague suggestion that financial responsibility will lie with the National Lottery offers the jazz cynic little hope of a bright financial future.

The funding situation in America is just as bleak. Although the National Endowment for the Arts was instigated in 1965, it took years for jazz to be considered seriously, trailing behind opera, ballet, orchestral music and the visual arts. Jazz never did catch up and in 1995 came the decision to slash funding by 40 per cent across the board for the coming fiscal year. A 40 per cent cut on something that was already an impoverished also-ran, when compared to other areas of the arts, was catastrophic. Just what this means for the future of jazz singing is impossible to evaluate but it certainly is not good news. What must be clear, given the experiences of jazz singers recounted in this book, is that the degree of commitment, the hard work, the enthusiasm, the dedication of jazz singers is certainly no less than that displayed by any singer in any other branch of the arts. Yet jazz singers remain disregarded, they are still treated shabbily, they are understood no better now than at any time in the past. It would be idle to pretend that simply throwing money at jazz would make any kind of sense, either commercial or artistic. But marketed and/or funded sympathetically and intelligently, it could benefit all participants.

Mike Campbell has considered the dichotomy between the artistic and commercial future of jazz singing: 'Artistically, the future is very bright. Commercially, I don't see a financial future. New young guys are coming along: Kurt Elling, Ben Sidran, Kevin Mahogany, Dianne Reeves, a lot of people are doing it – Madeline Eastman, she's just a killer. But the simpler kind of singers, the Carol Sloanes, they're not flashy singers. I don't think there is a future as we get into technology, instant gratification and flash. It's harder to gain an audience. Do you think that anyone would be listening to Nat Cole today? I don't think so. But small audiences who like taste don't want flash. Carol Sloane is about as unflash as it gets and is magnificent.'

Sloane herself is cautious about a strong future for jazz singing: 'Not the way I sing it. To be perfectly honest, I'm beginning to feel like a dinosaur.' Harry Connick Jnr also takes a negative view of latter-day audiences: 'If Billie Holiday walked on the stage of the Apollo Theater now, she would be booed off the stage because all that people want to hear today is tricks.' André Previn supports this line of thought. Writing a sleeve note for a recent Betty Bennett album he recalled once seeing Sarah Vaughan listening attentively to Bennett singing in a night club: 'Only when the set was over did she speak. Turning to her companion, she said: "the kid sings good." In today's market, such a statement wouldn't be tolerated as a genuine compliment. We live in an age of almost hysterical exaggeration. In publicity releases, *Rambo* is compared to *Citizen Kane*. Andrew Lloyd Webber has inherited the mantle of Mozart and Madonna is the reincarnation of Helen of Troy.' A more optimistic outlook is expressed by Susannah McCorkle who sees a bright future for jazz singing 'as long as people love it and youngsters discover it all the time'. Tina May agrees: 'I think jazz has a great future.' La Velle considers the future in a broader sense, introducing a philosophical view of the continuing role of singers in civilized society: 'There's always a future for music because it is the art that God gave man that will stand always. We are the troubadours, we are the people that carry on the story. We are here to make you feel good about being here.'

If the music industry planned for the future with music rather than money in mind it would today nurture young jazz singers and instrumentalists on a long-term basis and not cast them aside on the basis of poor initial sales. After all, if an artist was deemed good enough to sign in the first place the least the company should do is to have faith in its own judgment. Such actions would not be contrary to a company's own long-term self interest. As Tom Lellis says, 'It no longer has anything to do with talent; it is all to do with someone's ability to market something. Many choose to sell to the public, by massive hype, artists that are not worthwhile instead of hunting the marketplace for people that are worthwhile. The tradition of taking talent and nurturing it has been superseded by the businessman who will take anything that he thinks he can sell to the exclusion of many talented performers.'

Marguerite Juenemann ponders the same problem: 'It doesn't seem to be enough for the industry that your music is good and there is a public supporting you.' How would she like to see it changed? 'I would decrease the dollar's importance as motivation and enhance the importance of keeping creativity alive as a basic positive human necessity.' And Jan Ponsford backs this up: 'Jazz has got to have a future. It's the creative juice of music, an immediate source of creative music.' Tina May declares: 'I am appalled at how few people in the business side of jazz are prepared to market it. It has always been the case, particularly in Britain, that jazz has never been properly marketed, never been publicized.'

Although slow to encourage and promote contemporary jazz, the reissue programmes of major record companies have granted the accolade of appearing on compact disc to singers such as Monette Moore from the 1920s, Jerry Kruger from the 1930s, Lucy Ann Polk from the 1940s, Betty Bennett from the 1950s, all of whom were reluctantly granted occasional recording sessions at the height of their careers. Unfortunately, as such singers of true worth are to be found on compact disc, so too are the mediocre and bad.

The reissue programme does, of course, allow latter-day audiences and singers to listen to elements of the past they might otherwise have missed but, as we have seen, in the meantime few of the new singers are being recorded by major labels with any consistency. Can the singers do anything about this, apart from doing what they are already doing – making their own records and arranging their own gigs and acting as their own publicity agents and promotors? Well, if there is anything in the old adage about strength in numbers, perhaps they can. In late 1996 the recently formed London-based Jazz Singers Network had a membership in excess of 300 singers – and they were still a long way from being a nation-wide organization. Extrapolate this through Britain alone and the numbers become what politicians might regard as a significant lobby. Add those listed on the National Register of Jazz Vocalists in America and in similar organizations in Europe and the rest of the world and clearly the numbers of singers demanding to be heard must be huge – perhaps already reaching into five figures.

Can this significant number of individuals, banded together with a common purpose, achieve more than their fellows of the past? Perhaps they can, but wherever the singers of the future might take their music, it must be hoped that their predecessors are not forgotten. Carol Sloane remarks: 'Perhaps we will end up in some jazz archive somewhere.' If the experience and thoughts of singers like Sloane do end up in an archive, hopefully it will be a living one and not some musty old basement filled with dusty documents. Much better will be one that is freely accessible to newcomers who want to study and keep alive the traditions that have made jazz song such an important part of popular culture in the twentieth century. It doesn't seem too much to ask for a branch of popular culture that has given so much entertainment and pleasure to so many people for so many years. Whether or not it will, in fact, prove to be too much to ask remains to be seen.

Here, then, are three wishes for the future: a flourishing worldwide organization of jazz singers; an active movement by record companies to promote jazz singers; and a living research source for jazz singers.

In the meantime, in an uncertain world, one thing is certain; young women and men will continue to enter the tough and demanding profession of the jazz singer. Recognized or not, encouraged or not, popular or not, famous or not, rich or not, they will eagerly spend their days and nights doing something that they love – singing jazz.

Louis Armstrong with
Billie Holiday

Mildred Bailey

Lillian Boutté

Terry Blaine

Betty Bennett

Dee Dee
Bridgewater

Betty Carter

Cab Calloway

Mike Campbell

Laila Dalseth   Dardanelle

Elaine Delmar

Ella Fitzgerald

Dominique Eade

Dave Frishberg

Slim Gaillard

Shirley Horn

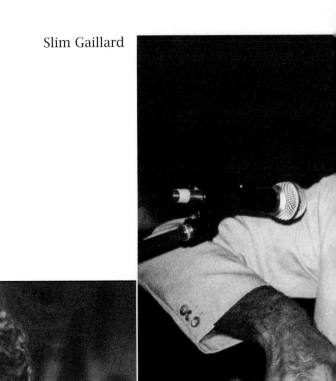

Helen Humes

Marguerite
Juenemann

Stacey Kent

Sue Kibbey

Barbara Lashley

Carol Kidd

Nickie Leighton-Thomas

Tom Lellis

Abbey Lincoln

Julia Lee

Chris McNulty

Susannah
McCorkle

Bobby
McFerrin

Claire Martin

Tina May

Helen Merrill

Carmen McRae

Marion Montgomery

Kitty Margolis

Nanette Natal

Mark Murphy

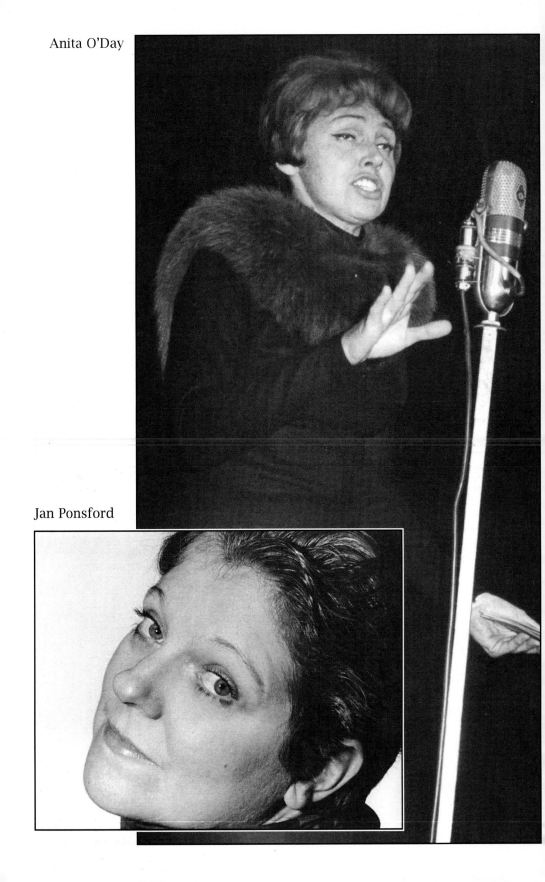

Anita O'Day

Jan Ponsford

Mark Porter

Dianne Reeves

Lucy Reed

Ellyn Rucker

Carol Sloane

Mel Tormé

Sister Rosetta
Tharpe

Sarah Vaughan

Marlene VerPlanck

Fats Waller

Ethel Waters

Magni Wentzel

Cassandra Wilson

Dinah Washington

Norma Winstone

Jimmy Witherspoon

This Directory is not an encyclopaedia. It is a list of artists, past and present, who are of interest in any study of the art of jazz singing and jazz-influenced popular singing. Some of the artists listed in the following pages indisputably warrant their inclusion here. Others might raise eyebrows; therefore, a word of explanation is required.

In the main text of this book some singers are discussed in detail and therefore these artists are mentioned only very briefly in this Directory: date of birth, or death, suggested records. In contrast, some artists had to be dealt with only briefly in the main text, or even omitted entirely, and this, therefore, is the place where they appear. Some names are quite clearly not jazz singers but they are here because they played a role, however unwitting or overlooked, in creating an atmosphere in which audiences could accept a form of music that was hitherto alien to them. And even today, some singers help form the bridge between popular song and jazz singing and hence appear here.

As is always the case in such ventures, space and personal taste will have coloured and affected selection. This is especially relevant to the records listed. Which out of hundreds of CDs by Billie Holiday do we include? They have to be only a sample. With a currently healthy reissue programme under way, the most recent labels are given, where possible, but the date is that on which the records were made, not released. This allows the reader to choose from a particular period of a singer's work. Label numbers are not included because these might vary from country to country.

In preparing this Directory we have been thankful for the existence of several important reference works. These are all listed in detail in the Bibliography but here we would like to express particular gratitude to *The Faber Companion to 20th-Century Popular Music*, Hugh Gregory's *Soul Music A - Z*, *The New Grove Dictionary of Jazz* and *The Guinness Encyclopedia of Popular Music*. Finally, we welcome readers' suggestions for additions or corrections to this listing which might be considered in future editions of *Singing Jazz*.

Alexandria, Lorez

b. Delorez Alexandria Turner, 14 August 1929, Chicago, Illinois, USA. First sang in church, then became a gospel singer. Late 50s, had successful albums and a spell with Ramsey Lewis, then turned to jazz. Recorded with Howard McGhee, Wynton Kelly. Rich contralto and a questing style result in truly professional performances that are always interesting, with often powerful interpretations.
Albums: *Lorez Sings Pres* (King, 1957), *A Woman Knows* (Discovery, 1978), *Harlem Butterfly* (Discovery, 1984).

Allen, Henry 'Red'

b. Henry James Allen, 7 January 1908, New Orleans, Louisiana, USA, d. 17 April 1967. Although much in Louis Armstrong's shadow throughout his career, he was a transitional musician. An expressive and rhythmic trumpet player, his singing echoed his eccentric instrumental work. He spent the second half of his life as a single, playing in New York clubs and touring internationally.
Albums: *The Henry Allen Collection Vols 1-4* (Collector's Classics, 1932-7), *Feeling Good* (Columbia, 1965).

Allen, Jackie

b. Milwaukee, Wisconsin, USA. Studied music at University of Wisconsin, Madison, where she concentrated on singing, having previously also learned French horn. In late 80s teamed with organist Melvin Rhyne, then in 1990 settled in Chicago but also sings and teaches in home town. Relaxed, she sings in a rhythmic, inventive style, with a pleasing, slightly nasal sound.
Albums: *Never Let Me Go* (Lake Shore Jazz, 1994).

Allison, Mose

b. Mose John Allison Jnr, 11 November 1927, Tippo, Mississippi, USA. Studied piano and trumpet and also wrote own material. Although born into a white middle-class family, is heavily influenced by black folk music. Played modern jazz with Stan Getz, Al Cohn, but became influential upon 60s and 70s pop singers. Composer of 'Parchman Farm', 'A Young Man's Blues'. Sings in casual, self-deprecating style.
Albums: *Back Country Suite* (Prestige, 1957), *Western Man* (Atlantic, 1971), *Middle Class White Boy* (Elektra, 1982), *My Backyard* (Blue Note, 1990).

Allyn, David

b. David Allen, 19 July 1923, Hartford, Connecticut, USA. Sang semi-professionally in mid-teens, then joined Jack Teagarden's big band in early 40s. After war joined Boyd Raeburn; briefly with Stan Kenton, then worked as a single. A highly skilled musician with good pitch and diction, his qualities are exceptional in the jazz-inflected post-Sinatra mould. Albums: *I Only Have Eyes for You* (Warner Bros, 1959), *In the Blue of the Evening* (Discovery, 1966), *Don't Look Back* (Xanadu, 1975).

Allyson, Karrin

b. Great Bend, Kansas, USA. Studied classical piano and after graduation in 1987 began singing in Minneapolis, Minnesota, clubs, often accompanying herself. A breathy delivery and rich sound brings interesting resonances to ballads and up-tempo songs.

Albums: *Karrin Allyson* (Concord, c.1992), *Azure Té* (Concord, 1994).

Anderson, Ernestine

b. Ernestine Irene Anderson, 11 November 1928, Houston, Texas, USA. Raised in Seattle, Washington, she began singing professionally at age thirteen with Russell Jacquet's band, then Johnny Otis, mostly performing r&b. In the 50s sang with Lionel Hampton, Gigi Gryce, toured Scandinavia with Rolf Ericson and recorded with Harry Arnold in Sweden. Resident in England during 60s, then settled on west coast of USA, singing in clubs and at festivals. Rich, wide-ranging voice and repertoire with strong affinity with the blues.

Albums: *Hot Cargo* (Metronome, 1956), *Moanin', Moanin', Moanin'* (Mercury, 1960), *Hello Like Before* (Concord, 1976), *When the Sun Goes Down* (Concord, 1984).

Anderson, Ivie

b. Ivy Marie Anderson, 10 July 1905, Gilroy, California, USA, d. 28 December 1949. Early in her career she sang with Earl Hines and toured USA and Australia before joining Duke Ellington in 1931. Made many fine records including the definitive 'It Don't Mean a Thing (If It Ain't Got That Swing)' and made an impact despite sharing stage with some of the finest soloists in all of jazz. Relaxed, with a delicately airy sound, she retired while still in her prime but came back for a 1946 recording.

Albums: *Ivie Anderson with Duke Ellington and His Famous Orchestra* (Jazz Archives, 1932–40) *An Introduction to Ivie Anderson* (Best of Jazz, 1932–42), *Ivie Anderson and Her All Stars* (Storyville, 1946).

Andrade, Leny

b. c.1939, Rio De Janeiro, Brazil. After studying piano, she turned to singing and in the 50s performed with many Brazilian artists including Sergio Mendes. Subsequently, she worked in Mexico, USA, Europe. A strong preference for Latin music is found in her repertoire and adds interesting colouring to her jazz work.

Albums: *Luz Neon* (Timeless, c.1990).

Andrews, Ernie

b. USA. Working mostly on the west coast, his blues style is effective whether with small jazz groups or with the big bands of the Los Angeles area. His ballad style is soulfully pleasing and overtly masculine.

Albums: *Juggernaut* (Concord, 1976), *From the Heart* (Discovery, 1980); *The Great City* (Muse, 1990).

Armstrong, Lil

b. Lillian Hardin, 3 February 1898, Memphis, Tennessee, USA, d. 27 August 1971. After studying music she worked with several bands and also played as a soloist. With King Oliver's band in Chicago in the 20s she met and married Louis Armstrong and played an important part in redirecting his career as a featured trumpeter. In the late 30s she made some delightful records with her own small band. A competent pianist and an appealing interpreter of songs.

Albums: *Lil Hardin Armstrong and Her Swing Orchestra* (Classics, 1936-40), *Lil Hardin and Her Orchestra* (Riverside, 1961).

Armstrong, Louis

b. 4 August 1901, New Orleans, Louisiana, USA, d. 6 July 1971. His career is assessed in detail in Chapter 2.

Albums: *The Hot Fives and Hot Sevens Vols 1-4* (CBS, 1925-8), *Young Louis Armstrong* (RCA, 1930-3), *Louis Sings the Blues* (RCA, 1933-47), *Town Hall Concert Plus* (RCA, 1947), *Louis Armstrong Plays W. C. Handy* (Columbia, 1954), *What a Wonderful World* (RCA, 1967).

Atwood, Eden

b. USA. A very accomplished young singer whose early promise was spotted by Concord Records who first reissued her own privately produced album, then recorded her afresh. She has a mature sense of interpretation and swings with effortless ease.

Albums: *There Again* (Concord, 1994).

Babs, Alice

b. Alice Nilson, 26 January 1924, Kalmar, Sweden. After singing in her own country she made an impression at the 1949 Paris Jazz Fair. In the 60s she began recording with Duke Ellington, her pure classical voice proving a perfect vehicle for his religious works. She studied classical singing, sang pop successfully and also the folk music of her native land. In a jazz context she swung effortlessly and interpreted ballads with flair.

Albums: with Ellington *Serenade to Sweden* (Reprise, 1963), *Far Away Star* (Phontastic, 1974-6).

Bailey, Mildred

b. Mildred Rinker, 27 February 1907, Tekoa, Washington, USA, d. 12 December 1951. Played piano in silent movie theatres and as a song demonstrator before playing and singing in clubs and on radio. Joined Paul Whiteman in 1929, recorded extensively, and had her own radio show. Her version of 'Rockin' Chair' was such a hit that she became known as the 'Rockin' Chair Lady'. After marrying Red Norvo, the pair were dubbed 'Mr and Mrs Swing'. She had a delicate, lightly flowing sound; her timing and phrasing made her a favourite of jazzmen and of many latter-day jazz singers.

Albums: *Mildred Bailey: Her Greatest Performances* (CBS, 1929-46), *Harlem Lullaby* (Living Era, 1931-8).

Bailey, Pearl

b. Pearl Mae Bailey, 29 March 1918, Newport News, Virginia, USA. d. 17 August 1990. After singing with the bands of Noble Sissle and Edgar Hayes, she attracted wide attention while with Cootie Williams. Played clubs and then appeared in Broadway shows. In the 50s she was in films and made many records. She married Louie Bellson who became her musical director. She won a special Tony Award for her leading role in the all-black version of *Hello Dolly*. Her stage act included wry patter in the black vaudeville tradition and occasional bursts of religious sermonizing amidst the songs.

Albums: *Pearl Bailey: 16 Most Requested Songs* (Columbia, 1945–50), *The Real Pearl Bailey* (Project, 1968).

Baker, Chet
b. Chesney Henry Baker, 23 December 1929, Yale, Oklahoma, USA, d. 13 May 1988. His low-key, laid-back singing, allied to an almost apologetic delivery, made him a beguiling singer. He was one of the few modern trumpeters to venture into vocals.

Albums: *Let's Get Lost* (Pacific Jazz, 1953–6), *Chet Baker Sings Again* (Timeless, 1984).

Baker, LaVern
b. 11 November 1929, Chicago, Illinois, USA, d. 10 March 1997. In the early 50s she hit the r&b bigtime, having previously recorded mostly ballads. At the end of the 50s she was seemingly well-suited to soul but began to drift from the spotlight. Although she had contracts with several major labels, including Columbia, Atlantic and Brunswick, there was never a forceful guiding hand behind her career.

Albums: *Real Gone Gal* (Charly, 1953–62), *Sings Bessie Smith* (Atlantic, 1958).

Beeks, Clarence
see **King Pleasure**

Benjamin, 'Sathima' Bea
b. 17 October 1936, Cape Town, South Africa. Sang in and around her home town, then met and married pianist Dollar Brand (who later became Abdullah Ibrahim). Met and recorded with Duke Ellington in early 60s. Later exiled and took up residence in USA. Wide-ranging repertoire and a pure, almost vibrato-free voice lend her a distinctive sound and style. Her work is imbued with the spirit of Africa.

Albums: *A Morning in Paris* (Enja, 1963), *Lovelight* (Enja, 1987), *Southern Touch* (Enja, 1992).

Bennett, Betty
b. 23 October 1921, Lincoln, Nebraska, USA. Sang with bands of Georgie Auld, Claude Thornhill and Charlie Ventura in the mid- to late 40s. In the 50s worked with her then-husband André Previn. Worked later mostly on the west coast, met and married Mundell Lowe in 1975, continuing to perform regularly into the late 80s. A developing interest in lyrics and the subtleties of songs resulted in her becoming a fine performer of jazz and popular standards. Albums: *Betty Bennett* (Trend, 1953), with Previn *Nobody Else But Me* (Atlantic, 1955), *The Song Is You* (Fresh Sounds, 1990).

Blaine, Terry
b. USA. Studied piano and other instruments formally before starting to sing. After college she sang with a rock band, then turned to jazz and developed a large repertoire with the aid of pianist Mark

Shane. A fine sense of phrasing imbues her work with great interest and a naturally joyous light shines through.

Albums: *Whose Honey Are You?* (Jukebox Jazz, 1994), *In Concert with the Mark Shane Quartet* (Jukebox Jazz, 1994).

Boswell, Connee

b. Connie Boswell, 3 December 1907, Kansas City, Missouri, USA, d. 11 October 1976. A gifted and well-trained instrumentalist, Boswell and her sisters, Martha and Helvetia, were raised in New Orleans and as children heard much black music. She was one of the first singers to recognize the potential of the microphone and to adapt her style accordingly. By the mid-30s she was a major influence upon many singers, black and white. After her sisters retired, she continued as a single and had a long and fruitful career despite the handicap of having to spend her active working life in a wheelchair.

Albums: *Connee Boswell and the Original Memphis Five in Hi Fi* (RCA, 1956).

Boswell Sisters, The

The outstanding vocal group of its time and the blueprint for many that followed, they were formed in New Orleans in the 20s. Connee (*qv*), Martha, b. 1908, New Orleans, Louisiana, USA, d. 1958, and Helvetia (Vet) b. 1909, New Orleans, d. 12 November 1988, were all instrumentalists and singers. They gained fame in New Orleans, then moved to Los Angeles and a nightly radio show. They recorded exten-sively in the early 30s, appeared on radio and on early television. All three married in the mid-30s and Martha and Vet retired, thus ending the group, but its influence lived on.

Albums: *Okay America!* (Jass, 1931-5), *You Oughta Be in Pictures,* (Conifer, 1932-5).

Boutté, Lillian

b. Lillian Theresa Boutté, 6 August 1949, New Orleans, Louisiana, USA. After singing in a church choir she began a career in r&b. Her musical interests widened her range and she was soon in the mainstream and also appeared on stage, notably in *One Mo' Time.* From the early 80s she appeared extensively in Europe, often with a group led by saxo-phonist Thomas l'Etienne, whom she married. Equally adept with ballads, blues, r&b, and gospel-flavoured songs, her reputation gained strength in the 90s, a period when she also conducted gospel clinics.

Albums: *Music Is My Life* (Timeless, 1984), *Lillian Boutté with Humphrey Lyttelton and His Band* (Calligraph, 1988), *Live in Tivoli* (Music Mecca, 1993).

Breach, Joyce

b. 27 February 1944, Alameda, Cali-fornia, USA. Studied piano as a child and started singing while at univer-sity. Her interest in the work of singers such as Mabel Mercer and Blossom Dearie was encouraged by singer-pianist Charles Cochran. She moved into cabaret work and spent twenty years in Pittsburgh's supe-rior nightspots. A deep yet soft voice and delightful diction helps her create admirable moods for the songs in her broad repertoire.

Albums: *Songbird* (Audiophile, 1985), *Lovers After All* (Audiophile, 1993).

Bridgewater, Dee Dee

b. Denise Garrett, 27 May 1950, Memphis, Tennessee, USA. Began singing in the 60s with University of Illinois big band. Married fellow band member Cecil Bridgewater and moved to New York where in the 70s she sang with the Thad Jones–Mel Lewis band and appeared on Broadway in *The Wiz*, for which she won a Tony Award. Sang on the west coast, mostly pop, then moved to Europe in the early 80s and re-entered the jazz world. By the early 90s was established internationally as a major jazz singer. A sensitive balladeer, she swings superbly on up-tempo numbers.

Albums: *Brains on Fire Vols 1 and 2* (Labor, 1966–7), *Dee Dee Bridgewater* (Elektra, 1980), *Live in Paris* (Affinity, 1986), *Keeping Tradition* (Verve, 1992), *Love and Peace: A Tribute to Horace Silver* (Verve, 1994).

Brooks, Hadda

b. Hadda Hopgood, 29 October 1916, Los Angeles, California, USA. While playing piano at a dance studio she was heard by Joe Bihari and hired for his nascent record company, Modern. She played boogie-woogie for Bihari, then in 1946 began singing with Charlie Barnet's band. She had hits with 'You Won't Let Me Go' and 'That's My Desire' and others and made

brief appearances in a number of Hollywood films in the late 40s and early 50s.

Albums: *Romance in the Dark* (Ace, 1940s).

Brown, Cleo

b. Cleo Patra Brown, 8 December c.1909, DeKalb, Meridian, Mississippi, USA. At the age of fourteen she was playing professionally in Chicago and soon had her own radio show. A gifted pianist and singer, she was popular in Chicago and New York, often playing boogie-woogie. Her singing style anticipated the light-voiced Rose Murphy and the rumbustious Nellie Lutcher. In 1953 she left music to become a nurse but twenty years later was back singing, though this time mostly in church, as C. Patra Brown. Albums: included on *Kings and Queens of Ivory* (MCA, 1935–40), *The Legendary Cleo Brown* (President, 1935/6).

Brown, Ruth

b. Ruth Weston, 30 January 1928, Portsmouth, Virginia, USA. She sang with Lucky Millinder in 1944, then married trumpeter Jimmy Brown and turned to r&b. Signed by Atlantic, she had five No. 1 hits in the 50s but by 1962 her style was out of fashion. In 1976 she came back from retirement, singing r&b and jazz. She appeared on Broadway in *Black and Blue* and won a Grammy for *Blues on Broadway*. An expressive ballad singer, she has an energetic, robust style. Albums: *Rockin' with Ruth* (Charly, 1950s), *Takin' Care of Business* (Stockholm, 1980), *Blues on*

Broadway (Fantasy, 1989), *Live at Ronnie Scott's* (Jazz House, 1994).

Brown, Walter
b. poss. August 1917, Dallas, Texas, USA, d. poss. June 1956. After singing semi-professionally through the late 30s in Texas, he moved to Kansas City and joined Jay McShann. He was with McShann for five years, where he became popular, leaving in 1945. Later, his career drifted and he battled unsuccessfully with drug addiction. He sang the blues with an unusual yet effective laid-back drawl.
Albums: with McShann *Hootie's KC Blues* (Affinity, 1940s).

Bryden, Beryl
b. Beryl Audrey Bryden, 11 May 1926, Norwich, Norfolk, England. An exuberant, larger-than-life fixture on the British trad jazz scene for many years, she sang with George Webb, Chris Barber and others in the 40s and soon had an enthusiastic following. In the 60s she became popular in Holland and Germany and happily ignored changing musical tastes. She was still singing and playing the washboard in the 90s, her earlier retirement never having quite come off.
Albums: *Way Down Yonder in New Orleans* (Elite Special, 1975), *Basin Street Blues* (CBS, 1991), *Big Daddy* (CBS 1991).

Cain, Jackie
b. Jacqueline Ruth Cain, 22 May 1928, Milwaukee, Wisconsin, USA. After singing ballads as a single, teamed up with Roy Kral in Chicago in the mid-40s. Billed as Jackie and Roy they joined Charlie Ventura's Bop for the People band in 1948, married the following year, and went out on their own. Heavily influenced by bop, they were also expert in vocalese. They continued performing into the 90s.
Albums: with Ventura *Jackie & Roy* (Regent/Savoy, 1948), *Spring Can Really Hang You Up the Most* (Storyville, 1955), *One More Rose* (Audiophile, 1980s), *High Standards* (Concord, 1982), *Full Circle* (Contemporary, 1988).

Calloway, Blanche
b. 1902, Baltimore, Maryland, USA, d. 16 December 1978. Sang as a child and toured extensively in the 20s. The following decade saw her leading her own band. Later she sang as a single then quit performing to work in other areas of show business, notably as manager of Ruth Brown. Her brother is Cab Calloway whom she pre-dated with her extrovert and cheerful style.
Albums: *Blanche Calloway* (Harlequin, 1931).

Calloway, Cab
b. Cabell Calloway, 25 December 1907, Rochester, New York, USA, d. 18 November 1994. After working as a dancer, drummer and singer, in 1929 he joined the Alabamians as front man. Later, in New York, he fronted the Missourians and in 1931 the band assumed his name when he took it into the Cotton Club as replacement for Duke Ellington. Calloway's singing was original, dramatic and extravagant and frequently wildly over the top.

He sang of drugs and drink and sex, dressed outrageously, and was hugely popular with the general audience. In later years he appeared extensively on stage and in films and on television.

Albums: *Minnie the Moocher* (RCA, 1930s), *Cruisin' with Cab* (Submarine, 1930s).

Campbell, Mike
b. Los Angeles, California, USA. He sings in cabaret and intimate jazz settings, carefully distilling the essence of his repertoire which draws from standards of the past and the post-bop songbook. He habitually works and records with leading contemporary jazz musicians, including Tom Garvin, his regular accompanist. He teaches in the USA, Canada and Europe. His singing voice is warm and his relaxed yet skilful manner lends intimacy and understanding to the songs he sings.

Albums: *Secret Fantasy* (Palo Alto, 1982), *Easy Chair Jazz* (Audiophile, 1982-90), *Blackberry Winter* (ITI, 1983-4), *Loving Friends* (Audiophile, 1994).

Carlisle, Una Mae
b. 26 December 1916, Xenia, Ohio, USA, d. 7 November 1956. Played piano on local radio before meeting Fats Waller in 1932. She worked with him and developed her piano style in his light. A sensitive singer of ballads, the late 30s found her in Europe but by the early 40s she was back in the USA, playing clubs and recording, often with leading jazzmen.

Albums: *Una Mae Carlisle and Savannah Churchill* (Harlequin, 1944).

Carroll, Joe
b. 25 November 1919, Philadelphia, Pennsylvania, USA, d. 1 February 1981. A Louis Armstrong follower at first, Carroll became one of few singers to adapt to bop. He sang with a hard edge to his voice and his natural exuberance and inventiveness made him an effective partner to Dizzy Gillespie in the late 40s and early 50s. Later he toured as a single.

Albums: with Gillespie *Dee Gee Days* (Dee Gee, 1951-2), *Joe Carroll: Man with a Happy Sound* (Charlie Parker, 1962), *Jumpin' at Jazzmania* (Jazzmania, 1978).

Carter, Betty
b. Lillie Mae Jones, 16 May 1929 (or 1930), Flint, Michigan, USA. Her career is assessed in detail in Chapter 8.

Albums: *I Can't Help It* (Impulse!, 1961), *Live at the Village Vanguard* (Verve, 1970), *The Audience with Betty Carter* (Verve, 1979), *Whatever Happened to Love?* (BetCar, 1982), *Feed the Fire* (Verve, 1993).

Charles, Ray
b. Ray Charles Robinson, 23 September 1930, Albany, Georgia, USA. Blind at seven, his early influences were Nat King Cole and Charles Brown and for a while he sang like them. By the late 40s he had found his own voice and was singing r&b in a way that emphasized the music's gospel roots although he himself was never a gospel singer. He built a huge

following for live concerts and records and had many hits. His stylistic range covers ballads, blues, r&b, country, soul and jazz, all of which he sings with flair and distinction.

Albums: *Ray Charles at Newport* (Atlantic, 1958), *Genius + Soul = Jazz* (Impulse!, 1961), with Cleo Laine *Porgy and Bess* (RCA, 1976).

Cheatham, Jeannie
b. Jeannie Evans, c.1936, Akron, Ohio, USA. She played piano as a child at church and when she was fourteen was with a sixteen-piece rehearsal band. In the early 60s she played jazz in small groups and also began singing as a group member. She developed a reputation as a pianist, singer and leader, then teamed up with Jimmy Colvin in the eastern states. When Colvin quit she continued until 1957 when she disbanded. The same year she married trombonist Jimmy Cheatham and continued working as a single or accompanist, mostly in New York. In 1977 the Cheathams moved to San Diego and continued to work and also recorded for Concord. A gifted piano player, she sings very well in the great spirit of the classic blues and is often backed by good jazz musicians.

Albums: *Sweet Baby Blues* (Concord, 1985), *Homeward Bound* (Concord, 1987), *Back to the Neighborhood* (Concord, 1988), *Gud Nuz Bluz* (Concord, l995).

Christy, June
b. Shirley Luster, 20 November 1925, Springfield, Illinois, USA, d. 21 June 1990. After working with Boyd Raeburn she joined Stan Kenton where her bright personality was contrasted with her detached singing style, the epitome of the west coast cool sound. After leaving Kenton she worked as a single and had a successful series of records for Capitol. She also sang and recorded with her husband, tenor saxophonist Bob Cooper. She sang into the 70s, then retired and suffered a period of ill-health.

Albums: *Daydreams* (Capitol, 1947-55), *Something Cool* (Capitol, 1955), *The Misty Miss Christy* (Capitol, 1956), *June Christy Recalls Those Kenton Days* (Capitol, 1959).

Citroen, Soesja
b. Holland. A rich and expressive contralto voice and a deep commitment to jazz mark this singer's work. Although she recorded several very good albums in the 80s, she did not make a breakthrough into the international scene. She has written lyrics for compositions by Thelonious Monk.

Albums: *To Build* (Coreco, 1980), *Key Largo* (Turning Point, 1982), *Soesja Citroen Sings Thelonious Monk* (Timeless, 1982-3), *Shall We Dance or Keep on Moping?* (Timeless, 1986).

Claassen, Fee
b. Holland. A well-trained singer with a repertoire of standards and originals. A singer to watch for in the future, she regularly works with alto saxophonist Carolyn Breuer.

Albums: *Simply Be* (Challenge, 1994).

Clooney, Rosemary

b. 23 May 1928, Maysville, Kentucky, USA. As the Clooney Sisters, she and her sister Betty sang in the early 40s and in 1949 joined Tony Pastor's band. She then went out as a single. She recorded extensively in the 50s but the following decade saw a decline in career and health. By the late 70s she was back on the scene, singing the great standards in her clear, ringing voice, often with good jazz backing and considerable jazz feeling.

Albums: *Rosie Solves the Swingin' Riddle* (RCA, 1960), *Here's to My Lady* (Concord, 1978), *Sings the Music of Harold Arlen* (Concord, 1983), *Sings the Music of Jimmy Van Heusen* (Concord, 1986), *Dedicated to Nelson* (Concord, 1995).

Cole, Holly

b. Canada. Although she has yet to achieve widespread attention, Cole has already built a small but deeply impressed following in the UK. She has a rich and sonorous sound which she uses to develop interesting concepts in a broad-based repertoire.

Albums: *Temptation* (Metro Cole, 1995).

Cole, Nat 'King'

b. Nathaniel Adams Coles, 17 March 1916, Montgomery, Alabama, USA, d. 15 February 1965. After playing jazz piano for many years his singing gradually became more popular. Although he was a major figure in the history of jazz piano, his singing was in the mainstream of popular music. He sang with a light rhythmic flair and a husky intimacy. His interpretations of many ballads became the standards by which others were measured. He had numerous hits during his lifetime and since his death many reissues have kept his name in front of audiences old and new.

Albums: *The Complete Capitol Recordings of the Nat King Cole Trio* (Mosaic, 1942–61), *After Midnight* (Capitol, 1956), *Welcome to the Club* (Capitol, 1959), *Live at the Sands* (Capitol, 1960).

Connor, Chris

b. 8 November 1927, Kansas City, Missouri, USA. She sang professionally in her home town before trying New York. She sang with several bands including Claude Thornhill's, where she was a member of the Snowflakes vocal group. She came to much wider attention when she joined Stan Kenton and thereafter sang as a single. Her career continued into the 90s. Melodically and rhythmically gifted, her husky voice has worn a little but her admirable technique has rarely faltered.

Albums: *Lullabies of Birdland* (Bethlehem, 1954), *Chris Craft* (Atlantic, 1958), *Sketches* (Stanyan, 1972), *London Connection* (Audiophile, 1993).

Cox, Ida

b. Ida Prather, 25 February 1896, Toccoa, Georgia, USA, d. 10 November 1967. Sang the blues from an early age and made records before a period in obscurity. In 1939 she reappeared to record with an all-star band, then more obscurity although blues *aficionados* kept her busy as a performer. A strong singer with a tough, nasal voice, her recordings, although sparse and well-spaced out, show her to be one of the most distinctive of her kind.

Albums: *The Uncrowned Queen of the Blues (BLack Swan, 1920s), I Can't Quit My Man* (Affinity, 1939-40).

Crosby, Bing

b. Harry Lillis Crosby, 3 May 1903, Tacoma, Washington, USA, d. 14 October 1977. He gained prominence after joining Paul Whiteman's Orchestra where he sang as a member of the Rhythm Boys vocal trio. By 1931 Crosby was out on his own and with numerous successful records and a career in Hollywood he soon became the most popular recording star in the history of the medium. More than any other popular singer of his generation, Crosby absorbed the lessons of jazz and helped spread a new style to an international audience for whom jazz itself was merely a word.

Albums: *The Jazzin' Bing* (Affinity, 1927-40), *The Victor Masters Featuring Bing Crosby (With Paul Whiteman and His Orchestra)* (RCA, 1927-31), *The Crooner: The Columbia Years* (Columbia, 1928-34), *Bing and Connee* (Decca, 1951), *Bing Crosby Sings While Buddy Bregman Swings* (Verve, 1956), *Bing and Satchmo* (MGM, 1960).

Cunninghams, The

Don Cunningham, b. 14 January 1931, St Louis, Missouri, USA, Alicia Cunningham, b. 5 October 1946, USA. He started out on drums and also played alto saxophone. She was a classically trained singer when they met in Los Angeles where they married in the 70s. Their duets are sparkling and dynamic and take full advantage of his urgent, rhythmic boppish style and her elegance and charm. Their stage presence is well-honed and stylish and they draw their repertoire from the standards and jazz.

Albums: *Make Me (A Sweet Potato Pie)* (Discovery, 1987), *Scat Tones 'n' Bones* (Discovery, 1989).

Dalseth, Laila

b. 1940, Norway. A self-taught singer, she has built her style upon that of Billie Holiday but has made her own distinctive contribution. She has played and recorded with jazz musicians of many nationalities and is married to saxophonist Totti Bergh. Extremely popular in her homeland, she deserves a much wider audience.

Albums: *Travelling Light* (Gemini, 1986), *The Judge and I* (Gemini, 1991).

Dandridge, Putney

b. Putney Louis Dandridge, 13 January 1902, Richmond, Virginia, USA, d. 15 February 1946. He sang and played piano in clubs in the north-eastern states before becoming a regular at New York jazz haunts. He recorded with many fine jazzmen, playing effective stride piano and singing in a light, pleasant voice.

Albums: *Putney Dandridge Vols 1-3* (Rarities, 1930s) *Putney Dandridge* (Timeless Historic, 1935-6).

Dane, Barbara

b. Barbara Jean Spillman, 12 May 1927, Detroit, Michigan, USA. Sang and played piano and guitar as a child. From the mid-40s she was involved musically and philosophically with labour, civil rights and feminist movements. She sang folk and jazz, working with Pete Seeger, Kid Ory, George Lewis, Turk Murphy and others. She appeared at jazz and folk festivals, sang on television and toured with Jack Teagarden's band. In the 60s and 70s she continued to ally her singing to political causes. A strong blues singer, her records are worth seeking out.
Albums: *Barbara Dane* (Dot, 1959).

Daniels, Maxine

b. Gladys Lynch, 2 November 1930, London, England. She won a talent contest at fourteen, then sang with Denny Boyce's dance band. During the 50s she sang in several superior London venues. Through ill health she was inactive for several years from 1962 but began a slow and successful return during the 80s. In the 90s appeared at jazz festivals and worked with Humphrey Lyttelton.
Albums: *A Beautiful Friendship* (Maxam, 1985), *Every Night About This Time* (Calligraph, 1986).

Dankworth, Jacqui

b. February, 1963, England. Her parents are John Dankworth and Cleo Laine and her brother is bassist Alec Dankworth. Although born into one of the most musical families in the UK, she made her own reputation decisively. Her repertoire draws heavily upon original material, much of which is self-composed. Her singing voice is light and floating with an ethereal sound which admirably suits much of her material.
Albums: *First Cry* (EFZ, 1994).

Dardanelle

b. Dardanelle Mullen, 27 December 1917, Avalon, Mississippi, USA. She began playing piano as a child and during the 30s played along the east coast. In New York in the early 40s she led a trio which included guitarist Tal Farlow. An accomplished pianist and vibraphonist, Dardanelle sings with elegant charm and has a deep and abiding interest in lyrics and in the roots of the music she performs.
Albums: *Colors of My Life* (Stash, 1978-82), *Dardanelle Echoes Singing Ladies* (Audiophile, 1980-90), *Swingin' in London* (Audiophile, 1994).

Dearie, Blossom

b. 28 April 1926, East Durham, New York, USA. After playing piano in a dance band she joined Woody Herman as a member of the Blue Flames vocal group, then was one of Alvino Rey's Blue Reys. In the early 50s she settled in Paris and formed her own Blue Stars vocal group. Later, she returned to the USA and found her niche in New York supper clubs and built a following as a sophisticated purveyor of witty songs and standards which she performs in a quietly undemonstrative manner.
Albums: *Blossom Dearie* (Verve, 1956), *My New Celebrity Is You*

(Daffodil, 1979), *Songs of Chelsea* (Master Mix, 1988).

Delmar, Elaine
b. Elaine Hutchinson, 13 September 1939, Harpenden, Hertfordshire, UK. Studying music from age six, she was influenced by her trumpet-playing father, Leslie 'Jiver' Hutchinson. She sings in clubs and has also played on the London stage in musicals and straight plays. Dynamic and highly entertaining, she regularly works with leading jazz musicians.
Albums: *Elaine Sings Wilder* (Columbia, 1966), *I've Got the World on a String* (Retrospect, 1976), *S'Wonderful* (Jazz House, 1992).

Dudziak, Urszula
b. 22 October 1943, Straconka, Poland. After studying piano, she was inspired to start singing upon hearing Ella Fitzgerald. She became one of Poland's best-known singers and after marrying jazz musician Michal Urbaniak travelled overseas. She sings largely wordless songs, using her five-octave range and electronic devices. Her work is ceaselessly exploratory and demanding. She also sings with the occasional group Vocal Summit.
Albums: *Urszula* (Arista, 1976), *Magic Lady* (In and Out, 1980), *Sorrow Is Not Forever ... But Love Is* (Keytone, 1983).

Eade, Dominique
b. 1959, USA. She studied at Vassar, Berklee College of Music and the New England Conservatory of Music, together with private study with jazz musicians such as Ran

Blake and Dave Holland. Since 1980 she has taught music both privately and in schools and colleges in the USA and Europe and in 1984 was appointed Instructor at the NEC of M. An elegant stylist with strong colourings of contemporary jazz makes her a singer who is always both entertaining and interesting.
Albums: *The Ruby and the Pearl* (Accurate, 1991), *My Resistance Is Low* (Accurate, 1994).

Eastman, Madeline
b. USA. Based in San Francisco, Eastman has developed a great reputation and attracted the admiration and respect of many other singers. She is especially noted for her facility with scat, a form that she uses with enormous intelligence and wit. She is co-owner, with Kitty Margolis, of Mad-Kat Records.
Albums: *Art Attack* (Mad-Kat, 1994).

Elling, Kurt
b. Chicago, Illinois, USA. Since signing with Blue Note he has attained an enviably high profile in a very short time. He began singing as a chorister but in college turned to jazz. He sings ballads, vocalese and ranges through standards and original material. A dynamic style and stage presence help build a reputation filled with great promise.
Albums: *Close Your Eyes* (Blue Note, 1995).

Ferrell, Rachelle
b. c.1961, USA. She first attracted attention in Philadelphia, mostly singing jazz standards. Later, she worked as a teacher in music colleges in New Jersey and also as a

session singer. Eager not to be pigeon-holed, in addition to singing jazz, she has also sung r&b, recording an album in this form before being signed by Blue Note. She has an astonishing multi-octave voice which she uses with great skill.
Albums: *First Instrument* (Blue Note, 1994).

Fitzgerald, Ella
b. Ella Jane Fitzgerald, 25 April 1917, Newport News, Virginia, USA, d. 15 June 1996. Her career is assessed in detail in Chapter 8.
Albums: *The Early Years, Part 1* (MCA GRP, 1935-8), *75th Birthday Celebration* (MCA GRP, 1938-55), *Ella Sings Gershwin* (Decca, 1950), *The Complete Ella Fitzgerald Song Books* (Verve, 1956-64), *Mack the Knife - Ella in Berlin* (Verve, 1960).

Freelon, Nnenna
b. USA. After singing in North Carolina, she was signed by Columbia. She has sung with Toshiko Akiyoshi and Yusef Lateef. Her achievements have been rewarded by praise from critics. At home and abroad she has been the recipient of several honours including the Billie Holiday Award from the French Académie du Jazz and the Eubie Blake Award in New York. She composes many of her songs and performs in a skilful and highly attractive manner.
Albums: *Heritage* (Columbia, 1993), *Listen* (Columbia, 1994).

Frishberg, Dave
b. 23 March 1933, St Paul, Minnesota, USA. He began his career in music as a pianist, working with leading jazz musicians. He was a regular accompanist for singers and also wrote songs which were performed by Blossom Dearie, Al Jarreau and others. Not until the early 70s did he begin singing his own songs in public. While his piano playing is solidly in the jazz tradition, his songwriting takes him into the parallel world of the sophisticated supper club performer.
Albums: *Getting Some Fun Out of Life* (Concord, 1977), *Can't Take You Nowhere* (Fantasy, 1985), *Where You At* (Bloomdido, 1993).

Gaillard, Slim
b. Bulee Gaillard, 4 January 1916, prob. Santa Clara, Cuba, d. 26 February 1991. After an adventurous early life, in the early 30s he entered vaudeville as a guitar-playing tap-dancer. Late in the decade he achieved great popularity with his jazz-tinged novelty songs which were couched in 'vout', Gaillard's highly individual version of jive talk. From the 50s onwards he appeared in films and on television, playing clubs and concerts, often in the UK where he became a resident in 1983.
Albums: *Slim and Slam* (Affinity, 1938-9), *Jazz At The Philharmonic: Opera in Vout* (Verve, 1946), *Anytime, Anyplace, Anywhere* (Hep, 1982).

Gallinger, Karen
b. USA. A strong-voiced expressive singer with good potential for the future.
Albums: *Live At The Jazz Bakery* (Sea Breeze, 1994).

Gibson, Harry 'The Hipster'
b. Harry Raab, 1914, New York City, New York, USA, d. May 1991. He played piano in jazz groups in New York, then formed a double act with singer Ruth Gibson whose name he took. His early 40s nightclub act caught with remarkable flair and precision the attitudes and language of the contemporary generations of zoot-suited streetwise hipsters. His frantic musicmaking was matched by a private life dogged by drugs and divorces.
Albums: *Everybody's Crazy But Me* (Progressive, 1940s), *Harry the Hipster Digs Christmas* (Totem, 1974), *Who Put the Benzedrine in Mrs Murphy's Ovaltine?* (Delmark, 1976, 1989).

Gonzales, Babs
b. Lee Brown, 27 October 1919, Newark, New Jersey, USA, d. 23 January 1980. After singing briefly with the big bands of Charlie Barnet and Lionel Hampton, he turned to bop in the mid-40s. His group, Babs's Three Bips and a Bop, included Tadd Dameron and he also worked with James Moody and Johnny Griffin in the 50s. He sang energetically, with often wildly over-the-top presentation, and did not always endear himself to jazz fans and other musicians.
Albums: *Cool Philosophy* (Jaro, 1959), *Sundays at Small's Paradise* (Dauntless, 1963).

Grace, Teddy
b. Stella Gloria Crowson, 26 June 1905, Arcadia, Louisiana, USA, d. 4 January 1992. She started singing professionally in 1931 and worked on radio. She recorded a fine set of blues with Charlie Shavers, and also made records with other jazzmen, but in 1940 she quit the music business. During World War Two she organized recruitment drive concerts but was taken ill and lost her voice. She never sang again. Grace could use her voice with delicate poise on ballads and be effectively growly when singing the blues.
Albums: *Teddy Grace* (Timeless CBC, 1937–40).

Greco, Buddy
b. Armando Greco, 14 August 1926, Philadelphia, Pennsylvania, USA. Starting out as a pianist, he began singing and led a successful trio in the mid-40s. After a spell with Benny Goodman, by the early 50s he was back as a single and/or trio leader. His repertoire and style was geared to the glitzy Las Vegas scene where he proved to be very popular for more than forty years.
Albums: *At Mr Kelly's* (Jasmine, 1955), *Body and Soul* (Epic, c.1966), *Macarthur Park* (Candid/Celebrity, c.1994).

Green, Lil
b. Lillian Johnson, 22 December 1919, Mississippi USA, d. 14 April 1954. After moving to Chicago she worked in various jobs before becoming a singing waitress. During the early 40s she sang and recorded with various artists, notably Tiny Bradshaw and Big Bill Broonzy. An effective singer of the blues and jazz repertoires, her best known songs were 'Why Don't You Do Right?', which was covered by Peggy Lee, and 'Romance in the Dark'. She

worked into the early 50s but was often inactive through ill health.
Compilations: *Romance in the Dark* (RCA, 1940–6).

Grimes, Carol
b. UK. Coming to prominence in 1969 with the blues band, Delivery, she had already built a localized reputation as a determined and forward-thinking singer. When Delivery disbanded she went solo for a while, then in 1972 formed her own band, Uncle Dog, then went out again as a single. Her success in the UK was mixed and she achieved more in Europe.
Albums: *Warm Blood* (1974), *Carol Grimes* (Charly, 1977), *Why Don't They Dance?* (Line, 1989).

Grosz, Marty
b. Martin Oliver Grosz, 28 February 1930, Berlin, Germany. His parents emigrated to the USA in 1933. He played banjo and guitar in various bands until the the mid-70s when he began to attract international attention due in part to his work with Soprano Summit. Favouring material from the 30s and earlier, and in particular the music of Fats Waller, he sings with engaging freshness and vigour and broad good humour.
Albums: *Hooray for Bix* (Riverside, 1957), *Extra! The Orphan Newsboys* (Jazzology, 1989), *Live at the LA Classic* (Jazzology, 1992).

Hadley, Dardanelle
see **Dardanelle**

Hall, Adelaide
b. 20 October 1901, New York City, New York, USA, d. 7 November 1993. Taught singing by her music teacher-father, she sang and danced in chorus lines in New York and Europe in the 20s. In 1927 she recorded 'Creole Love Call' with Duke Ellington. In the 30s she worked as a single, using Art Tatum among her accompanists. She eventually settled in Europe, worked with ENSA during World War Two, and after the war sang in British variety theatres and on radio. She continued to sing until shortly before her death, her voice retaining much of its early purity.
Albums: *That Wonderful Adelaide Hall* (Columbia, 1969), *Hall of Ellington* (Columbia, 1969–70).

Hardin, Lil
see **Armstrong, Lil**

Harris, Marilyn
b. USA. After spending twenty years in music as a composer, arranger and backing singer in radio and television, she released her first album in 1993, ten years after work first began on it. She sings in a clear, melodious voice and accompanies herself on keyboards. She writes intelligent lyrics and her repertoire ranges widely from contemporary pop to music with a hint of the blues.
Albums: *Between the Lines* (Wrightwood, 1983–93).

Hayes, Clancy
b. Clarence Leonard Hayes, 14 November 1908, Caney, Kansas, USA, d. 3 March 1972. A vaudeville singer and banjo/guitar player in the mid-20s, in the late 30s and early 40s he was a stalwart of the

Lu Watters revivalist jazz band. In the 50s he played and sang with Bob Scobey's Frisco Jazz Band. Although he sang ballads in a pleasant manner it was on up-tempo rhythmic songs that he came into his own and helped Watters and Scobey attain their widespread popularity.

Albums: *Clancy Hayes's Dixieland Band* (Audio Fidelity, 1960), *Live at Earthquake McGoon's* (ABC–Paramount, 1966).

Hendricks, Jon
b. John Carl Hendricks, 16 September 1916, Newark, Ohio, USA. On the advice of Charlie Parker he abandoned plans for a career in law and began singing in New York in the 40s. He met and teamed up with Dave Lambert and, later, Annie Ross to form a highly regarded trio, Lambert, Hendricks and Ross. Adept at scat and vocalese, Hendricks later spent much time in Europe singing solo, in groups, and also writing. His daughter Michelle is also a singer.

Albums: *Evolution of the Blues Song* (Columbia, 1960), *September Songs* (Stanyan, 1976), *Boppin' at the Blue Note* (Telarc Jazz, 1993).

Hibbler, Al
b. Albert Hibbler, 16 August 1915, Little Rock, Arkansas, USA. His first important engagement was with Jay McShann in 1942 and the following year he joined Duke Ellington. While still with Ellington he began recording as a single, turning towards r&b and had a hit with 'Unchained Melody'. He had an

expressive baritone and flamboyant stage presence.

Albums: *After the Lights Go Down Low* (Atlantic, 1956), *It's Monday Every Day* (Discovery, 1961), with Rahsaan Roland Kirk *A Meeting of the Times* (Atlantic, 1972), *For Sentimental Reasons* (Open Sky, 1982).

Holiday, Billie
b. Eleanora Harris, 7 April, 1915, Philadelphia, Pennsylvania, USA, d. 17 July 1959. Her career is assessed in detail in Chapter 4.

Albums : *The Complete Recordings : 1933-40* (Charly, 1933-40), *Quintessential Vols 1-9* (Columbia, 1930s-40s), *The Legacy* (Columbia, 1933-58), *Lady in Autumn* (Verve, 1946-59).

Horn, Shirley
b. 1 May 1934, Washington, DC, USA. After leading her own group for a while in the mid-50s she thereafter worked mostly as a single, accompanying herself at the piano. She spent much of the 60s in Europe and since then has toured extensively. Her piano playing is skilful and decidedly boppish. Her singing has an attractive quality and lends itself well to ballads.

Albums: *Embers and Ashes* (Hi-Life, 1961), *Travelin' Light* (Impulse!, 1965), *In the Garden of the Blues* (Steeplechase, 1984), *Light out of Darkness* (Verve, 1993), *I Love You Paris* (Verve, 1994), *The Main Ingredient* (Verve, 1995).

Horton, Joanne 'Pug'
b. Joanne Barbara Kitcheman, 30 May 1932, Sheffield, Yorkshire, UK. Sang locally as a child and later

worked as singer, dancer and model in England and Canada. During the 50s and early 60s was active in and out of music but gradually began to concentrate on singing. In the early 70s she was again outside music, operating her own fashion company. From the mid-70s onwards she was back on the jazz scene, often singing with Bob Wilber whom she married in 1978. She brings a strong voice and forceful personality to her work which often displays her liking for the blues.

Albums: *Kitchen Man*, (Fat Cat's Jazz, c.1978), *Don't Go Away* (Bodeswell, 1979).

Howard, Bob

b. Howard Joyner, 20 June 1906, Newton, Massachusetts, USA, d. 3 December 1986. In the late 20s he played piano and sang mostly in New York. In the 30s he also led a band, had a radio show and in the 50s moved into television. Like Putney Dandridge, he was a Fats Waller clone and is best represented for his 30s recordings. Mostly he sang in a light tenor but could descend into a rough baritone.

Albums: *Bob Howard* (Rarities, 1935).

Humes, Helen

b. 23 June 1913, Louisville, Kentucky, USA, d. 13 September 1981. Her first records were made when she was thirteen. In 1938 she joined Count Basie's band, then turned to r&b in the early 40s. She retired in the late 60s but was persuaded back by Stanley Dance for the 1973 Newport Jazz Festival. From then until her death she sang and toured endlessly. Her light, bell-like voice, faultless timing and phrasing was equally at home with ballads, blues, r&b, all of which she sang with great charm and originality.

Albums: *Be-baba-leba* (Whiskey, Women and Song, 1944-52), *T'Ain't Nobody's Biz-ness If I Do* (Contemporary, 1959), *Sneaking Around* (Black and Blue, 1974), *'Deed I Do* (Contemporary, 1976), *Helen Humes and the Muse All Stars* (Muse, 1979).

Hunter, Alberta

b. 1 April 1895, Memphis, Tennessee, USA, d. 17 October 1984. Raised in Chicago, she sang as a child in low dives and also worked in New York with leading jazzmen of the day. She retired in 1954 and took up nursing although she did record in 1961. At age eighty-two she was compulsorily retired from the hospital and, prompted by Barney Josephson, took up singing again. She sang in clubs, theatres, and on television, and revised some of her compositions for the soundtrack of the 1978 film, *Remember My Name*. A powerful and distinctive contralto allied to a pronounced but controlled vibrato allowed her to sing ballads and blues with equal authority.

Albums: *Classic Alberta Hunter: The Thirties* (Stash, 1935-40), *Alberta Hunter with Lovie Austin and Her Blues Serenaders* (Riverside, 1961).

Infascelli, Silvia

b. Italy. She sings with an attractive tuneful voice, building her repertoire largely from her own compositions. She also plays oboe and has studied vocal technique with Maggie Nicols.

Albums: *Blue Tracks* (Lion, 1994).

Jarreau, Al

b. 12 March 1940, Milwaukee, Wisconsin, USA. While at university he formed a vocal group, the Indigoes. He sang professionally from the mid-60s, making his first records in the mid-70s. Influenced by Lambert, Hendricks and Ross and the Hi-Lo's, he introduced African and Asian vocal techniques into his style and developed a large audience, especially in Europe. In the 80s he moved into jazz-rock fusion, increasing his audience accordingly, although he began to lose some of the more rock-orientated fans, but in the mid-90s his international following was still huge.

Albums: *We Got By* (Warner Bros, 1975), *Breakin' Away* (Warner Bros, 1981), *L Is for Lover* (Warner Bros, 1986), *Tenderness* (Warner Bros, 1994).

Jay, Barbara

b. UK. She began singing as a child, encouraged by her father, a jazz trumpeter. She sang with several leading jazzmen including Ronnie Scott, George Chisholm, and Tommy Whittle, whom she married. In 1970 she joined Benny Goodman for a European tour and she also sang in New York accompanied by Ellis Larkins. In the late 80s and 90s she regularly appeared in London and also toured the UK, sang on television and at several international festivals. Delightfully uncluttered, her style lends itself very well to the great standards which she favours in her large repertoire.

Albums: *The Nearness of You* (Tee-Jay, 1980s), *Memories of You* (Tee-Jay, 1990s).

Jefferson, Eddie

b. Edgar Jefferson, 3 August 1918, Detroit, Michigan, USA, d. 9 May 1979. He started out as a dancer but slowly turned to singing. He enjoyed musical experimentation, tried scat and also began writing lyrics to solos by instrumentalists. This form of singing, vocalese, was taken up by others, notably King Pleasure, and Jefferson's pioneering work was often overlooked. Despite some very good records he was increasingly marginalized and sometimes returned to dancing. He was filmed in performance in his hometown, *Eddie Jefferson: Live at the Showcase*, two days before he was shot to death outside the club.

Albums: *The Jazz Singer* (Evidence, 1962), *Body and Soul* (Prestige, 1968), *Things Are Getting Better* (Muse, 1974), *Keeper of the Flame* (Muse, 1978).

Johnson, Ellen

b. USA. After studying for a masters' degree in music at San Diego State University, she began singing professionally. Later, she returned to the same university to teach. She has a true, poised soprano voice which occasionally reveals traces of her operatic training. Her repertoire ranges over music by jazz composers such as

Duke Ellington, Charles Mingus, to some of whose work she has composed lyrics, and Bill Evans.

Albums: *Too Good to Title* (Nine Winds, 1993).

Jones, Etta

b. 25 November 1928, Aiken, South Carolina, USA. Early in her career she worked with jazz musicians but made her name in r&b. A recording contract with Prestige in the early 60s raised her profile and she continued to work in good company. From the mid-70s, she was often teamed with tenor saxophonist Houston Person.

Albums: *Something Nice* (OJC/Prestige, 1960-1), *So Warm* (OJC/Prestige, 1961).

Jordan, Louis

b. 8 July 1908, Brinkley, Arkansas, USA, d. 4 February 1975. After playing alto saxophone and occasionally singing in several bands during the 30s, notably that led by Chick Webb, he formed his own small group. By the mid-40s his band, the Tympany Five, had built a huge following with its repertoire of jump music and popular songs. Heavily featured were Jordan's infectiously lively and amusing vocals. His success was important in bringing r&b to the forefront of popular music and he was also one of the first black artists of the period to enjoy cross-over success with white audiences. In the 60s he toured Europe as a single.

Albums: *Louis Jordan and Friends* (MCA, 1940s-50s), *Louis Jordan with the Chris Barber Jazz Band* (Black Lion, 1960s).

Jordan, Sheila

b. Sheila Jeanette Dawson, 18 November 1928, Detroit, Michigan, USA. In her early teens she began singing in clubs in Detroit. Influenced by bop musicians she heard, among them Charlie Parker, in the early 50s she was in New York where she met and married pianist Duke Jordan. She studied with Lennie Tristano and Charles Mingus and recorded with George Russell. An uncompromising jazz singer, her repertoire includes musical settings of poetry, scat, freeform, religious liturgies and original material with a leavening of standards some of which she treats with enormous ingenuity. Her work is worthy of close attention which reveals an infinite variety of shading and layering.

Albums: *Portrait of Sheila* (Blue Note, 1962), *Confirmation* (East Wind, 1975), *Old Time Feeling* (Palo Alto, 1983), *Heart Strings* (Muse, 1993).

Juenemann, Marguerite

b. USA. After studying classical piano and clarinet she performed folk music. She then turned to jazz and in 1979 was a founding member of the vocal group Rare Silk, touring extensively, including a visit to Japan with Benny Goodman. In 1988 she began teaching at the University of Maine. Deeply interested in musical experimentation, she is particularly well-attuned to contemporary music and has written vocalese lyrics to several classics of modern jazz.

Albums: *By Whose Standards* (Juenetunes, 1994).

Kent, Stacey
b. c.1967, USA. After graduation in 1991 she visited England and impulsively took a post-graduate course in jazz. Having sung all her life she now began singing jazz and thanks to meeting many musicians was soon on the right path. Married to tenor saxophonist Jim Tomlinson, she tours extensively in the UK, broadcasts on radio, and has begun recording. A gifted singer with a deep affection for and understanding of the classic songbooks, she brings warmth and illumination to her wide repertoire.
Albums: *Stacey Kent* (Candid, 1997).

Kibbey, Sue
b. UK. After training as a dancer and becoming a qualified dance and drama teacher, she started singing jazz. She has also taught at the Royal Academy of Music's Summer Jazz Course. A warm, inventive singer, she has worked with Michael Garrick and also sings music from the traditional repertoire. She has performed a one-woman show and has sung in Europe and the Far East.
Albums: *Sue Kibbey with Teddy Fullick* (1990s).

Kidd, Carol
b. 19 October 1945, Glasgow, Scotland, UK. In her early teens she sang in talent shows and also worked with a traditional jazz band and at seventeen married the trombone player, George Kidd. She retired for four years but came back to work to great acclaim in mainstream jazz in the late 70s and throughout the 80s. In the 90s she continued to attract plaudits and good audiences and her records and broadcasts are always well received. Her poised singing style contrasts intriguingly with her easy-going rapport with audiences.
Albums: *All My Tomorrows* (Linn, 1985), *Night We Called It a Day* (Linn, 1990), *I'm Glad We Met* (Linn, 1992).

Kilgore, Rebecca
b. USA. Raised in New England, she played guitar and sang as a child. In 1979 she moved to Portland, Oregon, where she sang with a big band, a country and western group, and her own sextet, Beck-a-Roo. This group mostly performed country hits from the 60s. She has also worked in duo with Dave Frishberg and recorded with a mainstream band led by Dan Barrett.
Albums: *I Saw Stars* (Arbors Jazz, 1994).

King, Morgana
b. Morgana Messina, 4 June 1930, Pleasantville, New York, USA. After studying formally, she turned to popular music in the mid-50s. She combined her singing career with work as an actress in television and films. She sang into the 80s, her sweet voice blending nicely with jazz backings and she proved an interesting interpreter of popular songs.
Albums: *Stretchin' Out* (Muse, 1977), *Looking Through the Eyes of Love* (Muse, 1981).

King Pleasure
b. Clarence Beeks, 24 March 1922, Oakdale, Tennessee, USA, d. 21

March 1981. In the mid- and late 40s he began writing and performing vocalized versions of instrumental jazz solos. He also sang similar pieces composed by others, notably Eddie Jefferson's 'Moody's Mood For Love', with which Pleasure had a hit. Although the example he and Jefferson set did much to influence later vocalese singers, his career faltered during the 50s and never recovered.

Albums: *Sing* (OJC/Prestige, 1952–4), *Golden Days* (HiFi, 1960).

King, Sandra
b. 10 December 1950, London, England. She began singing semi-professionally at thirteen and early in her career she formed an important musical relationship with pianist Pat Smythe who remained her accompanist and musical director until his death in 1983. King sang with the National Youth Jazz Orchestra and also visited Europe and the USA. A sensitive and dignified interpreter of lyrics, King has a deep, expressive voice. In the 80s and 90s she divided her time between the UK and USA but has yet to achieve the audience her rich talent deserves.

Albums: *Sandra King in a Concert of Vernon Duke* (Audiophile, 1982), *The Magic Window* (Audiophile, 1986).

King, Teddi
b. Theodora King, 18 September 1929, Boston, Massachusetts, USA, d. 18 November 1977. She studied piano as a child, then sang professionally and studied voice mostly in her home town area. In 1952 she began a two-year spell with George Shearing, then sang as a single. For a while she sang pop but was back singing jazz in the early 60s. In 1970 she was diagnosed as having a seriously debilitating disease but continued to sing. A highly gifted singer and much respected among her fellow musicians, she sang in a fragile but melodious contralto and had superb phrasing and enunciation. A few weeks after recording rehearsal tapes for a projected album with Dave McKenna she died: the tapes were later released to great if late critical acclaim.

Albums: *Lovers and Losers* (Audiophile, c.1956), *This Is New* (Inner City, 1977).

Knowles, Pamela
b. Australia. Classically trained at the American Conservatory Theater and at London's Academy of Music and Dramatic Art, she has worked with both jazz and classical orchestras in Australia and New Zealand. She has toured Europe singing jazz. She is strong-voiced and has a dramatic flair.

Albums: *Love Dance* (Larrikin, 1993).

Kral, Irene
b. 18 January 1932, Chicago, Illinois, USA, d. 15 August 1978. Starting to sing professionally in her mid-teens, she joined Woody Herman for a brief spell, then sang with other bands and a vocal group, the Tattle Tales, before joining Maynard Ferguson in the late 50s. She also sang with Shelly Manne's group. Greatly admired by other singers, Kral was an outstanding

interpreter of ballads. She occasionally sang with her brother Roy.

Albums: with Ferguson *Boy with Lots of Brass* (EmArcy, 1957), *Better than Anything* (DRG, 1963), *Wonderful Life* (Mainstream, 1965).

Kral, Roy

b. 10 October 1921, Chicago, Illinois, USA. He played piano and sang with various small groups, with his sister Irene, and most importantly with Jackie Cain. They married after working with Charlie Ventura's Bop for the People orchestra in 1948. Singing as Jackie and Roy, they continued to work extensively over the following decades but he was also active writing and performing advertising jingles. A spirited bop-influenced singer, Kral's best work was in his duo performances with his wife.

Albums: *Jackie and Roy* (Brunswick, 1954), *Like Sing* (Columbia, 1962), *East of Suez* (Concord, 1980).

Krall, Diana

b. Nanaimo, British Columbia, Canada. At school she studied classical piano but played jazz in a band. Visiting Americans Ray Brown and Jeff Hamilton urged her to go to Los Angeles where she studied with Jimmy Rowles who encouraged her to sing more. In the 90s her albums attracted favourable attention. Krall's piano playing is crisp, deft and swinging. Her singing style is relaxed and intimate and she interprets ballads with warmth and persuasive charm.

Albums: *Only Trust Your Heart* (GRP, 1994), *All for You* (Impulse!, 1995).

Krog, Karin

b. 15 May 1937, Oslo, Norway. After singing for some years in her native land she made a big impact on international festival and club audiences from the mid-60s onwards. She recorded with such forward-thinking jazz musicians as Clare Fischer and Don Ellis. Adventurous, and with a range of musical interests that include Asian and African music, classics of the jazz repertoire and sophisticated nightclub material, Krog's appeal is to all tastes in jazz. She has also produced jazz shows on television.

Albums: *By Myself* (Philips, 1964), *Some Other Spring* (Sonet, 1970), *I Remember You* (Spotlite, 1981), *Krog Sings Gershwin* (Meantime, 1993).

Kruger, Jerry

b. USA. A distinctive singer with a clear admiration for Billie Holiday, she had only a brief time in the spotlight and then lived in relative obscurity. She made some records under her own name and with a small group featuring trumpeter Frankie Newton, then sang for a few months with Gene Krupa's first band.

Albums: with Newton *Emperor Jones* (Jazz Archives, 1937), with Krupa *Chronological* (Classics, 1938).

Laine, Cleo

b. Clementina Dinah Campbell, 28 October 1927, Southall, London, UK. First attracted attention with John Dankworth's bands in the early 50s. They married in 1958 and she later became an established solo attraction. Apart from an extensive career as a performing and recording artist, she has also been active as a music educator with Dankworth. Her distinctive, smoky, four-octave voice allows her to range over jazz, pop and classics with confidence and flair. Her popularity extends far beyond the boundaries of jazz. Her daughter, Jacqui Dankworth, is also a singer.

Albums: *Shakespeare and All That Jazz* (Affinity, 1965), *I Am a Song* (RCA, 1979), *Woman to Woman* (RCA, 1989), *Blue and Sentimental* (RCA, 1993), *Solitude* (RCA, l994).

Lambert, Dave

b. David Alden Lambert, 19 June 1917, Boston, Massachusetts, USA, d. 3 October 1966. He arranged for and occasionally sang scat with Gene Krupa's 1944/45 band. With Krupa he sang with Buddy Stewart and he continued to work in vocal groups, notably with Jon Hendricks and, later, with Hendricks and Annie Ross.

Albums: *Dave Lambert with Buddy Stewart,* (EmArcy, 1946).

Lambert, Hendricks and Ross

A vocal group formed in the late 50s by Dave Lambert, Jon Hendricks and Annie Ross. Their first album, *Sing a Song of Basie*, replicated the Basie band's instrumental performances, using wordless vocalized lines to reproduce the brass and reed sections of the band. Although the creative and improvisational elements of jazz were omitted from their work, the group's flair was exceptional and overcame this inherent drawback. In 1962 Ross was replaced by Yolande Bavan (b. 1 June 1940, Colombo, Ceylon/Sri Lanka). In 1964 the trio broke up.

Albums: *Sing a Song of Basie* (Impulse!, 1957), *The Swingers* (Pacific Jazz, 1958-9), *Lambert, Hendricks and Ross Sing Ellington* (Columbia, 1960), *Lambert, Hendricks and Bavan: Having a Ball at the Village Gate* (RCA, 1963).

Lashley, Barbara

b. c.1938, New York City, New York, USA. Although always interested in music, she did not begin her singing career until after she moved to California in 1974. She sang at clubs in San Francisco, built a reputation, and eventually travelled to overseas festivals. Drawing her repertoire from the full spectrum of jazz, she sings with depth and subtlety and is an excellent interpreter of lyrics.

Albums: *How Long Has This Been Going On?* (Shoestring, 1983), *Sweet and Lowdown* (Stomp Off, 1986).

Laurin, Anna-Lena

b. Sweden. She played piano as a child, studying the classical repertoire. Later she played alto saxophone, then began singing which proved to be her métier. She works with several bands, including Fee-Fi-Fo-Fum, with whom she sings as a full band member rather than as a featured singer. Her vocal lines are often wordless and she writes much of her own material.

Albums: *Dance in Music* (Dragon, 1994).

La Velle

b. La Velle McKinnie, 22 May 1944, Kankakee, Illinois, USA. She studied music from an early age and appeared on *The Ed Sullivan Show* at age five with the Little Black Angels gospel group. At eleven she was the youngest ever to study voice at Chicago's American Conservatory of Music and she later studied at Juilliard. She began her career in opera and appeared at La Scala, Milan. Although she sings blues and r&b she leans towards jazz and has worked with Joe Williams, Lionel Hampton, Ray Brown, Jacky Terrasson and Ray Charles. Based in Europe since the late 70s, she has been resident in Paris and Geneva. An articulate and flexible performer, her favourite singers are Ella Fitzgerald, Sarah Vaughan, Ethel Ennis, Della Reese and Dinah Washington.
Albums: *Straight Singin'* (OMD, 1991).

Lea, Barbara

b. Barbara LeCoq, 4 October 1929, Detroit, Michigan, USA. She majored in Music Theory at Wellesley College, and in the late 40s sang jazz in the north-eastern states. After graduation she worked professionally as a singer in the north-east and also made records. In 1956 she was voted *down beat*'s 'Best New Singer'. She then moved into acting, mostly on the stage. In the late 70s she returned to singing in clubs across the USA and sang at jazz festivals and also recorded again. In 1996 she was showing no signs of slowing up, appearing at festivals and recording. She sings in a deep, rich-toned voice with a pleasingly astringent sound which is especially effective in her meaningful interpretation of ballads.
Albums: *Barbara Lea* (Prestige/ Fantasy/OJC, 1956), *Remembering Lee Wiley* (Audiophile, 1979), *Do It Again* (Audiophile, 1983), *Pousse Café* (Audiophile, 1993), *Hoagy's Children Vols 1 & 2* (Audiophile, 1994), *Fine and Dandy* (Challenge, 1996).

Lee, Jeanne

b. 29 January 1929, New York City, New York, USA. Her first prominent work was with pianist Ran Blake in the mid-50s and since then has always been an uncompromising member of the avant-garde. She composes much of her repertoire which she sings in a striking and distinctively original manner. Since the mid-70s she has taught at the New England Conservatory of Music. In addition to performing as a single she is also a member of the occasional vocal group, Vocal Summit.
Albums: with Blake *The Newest Sound Around* (RCA, 1961), *Conspiracy* (Earthforms, 1974), with Blake *You Stepped Out of a Cloud* (1990).

Lee, Julia

b. 31 October 1902, Booneville, Missouri, USA, d. 8 December 1958. While still in her teens she sang with the band led by her brother, George E. Lee, in and around Kansas City. By the early 30s her reputation was strong enough to justify a solo career and by the end of the 40s she was a Capitol recording star. Essentially blues-orientated, she became known for her *double entendre* songs. Mostly, she accompanied herself at the piano.

Albums: *Kansas City Star Vols 1-5* (Bear Family, 1940s-50s).

Lee, Peggy
b. Norma Egstrom, 26 May 1920, Jamestown, North Dakota, USA. She first sang as a member of a vocal group, the Four of Us, working mainly in the mid-west. In 1941 she joined Benny Goodman and quickly had a hit recording and also began writing songs. In 1943 she quit the band following her marriage to guitarist Dave Barbour. A while later she returned to singing as a single. When she signed with Capitol she gained widespread attention. Since then she has toured extensively, appearing at concerts and on television around the world. Her repertoire ranges over Latin, folk and popular ballads, all tinged with a jazz-inflection. Her voice is light and carefully poised with a coolly detached quality.

Albums: *Sings for You* (Avid, 1940s-50s), *Black Coffee* (Jasmine, 1953-6), with George Shearing *Beauty and the Beat* (Capitol, 1959), *Basin Street East Presents...* (Capitol, 1960), *Mirrors* (A & M, 1969).

Leighton-Thomas, Nicki
b. UK. Has performed in and around London since the early 90s. She has a wide repertoire and features many songs by lyricist Fran Landesman with music by Simon Wallace. Has appeared at many top London jazz venues including The Vortex, 100 Club, Kettners and Pizza on the Park, and has featured at the Soho Jazz Festival.

Lellis, Tom
b. Cleveland, Ohio, USA. He began singing in his home town, later playing clubs and cruise ships, hotels and casinos. At twenty-four he began studying piano and also started to write lyrics to compositions by jazz musicians. During the 80s and 90s he worked extensively throughout the USA, singing and recording with leading jazzmen. A gifted singer with a great sense of swing, he draws his repertoire from many areas of music, preferring melodious songs and performing them without tricks and vocal excesses.

Albums: *And in This Corner* (Inner City, 1981), *Double Entendre* (Beamtime, 1991), *Taken to Heart* (Concord, 1993).

Lincoln, Abbey
b. Anna Marie Wooldridge, 6 August 1930, Chicago, Illinois, USA. She began singing professionally in Chicago in the early 50s and soon made her recording début, accompanied by Benny Carter. She married Max Roach in 1962 and often worked with bop musicians. After her marriage ended in 1970 she adopted the name Aminata Moseka. Her singing style is emotionally charged and although influenced by Billie Holiday she has her own highly distinctive sound. In the 80s and 90s she began singing more ballads and in addition to her own compositions she also draws music from her roots.

Albums: *Affair* (EMI, 1956), *That's Him!* (Riverside, 1957), *Straight*

Ahead (Candid 1961), *A Tribute to Billie Holiday* (Enja, 1987), *Devil's Got Your Tongue* (Verve, 1992), *A Turtle's Dream* (Verve, 1994).

Lutcher, Nellie

b. 15 October 1919, Lake Charles, Louisiana, USA. She played piano in her youth but did not attract widespread attention until 1947 and her million-selling 'Hurry On Down'. Throughout the 50s she had more record successes and appeared on radio, television and in clubs. The 60s were lean times and she worked as an AF of M official. In the early 70s her career was rejuvenated. She plays energetic, jumping piano and sings in an infectiously entertaining manner.

Albums: *Ditto from Me to You* (Jukebox Lil, 1947–55), *Nellie Lutcher and Her Rhythm* (Bear Family, 1996).

Lynne, Gloria

b. 23 November 1930 or 1931, New York City, New York, USA. She began singing at the local Mother AME Zion church and also sang at amateur talent contests, then studied for five years. In the early 50s she sang professionally, developing a wide stylistic range which drew upon the inspiration of Ella Fitzgerald, Mahalia Jackson, and the classical contralto, Marian Anderson.

Albums: *Miss Gloria Lynne* (Evidence, 1958), *I Don't Know How to Love Him* (ABC, 1975).

McCall, Mary Ann

b. 4 May 1919, Philadelphia, Pennsylvania, USA, d. 14 December 1994. She sang with several big bands, including those led by Buddy Morrow, Tommy Dorsey and Woody Herman, but it was not until the late 40s and a second stint with Herman that she stood out as a very good jazz singer. Although influenced by Billie Holiday, McCall's work with bop musicians gave her a more modern sound and style.

Albums: *An Evening with Charlie Ventura and Mary Ann McCall* (Norgran, 1954), *Detour to the Moon* (Jubilee, 1958), *Jake Hanna's Kansas City Express* (Concord, 1976), with Nat Pierce *5400 North* (Hep, 1978).

McCorkle, Susannah

b. 1 January 1949, Berkeley, California, USA. After starting a career as a translator, she began singing in the late 60s while in Europe. Her career blossomed first in England but later in the USA where she had a long residency at New York's Cookery in the late 70s. Over the years her voice has subtly darkened and she sings with enormous flair and vitality. An excellent interpreter of ballads, she often sings foreign-language songs, notably from Brazil, and swings admirably. She has written lyrics for songs and is also a published writer of fiction.

Albums: *The Quality of Mercer* (Black Lion, 1977), *No More Blues* (Concord, 1989), *I'll Take Romance* (Concord, 1992), *From Broadway to Bebop* (Concord, 1994), *Easy to Love* (Concord, 1995).

McFerrin, Bobby

b. 11 March 1950, New York City, New York, USA. His parents were both professional singers of classical music but after hearing Miles Davis and Keith Jarrett in concert in 1970 he turned to jazz. He studied at Juilliard and Sacramento State and in 1977 was staff pianist with the University of Utah Dance Department. Usually performing unaccompanied, he ranges widely over bop, jazz-rock, and ethnic musics, incorporating African singing devices and many sounds that are original, including pops and clicks and percussive effects caused by striking different parts of his body. He composes many of his own songs, music and lyrics, but wordless vocalizing is his main area.

Albums: *Bobby McFerrin* (Elektra Musician, 1982), *Spontaneous Invention* (Blue Note, 1986), *Simple Pleasures* (EMI Manhattan, 1990), with Chick Corea *Play* (Blue Note, 1992), *Bang! Zoom* (Blue Note, 1995).

McKinnie, La Velle
see **La Velle**

McNulty, Chris
b. 23 December 1953, Melbourne, Victoria, Australia. She sang professionally from age fifteen and in the early 70s studied music theory. She sang with a jazz-funk group and also sang on radio and television while singing in jazz clubs. In 1980 she moved to Sydney and five years later went to New York. Since the late 80s she has been based in New York and has also recorded. She sings in a tough contralto and with great flair and dedication and also writes lyrics to jazz songs.

Albums: *Waltz for Debby* (Discovery, 1990), *A Time for Love* (Amosaya, 1993).

McRae, Carmen
b. 8 April 1920, New York City, New York, USA, d. 10 November 1994. Her career is assessed in detail in Chapter 8.

Albums: *By Special Request* (Decca, 1955), *Sings Great American Songwriters* (GRP MCA, 1955-9), *Woman Talk: Live at the Village Gate* (Mainstream, 1965), *The Great American Songbook* (Atlantic, 1971), *You're Lookin' at Me* (Concord, 1983), *Carmen Sings Monk* (RCA Novus, 1990), *Sarah! Dedicated to You* (Novus, 1991).

Mahogany, Kevin
b. c.1958, Kansas City, Missouri, USA. He played baritone saxophone in Eddie Baker's New Breed Jazz Orchestra while studying in Kansas City. He won a church singing scholarship and also sang in a jazz choir while at university. He worked gigs in mid-western towns with a trio before striking out on his own and signing with Enja Records. The 'Baronial Baritone' has a rich melodic voice, singing standards with eloquent ease.

Albums: *Songs and Moments* (Enja, 1994), *You Got What It Takes* (Enja, 1995).

Manly, Gill
b. England. Based in London, she has been encouraged by Mark Murphy, John Dankworth, Cleo Laine and has guested at Ronnie Scott's club with singers Ian Shaw and Claire Martin. An invigorating singer, she has a

distinctive voice and a warm and insightful way with lyrics.

Albums: *Détour Ahead* (Parrot, 1994).

Margolis, Kitty
b. USA. Educated at Harvard and San Francisco State University, where she studied under jazz saxophonist John Handy, she began attracting close attention in San Francisco which she has made her base. She has appeared with distinction at festivals all over the USA, including Hawaii, and at Holland's North Sea Jazz Festival. She is also involved in jazz education. A rich contralto, she has a wide repertoire including ballads, Latin, blues and scat. She is co-owner, with Madeline Eastman, of Mad-Kat Records.

Albums: *Live at the Jazz Workshop* (Mad-Kat, 1992), *Evolution* (Mad-Kat, 1994).

Marsh, Tina
b. USA. She is nominal leader of the Creative Opportunity Orchestra, a contemporary big band formed in Texas in 1979. In addition to singing with the band, she also composes and arranges.

Albums: *The Heaven Line* (CreOp Muse, 1992).

Martin, Claire
b. 6 September 1967, Wimbledon, London, UK. While still a young teenager she became resident singer at a Bournemouth hotel. She then sang on Cunard cruise liners and in 1990 studied briefly with Marilyn J. Johnson in New York. The following year, leading her own band, she was a big hit in London, singing at many prestigious venues. Her repertoire ranges over r&b, mainstream, popular ballads and free music. Regularly accompanied by jazz musicians, her records have attracted much critical acclaim. She sings with warmth, commitment and great verve and vitality.

Albums: *The Waiting Game* (Linn, 1991), *Devil May Care* (Linn, 1993), *Old Boyfriends* (Linn, 1994), *Off Beat* (Linn, 1995).

May, Tina
b. UK. She began training as a singer at sixteen, eventually turning to jazz. She became popular on the UK club circuit and also built a successful teaching practice. A skilled improviser, she selects her repertoire with a careful eye for melody, lyric and mood. She is married to drummer Clark Tracey.

Albums: *It Ain't Necessarily So* (33 Records 1994), *So Nice* (33 Records, 1995), *Time Will Tell* (33 Records, 1996).

Melly, George
b. Alan George Heywood Melly, 17 August 1926, Liverpool, Lancashire, UK. He began singing in his late twenties, working mostly with traditional jazz bands and quickly built a reputation for the classic jazz and blues repertoire. In the 60s he was mostly active as a writer and critic on music and art but in the early 70s returned to singing. His frequent accompanist is trumpeter and noted jazz writer John Chilton who also contributes some original songs to Melly's wide-ranging repertoire.

Albums: *Nuts* (Warner Bros, 1971), *Anything Goes* (PRT, 1988), *George Melly and Mates* (One-Up, 1991).

Merrill, Helen

b. Helen Milcetic, 21 July 1930, New York City, New York, USA. She began singing professionally as a teenager, often working with noted bop musicians such as Charlie Parker, Bud Powell and Miles Davis, and in the 50s she worked memorably with Clifford Brown. Occasional albums followed over the years but the following her talent deserved never seemed to materialize. In the mid-90s she recorded a tribute album recalling Brown. Melodious, clear-voiced, with an understated yet passionate way with a lyric, her work is always imbued with a deep feeling for jazz.

Albums: *Helen Merrill Featuring Clifford Brown* (EmArcy, 1954), *A Shade of Difference* (Spotlite, 1965), *Chasin' the Bird* (Inner City, 1979), *Collaboration* (EmArcy, 1987), *Brownie: Tribute to Clifford Brown* (Verve, 1994).

Miller, Big

b. Clarence Horatio Miller, December 1922, Sioux City, Iowa, USA, d. 9 June 1992. He sang in church, then briefly led a band before army service in World War Two. After the war he sang with Lionel Hampton and Jay McShann. The poet Langston Hughes wrote a series of songs for him. In 1963 he moved to Australia, then eventually settled in Canada where he became a respected performer and educator. In 1981 the Canadian National Film Board produced a biographical film, *Big and the Blues*. His commanding style and deep, powerful voice excellently complemented his penchant for the blues.

Albums: *The Last of the Blues Shouters* (Southland, 1990).

Mills Brothers, The

One of the most popular vocal groups of the 30s and 40s, they sang in a smoothly sophisticated manner, slightly resembling earlier gospel harmonizers. Usually, they sang only to guitar accompaniment with added vocal sounds representing instruments, but were equally at home with small group or big band backing. They had several million-selling hits and were an influence upon many later doo-wop groups. The four were originally John, Herbert, Harry and Donald. When John died he was replaced by their father, John Snr, and on his retirement they continued as a trio: after Herbert's death, Harry and Donald sang on as a duo.

Albums: *Tiger Rag* (Patricia, 1931–8), *Paper Doll Vols 1 & 2* (ASV Living Era, 1931–42).

Montgomery, Marion

b. Marian Maud Runnels Montgomery, 17 November 1934, Natchez, Mississippi, USA. While still at school she sang on television in Atlanta, Georgia. In 1965 she became resident in England, meeting and marrying pianist Laurie Holloway who became her accompanist and musical director. A popular and frequent performer in clubs, she also appears regularly on television and at festivals and on the West End stage. Relaxed and with an intimate, persuasive sound, she has mostly worked as a single but some collaborations with pianist-composer-singer Richard Rodney Bennett led to audiences outside the jazz world.

Albums: *Sings for Winners and Losers* (Capitol 1963), *I Gotta Right to Sing* (Jazz House, 1987), *Mellow* (C5, 1992–3).

Moore, Marilyn

b. 16 June 1931, Oklahoma City, Oklahoma, USA, d. March 1992. She began singing and dancing as a three-year-old member of her family's vaudeville act. In her teens she concentrated on singing, turning to jazz, and in 1949 sang with Woody Herman and Charlie Ventura. During the 50s she worked in New York, mostly with small groups and with her husband, tenor saxophonist Al Cohn. Raising her family took her out of singing but despite an album in 1957 and being cast in a jazz show the following year, she never made a comeback. Deeply influenced by Billie Holiday, she sang in a style closely modelled on her idol.

Albums: *Marilyn Moore* (Affinity, 1957), with others *Oh Captain!* (MGM, 1958).

Morris, Sarah Jane

b. UK. Increasingly popular in the early 90s in England, she has also built a following in Europe and Japan. She sings with great dramatic flair and intensity, using her strong three-and-a-half octave voice to enormous effect. Her repertoire includes standards and music from the jazz avant-garde together with soul, Latin and neo-classical songs.

Albums: *Blue Valentine* (Jazz House, 1994).

Morse, Ella Mae

b. 12 September 1924, Mansfield, Texas, USA. She first sang in a band led by her parents, then, in 1939, sang with Jimmy Dorsey. In 1941 she joined Freddie Slack and had a huge hit with 'Cow Cow Boogie'. She continued to mine a profitable line in boogie-woogie songs and also performed with blues artists such as T-Bone Walker. She retired at the end of the 40s but returned to record another million-seller, 'Blacksmith's Blues', in 1952.

Albums: *The Hits of Ella Mae Morse* (Pathé Marconi 1940s), *The Morse Code* (Capitol, 1957).

Morton, Jelly Roll

b. Joseph Lemott, 20 October 1890, New Orleans, Louisiana, USA, d. 10 July 1941. A major figure in early jazz history, he is best known as a pianist, composer, arranger and bandleader. He sang with earthy directness, using a declamatory style, that was sometimes at odds with his highly sophisticated musicianship.

Albums: *The Centennial: His Complete Victor Recordings* (RCA, 1926–39), *Library of Congress Recordings Vols 1–8* (Swaggie, 1938).

Moseka, Aminata

see **Lincoln, Abbey**

Muldaur, Maria
b. Maria Grazia Rosa Domenica
D'Amato, 12 September 1943, New
York City, New York, USA. She sang
with a vocal group, the Cashmeres,
while still at school, then turned to
folk singing. In the early 60s she
added blues and ragtime to her
growing repertoire and then, in the
mid-70s, began including jazz in
her performances. She made some
festival appearances in a jazz
context but by the 80s was singing
gospel with a touch of soul. She has
a light, pleasant voice with some
reflection of her jazz interest
amidst all the other styles and
moods.
Albums: *Waitress in a Donut Shop*
(Reprise, 1974), *Gospel Nights*
(Takana, 1980), *Transblucency*
(Uptown, 1986).

Murphy, Mark
b. Mark Howe Murphy, 14 March
1932, Syracuse, New York, USA. He
first sang with a small band led by
his brother, then made a huge
impact on the jazz world with some
excellent mid- to late 50s albums.
In the middle of the next decade he
settled in Europe, performing a
ceaseless round of club and festival
dates and also teaching in Austria.
Between times he has made several
well-received albums. Enormously
zestful and with great vocal
dexterity, wit and intelligence, he
has been an important influence
upon many young singers and is
also much admired by his peers.
Albums: *Meet Mark Murphy*
(Brunswick, c.1956), *Rah!* (Original
Jazz Classics, 1961), *Stolen
Moments* (Muse, 1978), *Bop for*

Kerouac (Muse, 1981), *Night Mood*
(Milestone, 1986), *Very Early* (West
and East, 1993).

Myers, Amina Claudine
b. 21 March 1942, Blackwell,
Arkansas, USA. After singing gospel
music in church she went to
Chicago and in the mid-60s joined
the Association for the Advance-
ment of Creative Musicians. She
also formed an occasional gospel
trio with David Peason and Fontella
Bass. Despite her stylistic moder-
nity, gospel and blues roots are
always well in evidence in her work
even when she turned to jazz-rock.
In the late 80s she sang with
Charlie Haden's Liberation Music
Orchestra.
Albums: *Salutes Bessie Smith* (Leo,
1980), *The Circle of Time* (Black
Saint, 1983), *Country Girl* (Minor
Music, 1986).

Natal, Nanette
b. 6 October 1945, New York City,
New York, USA. After studying and
performing classical music, in the
60s she sang with rock and blues
bands. In the late 70s she began
singing jazz, quickly developing as
a gifted improviser. In 1980 she
founded her own record label,
Benyo Music, and around this same
time began teaching. She is also a
gifted composer. Her singing style
is polished, vibrant, poised and
exudes her great enthusiasm and
the enormous technical skills she
brings to her wide-ranging repertoire.
Albums: *My Song of Something*
(Benyo, 1980), *Wild in Reverie*
(Benyo, 1982), *Hi Fi Baby* (Benyo,

1986), *Stairway to the Stars* (Benyo, 1992).

Nicols, Maggie

b. 24 February 1948, Edinburgh, Scotland. She began her professional career as a dancer in London, then started singing and worked with many avant-garde musicians. She also led her own group, Okuren. Deeply committed to improvisational music, she has a warmly emotional style and her own lyrics display awareness and concern over humane issues.

Albums: with John Stevens *Oliv* (Marmalade, 1969), with Keith Tippett *Sweet and Sours* (FMP, 1982), *Live at the Bastille* (Sync Pulse, 1982), with Peter Nu *Nicols 'n' Nu* (Leo, 1985).

Niemack, Judy

b. USA. A distinguished interpreter of ballads, she performs with great insight and intelligence. Her tuneful voice is rich and deep and her phrasing is always imaginative and apposite.

Albums: *By Heart* (Sea Breeze, 1978), *Heart's Desire* (Stash, 1992), *Mingus, Monk and Mal* (Freelance, 1994).

O'Day, Anita

b. Anita Belle Colton, 18 October 1919, Kansas City, Missouri, USA. She began singing in Chicago clubs in the late 30s after enduring a short career as a marathon dancer and was eventually hired by Gene Krupa. Teamed with Roy Eldridge, she was important in fostering the band's popularity. In 1943 she joined Stan Kenton, went back to Krupa in 1945, and then went out as a single. A punishing schedule and years of serious addiction problems damaged her voice but she had already settled into a stylistic mode which did not require a demanding vocal range. She was still touring and recording in the mid-90s.

Albums: with Krupa *Drummin' Man* (Charly 1938–47), *Pick Yourself Up* (Verve, 1956), *Cool Heat* (Official, 1959), *I Told Ya I Love Ya Now Get Out* (Song Signature, 1960s), *Skylark* (Trio, 1978), *In a Mellow Tone* (DRG, 1989), *At Vine Street Live* (Disques Swing, 1991).

Page, Oran 'Hot Lips'

b. 27 January 1908, Dallas, Texas, USA, d. 5 November 1954. As a young man he played trumpet, accompanying blues singers such as Ma Rainey and Bessie Smith. His reputation as a trumpeter and singer grew and after a spell with Bennie Moten he was signed by Louis Armstrong's manager, Joe Glaser, ostensibly to take pressure off Armstrong. However, Page was relegated to second-string dates and his career was thus severely damaged. He was an effective singer, especially of the blues, and an outstanding trumpet player.

Albums: *Hot Lips Page* (Official, 1938-40), *Hot Lips Page in Sweden* (1951).

Paris, Barbara

b. 2 October 1954, Colorado, USA. She began singing folk but turned to jazz and was encouraged by tenor saxophonist Eddie Shu. She has sung in New York and Los

Angeles but chooses to remain based in Colorado. She has a clear, sensuous voice and selects her repertoire mainly from popular and jazz standards of the 40s and later.

Albums: *Where Butterflies Play* (Perea, 1992–3), *Happy Talk* (Perea, 1994).

Paris, Jackie

b. 26 September 1926, Nutley, New Jersey, USA. He worked as a guitarist and singer in New York in the early 40s and gradually became involved with bop. He recorded occasionally but through the next decade was mostly heard in hotels and clubs. He sings with rhythmic drive and a throaty delivery and his bop allegiances are always apparent. His career enjoyed a resurgence in the late 80s thanks both to albums which reissued earlier material and new record-ings. His wife is the singer Anne Marie Moss.

Albums: with Donald Byrd and Gigi Gryce *Modern Jazz Perspectives* (Columbia, 1957), *Jackie Paris* (Audiophile, 1988), *Nobody Else But Me* (Audiophile, 1988), *Jackie Paris/Marc Johnson/Carlos Franzetti* (Audiophile, 1994).

Parris, Rebecca

b. USA. Singing with great flair, driving and forceful on up-tempo songs and warmly poignant on ballads, she has attracted much praise from other singers. She is at her best with small groups but also enjoys the roar of a big band behind her.

Albums: *A Passionate Fling*

(Weston-Blair, c.1985), *Live at Chan's* (Weston-Blair, c.1986), *A Beautiful Friendship* (Altenburgh, c.1990).

Patterson, Ottilie

b. Anna-Ottilie Patterson, 31 January 1932, Comber, County Down, Northern Ireland. In the mid-50s she was prominent on the British traditional jazz scene and married bandleader Chris Barber. A strong, earthy delivery enhances her blues singing but she also has a more pensive side which she uses when appropriate, as for example in performances of poetry which she sets to music.

Albums: with Barber *40 Years Jubilee Vols 1–2* (Timeless, 1954–6), *Chris Barber at the London Palla-dium* (Columbia, 1961), *Madame Blues & Doctor Jazz* (Black Lion, 1983).

Peacock, Annette

b. New York City, New York, USA. She entered jazz following her marriage to bassist Gary Peacock. Her compositions were played by Paul Bley in whose trio her husband played. A pioneer of synthesized musical reproduction, she also plays piano, keyboards and bass. Her musical interests are wide, ranging through neo-classi-cism to the jazz avant-garde. Her compositions have emotional impact and deal often with inter-personal relationships. Her singing style is attuned to the special demands of the genre in which she performs.

Albums: *X-Dreams* (Aura, 1978), *Abstract Content* (Ironic, 1988).

Pollock, Marilyn Middleton

b. 26 October 1947, Chicago, Illinois, USA. She started out as a folk singer, then turned to rock. In 1985 she settled in Glasgow, Scotland, adding blues to her folk repertoire. At the start of the next decade she was singing the traditional jazz repertoire, vaudeville songs and blues. She sings ballads naturally and with sensitivity. She has performed one-woman shows based on vaudeville and jazz material.

Albums: *Nobody Knows You* (Fellside, 1988), *Those Women of the Vaudeville Blues* (Lake, 1990), with Steve Mellor *Red, Hot and Blue* (Lake, 1994).

Ponsford, Jan

b. 1954, UK. She became interested in jazz after hearing George Melly at the Reading Blues and Jazz Festival, but quickly expanded her interest into contemporary music by way of Archie Shepp. She joined the jazz-rock band, Big Chief, then developed a career as a single. She also teaches and is the founder of the contemporary singing group, Vocal Chords. An eclectic repertoire, an inventive musical mind, and the ability to take her singing where her mind goes, help make her one of the more interesting singers in the mid-90s.

Albums: *Vocal Chords* (ASC, 1995).

Porter, Mark

b. c.1962, Newbridge, Gwent, UK. Began singing at eighteen, after three years of music studies at school. He played organ by ear and sang for his own pleasure. His main influence was Vic Damone. From 1980 he sang semi-professionally in UK clubs, and in 1987 joined the New Squadronaires Orchestra. He has also sung with several Glenn Miller-style bands and has broadcast extensively.

Purim, Flora

b. 6 March 1942, Rio de Janeiro, Brazil. She played various instruments before deciding to concentrate on singing. In the late 60s she moved to the USA and worked with leading contemporary jazz musicians, eventually joining Chick Corea's Return to Forever band where she was reunited with Airto Moreira with whom she had co-led a band in the 70s. Frequently using wordless vocal lines which float airily above a sometimes thunderous accompaniment, much of her work has edged towards the nebulous world music classification.

Albums: *Stories to Tell* (Milestone, 1974), *Encounter* (OJC/Milestone, 1975–76), *The Magicians* (Crossover, 1986), *The Sun Is Out* (Crossover, 1989).

Rainey, Ma

b. Gertrude Malissa Nix Pridgett, 26 April 1886, Columbus, Georgia, USA, d. 22 December 1939. Singing in tent shows from childhood, she married Will 'Pa' Rainey in 1904 and toured with him, billed as 'The Assassinators of the Blues'. Eventually, she became a solo attraction, leading her own band, which included Thomas A. Dorsey, and was the most influential of the early classic blues singers. At the end of the 20s her reputation began to fade, affected in part by her repertoire which was almost exclusively blues songs. She retired in 1933. Although her recordings are of poor quality, when well remastered, the power and authority which made her the first great singer of the blues is apparent.

Albums: *Ma Rainey* (VJM, 1923-5), *Ma Rainey* (Milestones, 1920s).

Raney, Sue

b. Raelene Claire Claussen, 18 June 1940, McPherson, Kansas, USA. As a child she sang on radio and by her mid-teens had begun singing jazz. She sang with Ray Anthony and recorded critically successful albums with Nelson Riddle. Popular acclaim eluded her, however, and she sang mostly in comparative obscurity. In the 80s and 90s she made some excellent albums, often with leading jazz musicians. Her voice is finely textured and she sings with superb timing and subtlety.

Albums: *Sue Raney Sings the Music of Johnny Mandel* (Discovery, 1982), *Flight of Fancy* (Discovery, 1985), *In Good Company* (Discovery, 1990).

Rawls, Lou

b. 1 December c.1937, Chicago, Illinois, USA. Early in his career Rawls was influenced by Sam Cooke and he sang with him and in several gospel groups. By the end of the 60s his repertoire was an engaging mixture of pop, jazz, blues and gospel. His audience was very much the cabaret and hotel lounge set and he accordingly smoothed out his style to suit. He continued to sing through the 80s and also became active in television production.

Albums: *Stormy Monday* (Capitol, 1961), *Live* (Capitol, 1966), *A Natural Man* (MGM, 1974), *Close Company* (Epic, 1984), *It's Supposed to Be Fun* (Blue Note, 1990).

Reed, Lucy

b. c.1924, Marshfield, Wisconsin, USA. She began singing in Iron City, Michigan and after World War Two sang in Milwaukee and Duluth. She was heard by Woody Herman and joined his band, then went with Charlie Ventura before settling in Chicago. She quickly became a popular attraction in clubs, and apart from a short spell in New York in the mid-50s, has continued to sing in Chicago. A poised, clear voice, excellent diction and timing are allied to a deep understanding of lyrics. She often works with top-flight jazz musicians, including, in her 50s records, Bill Evans.

Albums: *The Singing Reed* (Fantasy, 1955-7), *Basic Reeding* (Audiophile, 1989-90).

Reese, Della

b. Dellareese Taliaferro, 6 July 1932, Detroit, Michigan, USA. In her teens she joined Mahalia Jackson's gospel troupe and later sang with Clara Ward and also led her own group, the Meditation Singers. In the mid-50s she sang with Erskine Hawkins and His Orchestra and then moved onto the fringes of r&b. In the 80s she was active in jazz-tinged pop singing, achieving some hits including pop versions of classics, one of which, 'Don't You

Know', based upon a Puccini aria from *La Bohème*, had given her a million-seller in 1959.

Albums: *One More Time* (ABC–Paramount, 1966), *The Classical Della* (RCA, 1980).

Reeves, Dianne

b. 1956, Detroit, Michigan, USA. Raised in Denver, Colorado, she sang in school but was spotted by Clark Terry while singing in Chicago. In the 70s she sang in Los Angeles, working clubs and studios while she studied with Phil Moore. In 1981 she toured overseas with Sergio Mendes and worked successfully for several years before attracting the attention of Blue Note Records. Although there are touches of soul and r&b in her work, she favours original material. Albums: *Welcome to My Love* (Palo Alto Jazz, 1982), *Dianne Reeves* (Blue Note, 1987), *Quiet After the Storm* (Blue Note, 1995).

Reys, Rita

b. Maria Everdina Reys, 21 December 1924, Rotterdam, Holland. As a teenager, she sang with various dance bands including one led by her father. In the late 40s she worked in various parts of Europe, sometimes as co-leader of bands, and in the 50s visited the USA where she worked with noted jazzmen such as Art Blakey and Jimmy Smith. From the 60s she sang as a single and extended her popularity in Europe. A fine rhythmic singer and a very good interpreter of ballads, Reys deserved far more attention in the jazz world at large during her long

career. She returned from retirement to sing on into the 1990s.

Albums: *Our Favorite Songs* (CBS, 1973), *That Old Feeling* (CBS, 1979), *Memories of You* (Utopia, 1983), *Great American Songbook Vols 1 & 2* (Music-All-In, 1992).

Richmond, June

b. 9 July 1915, Chicago, Illinois, USA, d. 14 August 1962. She sang briefly with Les Hite's band, then joined Jimmy Dorsey in 1938, one of the first occasions when a white band hired a black singer. Later, she sang with Cab Calloway and Andy Kirk. By the late 40s her popularity had widened and she went out as a single, but had to live mainly in Europe to achieve her potential. Her lightly rounded voice, allied to deft phrasing, helped give her a subtly swinging style.

Albums: *Andy Kirk at the Trianon* (Jazz Society, 1930s–40s).

Roché, Betty

b. Mary Elizabeth Roché, 9 January 1920, Wilmington, Delaware, USA. She was with Al Cooper's Savoy Sultans in the winter of 1939/40. In 1943 she joined Duke Ellington, then sang with Earl Hines before drifting a little. She rejoined Ellington in late 1951 and later had a career as a single. By the mid-60s she had slipped into obscurity and was for many years confined to a wheelchair. She had a pleasingly warm singing voice and exhilarating rhythmic delivery on up-tempo songs, comfortably moving from swing era styles to bop, becoming one of the best of the form's exponents.

Albums: with Ellington *Carnegie Hall Concert: January 1943* (Prestige, 1943), *Take the 'A' Train* (Bethlehem, 1956), *Singin' and Swingin'* (Prestige, 1960), *Lightly and Politely* (Prestige, 1961).

Ross, Annie
b. Annabelle Lynch, 25 July 1930, Mitcham, Surrey, UK. At the age of three she went to live in Hollywood with her aunt, singer Ella Logan. She made films but by the late 40s was back in Europe working as a singer. In the early 50s she teamed up with Jon Hendricks and Dave Lambert as Lambert, Hendricks and Ross. Back in Europe she continued to sing in clubs, at concerts and festivals into the mid-90s. Technically assured, she sings with warmth and commitment and interprets lyrics with rare perception.
Albums: *Annie Ross Sings* (OJC, 1953), *Annie by Candlelight* (Pye, 1956), *Gypsy* (Pacific Jazz, 1959), with Georgie Fame *In Hoagland* (Bald Eagle, 1981).

Rowland, Dennis
b. Detroit, Michigan, USA. His first impact was in 1977 when he joined Count Basie and sang on the band's Grammy Award-winning *On the Road*. In 1984 he went out on his own and also began a successful acting career in the theatre. He has a subtle and rhythmic style and uses his textured baritone to create impressive performances of standards and blues songs.
Albums: with Basie *On the Road* (Pablo, 1980), *Rhyme, Rhythm & Reason* (Concord, 1995), *Get Here* (Concord, 1995).

Rucker, Ellyn
b. 29 July 1937, Des Moines, Iowa, USA. She studied classical piano, then began playing jazz but did not become a full-time professional until she had turned forty. For many years she was in Denver, Colorado, until Mark Murphy persuaded her to expand her geographic horizons. Her piano style is eclectic and invigorating and, although less actively promoted, her singing is natural, unaffected and always pleasing.
Albums: *Ellyn* (Capri, 1987), *This Heart of Mine* (Capri, 1988), with Spike Robinson *Nice Work* (Capri, 1989).

Rushing, Jimmy
b. James Andrew Rushing, 26 August 1902, Oklahoma City, Oklahoma, USA, d. 8 June 1972. He studied piano, violin and singing, working with local bands, but by 1923 was singing semi-professionally in California. He returned to his home town to join Walter Page's Blue Devils, then Bennie Moten, joining Bill Basie in 1935. At the end of the 40s he embarked upon a solo career. Often recording, and touring endlessly, he made several fine studio and live albums. His singing voice was a high tenor and he sang the blues with a distinctively melodious quality.
Albums: with Basie *The Jubilee Alternatives* (Hep, 1943-4), *His Complete Vanguard Recordings (Goin' to Chicago/Listen to the Blues/If This Ain't the Blues)* (Vanguard/FNAC, 1954-7), *The Essential Jimmy Rushing* (Vogue, 1954-7), *The Jazz Odyssey Of*

James Rushing Esq. (Fresh Sounds, 1956), *Little Jimmy Rushing and the Big Brass* (CBS, 1958), *The You and Me That Used to Be* (Bluebird, 1971).

Schuur, Diane

b. Tacoma, Washington, USA. Blind from childhood, she sang professionally before she was ten years old. After singing with a band led by drummer Ed Shaughnessy, with whom she appeared at the Monterey Jazz Festival, she began a career as a single. She was encouraged by Stan Getz who helped to promote her. Her raw and energetic singing style appealed to pop crossover audiences and she won Grammy Awards in 1986 and 1987.
Albums: *Deedles* (GRP, 1984), *Deedles and Basie* (GRP, 1987), *Pure Schuur* (GRP, 1990), with B. B. King *Heart to Heart* (GRP, 1994).

Scott-Heron, Gil

b. 1 April 1949, Chicago, Illinois, USA. Raised in Texas, he visited New York at the age of thirteen by which time he had reportedly published two novels and a book of poetry. In 1972 he formed the Midnight Band with Brian Jackson, performing a heady blend of jazz, soul and proto-rap. A songwriter, much of his work is political and social protest.
Albums: *Small Talk at 125th and Lenox* (Flying Dutchman, 1972), *Moving Target* (Arista, 1982), *Spirits* (1994).

Shaw, Ian

b. 2 June 1962, St Asaph, North Wales, UK. He studied music at King's College, London. In 1987 he joined the soul-rock band, Brave New World, later touring with Carol Grimes. He has sung at Ronnie Scott's as a single, sometimes accompanying himself at the piano. An elegant interpreter of the great standards which he cloaks in contemporary sensibilities, he is also at ease with the latest trends in jazz. He sometimes appears as a member of Jan Ponsford's Vocal Chords.
Albums: with Grimes *Lazy Blue Eyes* (Offbeat, 1990), *Ghostsongs* (Jazz House, 1992), *Taking It to Hart* (Jazz House, 1995).

Simone, Nina

b. Eunice Waymon, 21 February 1933, Tryon, North Carolina, USA. She studied to be a classical pianist before accepting the futility of this as a career for a black woman of her times. Turning to popular music, she became established as a club player and singer during the 60s. She wrote songs in support of the Civil Rights movement and took a confrontational stance on issues of the day. Her singing style is declamatory, often displaying scant regard for the lyric content. Her piano playing is highly accomplished.
Albums: *Best of the Colpix* (Roulette, 1959–62), *It Is Finished* (RCA, 1972), *Baltimore* (CTI, 1978).

Sinatra, Frank

b. Francis Albert Sinatra, 12 December 1915, Hoboken, New Jersey, USA. He began singing in 1933, inspired by Bing Crosby's style and popularity. In 1939 he joined Harry James's band and the following year moved to Tommy Dorsey. He had many successful records and eventually left to start a career as a single. A masterful interpreter of lyrics, he always sang with confidence and an easy swing. Attuned to jazz through his big band apprenticeship, he worked particularly well with arrangers of similar mind, such as Axel Stordahl and Nelson Riddle, and his middle-period albums, on Capitol and Reprise, are classic examples of the art and craft of popular singing.

Albums: *The Formative Years* (Avid, 1939–42), *In the Wee Small Hours* (Capitol, 1955), *Songs for Swingin' Lovers* (Capitol, 1956), *I Remember Tommy...* (Capitol, 1961), *Sinatra-Basie* (Capitol, 1962), with Duke Ellington *Francis A. and Edward K.* (Reprise, 1968).

Sloane, Carol

b. 1937, Providence, Rhode Island, USA. At the age of fourteen she sang with a dance band and later worked with the Les and Larry Elgart Orchestra. Although popular in New York, her career did not take off and from the end of the 60s she worked outside music. In 1977 she returned to New York and since then has made records, toured extensively and has hosted her own radio show in Boston. Singing ballads with rare affection and in a calm melodious voice, she can also swing with effortless grace. In the 90s she has continued to prove that she is a major jazz talent.

Albums: *Out of the Blue* (Columbia, 1961), *Carol Sings* (Audiophile, 1978), *Heart's Desire* (Concord,

1991), *The Songs Carmen Sang* (Concord, 1995).

Smith, Bessie

b. 15 April 1894, Chattanooga, Tennessee, USA, d. 26 September 1937. After starting out as a dancer and singer in tent shows, by the 20s she was a star in her own show. Thanks to the spread of records she was soon acclaimed as the Empress of the Blues. By the end of the decade, however, changing musical times were leaving her behind. In 1933 she made more records and appeared at the Apollo Theater in New York and looked to be on her way back. She died following a road accident. Her rich contralto voice, stately delivery and powerful presence made her work an important part of American popular culture and a lasting exemplar for all blues singers.

Albums: *The Bessie Smith Story* (CBS, 1924–33).

Smith, Carrie

b. 25 August 1941, Fort Gaines, Georgia, USA. Raised in New Jersey, she sang in church and appeared as a chorister at the 1957 Newport Jazz Festival. Early in the 70s her solo career began to take off but she achieved more fame in Europe than in the USA. A deep, strong tone and forceful style and personality give depth and substance to her performances. A thread of blues and gospel runs through her broad repertoire.

Albums: *Fine & Mellow (Carrie Sings Billie Holiday/Carrie Sings Hoagy Carmichael)* (Audiophile, 1976), *When You're Down and Out* (Black and Blue, 1977), *Carrie Smith* (West 54, 1978), *Every Now and Then* (Silver Shadow, 1995).

Snow, Valaida

b. 2 June 1903, Chattanooga, Tennessee, USA, d. 30 May 1956. A good singer and dancer, she was an exceptionally good trumpet player. Throughout the 20s and 30s she toured internationally to great acclaim, making films and recording. In Denmark, in 1940, she was imprisoned following the German invasion but was eventually repatriated. She continued to perform but in relative obscurity. Her sisters were also musicians, two of them, Lavaida and Alvaida, becoming professionals.
Albums: *Valaida Vols 1-2* (Harlequin, 1935-40), *Hot Snow* (Rosetta, 1945).

Spirits of Rhythm, The

Ostensibly a novelty band, they made many excellent jazz recordings and in Leo Watson had a leading exponent of scat singing. In the 30s the group played New York clubs and also toured, attracting a wide audience thanks to their humorous approach. The group's distinctive sound was due to a combination of their vocal harmonizing, to their use of the tiple, a small, multiple metal-stringed guitar-like instrument, and to Watson's uniqueness. The other members were Teddy Bunn, guitar, Virgil Scroggins, drums and vocals, Wilbur and Douglas Daniels, tiples and vocals.
Albums: *The Spirits of Rhythm* (JSP, 1933-4).

Spivey, Victoria

b. Victoria Regina Spivey, 15 October 1906, Houston, Texas, USA, d. 30 October 1976. She had her first recording success when she was twenty with 'Black Snake Blues' and also appeared in the film *Hallelujah* (1929). She recorded regularly into the 40s, returning in the 60s and forming her own record company. She sang the blues with a high, nasal, somewhat threatening voice which gave her a highly distinctive sound.
Albums: *Jazz Sounds of the Twenties, Vol. 4: The Blues Singers* (Parlophone, 1923-31), *Songs We Taught Your Mother* (Prestige-Bluesville, 1961), *The Queen and Her Knights* (Spivey, 1963).

Squires, Rosemary

b. Joan Rosemary Yarrow, 7 December 1928, Bristol, UK. As a child she sang locally and during World War Two toured American Air Force bases in the UK. In the late 40s she sang with various bands including the British Force's Blue Rockets Dance Band. She also sang on radio and with Geraldo, turning down an offer to join Ted Heath. In the mid-60s she visited the USA and continued to appear on radio. In the 90s she was back on the scene touring with Barbara Jay and Maxine Daniels in a package celebrating the work of Ella Fitzgerald.
Albums: *My One and Only* (C5, 1950s-60s).

Stafford, Jo

b. 12 November, 1920, Coalinga, California, USA. After singing with a trio in Los Angeles and then the Pied Pipers vocal group, she came to prominence when a cut-down version of the Pipers joined Tommy Dorsey's band. In 1945 she began a solo career with many successful albums for Capitol, most of which were masterminded by her husband, arranger Paul Weston. She continued to tour until 1959 and made only a few later records before retiring. Her distinctive, almost vibrato-free voice was accurate and always a delight to hear.

Albums: *G. I. Jo* (Corinthian, 1950s), *Jo + Jazz* (Corinthian, 1950s).

Stallings, Mary

b. San Francisco, California, USA. She sang first in church, then in clubs when she was in her teens. She was briefly with Louis Jordan, then toured extensively and appeared at the 1965 Monterey Jazz Festival, singing with Dizzy Gillespie. For a year she was teamed with Billy Eckstine, then, in 1969, joined Count Basie for a three-year stint. Since then she has continued to sing in the USA and overseas.

Albums: *Mary Stallings & Cal Tjader* (Fantasy, 1961), *I Waited for You* (Concord, 1994).

Staton, Dakota

b. Aliyah Rabia, 3 June 1932, Pittsburgh, Pennsylvania, USA. After singing in clubs for several years, her career blossomed in the mid-50s. She toured extensively, as a single and with others, including Benny Goodman. In the late 60s she was resident in the UK but returned to the USA to enter the soul scene for which her dark, expressive voice

was ideally suited. Her varied repertoire has enabled her to move comfortably between jazz, soul and pop but has, at the same time, prevented her from attaining a high profile in any of these areas.

Albums: *The Late, Late Show* (Capitol, 1957), *Let Me Off Uptown* (Renaissance, 1958–60), *Spotlight on Dakota Staton* (Capitol, 1960s).

Stewart, Buddy

b. 1922, Derry, New Hampshire, USA, d. 1 February 1950. He sang with various vocal groups, in one of which his wife, Martha Wayne, also sang. With Gene Krupa's band in the mid-40s he recorded 'What's This?' with Dave Lambert, an early example of bop singing. He continued singing, sometimes with Lambert, but died following an automobile accident. He sang ballads in a relaxed manner but is best known for his boppish vocalizing.

Albums: *Dave Lambert & Buddy Stewart* (EmArcy, 1946).

Sullivan, Maxine

b. Marietta Williams, 13 May 1911, Homestead, Pennsylvania, USA, d. 7 April 1987. Recording with Claude Thornhill's band in New York, she had a surprise hit with a peppy version of 'Loch Lomond'. She then joined the small band led by John Kirby, to whom she was married. From the early 40s to the mid-50s she sang solo, then divided her time between music and work in the community. In the late 70s she was rediscovered and toured and made records with many jazz musicians, most fruitfully with Bob

Wilber and Dick Hyman. Sullivan, who also learned to play flügelhorn and valve trombone, sang with unfailing good taste and an airy sense of swing which never deserted her.

Albums: *It's Wonderful* (Affinity, 1937-8), *Seven Ages of Jazz* (Metrojazz, 1958), with Wilber *The Music of Hoagy Carmichael* (Audiophile, 1969), *Sullivan, Shakespeare, Hyman* (Audiophile, 1979), *Uptown* (Concord, 1985), *Maxine Sullivan and Scott Hamilton* (Concord, 1986).

Sweet Substitute

A vocal trio, formed in the UK in the mid-70s. Their initial style was based upon 30s and 40s American all-girl vocal groups. They expanded their repertoire to embrace current musical trends and worked with jazz musicians throughout the 80s. The group's members were originally Angie Masterson, Teri Leggett and Chris Staples, the latter being succeeded by Kate McNab.

Albums: *Sophisticated Ladies* (Black Lion, 1980).

Syms, Sylvia

b. Sylvia Blagman, 2 December 1917, New York City, New York, USA, d. 10 May 1992. As a youngster she hung out on 52nd Street and began singing in 1940. She worked in cabaret and also in the musical theatre. Throughout the 60s and 70s she sang mostly in clubs in New York. She had a tough and appealing vocal sound and her personal friendships with Billie Holiday and Mildred Bailey led to her absorbing elements of their craft. Her care with lyrics was a hallmark of her style.

Albums: *Sylvia Is* (Prestige, 1965), *A Jazz Portrait of Johnny Mercer* (DRG, 1990s).

Tania Maria

b. Tania Maria Correa Reis, 9 May 1948, São Luis, Maranhao, Brazil. She studied classical piano and played professionally for a few years but then attracted attention at the 1975 Newport Jazz Festival. She lived and worked in Paris for a while, then moved to New York in 1981. A vivid and exciting performer as pianist and singer, her early jazz work was strongly Latin-flavoured. Later, she developed a more overtly commercial approach.

Albums: *Piquant* (Concord, 1981), *The Real Tania Maria: Wild!* (Concord, 1985), *No Comment* (TKM, 1994), *Bluesilian* (TKM, 1996).

Teagarden, Jack

b. Weldon Leo Teagarden, 29 August 1905, Vernon, Texas, USA, d. 15 January 1964. After trying other instruments, at age ten he settled on the trombone. In his teens he began his professional career and in the late 20s made an enormous impact in New York with his remarkable trombone playing. He sang with a sleepy drawl, slurred diction and charm. In some respects he might be seen as a bridge between the sometimes raw black country blues singers and the urbane white crooners. He played in many bands, led his own for a while, and had a long association with Louis Armstrong which resulted in several good-natured vocal duets.

Albums: *King of the Blues Trombone* (Columbia, 1928-40), with Armstrong *Town Hall Concert Plus* (RCA, 1947), *The Jack Teagarden Sextet in Person* (Fanfare, 1963).

Terrell, Pha

b. Pha Elmer Terrell, 25 May 1910, Kansas City, Missouri, USA, d. 14 October 1945. He sang and danced in his home town before being signed by Andy Kirk. His singing with the band was popular, his delivery, which used a high tenor and occasional falsetto, having an appeal at that time. His style blended well with Kirk's sophisticated band but contrasted with that of most other black singers of the 30s. He sang as a single from 1941 until his premature death.

Albums: with Kirk *Walkin' and Swingin'* (Affinity, 1930s).

Tharpe, Sister Rosetta

b. Rosetta Nubin, 20 March 1915, Cotton Plant, Arkansas, USA, d. 9 October 1973. Raised in Chicago, she sang in church and also played blues guitar as a child. This combination of sacred and secular music remained a pattern of her career. She sang with Cab Calloway and Lucky Millinder but also had a successful partnership with gospel singer Sister Marie Knight. Her singing voice was cheerfully uplifting and her guitar playing earthily effective. Through the 50s she was one of the biggest draws in gospel and later toured the UK with Chris Barber.

Albums: with Millinder *Apollo Jump* (Affinity, 1941-2), *Live in Paris* (France's Concert, 1964).

Thomas, Leone

b. Amos Leon Thomas Jnr, 4 October 1937, East St Louis, Illinois, USA. He sang in New York from the late 50s, usually performing in an orthodox style. He then began to use a highly original style, employing scat in variations that took the form into new areas of inventiveness. Usually, he worked alone but on occasion teamed up with others including, somewhat surprisingly, Louis Armstrong in 1970.

Albums: *Spirits Known and Unknown* (Flying Dutchman, 1969), *Full Circle* (Flying Dutchman, 1973).

Thorson, Lisa

b. USA. She studied in Boston, where she still teaches. Deeply involved in education, and an active campaigner for rights for the disabled, she has been the recipient of many honours in and outside music. Actively encouraged in her singing by Sheila Jordan, she sings with a warm, fluid sound and interprets lyrics meaningfully. Since an injury in 1979 she is obliged to use a wheelchair for mobility.

Albums: *From This Moment On* (Brownstone, 1992-4).

Tormé, Mel

b. Melvin Howard Torme, 13 September 1925, Chicago, Illinois, USA. In show business from the age of four, he teamed up with a vocal group, the Mel-Tones, in the early 40s and recorded with Artie

Shaw's band. From the mid-50s onwards, he was a major nightclub star. In his youth his voice was light and carefree but he always sang with poise and accuracy. In later years his voice darkened into a pleasingly effortless baritone. He writes his own arrangements, is a multi-instrumentalist, and has also composed songs, including 'The Christmas Song', a hit for Nat King Cole. He has chosen to stay fairly close to the jazz path but his style and repertoire are such that throughout his career he has attracted audiences far outside the jazz world's usual confines with never a hint of compromise.

Albums: *Live at the Crescendo* (Bethlehem, 1957), *Mel Tormé and the Mel-Tones: Back in Town* (Verve, 1959), *Right Now* (Columbia, 1966), *An Evening with George Shearing & Mel Tormé* (Concord, 1982), *Mel & George 'Do' World War II* (Concord, 1990), with Rob McConnell *Velvet and Brass* (Concord, 1995).

Turner, Big Joe
b. Joseph Vernon Turner, 18 May 1911, Kansas City, Missouri, USA, d. 24 November 1985. He was a singing bartender in his home town where, at fifteen, he teamed up with pianist Pete Johnson. A blues shouter with a powerful rasping delivery, Turner shifted gear slightly in the late 40s to sing in the new jump style which evolved into r&b. In 1951 he had several major hits including, in 1954, 'Shake, Rattle and Roll', which was promptly covered by Bill Haley. Turner continued to make blues records, notably the outstanding *Boss of the Blues*. The 60s were lean years but from the early 70s, thanks to Norman Granz, Turner was on his way and shouting again. Despite ill health and a period of inactivity, he sang almost to the end.

Albums: *The Complete 1940-1944 Recordings* (1940-4), *Boss of the Blues* (Atlantic, 1956), with Count Basie *The Bosses* (Pablo, 1975), *The Trumpet Kings Meet Joe Turner* (Pablo, 1982), *Boogie Woogie Jubilee* (Vagabond, 1981).

Tyrrell, Christine
Based in London, of West Indian heritage, this engaging singer has concentrated her talents upon the traditional jazz and blues repertoire which she sings with great verve. Working clubs and festivals in the UK and parts of Europe, including the prestigious Cork Jazz Festival, she is usually with the Phil Mason band. She also sings gospel music with all the enthusiasm the genre demands.

Albums: with Mason *Spirituals and Gospel* (Lake,1995).

Vaughan, Sarah
b. Sarah Lois Vaughan, 27 March 1924, Newark, New Jersey, USA, d. 3 April 1990. Her career is assessed in detail in Chapter 8.

Albums: *The Essential Sarah Vaughan* (CBS, 1949-50), *Sarah Vaughan with Clifford Brown* (EmArcy, 1954), *Soft & Sassy* (Hindsight, 1961), *The Benny Carter Sessions (The Explosive Side of Sarah Vaughan/The Lonely Hours)* (EMI/Roulette, 1962-3), *Live in*

Japan (Mainstream, 1973–5), *How Long Has This Been Going On?* (Pablo, 1978), *Crazy and Mixed Up* (Pablo, 1982).

VerPlanck, Marlene
b. Marlene Pampinella, Newark, New Jersey, USA. She began singing at nineteen, first working with Tex Beneke, then Charlie Spivak and Tommy Dorsey. She met and married trombonist-arranger William J. 'Billy' VerPlanck who became her musical director. By the 80s she was highly popular on both sides of the Atlantic with numerous well-received albums to her credit. A sparkling technique, pure sound and flawless diction have helped make her one of the outstanding interpreters of the great standards.
Albums: *Marlene VerPlanck Loves Johnny Mercer* (Audiophile, 1978), *Pure & Natural* (Audiophile, 1987–9), *A Quiet Storm* (Audiophile, 1989), *Marlene VerPlanck Meets Saxomania* (Audiophile, 1993–4).

Vinson, Eddie 'Cleanhead'
b. 18 December 1917, Houston, Texas, USA, d. 2 July 1988. He played alto saxophone in territory bands and also accompanied Big Bill Broonzy who helped him develop his blues singing. Meanwhile, his saxophone playing was influenced by Charlie Parker. He led his own band in the mid-40s, playing bop and r&b but his career faltered in the 50s. From the mid-60s he was back on the scene and continued to tour internationally for the rest of his life. His singing, earthy and outrageous as it often was, was remarkably counterpointed by his direct bop saxophone style.
Albums: *Mr Cleanhead's Back in Town* (Bethlehem, 1959), *Kidney Stew* (Black and Blue, 1969), *Live at Sandy's* (Muse, 1978), *Roomful of Blues* (Muse, 1982).

Vocal Summit
A contemporary vocal group comprising: Urszula Dudziak (*qv*), leader, Jeanne Lee (*qv*), Bobby McFerrin (*qv*), Lauren Newton and Jay Clayton.
Albums: under Dudziak *Sorrow Is Not Forever ... But Love Is* (Keytone, 1983).

Walker, T-Bone
b. Aaron Thibeaux Walker, 28 May 1910, Linden, Texas, USA, d. 16 March 1975. A self-taught guitarist, as a teenager he toured with a tent show and then worked with various territory bands. He began to record under his own name in the 40s and had a huge hit with '(Call It) Stormy Monday'. He toured extensively, fought off ill health and continued to record, play festivals and make many appearances all over the world. A sophisticated singer and guitarist, he delivered lyrics almost conversationally, quite unlike his earthier contemporaries, and this might well have accounted for the impression he made upon the next generation's white and black rock 'n' roll singers.
Albums: *T-Bone Blues* (Atlantic, 1960), *Stormy Monday Blues* (Bluesway, 1967), *Good Feelin'* (Polydor, 1970), *Very Rare* (Reprise, 1973).

Waller, Fats

b. Thomas Wright Waller, 21 May 1904, New York City, New York, USA, d. 15 December 1943. After establishing a formidable reputation as a stride piano player in New York, he began to make a wider impression thanks to records. Many of his recordings featured his inimitable singing which extended his popularity far beyond the jazz world. He delivered lyrics in a slyly humorous manner, never afraid to send up those that were inadequate. He was also a composer of great distinction, writing '(What Did I Do to Be So) Black and Blue?', 'Ain't Misbehavin'', 'Honeysuckle Rose', 'I've Got a Feeling I'm Falling', and many others, often in collaboration with Andy Razaf. On some records, where the lyric was suitable and his mood was right, he proved to be a sensitive performer. He had all the qualities needed to make him a major entertainer of world-wide stature but he died suddenly on his way back to New York after appearances in California, including working on the film *Stormy Weather.*

Albums: *The Indispensable Fats Waller Vols 1-10* (RCA, 1930s-40s), *The Last Years* (Bluebird, 1940-3), *Live at the Yacht Club* (Giants of Jazz, 1940s).

Washington, Dinah

b. Ruth Lee Jones, 24 August 1924, Tuscaloosa, Alabama, USA, d. 14 December 1963. Raised in Chicago, she sang in church and also local clubs where she was heard by Lionel Hampton who hired her in 1943. She was with Hampton for three years and then embarked on a solo career and became hugely popular. Whether she sang blues or jazz, pop or r&b, she was clearly at ease and in command. Her singing voice, emphatically emotional and with a diamond-hard edge, was somehow in keeping with whatever she sang, adding resonance to blues and profound songs, acerbic wit to trite songs, and making many love songs unbearably moving. She remains one of the most versatile singers ever to have worked in popular music and was a major figure in black music.

Albums: *The Dinah Washington Story (The Original Recordings)* (Mercury, 1943-61), *For Those in Love* (EmArcy, 1955), *In the Land of Hi-Fi* (EmArcy, 1956), *The Best of Dinah Washington* (Roulette, 1962-4).

Waters, Ethel

b. Ethel Howard, 31 October 1896, Chester, Pennsylvania, USA, d. 1 September 1977. Raised in Philadelphia in conditions of abject poverty, she became a headline attraction in vaudeville by the time she was twenty-one. Starting out as a blues singer, she extended her repertoire and inclined towards a more lyrical and melodic approach. By the 30s she was widely known to white audiences. She made records, films, appeared on Broadway and in London. From the 40s her acting career, in films, on the stage, and later in television, took precedence and she became a distinguished and respected member of her profession. Her singing style was highly influential upon singers both black and white, female and male, and through artists such as Ella Fitzgerald has filtered through to the present day. Several of her recordings were among the first and definitive performances of songs: 'Sugar', 'Dinah', 'Am I Blue?' and 'Stormy Weather'.

Albums: *An Introduction to Ethel Waters* (Best of Jazz, 1921–40), *Her Greatest Years* (Columbia, 1925–34).

Watson, Leo

b. 27 February 1898, Kansas City, Missouri, USA, d. 2 May 1950. He first worked alone but in the 30s teamed up with a novelty band which eventually became the Spirits of Rhythm. In addition to singing he played drums and tiple. His vocal style, original and sensational for its time, was an astonishing blend of scat, story-telling and straight singing and was all largely spur-of-the-moment improvising. He worked briefly and recorded with the bands of Artie Shaw, 'Freewheeling' (1937), and Gene Krupa, 'Nagasaki' (1938). In the 40s he returned to the Spirits, but mostly worked as a single again.

Albums: *The Spirits of Rhythm* (JSP, 1933–4).

Wentzel, Magni

b. 28 June 1945, Norway. Her parents were musical and she first sang professionally at the age of twelve. Inspired by Ella Fitzgerald, Peggy Lee, June Christy and others, she turned to jazz. However, she also studied classical guitar and has performed publicly on this instrument, playing guitar concertos with symphony orchestras. She has also sung from the classical repertoire after studying at the Norwegian Opera School. She has a four-octave range but when performing standards and jazz songs she uses it without artifice.

Albums: *Come Along with Me* (Gemini, 1993).

Whitfield, Weslia

b. California, USA. She began singing in a trio with her sisters when she was about four and at seven studied piano for six years, then voice. She was a member of the San Francisco Opera Chorus for four seasons, then sang professionally in church. Her jazz work was encouraged by Mike Greensill, whom she married. Her love for jazz and the great songs from the standard repertoire is evident in all that she does. Her voice is fluid and resonant and she brings depth and charm to ballads.

Albums: *Seeker of Wisdom and Truth* (Cabaret, 1993), *Nice Work* (Landmark, 1994), *Nobody Else but Me* (Landmark, 1996).

Wiley, Lee

b. 9 October 1915, Fort Gibson, Oklahoma, USA, d. 11 December 1975. As a teenager she sang with Leo Reisman's band, recording with Paul Whiteman, and the Casa Loma Orchestra. In the early 40s she made many fine records, usually with small jazz groups. Later, she sang with a big band led by pianist Jess Stacy, to whom she was married for a while, then again with small groups. The 50s and 60s were quiet times but in 1972, with her voice deteriorating, she was received with great acclaim at the New York Jazz Festival. Hers was a small, fragile voice and she delivered lyrics with cautious warmth and wistfulness which created an atmosphere of low-key intimacy. Over the years she has proved to be influential upon singers hearing her records for the first time long after her death.

Albums: *Lee Wiley on the Air, Vol. 1* (Totem, 1932-6), *Lee Wiley on the Air, Vol. 2* (Totem, 1944–5), *Sings the* Songs of *Rodgers & Hart and Arlen* (Audiophile, 1940s), *Porter and Gershwin* (Audiophile, 1940s), *Back Home Again* (Audiophile, 1971).

Williams, Joe

b. Joseph Goreed, 12 December 1918, Cordele, Georgia, USA. Raised in Chicago, he sang with a gospel group but by the end of the 30s was singing with jazz musicians. He spent a decade with various bands and in 1951 had a minor hit with 'Every Day I Have the Blues'. In 1954 he re-recorded the song with Count Basie which resulted in a major hit and sealed their partnership. He stayed with Basie for a decade, then resumed his solo career. Over the years his voice matured and mellowed and showed none of the usual signs of wear and tear. He sings the blues with a tuneful polish which has helped attract a large following. His ballad singing is urbane and sincere and throughout all his work are signs of abiding good humour.

Albums: *Joe Williams Sings Everyday* (Regent, 1950-1), *Count Basie Swings, Joe Williams Sings* (Verve, 1955-6), *Joe Williams at Newport '63* (RCA, 1963), *Joe Williams Live* (Fantasy, 1973), *Nothin' but the Blues* (Delos, 1983), *I Just Want to Sing* (Delos, 1985).

Williams, Midge

b. c.1908, California, USA, d. unknown date. She first sang with a family vocal group, then became a single in the late 20s. In the early 30s she sang in China and Japan, then went back to the USA to host a radio show and work with Fats Waller. She recorded with various bands, sometimes using the name, Midge Williams and Her Jazz Jesters. At the end of the 30s she sang with Louis Armstrong's big band then went solo before disappearing from the scene. She is believed to have died some time after the mid-40s. She sang in a relatively straight manner in an engaging light voice.

Albums: *Midge Williams and Her Jazz Jesters* (Classics, 1937–8).

Wilson, Cassandra

b. 4 December 1955, Jackson, Mississippi, USA. Until the mid-70s she sang mostly in and around her home town. Her repertoire was an amalgam of folk, blues and r&b but she gradually turned to jazz. After a spell in New Orleans, she went to New York where, in the early 80s, she began making an impact. Associating with contemporary jazz musicians and directing her work at the same audience, she made some adjustments to accommo-

243

date the mainstream and by the 90s was on the edge of international stardom. Her warm, smoky voice and careful, often richly arranged accompaniments, make her an always interesting, sometimes mesmerizing singer. Clearly, she is a singer who will continue to make her mark.

Albums: *Point of View* (JMT, 1986), *Blue Skies* (JMT, 1988), *Live* (JMT, 1991), *Blue Light 'Til Dawn* (Blue Note, 1993), *New Moon Daughter* (Blue Note, 1996).

Winstone, Norma

b. Norma Ann Winstone, 28 September 1941, London, UK. After studying piano and organ she began singing in mainstream jazz and the jazzier end of pop. By the 60s, however, she was firmly associated with the jazz avant-garde. Her wordless improvisations, sometimes with Michael Garrick's sextet, helped spread her reputation as a remarkable and innovative singer. In the 70s she became a founder member of Azimuth, a trio which also featured Kenny Wheeler and John Taylor. Late in the 80s she frequently worked with Tony Coe and in the mid-90s was with Jan Ponsford's Vocal Chords and also fronted her own new band, New Friends. Winstone's repertoire is wide and varied and periodically she re-invents herself, deliberately changing styles to further test her seemingly boundless limits. Consistently interesting and with high standards of musical excellence, she is a major figure of international jazz singing in the 90s.

Albums: *Edge of Time* (Argo, 1971), *Azimuth* (ECM, 1977), *In Concert* (Enodoc, 1988), *Well Kept Secret* (Hot House, 1993), *Azimuth '95* (1994).

Witherspoon, Jimmy

b. 8 August 1923, Gurdon, Arkansas, USA. He sang in church, then began singing professionally. Until war service he sang ballads but while in India with the US Navy he heard Teddy Weatherford's band and thereafter turned increasingly to the blues. After the war he sang with Jay McShann, then led his own band and had some success in r&b. The 50s were hard times but he came back to an international following. A powerful singer with the earthy directness of Joe Turner but with a slightly more mellow sound, he customarily works with jazz musicians.

Albums. *Jimmy Witherspoon at Monterey* (HiFi, 1959), *Roots* (Reprise, 1962), *Spoonful* (Blue Note, 1975), *Jimmy Witherspoon and the New Savoy Sultans* (Black and Blue, 1980).

Zetterlund, Monica

b. 20 September 1938, Hagfors, Sweden. First singing in Scandinavia, her records with Arne Domnérus in the late 50s, then with Bill Evans, led to international acclaim. She also sings folk music of her native land and classical music. Her jazz style is clean and well-ordered. Alongside her singing career she also acts in films and on the stage.

Albums: with Evans *Waltz for Debby* (Philips, 1964), *It Only Happens Every Time* (EMI, 1977).

Limited by space as it is, the foregoing A–Z is quite clearly only a partial listing of the many singers who have worked or are still working in jazz and jazz-influenced popular music. Many of those not listed therein are well worth seeking out, either in person or on record and a few more names are therefore given below. Perhaps at some future date these will form the basis of an expanded listing.

Patricia Barber, Fontella Bass, Germaine Bazzle, Tony Bennett, Theo Blackman, Angela Bofill, Kysia Bostic, Carmen Bradford, Tiny Bradshaw, Teresa Brewer, Charles Brown, Deborah Brown, Marie Bryant, Willie Bryant, Donna Byrne, Gerard Carelli, Thelma Carpenter, Inez Cavanaugh, Jay Clayton, Mary Coughlan, Randy Crawford, Meredith D'Ambrosio, Litsa Davies, Matt Dennis, Bob Dorough, Roy Eldridge, Anita Ellis, Ethel Ennis, Samirah Evans, Peter Fessler, Karen Francis, Maureen Francis, Aretha Franklin, Laura Fygi, Cecil Gant, Georgia Gibbs, Astrud Gilberto, Gabrielle Goodman, Norbert Gottschalk, Anita Gravine, Sue Harker, Allan Harris, Marion Harris, Wynonie Harris, Nancy Harrow, Johnny Hartman, Honor Heffernon, Lucille Hegamin, Bill Henderson, Jacqui Hicks, The Hi-Lo's, Linda Hopkins, Etta James, Denise Jannah, Maria João, Christine Jones, Salena Jones, Beverley Kenney, Marie Knight, Jeanne Lambe, Denise Lawrence, Ranee Lee, Caroline Loftus, Ella Logan, Sandy Lomax, Martha Lorin, Carmen Lundy, Maureen McGovern, Manhattan Transfer, Marianne Mendt, Mabel Mercer, Audrey Morris, Barbara Morrison, Lee Morse, Anne Marie Moss, Ray Nance, Lauren Newton, Carla Normand, Clay Osborne, Lucy Ann Polk, Arthur Price, Louis Prima, Arthur Prysock, Kenny Rankin, Bertice Reading, Irene Reid, Terrie Richards, Mavis Rivers, Vanessa Rubin, Patrice Rushen, Daryle Ryce, Annette Sanders, Hazel Scott, Helen Shapiro, Linda Sharrock, Daryl Sherman, Ben Sidran, Clara Smith, Mamie Smith, Trixie Smith, Helen Sorrell, Kay Starr, Sandy Stewart, Terry Thornton, George 'Bon Bon' Tunnell, Jenny Tyrrell, Gino Vannelli, Roseanna Vitro, Helen Ward, Carla White, Georgia White, Margaret Whiting, Ronny Whyte, Nancy Wilson, Eleanor Winston, Val Wiseman, Elly Wright, Gail Wynters.

BIBLIOGRAPHY

Reference

Carr, Ian, Fairweather, Digby and Priestley, Brian, *Jazz: the Essential Companion*, Grafton, London, 1987

Chilton, John, *Who's Who of Jazz: Storyville to Swing Street*, Chilton, London, 1985

Gregory, Hugh, *Soul Music A–Z*, Blandford, London, 1991

Hardy, Phil, and Laing, Dave, *The Faber Companion to 20th-Century Popular Music*, Faber, London, 1992

Kernfeld, Barry (ed.), *The New Grove Dictionary of Jazz*, Macmillan, London, 1995

Larkin, Colin (ed.), *The Guinness Encyclopedia of Popular Music*, Guinness, London, 1995

Autobiographies, biographies, general

Albertson, Chris, *Bessie*, Stein and Day, New York, 1972

Applebaum, Stanley, and Comner, James (eds), *Stars of the American Musical Theater*, Dover, New York, 1981

Balliett, Whitney, *American Singers*, Oxford University Press, New York, 1979

Broughton, Viv, *Black Gospel: an Illustrated History of the Gospel Sound*, Blandford, Poole, Dorset, 1985

Carr, Roy, Case, Brian and Dellar, Fred, *The Hip: Hipsters, Jazz and the Beat Generation*, Faber, London, 1986

Colin, Sid, *Ella: the Life and Times of Ella Fitzgerald*, Elm Tree, London, 1986

Crowther, Bruce, and Pinfold, Mike, *The Jazz Singers: From Ragtime to the New Wave*, Blandford, Poole, Dorset, 1986

Ellington, Duke, *Music Is My Mistress*, W. H. Allen, London, 1974

Ellison, Ralph, *Shadow and Act*, Vintage, New York, 1972

Ewen, David, *All The Years of American Popular Music*, Prentice-Hall, Englewood Cliffs, NJ, 1977

Feather, Leonard, *The Book of Jazz*, Horizon, New York, 1965

—-, *The Encyclopedia of Jazz in the Seventies*, Quartet, London, 1978

Fox, Roy, *Hollywood, Mayfair and All That Jazz*, Leslie Frewin, London, 1975

Gourse, Leslie, *Sassy: the Life of Sarah Vaughan*, Scribner's, New York, 1993

Grime, Kitty, *Jazz Voices*, Quartet, London, 1983

Hammond, John, Jnr., with Townsend, Irving, *John Hammond on Record: an Autobiography*, Penguin, London, 1981

Jackson, Arthur, *The Book of Musicals*, Mitchell Beazley, London, 1977

Jones, Max, *Talking Jazz*, Macmillan, London, 1987

Kirkeby, W. T. Ed, *Ain't Misbehavin': the Story of Fats Waller*, Peter Davies, London, 1966

Laine, Cleo, *Cleo*, Simon and Schuster, London, 1994

Larkin, Philip, *All What Jazz - a Record Diary 1961-1971*, Faber, London, 1985

Lee, Peggy, *Miss Peggy Lee*, Bloomsbury, London, 1990

Lees, Gene, *Singers and the Song*, Oxford University Press, New York, 1987

Nicholson, Stuart, *Ella Fitzgerald*, Scribner's, New York, 1994

—, *Billie Holiday*, Gollancz, London, 1995

O'Day, Anita, and Eells, George, *High Times, Hard Times*, Corgi, London, 1983

Pinfold, Mike, *Louis Armstrong: His Life and Times*, Spellmount, Tunbridge Wells, Kent, 1987

Schuller, Gunther, *The Swing Era: the Development of Jazz 1930-1945*, Oxford University Press, New York, 1989

Shaw, Arnold, *52nd St: the Street of Jazz*, Da Capo, New York, 1977

—, *Honkers and Shouters: the Golden Years of Rhythm & Blues*, Collier, New York, 1978

Shapiro, Nat, and Hentoff, Nat, *Hear Me Talkin' to Ya: the Story of Jazz by the Men Who Made It*, Penguin, London, 1962

Simon, George T., *The Big Bands*, Collier Macmillan, 1974

Sinatra, Nancy, *Frank Sinatra: an American Legend*, Virgin, London, 1995

Smith, Joe, with Fink, Mitchell (ed), *Off the Record: an Oral History of Popular Music*, Warner Brothers, New York, 1988

Stokes, W. Royal, *The Jazz Scene*, Oxford University Press, London, 1991

Stowe, David W., *Swing Changes: Big Band Jazz in New Deal America*, Harvard, Cambridge, Massachusetts, 1994

Taylor, Arthur, *Notes and Tones*, Quartet, London, 1988

Thompson, Charles, *Bing: the Authorised Biography*, Star, London, 1976

Waters, Ethel, *His Eye Is on the Sparrow*, W. H. Allen, London, 1951

White, John, 'Veiled Testimony: Negro Spirituals and the Slave Experience', *American Studies* Vol. 17 No. 2, 1983

Wilder, Alec, *American Popular Song: the Great Innovators 1900-1950*, Oxford University Press, London, 1972

Williams, Martin, *Jazz Heritage*, Oxford University Press, New York, 1987

Magazines referred to in the text include various editions of *Coda*, *Crescendo International*, *down beat*, *Jazz Journal International*, *Jazz on CD*, *JazzTimes*, *Melody Maker*, *The Music Paper*, any or all of which are recommended to readers. We have also referred to numerous sleeve notes on albums by many of the artists discussed in *Singing Jazz*.

INDEX

INDEX OF SONG TITLES

255